# HEALTHY,
# WEALTHY,
# & FAIR

# HEALTHY, WEALTHY, & FAIR

## Health Care and the Good Society

EDITED BY

JAMES A. MORONE AND

LAWRENCE R. JACOBS

OXFORD

UNIVERSITY PRESS

2005

# OXFORD
### UNIVERSITY PRESS

Oxford University Press, Inc., publishes works that further
Oxford University's objective of excellence
in research, scholarship, and education.

Oxford   New York
Auckland   Cape Town   Dar es Salaam   Hong Kong   Karachi
Kuala Lumpur   Madrid   Melbourne   Mexico City   Nairobi
New Delhi   Shanghai   Taipei   Toronto

With offices in
Argentina   Austria   Brazil   Chile   Czech Republic   France   Greece
Guatemala   Hungary   Italy   Japan   Poland   Portugal   Singapore
South Korea   Switzerland   Thailand   Turkey   Ukraine   Vietnam

Copyright © 2005 by Oxford University Press, Inc.

Published by Oxford University Press, Inc.
198 Madison Avenue, New York, New York 10016

www.oup.com

Oxford is a registered trademark of Oxford University Press

Library of Congress Cataloging-in-Publication Data
Healthy, wealthy, and fair / health care and the good society /
edited by James A. Morone and Lawrence R. Jacobs.
p. cm.
Includes bibliographical references.
ISBN-13 978-0-19-517066-5
ISBN 0-19-517066-0
1. Health—Social aspects—United States. 2. Medical economies—United States.
3. Equality—Health Aspects—United States. 4. Capitalism—Health aspects—United States.
5. Medical policy—United States.
[DNLM: 1. Health Policy—United States. 2. Delivery of Health Care—economics—
United States. 3. Health Planning—United States. 4. Insurance, Health—economics—
United States. 5. Politics—United States. 6. Socioeconomic Factors—United States.
WA 540 AA1 H4858 2004]   I. Morone, James A., 1951–   II. Jacobs, Lawrence R.
RA418.3.U6H436   2004
362.1'0973—dc22       2004002575

1  3  5  7  9  8  6  4  2

Printed in the United States of America
on acid-free paper

To LAWRENCE D. BROWN

# Acknowledgments

This book began as a passionate conversation. *Healthy, Wealthy, and Fair* is our effort to spread the alarm about Americans' poor health. We describe the trouble, explain how it developed, and suggest what the United States can do about it.

The authors came together thanks to an extraordinary program. The Robert Wood Johnson Foundation's Investigator Awards gives scholars several years to think hard about creating a healthier society. Barbara Krimgold (our intellectual godmother) and Al Tarlov (our godfather) directed the program and inspired, advised, and cheered us. David Mechanic and Lynn Rogut took over the program halfway through our project and offered us splendid guidance, encouragement, and support. At Oxford University Press, Dedi Felman was a dream editor and Heather Hartman transformed our manuscript into this elegant volume.

Many colleagues pitched in with suggestions. Thanks to Jason Barnosky, Phil Brown, Dalton Conley, Jim House, Rick Mayes, Ted Marmor, Larry Mishel, Andre Schiffrin, and Leo Wiegman. Kelli Auerbach, Jason Barnosky, and Michael Illuzzi researched, shaped, and polished the manuscript. Special thanks to Jim Knickman and David Colby at the Robert Wood Johnson Foundation. And we all fondly remember Sol Levine, former director of the Investigator program, as a wise mentor and kind friend.

We dedicate the book to our friend and colleague, Larry Brown of Columbia University. Larry chaired our first meetings, helped organize the book, and kept reminding us of both the forest and the trees. More important, for the last quarter century, Larry has been our intellectual model. One after another he whips off his snappy, elegant, edgy, droll, sober, razor-sharp essays about American politics. Larry manages to be wise and funny, cool and kind. Through it all, he remains a steadfast realist while never forgetting the great prize—a good and generous community.

And that, finally, is what brought us together and inspired our book: imaging a better society and a healthier community. As you'll see, this is a collection of essays that sums to something more. It is also an invitation to join the authors in the quest for an America that is genuinely healthy, wealthy, and fair.

# Contents

ix

## Part IV. Chaotic Institutions

## Part V. The Territory Ahead: Little Victories

## Part VI. Thinking Big

# Contributors

LAWRENCE D. BROWN
Professor of Public Health, Columbia University

MARIE GOTTSCHALK
Associate Professor of Political Science, University of Pennsylvania

COLLEEN GROGAN
Associate Professor, School of Social Services Administration,
University of Chicago

LAWRENCE R. JACOBS
Professor of Political Science, University of Minnesota

PETER D. JACOBSON
Professor, University of Michigan School of Public Health

ICHIRO KAWACHI
Professor of Social Epidemiology, Harvard University

ELIZABETH H. KILBRETH
Associate Research Professor, University of Southern Maine

JAMES A. MORONE
Professor of Political Science, Brown University

CONSTANCE A. NATHANSON
Professor of Clinical Sociomedical Science, Columbia University

BENJAMIN I. PAGE
Professor of Political Science, Northwestern University

ERIC PATASHNIK
Associate Professor of Politics, University of Virginia

MARK A. PETERSON
Professor of Public Policy, University of California, Los Angeles

MARK SCHLESINGER
Professor of Public Health, Yale University

ELIZABETH SELVIN
Ph.D. candidate, Bloomberg School of Public Health,
Johns Hopkins University

DEBORAH STONE
Research Professor of Government, Dartmouth College

# HEALTHY, WEALTHY, & FAIR

# Introduction: Health and Wealth in the Good Society

## JAMES A. MORONE AND LAWRENCE R. JACOBS

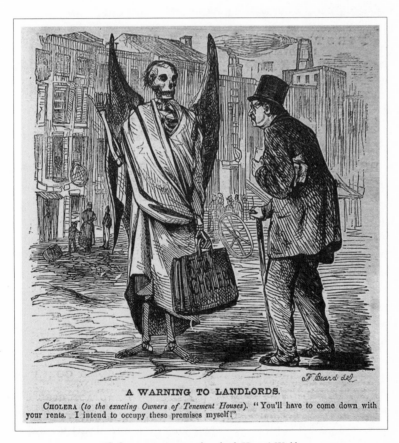

Cholera moves in on a slum lord. *Harper's Weekly,*
September 12, 1896.

Most Americans believe they live in a generous nation, brimming with opportunity. Even poor people cling to the American dream—work hard and you'll get ahead. If trouble hits, the neighbors are usually quick to lend a hand. When terrorists plowed into the World Trade Center, New Yorkers immediately crowded the hospitals to donate blood. Emergency workers from around the nation rushed to New York to pitch in. The community spirit runs deep in the American grain. In 1835, Alexis de Tocqueville marveled at how "an enlightened self love continually leads [Americans] to help one another." If your barn burned down, the townspeople helped you raise a new one. From this angle, Americans are a vibrant, energetic people with a long, deep sense of community. We are there to catch our neighbors if they fall on hard times.[1]

But there is also a darker picture of America. Many people around the world see a county of tight fists and hard hearts. Americans, they believe, valorize wealth, scorn failure, and look out mainly for number one. The richest nation in history tolerates extraordinary poverty. We cut taxes, cheer as the rich get richer, and look the other way as the social safety net decays. Critics see an America enthralled by hard-knuckle capitalism, a land of multimillionaires and hungry children.

Which is the real United States? Both are. We are powerful, rich, and generous. One penny out of every American dollar goes to charity—no other nation comes close. But we also tolerate extremes of wealth and poverty that are hard to fathom. By the mid-1990s, the wealthiest 1% of our households controlled almost half the nation's financial assets. Most of the world's billionaires live in the United States. The heads of our largest corporations make more than 300 times as much as the typical American worker and roughly 500 times more than the lowest paid (the numbers vary, depending on how you count—but our ratio stands out in every tally of industrial nations). Contrast this with Japan, where the top executives make about 20 times more than the lowest-paid workers. For that matter, compare American wages today to those of a generation ago: In 1965, the typical (or median) American chief executive officer made 26 times more than a typical worker; by 1989, the ratio had risen to 72:1 and by 2000 it stood at 310:1.[2]

Meanwhile, at the other end of the spectrum, poor Americans lead hard lives without much help from their more affluent countrymen. Compared to poor people in other industrialized countries, America's poor work harder and get less assistance—a lower minimum wage, fewer unions, and far less government support. Some seven million Americans are in immediate danger of becoming homeless. Most of them have jobs. And children. Forty-three million people have no health insurance at all; some thirty million have too little to cover a serious illness. Almost one in five children lives below the poverty line—almost two in five for black kids. Poor children grow up with the odds stacked heavily against them. Teachers will tell you why Jane can't read—she's hungry. Or perhaps she does not see well. An army of people without health insurance adds up to millions of parents who can't afford the frills—like eye examinations or visits to the dentist.

A look at Americans' health reveals the astonishing consequences. American girls are born with a life expectancy that ranks nineteenth in the world. (In another survey they fall to twenty-eighth.) Male babies weigh in at thirty-first—in a dead tie with Brunei Darussalam. The average American boy lives 3.5 years less than the average Japanese baby—though the Japanese child is a lot more likely to grow up smoking cigarettes. The American adolescent death rate is twice as high as England's. These dismal American averages mask vast differences across our population. A male born in some sections of Washington, DC, has a life expectancy 40 years lower than a woman born in rural Minnesota.[3] But add us together—look at the whole nation—and our health statistics land us far below the rest of the industrial world. In short, great differences in wealth equate to great differences in health. Surely Tocqueville's community-minded America would not tolerate such dismal prospects for so many people. Surely a good community would do something.

The American dream imagines a real chance for every person. President Abraham Lincoln put it famously before the Civil War: Any person who is "honest," "sober," "industrious," and "prudent," he said, would soon get ahead and become a success. But that famous vision of opportunity fades in and out over American history. In today's political economy, it is slipping completely out of sight for many people. With this volume, we aim to rouse the American spirit of generosity so emblematic of that first America. We focus on the most fundamental inequity: differences in health across our population. This volume charts the inequalities in health, explains why they exist, and suggests what we might do to regain balance. The same underlying message runs through every chapter. A rich and generous nation should not sanction such disparities in life and death, health and disability.

## American Troubles

Why do Americans fare so badly in the cross-national health statistics? Why don't our men live as long as those in, say, Croatia? Our health troubles are the result of three interrelated causes: inequality, poverty, and the way we organize our health care system.

## Inequality

A now famous study of the British civil service found that with each rung up the bureaucratic ladder, people suffered fewer fatal heart attacks—the clerks and messengers at the bottom were four times more likely to die than the executives at the top. As Ichiro Kawachi explains in chapter 1, health scholars following up this study uncovered a surprising finding that seemed to hold true for one nation after another: the higher the levels of inequality—the more rungs on the economic scale, the greater the distance between richest and poorest—the worse the nation's health. Longevity seems to be greater in more egalitarian settings.[4]

Why is this? Perhaps greater equality builds support and trust. Proponents of this view think equality makes for tighter communities and stronger institutions ranging from churches to government. In egalitarian communities, people feel more effective, more empowered. In contrast, inequality generates trouble right down the social ladder. It strains the culture of shared community and creates social stresses. By now, a host of international studies suggest that falling behind creates physiological and psychosocial damage. From this perspective, America's high mortality rates are the price we pay for the great gap between rich and poor. Fierce economic competition produces winners, losers, and plenty of social troubles.

How should we respond? Some public health advocates draw the simple conclusion: Attack inequality. "Reducing socio-economic and racial-ethnic disparities," argues sociologist James House, is "the major opportunity for improving health," both in the United States and around the world.[5] But that's no small job. After all, inequalities do not spring up by accident. Rather, societies build them up through countless political and economic decisions. For example, what kind of safety net protects the poor? Where do we peg the minimum wage? Do we tilt our business policies to encourage or discourage labor unions? Who do we tax, and how much do we tax them? (This may be the single most important question, for it defines how much we will redistribute income.) How do we organize and regulate business competition? How do we oversee our national markets? What do we do about immigration? How do we distribute corporate tax breaks, farm subsidies, low-income housing, kindergartens, and tonsillectomies? The answers to thousands and thousands of basic political and economic questions add up to our distribution of wealth and poverty. And, of course, the final tally is a constantly contested work in progress.

A great historical pendulum sometimes swings the United States toward greater equality; at other times toward great disparities. In the past 150 years, there have been two major bursts of inequality: from 1870 to 1910 and from 1979 to today. These eras have been tagged American gilded ages.[6]

In chapter 2, Lawrence Jacobs explains just how the United States developed its new Gilded Age. Three factors enabled powerful interests to overwhelm egalitarian politics. Well-organized interests wield disproportionate power; the poor participate less; and American labor plays a comparatively weaker hand. To understand the contemporary American political economy, argues Jacobs, start with these three cold political dynamics.

In the past, bursts of inequality eventually triggered egalitarian backlashes. "If I read the temper of our people correctly," said President Franklin D. Roosevelt at his first inaugural, "we now realize as we have never realized before our interdependence on each other; that we cannot merely take but we must give as well." Below the quest for wealth, Roosevelt reminded his countrymen, lie the "old and precious moral values" of sharing, of ministering to fellow citizens.[7]

Of course, egalitarian surges do not simply spring out of moralistic rhetoric. Great concentrations of wealth eventually inspire popular rebellions and provoke populist leaders. President Roosevelt unveiled Social Security looking nervously over his shoulder, as Governor Huey Long stormed out of Louisiana with a jarring scheme to soak the rich— he proposed an income tax rate of 100% on anything over $1 million; a generation later, President Lyndon Johnson signed the Civil Rights Act as black demonstrators thronged the streets. Again and again, rebellions against concentrated wealth and privilege have pushed our leaders to challenge inequality and injustice. Read this way, American history swings between the power of big money (dominating both economics and politics) and a formidable egalitarian tradition that insists on reducing inequities.

Public health advocates who trace our poor health data to inequality are, in effect, calling for a resurgence of the great American egalitarian tradition. As they see it, our health statistics won't improve, relative to other nations, until we make a new commitment to equality. However, the contemporary global economy pushes us in just the opposite direction—the disparities are growing rapidly and neither political party seems ready to resist the trend. Is there a more accessible path to better national health?

## Poverty

Many scholars argue that those alarming health statistics flow not from general inequality but, much more directly, from the army of poor and near-poor Americans.[8] After all, more than one in ten Americans (almost 33 million) is poor. The Census Bureau labels 40% of them (13.4 million) "severely poor"—they don't even make it halfway to the poverty line. The numbers are worse for minorities; more than a fifth of blacks and Hispanics are poor. And poverty is shadowed by all kinds of trouble, like hunger (33 million Americans live with food insecurity) and homelessness (perhaps as many as 3.5 million a year; about 40% are children).[9]

In addition, poor neighborhoods face high crime and inadequate education. There are few (safe) parks, well-paying jobs, reliable transportation links, or health care clinics. Instead, poverty attracts danger—too much alcohol and tobacco, illegal drugs and fast foods. One observer after another has gone off to study poor communities and come back with the same report: poor lives are full of stress and the struggle to get by. Jobs are scarce and pay is low. Despite the odds, almost 40% of poor Americans hold jobs—and one in ten (11.5%) manages to work full time all year round. People die younger in Harlem than in Bangladesh. Why? It is not what most people may think—homicide, drug abuse, and AIDS are far down the list. Rather, as the *New England Journal of Medicine* summed up the evidence, the leading causes of death in poor black neighborhoods are "unrelenting stress," "cardiovascular disease," "cancer," and "untreated medical conditions."[10]

From this perspective, the answer to our health dilemma lies in fighting poverty. Conservatives and liberals disagree on the ideal distribution of income and on the best approach to fighting poverty. But most wealthy nations find ways to shelter their citizens from the extreme vicissitudes of global competition. Their success appears to be reflected in their people's health.

## Health Care

It has become fashionable to disparage health care's contribution to health. The medical system, wrote Aaron Wildavsky in 1977, "affects about 10% of the usual indices for measuring health . . . most of the bad things at happen to people are at present beyond the reach of medicine."[11] A some public health advocates have adopted this medical nihilism. ated attack on health disparities, they argue, would require a larger fight against poverty. As people's lives improve, our health indices will take care of themselves.

But even if poverty is a primary cause of acute illness and early death, this lesson overlooks the basics. Simple health care—annual check-ups, screenings, vaccinations, eyeglasses, dentistry—saves lives and improves well-being. People in poor neighborhoods are familiar with the rush of wonderful, long-delayed health care services that come when someone lands a good job. It's a uniquely American experience.

No other industrial nation has such yawning gaps in health insurance—43 million without any, 30 million with not enough. The numbers reflect a lot of trouble: uninsured people are slow to seek treatment. Even middle-class parents worry about the next medical emergency or, in many cases, the routine trip to the doctor's office. Life without health insurance means constantly measuring aches and fevers against the next payday. Changing jobs brings a new set of anxieties about losing medical coverage.

Of course, no health care system treats everyone the same way. But our disparities in care are unusually wide and deep. Emergency-room psychiatrists confront attempted suicides with different protocols. Well-insured people get assigned hospital beds; the uninsured get patched up and sent back to the streets. From diagnostic procedures (prostate screenings, mammograms, and pap smears) to treatment for asthma, the uninsured get less care; they get it later in their illness episodes; and they are roughly three times as likely to have an adverse health outcome. The Institute of Medicine blames gaps in insurance coverage for 17,000 preventable deaths a year.[12]

The number of uninsured Americans keeps growing. The problem threatens to overwhelm our hospitals and doctors. It loads another stress onto working families. The costs of the system put pressure on employers who inch out of the health insurance business by pushing costs onto their employees. The workers, in turn, risk financial ruin if a member of their family ends up in the hospital. Health bills are America's largest cause of personal bankruptcy.

These three problems—inequality, poverty, and inadequate health insurance coverage—are all related. Timid reformers often imagine that small changes might add up to serious reform. However, health care is America's trillion-dollar industry. Coverage for more than 40 million people will be wickedly expensive, requiring a massive redistribution of income from the haves to those who have less. Moreover, from a medical perspective, decent health insurance coverage ought to come with renewed efforts to address the worst consequences of poverty—hunger, homelessness, poor education, and bad health habits.

These kinds of reforms will not sneak quietly through the system. They will not come through incremental steps—though small changes can help. Rather, real reform will require powerful grassroots movements and committed leaders. However, before even imagining a path to change, reformers have to face up to the obstacles.

## The Barriers to Reform

The sheer size of the inequality problem raises a classic puzzle. Why does the American majority accept political and economic rules that deliver enormous wealth to a small minority? Why do we skew wealth—and health—so much more dramatically than other industrial nations? After all, early American theorists had worried about just the opposite—the majority would use the tax system to soak the rich. "Every shilling with which they overburden the inferior number [of wealthy people]," wrote James Madison, "is a shilling saved to their own pockets."[13] What happened?

### Market Power and Horatio Alger Dreams

Many Americans believe that, even if the consequences are painful, a race for riches makes the entire nation more prosperous. After all, look at our own record—great inequality matched by great economic growth. But there is little real evidence for this connection. Cross-national data suggest no link between prosperity and inequality. In fact, just the opposite seems true. The less prosperous nations—Russia and Mexico, rather than France and Italy—are generally the ones that permit vast gulfs between haves and have-nots.[14] The data—both across other nations and down through our own history—suggest that the United States might do even better if we once again buffered the markets' worst consequences.[15]

Part II addresses the market question directly. In chapter 3, Deborah Stone juxtaposes two sets of values—equality versus markets. Market thinking, she argues, has spread too far into our social realm. It undermines important ideals—like racial justice and decent health care. We can achieve those goals only by reining in and properly overseeing our markets. In chapter 4, Mark Schlesinger shows how American health care has long featured alternate values grounded in medical science and social welfare. However, contemporary political elites have overwhelmed those norms by applying a powerful and corrosive kind of market thinking to health policy. He tells us that the market metaphor undermines our own traditional values. Both chapters end with the same forceful claim: Reformers worried about health will have to impose limits on market competition.

Of course, the call to market goes beyond ideology and often reflects blunt self-interest. Market winners are frequently reluctant to share their wealth. They fight fierce battles with less privileged groups—most notably, organized labor and racial minorities. However, today we are witnessing an odd twist in the old class conflicts: market thinking filters into the calculations of the very interests who normally lead the charge for social justice.

In part III, we explain why. Marie Gottschalk argues in chapter 5 that American social policy is not a purely public enterprise but a complicated public-private arrangement. Benefits are not tied to citizenship and overseen by the state; rather, they are often linked to jobs, administered by employers, and supported by public policies. Private employers offer pensions, health insurance, and disability benefits, all backed up by government regulations and tax policies. In most nations, organized labor emerged as a great political champion of universal social policies like national health insurance. In the United States, however, the public-private welfare state reshaped organized labor's interests. It is not that American labor is politically weak, argues Gottschalk; rather, it has been co-opted by the once generous employee benefit system it helped create. American labor is invested in the market-driven, public-private welfare state.

Market thinking also subtly subverts the power of disadvantaged groups like racial minorities. In chapter 6, Constance Nathanson shows how American interest groups censor themselves. They are constrained by the powerful idea of the market as a grand metric of social worth. Moreover, many diseases have social stigmas. Minority groups, eager to win respectability, do not fight for reform. They overlook their own sick members and fail to push alternative goals and programs.

Taken together, parts II and III describe the powerful, increasingly unbridled force of self-seeking. Market economics overrun our egalitarian norms. Restoring American social justice—addressing American health disparities, mending our community—means taking on and limiting the consequences of those formidable markets.

## Chaotic Government

Of course, market ideology and powerful economic interests do not always win. Cries of "socialism" did not stop Medicare, for example. The program passed and became enormously popular. In fact, Medicare and

Social Security became known as "third rails" of American politics—just touching them could be politically hazardous. Americans may celebrate economic markets. They may be primed to attack government. But that is only one part of the story.[16]

A more subtle interpretation of American politics focuses on the government itself. "No other nation organizes its government as incoherently as the United States," concludes one English study of American antipoverty programs. The political chaos—sometimes celebrated as checks and balances—"leaves most reforms sprawling helplessly in a scrum of competing interests." Political programs must pass through the executive branch, two independent houses of Congress, the federal bureaucracy, and the many layers of American federalism. Courts intervene at every stage. To pass this kind of gauntlet, proposed programs are first oversold and then heavily compromised. [17]

The chaotic organization of American politics—full of institutional back alleys in which to mug reforms—is often misread as simple hostility to government action. Consider national health insurance. While Americans have long been skeptical about the idea, both Harry Truman (in 1948) and Bill Clinton (1992) won the presidency touting universal health insurance as a major domestic initiative. What played well on the campaign trail got defeated in Congress. In a parliamentary system, free of checks and balances, one party (or coalition) would control the executive, the legislature, and the bureaucracy. In such a setting, the Truman or Clinton administration would have had the opportunity—in fact, would have been expected—to legislate the reform it promised during the election. If the United States operated under British (or Canadian or German) political rules, it likely would have won national health insurance several times over. [18]

Over time, the American government has grown increasingly maladroit at winning big policy changes. Instead, it has become geared to deliver narrow benefits to well-organized interests. This is a system that brilliantly services clients. Our government dispenses a steady stream of tax breaks, subsidies, narrowly framed programs, regulatory relief, and special favors. The intricate system spans public and private sectors. Sophisticated analyses of inequality have to be rooted in this American institutional reality. So do calls for action.

Part IV delves into the institutional details. Any major American reform must pass through Congress. In chapter 7, Mark Peterson shows just how and why Congress has become the reformers' graveyard. But this is a fluid story; Congress is always changing—Truman's failure in 1946 was very different from Bill Clinton's in 1993. Each generation of reformers faces new challenges and, if they read the institution correctly, fresh possibilities.

A generation ago, reforms stalled in legislatures sometimes won in the courts. In chapter 8, Peter Jacobson and Elizabeth Selvin explain how the era of liberal judicial intervention came to an end—replaced by a cautious judiciary that defers to market winners (with a growing minority eager for a more ambitious conservative activism). Both chapters end on the same note: political institutions will not lead the way to social reform until a powerful popular movement shakes up the current political calculations. Each institutional analysis yields the same advice: Think big.

## The Territory Ahead

How to start building the good society? Two classic political strategies point in different directions. Conventional wisdom counsels incremental reform. Take one small step at a time and eventually the little advances will add up. The bold alternative pushes short-term political considerations aside. Only great aspirations will galvanize populist politics and leverage our reluctant state. Throughout American political history, great reforms began with a small group of believers, tirelessly pushing against all the odds.

Which path to follow? As Yogi Berra famously advised, "When you come to a fork in the road, take it." Parts V and VI examine both strategies: Build on past successes and propose bold departures.

The incrementalists begin with a classic bit of political science wisdom: Every policy changes the ensuing politics. Launching a new program—large or small—shifts the constellation of interests working in the area. Beneficiaries and providers organize to protect and extend their gains. Build onto existing programs, argue proponents, and reform American society one small achievable step at time.

In chapter 9, Colleen Grogan and Eric Patashnik illustrate prospects—and the pitfalls—by tracing Medicaid's great political arc. The program began inauspiciously. Medicare's enemies, casting about for a smaller (and frankly less popular) program with which to deflect reformers, proposed Medicaid—"welfare medicine" for the needy. However, once it passed, Medicaid began drifting toward the mainstream. Public officials looking to increase health care coverage repeatedly expanded the program through the late 1980s and 1990s. Today, Medicaid seems poised between mainstream medicine and the welfare program. Some health advocates think Medicaid offers a promising path to reform by slowly adding beneficiaries and expanding health services—a politically simple way to get care to more children, uninsured workers, immigrants, and others.

Even very small, local programs—those flying far below the media radar—can add up to meaningful change. In chapter 10, Elizabeth Kilbreth and James Morone investigate a program (operating with state, local, and private funds) that opened health care clinics in poor schools. Because it raised issues like parental control, reproductive health, and substance abuse, the school-based health centers generated enormous opposition around the country. However, against all odds, the programs grew and prospered. Their success stands as a parable for a new generation of activists. The clinics found unlikely champions in state-level public health bureaucrats. The public officials, in turn, organized local parent groups. The new grassroots coalitions cut across race, class, and (sometimes) political ideology. Thanks to these unlikely innovations, a little political jolt—spanning education, health care, and other youth issues—is stirring at the grass roots.

Still, it will take much bolder breakthroughs to squarely address the problems we posed at the start of this volume. As Lawrence Brown suggests in chapter 11, incrementalism is a long, slow, often very helpful, and ultimately inadequate response to American inequality. The task we set ourselves at the start—improving America's health—will require more than tinkering on the political margin. Small reforms will not remake a political economy that reverberates with self-interest. Each author in this collection independently returns to the same policy advice: seek bold changes. In chapter 12, Benjamin Page suggests how we might begin to do so. He breaks away from conventional thinking and imagines what our government might do—based on what it has done well in the past.

This kind of thinking runs counter to all conventional wisdom. The political mood is unambiguous—this is no time to dream of great societies or bold new deals. However, we confront a galloping inequality that leaves entire groups and neighborhoods far behind. Wealthy people segregate themselves and prosper. As we show in the concluding essay, a global economy powerfully exacerbates the gap between rich and poor. Reversing such formidable trends requires radical rethinking. It cannot happen without a bold assault on those three main interrelated problems—inequality, poverty, and health care coverage.

A long, populist tradition stretches back to America's founding. Tocqueville celebrated vibrant American communities where people understood that their own best interest—their "self-interest rightly understood"—required the whole community to pitch in and help one another, to work together, to see their fates as deeply interconnected. There was nothing in Europe, averred Tocqueville, like the vibrant American sense of community. Our current dilemmas call for a return to that robust, egalitarian spirit of help-your-neighbor.

And that return will require leaders who seize on big reforms and champion them against a contemporary antitax, promarket tide. Along with committed leaders, real change will require another surge of American populism. The final chapters suggest how we might begin to foster that venerable American energy.

We do not enter our calls for change naively. The following chapters detail the many barriers that confront reformers. However, this book is more than a text about equality and health. It is also a manifesto to think big about making a good society. The authors invite you to join us in pushing for an America that is healthy, wealthy, and fair.

## Notes

1. Alexis de Tocqueville, *Democracy in America* (1835; Garden City, NY: Doubleday, 1969), 526; Jennifer Hochschild, *Facing Up to the American Dream: Race, Class and the Soul of the Nation* (Princeton, NJ: Princeton University Press, 1995), chapter 3, on poor people clinging firmly to the American dream. For a discussion of the basic mindsets, see James A. Morone, *Hellfire Nation: The Politics of Sin in American History* (New Haven, CT: Yale University Press, 2003).

2. Philanthropic contributions reported in "The New Wealth of Nations," *The Economist* (Suppl. 16 June 2001): 15. The data on concentration of wealth gets cut many different ways. See Larry Mishel, Jared Bernstein, and Heather Boushey, *The State of Working America: 2002–2003* (Ithaca, NY: Cornell University Press, 2002); they report that the wealthiest 1% of households controls 47.3% of "net financial assets" and 16.6% of household income, 278; median CEO income, 7. Relative income computed by comparing median annual pay for the CEOs of America's largest 100 corporations and the median annual earnings of full-time workers reported in Ichiro Kawachi, Bruce Kennedy, and Richard Wilkinson, *The Society and Population Health Reader: Income Inequality and Health* (New York: New Press, 1999), xi; total wealth, xii. See also Stephen Bezruchka, "My Turn: Is Our Society Making You Sick?" *Newsweek* (26 February 2001): 14; cross-national data on poor (hours worked) from Christopher Jencks, "Does Inequality Matter?" *Daedalus* 131.1 (Winter 2002): 53.

3. Data computed from the United Nations Secretariat, Population Statistics Division, *Indicators on Health, 1999*; Lynnley Browning, "U.S. Income Gap Widening," *New York Times* (25 September 2003): C2.

4. Michael Marmot, M. J. Shipley and G. Rose, "Inequalities in Death—Specific Explanation of a General Pattern?" *Lancet* (5 May 1984): 1003–1006; James

Auerbach and Barbara Kivimae Krimgold, eds., *Income, Socioeconomic Status and Health* (Washington, DC: National Policy Association, 2001), 87.

5. James House, "Relating Social Inequalities in Health and Income," *Journal of Health Politics, Policy and Law* 26.3 (June 2001): 524.

6. See Kevin Phillips, *Wealth and Democracy: A Political History of the American Rich* (New York: Broadway Books, 2002).

7. Franklin Delano Roosevelt, "Inaugural Address," March 4, 1933, *The Public Papers and Addresses of Franklin D. Roosevelt II* (New York: Random House, 1938), 11–16.

8. House, "Relating Social Inequalities," 527. For an example of the income, race, and health tangle, see David Williams, "Race and Health: Trends and Policy Implications," *Income, Socioeconomic Status and Health*, ed. James Auerbach and Barbara Kivimae Krimgold (Washington, DC: National Policy Association, 2001), 67–85.

9. Bernadette Proctor and Joseph Dalaker, U.S. Census Bureau, Current Population Reports, *Poverty in the United States, 2001* (Washington, DC: U.S. Government Printing Office, 2002).

10. Arline Geronimus, John Bound, Timothy A. Waidmann, Marianne M. Hillemeier, and Patricia B. Burns, "Excess Mortality among Blacks and Whites in the United States," *New England Journal of Medicine* 335 (1996): 1552–1558; see also Geronimus, "To Mitigate, Resist or Undo: Addressing Structural Influences on the Health of Urban Populations," *American Journal of Public Health* 90.68 (June 2000): 867–872; and C. McCord and H. P. Freeman, "Excess Mortality in Harlem," *New England Journal of Medicine* 322 (1990): 173–177.

11. Aaron Wildavsky, "Doing Better and Feeling Worse: The Political Pathology of Health Policy," *Daedalus* 106.1 (Winter 1977): 105.

12. Institute of Medicine, National Academy of Sciences (Washington, DC: National Academy Press, January 14, 2004).

13. James Madison, *Federalist Number 10*.

14. For an overview of the relationship between national wealth and inequality, see Jencks, "Does Inequality Matter?" 49–65.

15. On the American historical experience, see, for example, Robert Kuttner, *Everything for Sale: The Virtues and Limits of Markets* (New York: Knopf, 1997).

16. On the political difference between winning and maintaining social policies, see Lawrence Brown, *New Politics, New Policies* (Washington, DC: Brookings Institution, 1982).

17. Peter Marris and Martin Rein, *Dilemmas of Social Reform: Poverty and Community Action in the United States* (Chicago: Aldine, 1973), 7.

18. This argument is from James A. Morone, *The Democratic Wish: Popular Participation and the Limits of American Government.* (New Haven, CT: Yale University Press, 1998), chapter 8.

# Part I

# AN AMERICAN DILEMMA

# Why the United States Is Not Number One in Health

ICHIRO KAWACHI

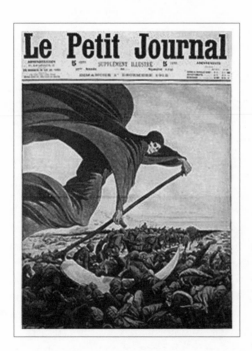

Americans are quite accustomed to seeing their country rank at the very top of the medal chart at the Summer Olympic Games. Imagine our surprise, then, upon discovering that our health status ranks near the bottom among the 13 most economically advanced countries of the world. In the health Olympics, we rank twelfth overall on sixteen indicators of health status—behind Japan, Sweden, Canada, France, Australia, Spain, Finland, the Netherlands, the United Kingdom, Denmark, and Belgium.[1] On specific indicators, we rank as follows:

- 13th (bottom) for percentage of low birth weight
- 13th for neonatal mortality and total infant mortality
- 13th for years of potential life lost
- 11th for life expectancy at age 1 for females, 12th for males
- 10th for life expectancy at age 15 for females, 12th for males
- 10th for life expectancy at age 40 for females, 9th for males
- 7th for life expectancy at age 65 for females, 7th for males

About the only health indicator for which we rank near the top of the medal chart is life expectancy, at age 80 (third for both females and males).[2] If this were the sports Olympics, our Senate would order urgent public hearings to get to the bottom of our dismal performance and Congress would immediately pump millions of extra dollars into athletic programs to correct this source of national shame.

Why, then, do we not see a comparable level of outrage when it comes to our performance in the health Olympics? This chapter outlines three possible explanations for our curious complacency. First, the American public may be ignorant of its dismal health performance because the issue does not receive regular coverage on the nightly news in the way that our economic performance does. Second, even if we were aware of our health performance, some members of the public might not care about our relative rank compared to other rich nations, so long as average life expectancy continues to improve. Third, the public might ignore the problem because it is misinformed about the causes of our poor health performance and, hence, what can be done about it.

## The Dow Jones versus the Doug Jones

It is quite understandable that most Americans mistakenly assume we rank first in the world on indicators of longevity and good health. After all, we are the wealthiest nation in the world, and everyone knows that a higher standard of living allows longer and healthier lives. We also spend by far the most of any nation on health care. We make up just 4% of the world's population, yet we expend about half of all the money spent on medical care across the globe.[3] But contrary to most people's assumptions, even as far back as 1970, the United States ranked about fifteenth in the world in health indicators like life expectancy and infant mortality. Twenty years later, our position had slipped to about twenty-second, or near the bottom of the OECD (Organization of Economic Cooperation and Development) countries—behind almost all rich countries and even a few poorer ones. Japan, by contrast, started out near the bottom (twenty-third) of the health Olympics in 1960, but overtook the rest of the world by 1977.[4]

If the American public was more generally aware of these kinds of comparisons, we might feel less smug about being the richest, most successful economy in the world. However, in contrast to the compulsive way in which we track the performance of our economy, Americans remain largely ignorant about the state of the nation's health, because there is no equivalent of the Dow Jones Industrial Average by which we can monitor our health performance. We are quite accustomed to following the ups and downs of the Dow Jones on a minute-by-minute basis. However, "in contrast to the tools, structures, and mechanisms of the economic sphere, the richness and variety of its indicators, and the regularity with which they are reported, our vision of the social sphere is far more obscure. Social data are collected once a year at best, rather than daily, weekly, monthly, or quarterly, as in economics."[5]

Texas populist Jim Hightower has argued that our nation should develop an alternative to the Dow Jones index, one that better describes what is happening to ordinary people. Such an index might track a combination of social indicators such as wages, unemployment, and benefits like health insurance. Hightower suggests calling it the "Doug Jones index," in honor of the working-class man.[6] As it happens, the Miringoffs at the Fordham Institute for Innovation in Social Policy have developed exactly such an index, which they have dubbed the Index of Social Health.[7] This index is made up of health indicators such as infant mortality, teenage suicide, homicides, health insurance coverage, drug abuse, rates of child abuse, and alcohol-related traffic fatalities, as well as broader social indicators such as children in poverty, high school dropouts, and affordable housing. When stacked up against our nation's market performance, the unavoidable conclusion is that our nation's health and social performance have stagnated, even as our economy has taken off.

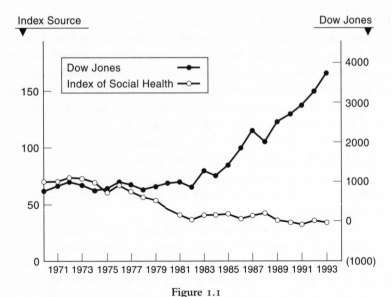

**Figure 1.1**

**Index of Social Health and the Dow Jones Industrial Average, 1970–1993.**
Sources: Fordham Institute for Innovation in Social Policy; Statistical Abstract of
United States; Survey of Current Business.

In Figure 1.1, we see that our nation's Index of Social Health closely
tracked the performance of the Dow Jones index up until the late 1970s.
Since then, however, the two lines have diverged: our social health has
slumped, while the Dow Jones currently hovers around 10,000. The
same pattern is repeated when we substitute a broader indicator of economic performance, such as growth in the per capita gross domestic
product.

Granted, some indicators that comprise the Miringoffs' index have
improved in recent years; for example, homicide rates. Even so, current
rates of firearm homicide remain at levels above the rates that prevailed
prior to the 1980s. Other health indicators not included in the Index of
Social Health, such as rates of low birth weight, demonstrate little or no
improvement over the past two decades. In fact, on a state-by-state basis,
only New Hampshire did not record an increase in low birth-weight
babies between 1985 and 1996. For the United States as a whole, rates
increased by 9%, while in some midwestern states such as Minnesota,
Iowa, and Indiana, rates rose by as much as 20%.[8]

## Different Yardsticks:
## Absolute versus Relative Health Achievements

Even if Americans were made aware of our dismal health performance, some of us might argue that we need not be concerned about our relative ranking in the health Olympics, so long as, on average, everyone is living longer. In other words, our performance should be judged in terms of *absolute* gains in life expectancy and not with reference to our comparative performance vis-à-vis other rich countries. While this argument has superficial merit (we shouldn't envy the achievement of others), it falls down on the hard facts. Thus, while it is true that life expectancy for Americans has been improving *on average*, averages can obscure dramatic differences between groups. For African-Americans, life expectancy actually slid backward during the 1980s, even as the longevity for white Americans continued to rise (see Table 1.1).[9]

Even though the *average* life expectancy of Americans continues to improve, it is impossible to ignore the staggering disparities in longevity that have been documented across groups and regions of the United States. An African-American born in the District of Columbia can expect to live 57.9 years—lower than the life expectancy of the male citizens of Ghana (58.3 years), Bangladesh (58.1 years), or Bolivia (59.8 years). By contrast, an Asian-American woman born in Westchester County, New York, can expect to live on average for 90.3 years.[10] Regardless of one's views about how best to judge comparative health performance, the sheer magnitude of these disparities ought to cause alarm and concern.

Table 1.1
U.S. Life Expectancy at Birth, 1984–1992

| Year | White | Black |
|------|-------|-------|
| 1984 | 75.3 | 69.5 |
| 1985 | 75.3 | 69.3 |
| 1986 | 75.4 | 69.1 |
| 1987 | 75.6 | 69.1 |
| 1988 | 75.6 | 68.9 |
| 1989 | 75.9 | 68.8 |
| 1990 | 76.1 | 69.1 |
| 1991 | 76.3 | 69.3 |
| 1992 | 76.5 | 69.6 |

*Source:* Williams, 2001, p. 74

## Myths about Lagging U.S. Health Performance

Supposing that the American public came to acknowledge our dismal health performance, there still remain some powerful myths about what can be done to improve our health status. These myths have attained the status of shibboleths. The first is that our poor health performance, especially with respect to racial disparities in health, reflects inherited differences in health stock. The second myth is that our poor health performance comes from poor people behaving badly. A third myth puts all the blame for our health status on the lack of universal access to health care. These myths warrant careful scrutiny.

### Poor Health Equals Bad Genes

The "bad genes" line of argument will be familiar to readers who have followed the infamous "bell curve" controversy.[11] According to this line of argument, our nation's lackluster health performance can be explained by the distribution of flawed genes in the population. For instance, the high incidence of obesity, hypertension, diabetes, and low birth weight can all be explained by a higher genetic predisposition within our communities (especially African-American communities) to develop these maladies. Although this unfortunate perception is still highly prevalent in our society (and we devote large sums of research dollars to pursue this hypothesis), the idea has been thoroughly discredited. In other words, while not denying the existence of an inherited predisposition to these diseases, we can reject the notion that our overall health performance can be blamed on the disproportionately high prevalence of individuals with such predispositions in our society.

We owe this insight to the work of researchers who have carefully compared the occurrence of these diseases across populations sharing the same genetic stock, but living in different societies. For instance, U.S.-born black women have twice the incidence of low birth-weight babies compared to white American women. However, when the birth weight patterns of *African-born* black women are compared to American black women, they much more closely resemble the distribution among U.S. *white* women than among U.S.-born black women. In other words, it is U.S.-born black women who exhibit a different pattern of birth weights compared to the other groups, even though African-born and U.S.-born black women presumably share the same genetic stock.[12] Similar findings have been reported for the distribution of blood pressure and hypertension among U.S.-born blacks compared to West African populations,[13] as well as the prevalence of diabetes.[14] These kinds of data refute the "bad genes" argument as an explanation for poor health status in our country.

Instead of blaming the flawed genes of our citizens, we ought to be searching for what it is about American society that is toxic to health. Even the longevous Japanese are not immune to the toxic influence of American society. According to the famous NiHonSan Study, which followed Japanese immigrants to the United States, the closer they settled to the American mainland, the higher their risk was of suffering a heart attack.[15] Death rates from heart attack were lowest among the Japanese who stayed behind, intermediate among those who settled in Honolulu, Hawaii, and highest among immigrants who moved to San Francisco.

## Poor People Behaving Badly

The second, and in some ways most culturally ingrained, myth about our nation's health is that sick people—especially poor and uneducated people—bring poor health upon themselves through ill-informed or irresponsible risk-taking behaviors.[16] This line of reasoning owes its enduring appeal to other values that are held sacred in American culture, such as liberty, individualism, and moralism.[17] According to this view, individuals are free to choose their "lifestyles," as long as they take responsibility for the consequences of their own choices and don't expect others to pay for them. Some would even assert that our poor health status is the price we pay for maintaining our values—but a worthwhile one for the liberty and opportunity guaranteed by the American way of life. If you don't like the American way, you can always defect to Cuba, where people live long (and, many would add, where life *feels* long).

The flaw in this logic is that people don't always *choose* to behave badly (by ignoring the doctor's advice to stop smoking, indulging in fast foods, or putting off regular exercise). Nobody denies that some "risky" behavior is freely chosen or that individuals should take some responsibility for their own actions. However, *how much* individual responsibility should be assigned to bad behaviors lies at the crux of the disagreement between those who say nothing can (or needs to) be done about our poor health status, versus those who see it as an avoidable blemish on our national record.

Adopting a life-course perspective often helps tease out the issues of individual freedom and responsibility from the claims of collective responsibility. For instance, in the case of cigarette smoking and its adverse health consequences, adult smokers are typically held accountable for their habits. But this ignores the reality that an overwhelming majority of adult smokers initiated their lifelong addiction as underage minors. Over 80% of smokers become addicted to nicotine before the legal age of purchase. Even staunch libertarians would concede that minors are not capable of making responsible decisions that may affect their future welfare. Yet American lawmakers (until very recently at least) routinely permitted tobacco manufacturers to peddle their products to children through the medium of cartoon characters, as well as advertising in youth-oriented magazines and public venues. The tobacco industry goes even further by systematically targeting its outdoor advertising to low-income and minority ethnic neighborhoods. In other words, the high prevalence of health-damaging behaviors (like smoking) among poor people is less a sign of their moral turpitude than a consequence of the workings of the not-so-invisible hand of the free market.

Similar arguments could be made about the deliberate decisions of fast food manufacturers to open their businesses near schools in low-income neighborhoods, or the lack of availability of healthy food choices where poor people shop. The ability to choose regular physical activity is also socially constrained. Parents may discourage their children from exercising outdoors in high-crime neighborhoods. Public exercise facilities, like playgrounds and bike paths, are more accessible, appealing, and safer in middle-class as opposed to impoverished neighborhoods. High-status employees have more flexible work schedules that permit them to take long lunch-hour workouts at the gym. Joining a health club requires membership fees that many low-income individuals cannot afford without sacrificing money needed for food, clothing, and other necessities. The long list of barriers to adopting a healthy lifestyle should give pause to those among us who would blame the poor health habits of fellow citizens on ignorance, sloth, or indifference.

## Lack of Access to Health Care

A third persistent misconception about our lagging health performance is our lack of access to universal health care. The United States is unique among the world's rich countries in failing to assure universal access of citizens to medical care. And there can be no gainsaying that universal access to health care would improve the health of millions of Americans currently without coverage. Nor can there be denying that medical care makes a difference to the health status of sick individuals (sometimes dramatically so, as in fixing a broken limb).

However, the fallacy of ascribing our health performance to lack of universal coverage lies in the assumption that health care can account for variations in health status. It is the fallacy of confusing the cure with the cause of the illness—like blaming a patient's fever on a deficiency of aspirin.

Sometimes the (important) goal of achieving universal health care in this country is discussed as if it were an *alternative* to doing something about the non-medical determinants of health (and vice versa). This is a myth that ignores the fact that the two goals are, in fact, complementary. Inequality in access to medical care is, after all, just another manifestation of inequalities in access to broader resources (such as wealth, credit, employment, and education), all of which contribute to our ability to lead healthy lives. Nor is inequality in access to medical care a simple yes/no phenomenon (you either have health insurance or you don't). Even in countries with a national health care system, such as Great Britain, there are lingering disparities in the quality of medical care, the geographic distribution of doctors and medical facilities, and so on. Additionally, what *type* of health care we get may matter. According to some analyses, lack of primary care accounts for a significant part of the dismal American health care performance.[18] This implies a radical redirection of current efforts to reform health insurance, including restructuring medical care priorities in a system that is overwhelmingly focused on the delivery of specialist and hospital-based care.

## If It's Not Bad Genes or Bad Behaviors, Then What Is It?

If bad genes and bad behaviors can't explain America's dismal state of health, then what can? The answer lies in much more fundamental social causes.[19] We now understand that the prerequisites for the health and well being of a population consist of fundamental social conditions, such as a fair distribution of resources as well as robust support for our self-respect.[20] Translated into concrete terms, the social determinants of health include access to safe neighborhoods, productive employment, freedom from discrimination, and full participation in the life of communities. In turn, people's access to health-promoting social conditions is played out through the political process. Politics determine who gets what, how much, and when. As Rudolf Virchow famously asserted, "Medicine is a social science, and politics is nothing else but medicine on a grand scale."[21] To illustrate this point, consider the paradox identified at the beginning of this chapter, i.e., why, despite being the wealthiest country in the world, we are not the healthiest.

## Economic Prosperity and Health

As it turns out, there is almost no correlation among the world's richest countries between their per capita wealth and life expectancy. A comparison of countries with roughly the same level of economic prosperity reveals dramatic differences in life expectancy (see Table 1.2).

Among rich countries, then, economic prosperity alone is no guarantee of stellar health performance. That is not to say that economic growth does not matter. Three-fifths of the world's people still live on less than $2 per day, and there is no denying that in poor countries, raising people's incomes, even by a small amount, would dramatically improve their life chances. That said, even among countries of middle economic development, we can find dramatic disconnects between the material standard of living and life expectancy. Amartya Sen has repeatedly pointed out the unexpected success of countries such as China, Sri Lanka, and the Kerala region of India, which have less than one-sixth the per capita gross national product of wealthier countries such as Brazil, Namibia, South Africa, and Gabon—but nonetheless record much higher performance on health indicators such as life expectancy.[22]

A major reason why the average income of a country is not correlated with its average health is because averages can hide deep divisions within society. For example, countries like Brazil and South Africa have much higher average incomes than Sri Lanka or China, but their wealth tends to be concentrated in the hands of the fortunate few. China and Sri Lanka, despite much lower average incomes, tend to spread their

Table 1.2
**Comparison of Per Capita GNP in Selected Countries and Their Life Expectancies**

| Country | Per Capita GNP (U.S. $) | Average Life Expectancy (Years) |
| --- | --- | --- |
| United States | 29,080 | 76.7 |
| Sweden | 26,210 | 78.5 |
| Netherlands | 25,830 | 77.9 |
| United Kingdom | 20,870 | 77.2 |
| France | 26,300 | 78.1 |
| Germany | 28,280 | 77.2 |

*Source:* 1999 Human Development Report.

economic gains more evenly throughout the population, and economic growth is also plowed back into social spending that benefits all.

To turn to the United States, our spectacular economic growth in recent decades has not been equally shared across segments of the population. Beginning in the mid-1970s (incidentally, about the time that our Index of Social Health started to diverge from indicators of market performance—see Figure 1.1), the American economy began registering sharp increases in both earnings and income inequality. Over the past two and a half decades, the affluent sections of society have been pulling away sharply from the middle class and poor.[23] Between 1977 and 1999, the average after-tax incomes of the top fifth of American families rose by 43%. By contrast, the average incomes of the middle fifth of families rose by a meager 8% over the same 22-year period, or less than 0.5% per year. At the bottom, the incomes of poor families actually fell by 9%. Forty percent of American families are either no better off or worse off today in real terms than they were in 1977. But at the very top, the incomes of the wealthiest 1% of the population rose by a staggering 115% after adjusting for inflation.[24]

In other words, if you happened to have been born into the top fifth of the population (better still the top 1%) during the past 25 years, you probably lived the American dream. Conversely, if you happened to have been working class or poor, you would be justified in believing that life had not improved, or had possibly even gotten worse. Despite the sustained economic growth during recent years and the longest bull market in postwar history (which ended in 2001), America has scarcely made a dent on the number of households living in poverty. We may crow about our economic performance to the rest of the world, but our pattern of growth has been spectacularly lopsided.

## Inequality, Poverty, and Health

Prosperity, by itself, cannot guarantee health. The Achilles' heel of the American economy is the high degree of economic inequality we tolerate in our society.[25] A direct consequence of economic inequality is that people near the bottom of the income distribution are poorer than they otherwise would be. Poverty in America (and for that matter, anywhere else in the world) means that people lack the resources to purchase the necessary goods and services to maintain good health.

The mediocre performance of the economy for poor and working-class Americans might be sufficient to account for our dismal health performance as a nation. However, health research suggests that the deleterious consequences of economic inequality are not just confined to the officially poor. According to this new view, the unequal distribution of income and wealth—as distinct from the low absolute standard of living among the poor—exerts an independent, detrimental influence on population health.[26] As it happens, the United States is one of the most unequal societies among developed countries. According to the Luxembourg Income Study, the distribution of incomes in this country is the most unequal of 22 industrialized countries that belong to the OECD— by quite a margin.[27] Wealthy Americans make considerably more money than their counterparts in other wealthy countries, while the bottom 10% of our households make considerably less than poor people in Europe or Japan. Consequently, the size of the gap between rich and poor is substantially wider in this country than in other societies.

An impression of the extent of inequality in this country can be swiftly, and vividly, gained by comparing the façade of public life in American cities compared to other countries. The visitor to any sizable American city is likely to be accosted by desperate panhandlers on the sidewalks and intersections. Homeless people are less noticeable in the major cities of other rich countries, or in the case of some places like Osaka, Japan, municipal authorities have gone to the extent of setting aside land in public parks to build temporary housing for itinerant populations. Americans drive around cities in hulking, gas-guzzling sport utility vehicles, while most Europeans, even wealthy ones, get by on more modest vehicles or take public transport. The enormous gulf between the rich and poor in this country has led over time to what John Kenneth Galbraith once dubbed the paradox of private splendor amidst public squalor.[28] As private wealth becomes more concentrated, the quality of public life suffers.

Across the American states, researchers have found a striking association between the degree of household income inequality and mortality rates: The more inegalitarian the distribution of income, the more unhealthy people tend to be.[29] Figure 1.2 shows the correlation between one measure of income inequality (aptly called the Robin Hood Index) and the mortality rate at the state level.[30] The Robin Hood Index is equivalent to the proportion of total income earned by all the households within a state that would need to be redistributed from the well-off to the less well-off in order to achieve income equality. Consequently, the higher the Robin Hood Index value, the more unequal the distribution of income in a given state.

As Figure 1.2 shows, the more unequal the distribution of income in a state, the higher the death rate. Other studies have shown that economic

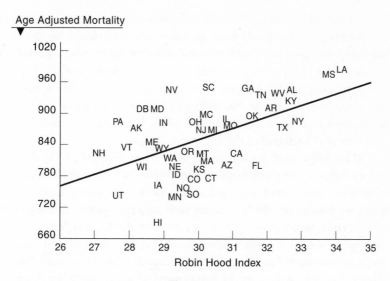

Figure 1.2

The relationship of income inequality to mortality rates
across the United States.

inequality is associated with higher rates of depression,[31] higher prevalence of hypertension and smoking,[32] and higher rates of teen pregnancy
and birth,[33] as well as lower self-rated health (i.e., people reporting that
their health is only fair or poor, as opposed to excellent or very good).[34]

Correlations of this type do not prove causation, and so the evidence linking economic inequality to poor health status is not universally
accepted.[35] In particular, many economists remain skeptical about such a
link, primarily because other factors besides economic inequality (such as
poverty or racial discrimination) might be driving the apparent association between income inequality and poor health status.[36] According to
these views, the real culprit behind America's poor health performance is
not economic inequality per se, but our persistent rate of poverty and/or
history of strained race relations that have produced massive health disparities. These arguments are important and warrant scrutiny.

First of all, there is no contradiction in stating that persistent poverty,
racism, and economic inequality are each, in and of themselves, important
contributors to the poor health of Americans. There can be no gainsaying that the poorest Americans bear a disproportionately high burden of illness and premature mortality compared to the rest of society.
However, the officially poor represent only 11% of the population, so we

can't blame all of our lackluster health performance on that segment of the population. The health status of Americans is mediocre for the near poor, the working poor, and even middle-class Americans, especially if you happen to belong to a minority race/ethnic group, or if you happen to live in a deprived community. Living in an unequal society is toxic to just about everybody's health, and our poor ranking against other economically advanced countries can't simply be blamed on the misbehaving minority at the tail end of the bell curve.

More important, for the critics who assert that poverty is the real culprit behind our poor health achievement, not economic inequality, what they conveniently leave out is that income inequality is one of the major *mechanisms* by which a society ends up with a persistently high rate of poverty. Consider the case of Sweden and the United States, which look rather similar in terms of their family poverty rates prior to government intervention (20.7% and 23.2%, respectively). After redistributive taxes and transfer payments, the two countries look dramatically different. Compared to the United States, Sweden ends up with a more egalitarian distribution of income, a much lower rate of family poverty (3.8% compared to 18.9%), as well as a higher level of life expectancy.[37] In other words, if our politicians are serious about tackling poverty, someone has to pay for the health care of low-income families, their prescription drug costs, their child care and children's education, and so forth. Leaving this to laissez-faire markets and trickle-down policies simply will not suffice. Tackling poverty and reducing income inequality are therefore complementary policy objectives; they are not mutually exclusive, as some critics appear to imply.

The question of reducing racial inequalities has also been posed as an alternative to tackling economic inequalities—to the detriment of both agendas. In the ongoing debate about whether economic inequality is harmful to health, some researchers have noted that the effects of income inequality on excess mortality are not robust after taking into account racial heterogeneity in the population.[38] In other words, it is America's racial heterogeneity (and presumably the resulting strained racial relations) that is to blame for our poor health achievement, not our degree of economic inequality. Once again, this is a false dichotomy. Racial heterogeneity and prejudice are surely part of the historical mechanism by which this country has ended up with, and continues to tolerate, high degrees of economic inequality. Racial heterogeneity is itself a marker for many kinds of inequality in access to resources, including not only wealth and income, but also education, health care, and residential quality. Furthermore, whereas government policy can alter the distribution of income, it can hardly influence the distribution of race (at least not democratically).

## Conclusion

Considering all of the evidence, there is a good case to be made for implicating economic inequality as a major culprit behind America's mediocre health performance. Several lines of reasoning suggest why economic inequality is detrimental to our nation's health. In the realm of politics, income inequality translates into poor health via the polarized politics of rich and poor. That is, when the social distance widens between the rich and poor in society, governments tend to invest less in social infrastructure, such as public transport and amenities, public education, public health, and social welfare. In addition, our poor health performance reflects exposure to a variety of other adverse social circumstances as well, including residential segregation, racism, job insecurity, and the erosion of community bonds.

Health is an exquisitely sensitive mirror of our social conditions and political arrangements. It stands to reason, therefore, that improving our collective health requires investments to improve the circumstances of our families, communities, and workplaces.

## Notes

1. Barbara Starfield, "Is U.S. Health Really the Best in the World?" *Journal of the American Medical Association* 284 (2000): 483–484.

2. Ibid.

3. Stephen Bezruchka, "Is Our Society Making You Sick?" *Newsweek* (26 February 2001): 14.

4. Ibid.

5. Marc Miringoff and Marque-Luisa Miringoff, *The Social Health of the Nation: How America Is Really Doing* (New York: Oxford University Press, 1999), 12.

6. Hightower quoted in Nancy Folbre, *The Invisible Heart* (New York: The New Press, 2001), 64.

7. Marque-Luisa Miringoff, Marc Miringoff, and Sandra Opdycke, "The Growing Gap between Standard Economic Indicators and the Nation's Social Health," *Challenge* (July–August 1996): 17–22.

8. Annie E. Casey Foundation, *Kids Count Data Book* (Baltimore: The Annie E. Casey Foundation, 1999); George A. Kaplan, Susan A. Everson, and John W. Lynch, "The Contribution of Social and Behavioral Research to an Understand-

ing of the Distribution of Disease: A Multilevel Approach," *Promoting Health: Intervention Strategies from Social and Behavioral Research*, ed. Brian D. Smedley and S. Leonard Syme (Washington, DC: Institute of Medicine, National Academy Press, 2000), 46.

9. David Williams, "Race and Health: Trends and Policy Implications," *Income, Socioeconomic Status, and Health: Exploring the Relationship*, ed. James A. Auerbach and Barbara Kimivae Krimgold (Washington, DC: National Policy Association and the Academy for Health Services Research and Health Policy, 2001), 74.

10. Christopher J. L. Murray, Catherine M. Michaud, M. T. McKenna, and James S. Marks, *U.S. Patterns of Mortality by County and Race, 1965–1994* (Cambridge, MA: Harvard Burden of Disease Unit, Harvard Center for Population and Development Studies, and the Centers for Disease Control and Prevention, 1998).

11. Richard Hernstein and Charles Murray, *The Bell Curve: Intelligence and Class Structure* (New York: Free Press, 1995).

12. Richard J. David and James W. Collins, "Differing Birth Weight among Infants of U.S.-Born Blacks, African-Born Blacks, and U.S.-Born White Women," *New England Journal of Medicine* 337 (1997): 1209–1214.

13. Richard Cooper, C. N. Rotimi, S. Ataman, D. McGee, B. Osotimehin, S. Kadiri, W. Muna, S. Kingue, H. Fraser, T. Forrester, et al., "The Prevalence of Hypertension in Seven Populations of West African Origin," *American Journal of Public Health* 87 (1997): 160–168.

14. Richard Cooper, C. N. Rotimi, J. S. Kaufman, E. E. Owoaje, H. Fraser, T. Forrester, R. Wilks, L. K. Riste, and J. K. Cruickshank, "Prevalence of NIDDM among Populations of the African Diaspora," *Diabetes Care* 20 (1997): 343–348.

15. Michael Marmot and S. Leonard Syme, "Acculturation and Coronary Heart Disease in Japanese Americans," *American Journal of Epidemiology* 104 (1976): 225–247.

16. Sally Satel, *P.C., M.D.: How Political Correctness Is Corrupting Medicine* (New York: Basic Books, 2000).

17. James A. Morone, "Enemies of the People: The Moral Dimension to Public Health," *Journal of Health Politics, Policy and Law* 22 (1997): 993–1020.

18. Barbara Starfield, "Is U.S. Health Really the Best in the World," *Journal of the American Medical Association* 284 (2000): 483–485.

19. Bruce Link and Jo Phelan, "Social Conditions as Fundamental Causes of Disease," *Journal of Health and Social Behavior* (1995, extra issue): 80–94.

20. Norman Daniels, Bruce Kennedy, and Ichiro Kawachi, *Is Inequality Bad for Our Health?* (Boston: Beacon Press, 2000).

21. Anonymous, "Rudolf Virchow on Pathology Education," available at www.pathguy.com/lectures/virchow.htm.

22. Amartya Sen, *Development as Freedom* (New York: Alfred A. Knopf, 1999).

23. Lawrence Mishel, Jared Bernstein, and John Schmidt, *The State of Working America, 1998–1999* (Washington, DC: Economic Policy Institute, 1999).

24. Figure 6, data from Mishel et al., *Working America*.

25. Richard Freeman, "Is the New Income Inequality the Achilles' Heel of the American Economy?" *The Inequality Paradox: Growth of Income Disparity*, ed. James A. Auerbach and Richard S. Belous (Washington, DC: National Policy Association, 1998), chapter 12, 219–229.

26. Ichiro Kawachi, Bruce P. Kennedy, and Richard G. Wilkinson, *Income Inequality and Health: A Reader* (New York: The New Press, 1999).

27. Timothy M. Smeeding, "U.S. Income Inequality in a Cross-National Perspective: Why Are We So Different?" *Inequality Paradox: Growth of Income Disparity*, ed. James A. Auerbach and Richard S. Belous (Washington, DC: National Policy Association, 1998), 194–217.

28. John Kenneth Galbraith, *The Affluent Society* (Boston: Houghton Mifflin, 1958).

29. Kawachi et al., *Income Inequality and Health*.

30. Bruce P. Kennedy, Ichiro Kawachi, and Deborah Prothrow-Stith, "Income Distribution and Mortality: Cross-Sectional Ecological Study of the Robin Hood Index in the United States," *British Medical Journal* 312 (1996): 1004–1007. See also erratum, *British Medical Journal* 312 (1996): 1253.

31. Robert S. Kahn, Paul H. Wise, Bruce P. Kennedy, and Ichiro Kawachi, "State Income Inequality, Household Income, and Maternal Mental and Physical Health: Cross-sectional National Survey," *British Medical Journal* 321 (2000): 1311–1315.

32. Ana V. Diez-Roux, Bruce G. Link, and Mary E. Northridge, "A Multilevel Analysis of Income Inequality and Cardiovascular Disease Risk Factors," *Social Science & Medicine* 50 (2000): 673–687.

33. Rachel Gold, Ichiro Kawachi, Bruce P. Kennedy, John W. Lynch, and Frank A. Connell, "Ecological Analysis of Teen Birth Rates: Association with Community Income and Income Inequality," *Maternal and Child Health Journal* 5 (2001): 161–167.

34. Bruce P. Kennedy, Ichiro Kawachi, Roberta Glass, and Deborah Prothrow-Stith, "Income Distribution, Socioeconomic Status, and Self Rated Health in the United States: Multilevel Analysis," *British Medical Journal* 317 (1998): 917–921.

35. Christopher Jencks, "Does Inequality Matter?" *Daedalus* (Winter 2002): 49–65.

36. Jennifer Mellor and Jeffrey Milyo, "Re-examining the Evidence of an Ecological Association between Income Inequality and Health," *Journal of Health Politics, Policy and Law* 26 (2001): 487–522.

37. Clyde Hertzman, "The Case for an Early Childhood Development Strategy," *Isuma* 1 (2000): 1–19.

38. Angus Deaton and Darren Lubotsky, "Mortality, Inequality and Race in American Cities and States," *Social Science & Medicine* 56 (2001): 1139–1153.

# Health Disparities in the Land of Equality

## LAWRENCE R. JACOBS

*From the Depths.* Photogravure
by William Balfour Kerr, 1906.

Elliot Wilson is an African-American music writer and editor who grew up in a housing project in New York City. He landed a job with an up-and-coming magazine that paid him in the low six figures. But the high salary did not bring elation or good health. He was troubled by guilt for "selling out," knowing that most African-Americans have a "short expectancy of life. . . . [and] don't feel [they] can be on a five-year plan to success." His ambivalence about "making it" was also complicated by the racial tension at his new job. As he wrestled with feelings of guilt, he discovered that he had "the black man's disease," high blood pressure. He attributed it to bad diet, the pressure of his job, and the struggle for survival in white America.[1] Wilson's story illustrates a common pattern: being black in America is dangerous to your health even if you are relatively affluent.[2]

In 1994, Sergeant Harry Feyer was a mechanic in the U.S. Army who faced a stark situation: the Army informed him that he would be discharged as it cut "dead wood" to reduce costs, and yet his family—his pregnant wife and his 5-year-old son—needed medical benefits. Fear of whether he could support his family and cover their medical care kept him awake at night and convinced him that he had no choice but to volunteer to work in an area that scares off most soldiers: nuclear, biological, and chemical warfare. "I took it," Feyer explained, "because I didn't want to throw away 8 years of being in the Army." And he needed the medical benefits for his family.[3] The immediate pressures on Feyer, who is white, overwhelmed any concern about the health risks of working with hazardous materials. Feyer illustrates the bind faced by many Americans who are locked into relatively low-paying jobs and who struggle to gain medical benefits, even if it means exposing themselves to potentially serious health risks at work.

Americans embrace democracy and yet tolerate disparities in health due to the stress of race relations, economic deprivation, and inadequate medical care. Why? How could the richest country in the world (perhaps, the richest ever known) leave hardworking citizens like Elliot Wilson and Sergeant Feyer in such agonizing situations? Why does a country that guarantees equal rights to all Americans regardless of skin color or income put up with Sergeant Feyer's dilemma (take that hazardous job if you want health insurance) and with a level of racial tension that literally kills people of color?

One popular view blames Wilson, Feyer, and Americans like them for their own problems. After all, Wilson concedes that his high blood pressure stems, in part, from poor diet, and Feyer's unappealing specialty choice reflects his failure to demonstrate skills that made him more than "dead wood." Indeed, this view of their conundrums fits with a long American tradition of individual self-reliance: Wilson and Feyer (and other Americans facing similar circumstances) are in a bind because they made bad decisions and are now suffering the consequences. Put simply, individuals make their own health through their personal choices—smoking, using drugs, engaging in risky sexual behavior, abstaining from exercise, eating high-fat foods, and failing to develop the skills that earn them employer health insurance benefits.

Chalking up Wilson's and Feyer's problems to their own flawed personal choices has an understandable allure to Americans raised on a thick porridge of individualism and, yet, it misses an important part of the story. The reality is that income, occupational position, race, and other factors constrain and influence individual choices. Neighborhoods where lower-income and black Americans live offer fewer opportunities for individuals to choose healthier behaviors than more affluent white communities. In place of large supermarkets with fresh vegetables, convenience and liquor stores dot the landscape of disadvantaged neighborhoods. Exposure to violence as well as to environmental threats—crumbling buildings, chemical pollution, and biological threats—is also more likely. Even individuals intent on making "good" decisions find fewer opportunities to make those choices in poor neighborhoods. Even relatively affluent African-Americans like Wilson often find their housing options limited by racial segregation and experience the stress of living with race—whether it is tension at work or being singled out by police for scrutiny.[4]

Although he is white, Feyer's predicament also reflects forces beyond his control: The restructuring of the global economy toward information and knowledge industries has reduced job opportunities for low-skilled workers who once enjoyed high wages and good health insurance. Between 1979 and 1993, the real hourly wages of males with 12 years of education fell by a fifth; those with entry-level jobs have declined by a third.[5] One out of seven Americans (43.6 million) lacks health insurance, even though many hold regular jobs. More than 1 million Americans in 2002 joined the growing numbers whose employers no longer offered them health insurance (the American alternative to government coverage found in all other industrialized countries). Cost cutting by business has slashed the proportion of Americans covered by employer-sponsored insurance to 61%. The bottom line is that while the choices of individuals are of course important, they are made within a broader environment that is beyond the control of any individual.

Many Americans may not be alarmed about the plight of folks like Elliot Wilson and Sergeant Feyer because they believe that "big government" steps in to solve the problem. Indeed, the United States spends more money on medical care (one-seventh of the economy) than any other country in the world; the government has established expensive programs to widen access to medical care and improve health. About one-fifth of the federal government's budget is devoted to two efforts to help the vulnerable: Medicaid and Medicare. Medicaid opens the door to the poorest citizens, while Medicare finances care for retirees, the disabled, and those with designated medical afflictions (especially end-stage renal disease).

Government is "big," but its money and authority are not used to coddle millions of working Americans who lack health insurance. Nor is the government's major focus helping individuals who fail. A number of studies have demonstrated that the health of African-Americans and individuals with limited income is most affected by medical care and, yet, these people have less access to medical care than financially better-off groups: they receive less preventive care and fewer diagnostic procedures (e.g., prostate and colorectal screening, pap smears, and mammograms). Programs like Medicare and Medicaid have made a big difference in improving the health and medical treatment of some Americans, but they have not prevented these discrepancies in the treatment of African-Americans and the less affluent. Furthermore, no government assistance is provided to millions of Americans who work full time for employers who do not offer health insurance.

The critical question is this: How are the government's vast resources being used and why isn't the government doing more to protect citizens who play by the rules? The enormous human costs of inadequate or missing government policies give urgency to answering this question.

In all industrialized countries, market competition intensified during the 1980s and 1990s as changes in finance and technology altered the global economy, escalated the demand for high-skill workers, and widened the gap between the affluent and the rest of the population. Governments in the United States, Canada, and Western Europe attempted to protect their citizens through policies on income, education, occupational conditions, and other areas. The purpose was to lessen the kind of gross inequalities that Charles Dickens portrayed in *Oliver Twist* and to lift citizens above a desperate fight for survival.

In Western Europe and Canada, governments tempered pressures that would have widened economic inequality and disparities in health by erecting, maintaining, or strengthening a wide range of policies— increased funding for education to expand the supply of skilled workers, cash assistance, higher minimum wages, and continuation of taxation rates and programs to encourage unionization through centralized wage bargaining.

In the United States, by contrast, the kind of economic changes that swept Western Europe and Canada over the past few decades had a more immediate, powerful, and unbuffered impact on income and wealth distribution than they did in other industrialized countries. American policy makers were not asleep. They did substantially increase tax rebates to low-income workers under the earned income tax credit beginning in the mid-1980s and, as subsequent chapters will show, established or expanded existing programs to expand medical care to children and the poor. These efforts fell short, however, of responding adequately to the crushing changes brought about by new economic pressures and increased insecurity. From the late 1970s to the middle 1990s, inequality in the distribution of income increased by 24% in the United States; the increases among our allies were far smaller—11% in Sweden and Italy and about 7% in Canada, Germany, Finland, and Norway.[6] The impact of government programs is starkly illustrated by comparing the poverty rates *after* government steps in: 16.9% of the total American population is poor compared to about half that rate in northern Europe, Germany, and France; a staggering one out of five American children (22%) are poor compared to 3% in Sweden, 4% in Norway and Finland, and about 8% to 10% in Denmark, France, and Germany.[7]

Large and exceptional levels of economic inequality and poverty make Americans sick and lead to their premature deaths. In 1995, the growing gaps in the distribution of income accounted for the *combined* loss of life resulting from lung cancer, diabetes, motor vehicle crashes, human immunodeficiency virus infection, suicide, and homicide.[8]

Governments have two tools to protect the health of their citizens— they can finance access to medical care and they can buffer the push of markets to widen economic inequality. The comparatively poor health of Americans, documented in chapter 1, results from the relatively tepid use of the tools of *medical access* and *market management* by U.S. policy makers. Health is affected not only by low income but also by the occupations that low pay is often associated with—think of Sergeant Feyer as he dons protective equipment to go to work. Millions of low-income Americans are dying or becoming sick at higher rates than the more affluent because they face everyday experiences more easily avoided by insured and more affluent individuals: illnesses that go untreated or that are treated after they have become acute (as in the case of asthma); low or modest incomes that prevent a healthy diet, housing, and other necessary living conditions; and membership in a racial or ethnic minority.

We think of our own health as deeply personal. We blame our colds on a friend or relative who sneezed, and we trace our stomachaches to the food we ate. The health of an entire population is affected by these kinds of individual circumstances, but more than that, it is the product of our choices as a society. Economic and racial conditions, along with access to essential medical care, can (if not properly treated) become social germs that infect and kill.

The puzzle is explaining why America has taken halting and ineffective steps to protect the health of its citizens. American citizens possess the right to vote and to engage in other forms of political activities— indeed, they pioneered democratic vehicles for mobilizing voters such as the political party—and yet their government has tolerated the largest and fastest growing disparities in income, wealth, and health among advanced industrial countries. Why haven't a majority of voters banded together to elect a government that would protect them from the kind of harsh treatment by markets that citizens in Western Europe and Canada have escaped? Why would *elected* government officials in the United States be reticent (compared to their colleagues in Western Europe and Canada) to use the tools of medical access and market management to prevent large increases in the economic inequality and health problems of many of their constituents? How can a structure of inequality in income and health develop and be tolerated in a political system that guarantees political equality and empowers citizens and their elected government to manage markets and provide assess to medical care?

This chapter argues that the political rights enjoyed by all U.S. citizens are used disproportionately by the better organized and better established. In American politics, *three trenches* prevent the largesse of government from being devoted to raising the health of all Americans—business and interest groups wield disproportional power, the less advantaged do not participate, and workers are poorly organized.

## Government Policy as War Bounty

You don't need a degree in political science to see the armies of special interests that descend on government to get their share of the "take." When members of Congress or the president consider changing Medicare, for instance, you can count on the presence of lobbyists for pharmaceutical companies, managed care organizations, insurance companies, medical equipment suppliers, nursing home operators, seniors (the American Association of Retired Persons), hospital representatives

(American Hospital Association), doctors (the American Medical Association), and organizations representing many medical specialties. Often these groups operate in a way that is invisible to most Americans; once in awhile the curtain of silence is parted to show, for instance, pharmaceutical manufacturers using campaign contributions to shape legislation on Medicare's drug benefit.[9]

## Interest Groups as the Tool of Democratic Government

Although many Americans revile special interests as a corrupting influence, the very fact that they are plentiful and diverse could offer a self-correcting mechanism for an open and responsive democratic government. In fact, one set of observers of American politics (known as the "pluralists") has long argued that ordinary citizens from across American society organize into numerous, diverse groups that engage in continuous bargaining; the competition of these multiple and competing pressure groups prevents any one group from monopolizing power. Government policy becomes a kind of cash register recording the balancing of these competing demands. The resulting form of government is relatively open, allowing citizens to exert a relatively high degree of control over issues of concern to them.[10]

The optimistic view of interest groups is illustrated by the contending efforts in 2002 to simultaneously expand Medicare benefits and payments to medical care providers at a time when government budgets were constrained by large new expenditures on national security after September 11 to defend against terrorist attacks. Rather than any one group monopolizing Medicare policy, the ambition of one set of interest groups fighting to expand Medicare's benefits for seniors was counteracted by the ambition of lobbyists for doctors and hospitals to increase their reimbursement. Eventually, they compromised and both got something—but not everything—that they wanted.

The mere presence of interest groups, then, is not necessarily harmful or even hostile to democratic government. Interest groups representing the less affluent and African-Americans could (and do, to some extent) organize and press for policies that would benefit their health.

## Interest Groups as an Organization of Bias

Interest groups rarely deliver, however, on the promises of their proponents—representation of American society, intense competition, and articulation of the broad public's concerns. The all too common result is that big government becomes an appetizing watering hole for well-organized pressure groups skilled at making deals to satiate their own appetite.

The implications for health policy are significant: Huge government expenditures on health care and on programs that affect health more broadly originate in a commitment to help all of American society, but during the legislative process they are often shaped and implemented to favor the well organized.[11] The nitty-gritty work of building coalitions to enact legislation invariably produces programs that reward different sections of American society in proportion to their existing power and resources. Those who benefit most are often those who are already influential in the halls of government and successful within the walls of boardrooms. Society's broad commitment to creating a healthy society is undermined in three ways by interest groups: business groups dominate, the well organized collude, and market winners silence important policy debates.

*The Best Organized Are the Biggest Winners.* In American society, not all interests are organized or represented. There has been a significant rise in the number of interest groups plying their trade in Washington, but far more of them represent businesses and large institutions than the public interest and the disadvantaged; the watchdogs for the vulnerable lack the financial and organizational resources of their adversaries.[12] In chapter 6, Constance Nathanson offers a telling study of advocates for the disadvantaged who did organize (from campaigners against tuberculosis in the black community and medical profession during the early twentieth century to more recent community organizing to combat AIDS) but were thwarted by insufficient financial, political, or public support (even within the disadvantaged communities themselves).

The overrepresentation of the better established can be cumulative over time. Efforts to enact health insurance for all Americans were made throughout the twentieth century—in the early 1900s (especially in several states, most notably New York), the New Deal in the 1930s, Harry Truman's fiery campaigns in the 1940s and early 1950s, and the efforts of Richard Nixon and Bill Clinton over the past three decades. The failed battle to enact universal health insurance is like a folk ballad in which the details in each stanza change but the stock refrain remains largely unchanged: Americans who supported or stood to gain from the legislation were outgunned or unnerved by well-financed representatives of business, doctors, hospitals, and conservative politicians who capitalized on Washington's legislative labyrinth and the uneasiness of Americans with "big" government.

The one significant blemish on this consistent record of failed reform is the passage of Medicare in 1965.[13] Reform opponents were every bit as ferocious and dogged when President John F. Kennedy fulfilled his campaign promise and introduced legislation in 1961. But during this one episode, the opponents of reform were foiled by the confluence of increasing hospitalization costs; the landslide victory in the 1964 election for the Democratic Party (Lyndon Johnson swamped Barry Goldwater and the Democrats won large majorities in the House and Senate); and the strategic decisions of determined health care reforms to pull back from national health insurance to target one widely admired part of the population (seniors), a narrow set of medical care (largely hospitalization), and one of the most popular government programs as a programmatic foundation (Social Security).

Medicare is living proof that the United States can and does use one of the two government tools for protecting citizens—expanding access. Medicare has expanded access to health care, improved health and life expectancy, and reduced poverty among seniors and the disabled.

So often in the United States, the problem is not the complete failure to act but the incompleteness of the actions that are taken. As much as Medicare is a tribute to the powerful impact of government in improving the lives and health of Americans, it is also a testament to the limitations of government actions owing to the disproportionate influence of the organized and better established.

Medicare expanded access to seniors and the disabled at a financial cost ($200 billion per year) and manner that were directed, ironically, at accommodating the opponents of national health insurance and some of the harshest critics of widening the scope of government. The history of Medicare is, in part, a tale of "big" government benefiting the very special interests that initially opposed the program.[14] The accommodation of reform opponents began during the initial design of Medicare's administrative structure. Soon after Kennedy's election in 1960, influential civil servants argued for "direct federal administration" to control reimbursement of doctors, hospitals, contractors, and others. They explicitly warned against arrangements that would "not be strong from an administrative point of view ... for a program where ... the costs are to be paid by the Federal Government." The combination, however, of vociferous opposition to "government interference" by groups representing business, doctors, and hospitals, along with public uneasiness about major new government functions, prompted Democratic presidents and legislators to overrule the recommendation of the civil servants and deliberately undermine government administration of public funds. The godfathers of Medicare simultaneously committed huge sums of new public money and promised to "protect completely against Federal interference" both by putting the determination of reimbursement in the hands of providers (who could charge what they deemed "reasonable") and by ceding oversight to private agencies who would handle claims, inspect providers, and review billed costs.[15] Imagine painting your parent's house and then, after the fact, setting your price and having it paid (without question) by your local government.

Soon after Medicare was signed into law in 1965, its costs (not surprisingly) far exceeded the projections of its promoters. The abdication to special interests and failure to establish government budget authority over public funds in the mid-1960s was followed, as civil servants had predicted, by generous reimbursement for doctors, hospitals, and medical equipment suppliers. The program's architects (at the height of their political power) knowingly caved in to the demands of health care providers; it would take two decades to reestablish financial control.

By the 1980s and 1990s, presidents Ronald Reagan, George H. W. Bush, and Bill Clinton moved in the direction of the original civil servant recommendation by establishing "prospective payment systems" for Medicare's spending on hospitals, doctors, and outpatient services, which ended the ability of providers to set their own reimbursement.[16] The delayed assertion of government authority over public funds did not, however, end the accommodation of Medicare service providers. Hospitals, doctors, medical equipment suppliers, medical laboratories, agencies that provide home care and physical and occupational therapy, and others all depend on Medicare as their largest single source of income. The intense stakes of service providers combined with the understandable apathy and limited information of most Americans regarding the detailed administration of Medicare have translated into enormous influence for the organizations that represent service providers. Here are some of the myriad ways in which providers of service have benefited from the annual distribution of Medicare's $200 billion:[17]

• Representatives of the medical equipment suppliers, medical laboratories, and the agencies that provide services to Medicare beneficiaries have swayed lawmakers to mandate how and how much they are paid. This explains why Medicare sports its own equivalent to the $400 toilet seats bought by the Defense Department and why efforts by Democratic and Republican presidents to improve Medicare's purchasing have been defeated by influential members of Congress.

- Health maintenance organizations and managed care firms continue to enjoy enormous support among lawmakers even as they have stripped tens of thousands of Medicare beneficiaries from their programs because they were no longer profitable. Congressional leaders are now talking about buying their participation, even if it costs more than the per-patient expenditures on beneficiaries in the traditional Medicare program.

- Although the American Medical Association is no longer the dominant interest group representing the medical profession, it has switched from leading the opposition to Medicare (along with national health insurance) when it was first proposed in the 1960s to literally living off of its operations, in part because it holds the quite profitable copyright on the prospective payment system for physicians.

- Medical providers no longer enjoy the professional autonomy they once did,[18] but hospitals take advantage of Medicare's prospective payment systems and doctors have continued to prosper—compared to their counterparts in Western Europe and Canada—as their representatives have continued to influence the executive branch's decisions about Medicare payments to them.[19] Compared to their counterparts in Western Europe and Canada, the payment of American doctors by private and government sources remains very generous.

The well organized and vigorously represented exert a disproportionate "voice" in the making of health policy. The playing field is not even; many teams never form; many that form lack the resources to show up consistently and at the right time; and others are just chased off the field. This was all too apparent to the supporters of President Clinton's efforts in 1993 and 1994 to redistribute resources from the affluent to those who were uninsured or underinsured. The President and his allies blame their defeat on the imbalance in interest-group organization and pressure. Although this account is self-serving because it shifts the spotlight off of their own errors, it does describe one part of the 1993–1994 legislative battle: the most vocal and visible groups represented well-organized interests that were intent on protecting their stakes in the current system and preventing reform by instilling uncertainty in members of Congress and in the minds of many Americans:[20]

- Big businesses as a whole stood to gain from Clinton's controls on health expenditures, but their umbrella organizations—the Business Roundtable and the National Association of Manufacturers—

opposed the president's plan because of intense pressure from a few members (namely, health insurers) who had large stakes in the existing system.

- Health maintenance organizations rallied against government regulations and requirements about accepting poor people.
- Small businesses, pharmaceutical companies, and small and medium health insurers threw themselves into defeating Clinton's plan because they (accurately) saw it as a dire threat to their survival.
- Representatives of doctors mobilized to voice concern about reductions in their income and further encroachment on their autonomy to make clinical decisions.
- Health care centers at universities around the country organized to complain about cuts in their financing.
- The Northeast formed a coalition to continue to get a disproportionate share of government health expenditures at the expense of states like Minnesota, which had lower expenses.

There were, of course, representatives of unions and Medicare beneficiaries that backed reform as a whole. But even they failed to match the intensity of reform opponents due to their own concerns about protecting the benefits of their constituents.

In short, when American policy makers attempted to use government to expand access and to claw back government money in Medicare to fund care for individuals with lower incomes, they often found doctors, hospitals, and an array of other stakeholders well organized and aggressive in pressing their interests while the potential (and more diffuse) beneficiaries of reform were unorganized or drowned out. Despite this record of dominance by powerful interests, the 1965 passage of Medicare demonstrates the potential for significant breakthroughs when real-world problems, political upheaval, and realistically calibrated strategy by determined reformers come together.

*Interest Group Collusion.* The hopeful interpretation of interest groups as a tool for open democratic government rests on the assumption of competition—the battle of lobbyists will serve as a kind "hidden hand" that counteracts any one group's grab for domination and allows policy to emerge that represents the diverse perspectives in the country. The reality of American politics, however, is that the most powerful interest groups often establish cooperative relationships among themselves and with legislators and bureaucrats. Interest groups (like big business) spend much of their time trying to avoid competition; interest groups join with legislators and civil servants to form largely independent fiefdoms or "iron triangles" that control government decisions in narrow policy areas.[21]

The secret to the effectiveness of Medicare service providers is the symbiotic relationships they form with members of Congress and Medicare administrators. What may seem like watchdogs from afar are, in fact, lapdogs of special interests. Obviously, Medicare needs hospitals, doctors, therapists, equipment, and many other essential goods and services. The question, however, is how much medical providers, suppliers, and contractors are paid and the volume and kind of services they provide. Members of Congress treat the distribution of Medicare's largesse as a valuable political tool to "bring the bacon" back home to constituents, but also to reward contributors and lobbyists that support them. One of the most remarkable statements about Medicare is that its fiery beginning in the legislative battles of the early 1960s has been replaced by bipartisan cooperation in distributing the program's billions of dollars to health care providers, suppliers, and contractors.

Not surprisingly, lobbyists for Medicare's providers, suppliers and contractors are eager to support their friends in Congress with campaign contributions, political help in advertising their good deeds to constituents back home, and jobs in their districts. For their part, the civil servants who administer Medicare in the Department of Health and Human Services facilitate the feeding of providers, suppliers, and contractors as a welcome opportunity to curry favor with allies who will work to protect their budgets and expand their authority and personnel—members of Congress and special interest groups.

On occasion, representatives of Americans with poor health are able to work with the institutional forces that live off of Medicare or, when necessary, to challenge them. In chapter 9, Colleen Grogan and Eric Patashnik show how determined reformers expanded the base of support for Medicaid (which began as a program for the poor) and its services. Coalition building and well-timed interventions by advocates for the poor have spared Medicaid from the budgetary and programmatic cuts that often meet programs for the poor—such as "welfare"—and expanded its assistance to mothers and children.

Competition among interest groups, though, rarely drives the distribution of huge government expenditures on medical care. Instead, interest groups cooperate with members of Congress and civil servants to shut out opposing interests and undermine the competitive nature of the political marketplace. The result is that big government and well-established sectional interests work together to create "socialism for the organized."[22]

*Controlling the Agenda to "Safe" Issues.* There is almost no limit to the set of issues and problems that government officials could discuss. Not surprisingly, governments regularly fail to address many pressing real-world problems. Which issues and subjects from this nearly infinite pool actually receive sustained attention by government officials? What explains the silences in American policy discussions?

Today's policy debate on health and health care skips past the urgent problem of more than 40 million uninsured Americans and instead focuses on expanding Medicare benefits to drugs and a nebulous "Patient's Bill of Rights." Chapters 3 and 4 (by Deborah Stone and Mark Schlesinger, respectively) suggest that economic and racial inequalities in health and access to medical treatment are not recognized or accepted as problems that demand urgent policy responses. One reason may be the predominance of market principles, which convert troubling disparities into technical questions about "efficiency," "consumer choice," and health care "producers" and hide the larger social and distributional consequences. These chapters raise an important question: Why aren't Americans morally outraged by the racial discrimination that Stone points to and why don't they punish policy makers who embrace markets in defiance of the public's reservations (as Schlesinger shows)?

The *silences in policy debates* about the uninsured and racial and economic inequalities result from a number of interrelated factors: cultural traditions that gravitate toward definitions of equality in terms of opportunity rather than outcome and continue to express uneasiness with government interventions to alter distributions by markets; established institutional arrangements (such as the provision of health insurance through employers) that reflect and reinforce individualist and antistate traditions; and the polarization of the political parties regarding the role and scope of government.

Effective interest groups exploit the existing cultural, institutional, and political tendencies to affect the subjects of policy discussions long before a particular proposal is initiated, debated, or even decided. Their objective is to exclude issues that significantly threaten the status quo and their interests from full discussion by government officials and in the mass media.

Of course, interest groups cannot censor discussion of threatening issues, but they do have an imposing arsenal for discrediting them by drawing on cultural, institutional, and political legacies:[23]

- They can invoke an existing stigma or bias: they warn about waste and market inefficiencies (as Stone observes) and castigate the "undeserving" poor as a justification for shifting a large segment of expenditures on Medicaid—a program created to aid the indigent—to individuals who were in the middle class during their working years but have become confined to acute-care or long-term facilities like nursing homes. Chapter 9 by Grogan and Patashnik explores the remarkable repositioning of Medicaid to serve the non-poor.
- Established interest groups can use entrenched procedures (such as the congressional legislative process) to discredit unwelcome changes as "budget busting"—even as they continue to accept large government expenditures.
- They use paid advertisements to capitalize on Americans' widespread distrust in government, discrediting unwanted reforms as "inefficient" or "wasteful"—critiques that, of course, do not apply to their activities. The Health Insurance Association of America carefully calibrated a series of advertisements based on a mythical folksy couple, "Harry and Louise," to evoke unease among the public and Washington policy makers that the Clinton reform would introduce "big government" and threaten the care of everyday Americans.

Interest groups deploy these tactics to restrict the scope of government policy discussions to "safe" subjects. The relative silence about the uninsured, the acceptance of market principles, and the logic and calculations that flow from them (especially among policy makers) are the products of American institutions, partisan politics, and cultural patterns. In addition, interest groups effectively channel health policy discussions away from sustained debates about the redistribution of existing health expenditures from the currently insured and well-paid contractors, providers, and suppliers of medical services.

In short, the successful individuals use interest groups to magnify their success. Americans who are successful in private markets are most likely to join and fund established interest groups who develop cooperative relations with government officials and, in turn, win government tax exemptions and subsidies for their members. By contrast, the unorganized and less well established receive less not only from their employers but also from their government. The result is that health care policies affecting broader living conditions in society *expand* (rather than lessen) inequalities. Political rights are equal (each citizen has only one vote), but the most advantaged use their rights more extensively and with greater success.

## The Contested Rights to Medical Care and Good Health

Americans have long battled over how to define their "rights." Think of an issue and you can probably quickly associate a "right" with it. Some of the most intense battles in American history have been fought over establishing the "rights" of women and African-Americans to vote. There's also been a 100-year struggle to win the "rights" to government financing for American medical care.

The great variety of rights that Americans claim falls into three clusters.[24] One set includes civil rights—namely, the use of courts to conduct commercial interests and other private affairs. After you sign a contract with a business to receive a service, you are obligated to make good on your end of the deal (usually by paying you bill). If you meet your end of the contract, you have a "right" to expect the service or you can sue in court. Managed care organizations, for instance, must provide promised health services to their customers who pay their premiums or they can be taken to court and sued to provide the service and, perhaps, to pay a penalty. The second cluster of rights is political—the right to participate in representative government, enshrined in the notion of "one person, one vote." The third cluster is social rights—government programs that provide services and cash assistance that guarantee a basic standard of living. Government payments to Social Security recipients provide a minimum income for retirees; Medicare guarantees health services for seniors and the disabled.

### Restricting Rights

The three clusters of citizenship rights could feed off each other to promote their expansion. One of the great fears among the framers of the U.S. constitution was that majorities would use the vote to seize property and land—that is, use political rights to redistribute wealth. Indeed, in Western Europe, citizens extensively use their political rights—with 70% or more voting in national elections—to support governments that have established social rights to universal access to medical care and a number of policies (from generous unemployment benefits and allowances for children and housing to progressive taxation) that guarantee living standards against the swings of private markets. In Western Europe, political rights have been the engine driving the expansion of social rights.

In the United States, though, rights have interacted in ways that often hem in and restrict citizenship rights. In chapter 8, Peter Jacobson and Elizabeth Selvin suggest that a "conservative judicial counterreformation" over the past several decades has allowed health maintenance organizations and insurance companies, for instance, to use their construction of civil rights to fend off challenges against both their use of financial incentives to discourage certain treatments and their decisions to delay or deny medical care. This string of decisions by the judiciary is preventing citizens from using civil rights to broaden social rights to medical services by managed care organizations, health care providers, and the government. The muffling of the connection between civil and social rights is only one missed link, however. The interaction between political and social rights is another.

Americans' low voting rate and their often incomplete knowledge of about government policy is often portrayed as a failing of citizenship. But the truth is that the exercise of political rights does not occur in a social and economic vacuum. Social rights that promote governments' policies to help house, feed, and keep their constituents healthy give citizens some relief from the struggle for survival. They better enable citizens to devote time and energy to becoming informed and vigilant monitors of their elected representatives and thereby meaningfully exercise their formal political rights. Higher voting rates and political participation throughout Western Europe reflect, in part, the economic and social support that citizens receive (including a holiday to vote in national elections). While social rights encourage and promote the exercise of political rights in Western Europe, the comparatively ungenerous benefits in the United States put a drag on political participation. Americans are beleaguered voters. For many Americans (especially at the lower end of the income spectrum), exercising their right to vote requires a hurried trip to the ballot box, squeezed into a long day at work already overshadowed by other nagging concerns: perhaps a virus they cannot afford to have treated by a doctor, or worries about how to stretch a paycheck to cover their expenses.[25]

Voting, lobbying, and exercising other political rights create an important—but comparatively untapped—means for American citizens to expand the generosity of government cash benefits, medical care, and other services. Americans with lower income and blue-collar occupations are most in need of government assistance and most supportive of government activism. The hitch is that the very citizens who stand the most to gain from using their political rights to expand social rights (the less affluent and less well established) are also the least likely to vote, attend political meetings, join political organizations, write to their elected officials, contribute to candidates, and influence policy makers.[26]

As a result, those most needy and supportive of expanded social rights and government assistance are among the least visible in the political process. Even activists drawn from the ranks of less well-established Americans do not accurately represent their needs and preferences for government help.[27] Put simply, American government officials hear from the more affluent more often and clearly than they do from the less affluent. When elected officials hear from the less affluent, their "voice" is often distorted. The outcome is well documented: the depressed turnout by America's low-income citizens is associated with government benefits and services that are less generous toward them than those found in Western Europe and Canada where the less well-established participate in politics more extensively.[28]

There are, however, notable exceptions to the general pattern in the United States of civil and political rights failing to fuel the kind of social rights and egalitarian policies found in Western Europe and Canada. Seniors vote at relatively higher levels, which has sustained the most effective antipoverty programs in the United States—Social Security and Medicare. Indeed, these programs suggest that citizenship rights can reinforce each other in the United States: consistently higher voting by seniors has buoyed Social Security and Medicare, and the existence of these programs has given seniors motivation to remain acutely engaged in government policy.[29] In addition, when the poor and other disadvantaged groups have mobilized at critical junctures, such as during the 1960s, government assistance for these groups improved at the national and state levels. In chapter 3, Stone reminds us that the civil rights movement transformed medical care by desegregating many facilities. Moreover, Theda Skocpol shows that very large voluntary associations have been quite successful since the eighteenth century in mobilizing a cross-section of Americans to energetically exercise their political rights to bring about government reforms, including the expansion of social rights.[30]

## Liberal and Conservative Impulses

The decision of citizens (especially from lower-income groups) to not exercise their political rights raises fundamental questions about American culture and beliefs. Why don't the less affluent and less well established consistently deploy their political rights to drive out their lawmakers when they realize that their illness and mortality rates are higher than their better-situated counterparts? Health can be improved by access to essential medical care and other social benefits, but why don't we see the afflicted more frequently take extreme measures, like Denzel Washington's character in Hollywood's *John Q*?

The short answer is that large numbers of Americans are ambivalent or opposed to the general idea of using government to redistribute resources (though they do support concrete steps to alleviate what are seen as excesses of the private market system).[31] The source of that uneasiness with a philosophical embrace of egalitarian redistribution lies in the long-standing understanding of the rights of citizenship as guaranteeing equality of *opportunities* more than equality of *results*.

The rights of citizenship deliver concrete benefits like health insurance and cash allowances—quantitative benefits—but they also affect the quality of our lives in a public community by bestowing *equal status* on each of us. Regardless of background or current living conditions, all citizens are treated as full, participating members of the community, with fair access to society's way of life. The paychecks that you and I receive may be different, as may be the color of our skins, but we are each citizens with equal rights to a fair trial and to having one vote; neither of us can point to a hereditary title and expect to win preferential treatment by a judge or to have our ballots counted over someone else's.

The now widespread agreement that all Americans are equal reinforces the long-standing belief that America is a *meritocracy*——that status equality allows each citizen to rise or fall on his or her own. All citizens start life at the same point and have the opportunity, through education and other rights, to go as far as their intelligence, work effort, and other elements of merit will take them. Low income or, as in Sergeant Feyer's predicament, lack of health insurance is often attributed to flaws in the individual because all citizens start with the same basic rights and opportunities.

The result is that Americans tolerate inequality of economic *results*, especially in the abstract. Large majorities of Americans support private property and free enterprise and believe that having rich people benefits the country. Few approve of a substantial redistribution of income or wealth, and polls indicate that most agree that "[p]eople should be allowed to accumulate as much wealth as they can, even if some make millions while others live in poverty." Citizens in other industrialized countries are far more supportive of government policies that redistribute income and wealth in a more equal direction.[32]

An important reason that the disadvantaged do not regularly use their political rights to revolt to redistribute resources in their favor is that most Americans (including the less affluent) embrace the notions of meritocracy and equal opportunity. African-Americans and Americans with low incomes embrace the creed of a meritocracy as the savior for themselves and their children.[33] These sturdy beliefs put a "stamp of legitimacy" on the economic and social inequalities that are produced by the private market system. Citizenship rights provide the "foundation of equality on which a structure of inequality could be built."[34]

The powerful hold of citizenship rights in legitimizing inequalities is so often revealed by what does *not* happen—that is, by quiescence and passivity. The less well established do not take over hospitals like John Q.

The allure of meritocracy is intoxicating and enduring, and yet, American history is marked by startling episodes of popular eruptions that do redistribute resources—such as the New Deal and the Great Society—as well as by huge government programs that pump some money every day from the pockets of the most well off to the least well off (e.g., the Earned Income Tax Credit and other programs for the working poor, but most notably Social Security and Medicare).

The philosophical embrace of equality of opportunity coincides with strong support for government actions to interfere with private markets to protect citizens against clear threats.[35] Social Security, Medicare, and a host of other concrete and focused government programs that redistribute income enjoy the support of super-majorities of eight or nine out of ten Americans, and most Americans oppose unfair economic disparities that do not reflect merit or effort. There is growing anxiety about the threat of managed care to medical treatment, rising doubts about its positive contributions, increasing support for targeted government reforms, and strengthening opposition to expanding the role of managed care in Medicare.[36]

America is torn between philosophical impulses: we oppose intrusive and extensive government interventions to redistribute income and wealth while we pragmatically accept the need for concrete government protections against clear and specific threats from private markets. The natural inclination of even the disadvantaged is not to reach for their right to vote to push through massive redistribution, but Americans are not wooden caricatures of idealized individualists either. At particular moments, large majorities of Americans have been rallied to support targeted government reforms by large voluntary organizations and popular social movements.

## Keeping Politics Out of the Workplace

Many of the rights bestowed by citizenship are checked at the door when Americans walk into their place of employment. In her best-selling book *Nickel and Dimed*, Barbara Ehrenreich recounts how her coworkers in low-wage jobs "spend half their waking hours in what amounts . . . to a dictatorship." All citizens are armed with constitutional

protections against random searches, wiretaps, and threats and intimida-
tion by autocratic government officials. But when Ehrenreich walked
through the door to Wal-Mart, she surrendered those rights and came
under constant surveillance, abuse from managers intent on intimidating
her, and the possibility of arbitrary and immediate dismissal. Workplaces
run under the iron fists of authoritarians.

The "workplace authoritarianism" that Ehrenreich chronicles points
to a critical third explanation for the relatively restrained government
presence in securing the health of Americans—the comparatively weak
organization of workers in their jobs and the correspondingly weak political organization of workers in the government policy-making process.
In Western Europe, Ehrenreich's coworkers would have organizations
(namely, unions and a labor party) to help protect them. There, management lacks the prerogative (accepted without question in the United
States) to fire workers, and the government is often involved in organizing bargaining between labor and employers and setting wages.[37] Citizenship rights extend *into* the workplace.

The decisive power in the private sector is control over capital assets
(as exercised through decisions about wages and working conditions),
and the principal beneficiaries are the owners of those assets—whether
they are invested in a factory that produces cars or a restaurant that serves
food. By contrast, the decisive power in the sphere of politics comes from
voting and is wielded by assembling majorities. It is through the public
sphere of politics where citizens reside that individuals who are isolated
and disconnected in the workplace can be organized into an effective
bloc that checks the autocrats of the workplace.

The power of politics over markets varies across industrialized countries, adding to our explanation of why Americans (even the less well off)
do not regularly use their political rights to expand their social welfare
benefits. In countries where the rate of unionization and the number of
seats held by organized labor in the legislature and cabinet is comparatively
high, government policy toward taxation and spending are friendlier to
workers.[38] In the northern European countries of Sweden and Norway,
where most workers are unionized and organized labor is well represented
in the legislature and often in the cabinet, workers deploy their political
rights as citizens to gain generous government assistance inside and outside the workplace. The effective use of political power equips workers
with generous government benefits that emancipate them from relying
on their employers for their survival. The chain reaction resembles falling dominos: the political organization of workers expands social rights,
reduces dependence on employers, and checks workplace autocrats with

government rules or the prospect of losing workers. Unlike Ehrenreich's cowed and meek coworkers, Swedish and Norwegian employees have less reason to fear retaliation and more incentives and opportunities to organize in the workplace and in the political process.

Ehrenreich and her colleagues work under authoritarian regime precisely because of how they exercise political rights. American workers are not widely unionized compared to their western counterparts and lack an effective political organization like a European labor party. The result is that means-tested public assistance and social insurance programs that adhere to the individual success of employees are comparatively prominent. The context for Marie Gottschalk's discussion of union cooperation with employers in chapter 5 is the emaciated political organization of labor in the United States: its limited unionization and ineffective political organization (i.e., relying on a troubled marriage with the Democratic Party). Unions have used their financial and organizational resources to support workplace benefits for their members and unsteady private-public partnerships precisely because they lack the kind of political resources and power that their counterparts in Western Europe enjoy.

American workers—compared to their counterparts abroad—are especially dependent on their employers, particularly vulnerable to retaliation, and prone to abdicating to the demands of employers (as was the case with Ehrenreich's coworkers). Women are particularly vulnerable: They earn less than men at the workplace and provide unpaid care in the home, which curtails their eligibility and level of government assistance through such programs as Social Security.[39]

## The Triple Trench

Variations in health are not simply the "natural" product of individual choices and behaviors. Instead, they result from collective decisions about how we organize work and government policies. The government does devote huge sums of money to health, and yet the monies are not targeted at narrowing the disparities in health among economic and racial groups. The explanation for the peculiar mix of political equality, enduring disparities in health, and big government lies in the nature and degree of political participation in America.

Political rights are distributed equally but are disproportionately used by the better organized and better established. The selective use of political rights has, in turn, retarded the development of social rights. Put simply, weakly organized workers, constrained citizenship rights, and the disproportionate power of business and institutional interest groups form three trenches that protect the largesse of government from being consistently devoted to raising the health of all Americans.

But the triple trenches that disproportionately benefit the already advantaged are not insurmountable. Medicare and Medicaid, as well as Social Security, redistribute resources and are effective in reducing poverty and improving health; all were established after overcoming the same set of tripartite hurdles. The chapters in this volume reveal the hurdles that contribute to the poor health of Americans as well as the strategies and political conditions that produced successful efforts to expand access to medical care and improve living conditions in the past. The concluding chapters by Lawrence Brown, Benjamin Page, and Lawrence Jacobs and James Morone offer a menu for future strategies.

## Notes

Jim Morone offered provocative comments that strengthened this chapter.

1. N. R. Kleinfield, "Guarding the Borders of the Hip-Hop Nation," *New York Times* (6 July 2000): A1.

2. James House and David Williams, "Understanding and Reducing Socioeconomic and Racial/Ethnic Disparities in Health," paper prepared for the conference on "Capitalizing on Social Science and Behavioral Research to Improve the Public's Health" sponsored by The Institute of Medicine of the National Academy of Sciences and the Commission on Behavioral and Social Sciences and Education of the National Research Council, April 2000.

3. Steven Holmes, "Which Man's Army," *New York Times* (7 June 2000): A1.

4. Douglas Massey and Nancy Denton, *American Apartheid: Segregation and the Making of an Underclass* (Cambridge, MA: Harvard University Press, 1993).

5. Richard Freeman, "Are Your Wages Set in Beijing?" *Journal of Economic Perspectives* 9 (Summer 1995): 15–32.

6. Lawrence Mishel, Jared Bernstein, and Heather Boushey, *The State of Working America* (Ithaca, NY: Cornell University Press, 2003), 413–415.

7. Ibid., 416. These figures are based on the standard approach for comparing poverty rates across countries—namely, the proportion of individuals receiving 50% or less of the median (or middle) income in each country.

8. John Lynch, George Kaplan, Elsie Pamuk, Richard Cohen, Katherine Heck, Jennifer Balfour, and Irene Yen, "Income Inequality and Mortality in Metropolitan Areas of the United States," *American Journal of Public Health* 88 (July 1998): 1074–1080, 1079.

9. Sheryl Gay Stolberg and Gardiner Harris, "Industry Fights to Put Imprint on Drug Bill," *New York Times* (5 September 2003): A1.

10. David Truman, *The Governmental Process* (New York: Knopf, 1951); Robert Dahl, *A Preface to Democratic Theory* (Chicago: University of Chicago Press, 1956).

11. Richard Titmuss, "The Social Division of Welfare," *Essays on the Welfare State* (Boston: Beacon Press, 1969), 34–55.

12. E. E. Schattschneider, *The Semi-Sovereign People* (New York: Holt, Rinehart and Winston, 1960); Robert Salisbury, "The Dominance of Institutions," *American Political Science Review* 78 (1984): 64–76; Jack Walker, "The Origins and Maintenance of Interest Groups in America," *American Political Science Review* 77 (1983): 390–406; Virginia Gray and David Lowery, "The Diversity of State Interest Group Systems," *Political Research Quarterly* (March 1993): 81–97; Kay Schlozman and John Tierney, *Organized Interests and American Democracy* (New York: Harper & Row, 1986), 57.

13. Lawrence Jacobs, *The Health of Nations: Public Opinion and the Making of American and British Health Policy* (Ithaca, NY: Cornell University Press, 1993).

14. The accommodation of health care providers and, especially, the deliberate decision to avoid concentrated government authority over Medicare's budget and the quality of provided services can be found in Jacobs, *Health of Nations*.

15. The proponents of "direct Federal administration" were senior administrators in the Department of Health, Education, and Welfare and the Bureau of the Budget beginning in December 1960 (Jacobs, *Health of Nations*, 155–157, and 208–210).

16. Jonathan Oberlander provides an excellent history of Medicare since its founding. See *The Political Life of Medicare* (Chicago: University of Chicago Press, 2003).

17. These illustrations are drawn in part from Bruce Vladeck, "The Political Economy of Medicare: Medicare Reform Requires Political Reform," *Health Affairs* 18:1 (January–February 1999): 22–36.

18. Paul Starr offers a magisterial overview of doctors' fall from professional grace in *The Social Transformation of American Medicine* (New York: Basic Books, 1982).

19. Steven Balla, "Medicare Physician Payment Reform: The Influence of Legislators, Interest Groups, and Citizens in Agency Rulemaking," presented for the 1994 Annual Meeting of the American Political Science Association, 1–34; Susan Foote, *Managing the Medical Arms Race* (Berkeley: University of California Press, 1992).

20. Although the imbalance in interest group intensity contributed to the defeat of Clinton's health reform plan, a number of other factors played an important (and perhaps greater) role including fierce partisan polarization (as Mark Peterson discusses in chapter 7) and political miscalculations by the White House in the designing and scope of its plan and strategy for enacting it. Portmortems on the Clinton health reform episode—including the mea culpas by Clinton supporters and their arguments for blaming the defeat of the president's plan on the imbalance of interests—can be found in the following: Lawrence

Jacobs, "Politics of America's Supply State: Health Reform and Technology," *Health Affairs* 14 (Summer 1995): 143–157; Lawrence Jacobs and Robert Shapiro, *Politicians Don't Pander: Political Manipulation and the Decline of Democratic Responsiveness* (Chicago: University of Chicago Press, 2000); Theda Skocpol, *Boomerang: Clinton's Health Security Effort and the Turn Against Government in U.S. Politics* (New York: W. W. Norton, 1996); Haynes Johnson and David Broder, *The System: The American Way of Politics at the Breaking Point* (Boston: Little, Brown, 1996).

21. Theodore Lowi, *The End of Liberalism* (New York: Norton, 1979); Grant McConnell, *Private Power and American Democracy* (New York: Knopf, 1966).

22. Lowi, *End of Liberalism*.

23. Schattschneider, *The Semi-Sovereign People*; Peter Bachrach and Morton Baratz, *Power and Poverty: Theory and Practice* (New York: Oxford University Press, 1970); John Gaventa, *Power and Powerlessness: Quiescence and Rebellion in an Appalachian Valley* (Urbana: University of Illinois Press, 1980); Anne Schneider and Helen Ingram, "Social Construction of Target Populations: Implications for Politics and Policy," *American Political Science Review* 87 (June 1993): 334–347.

24. This discussion is based on T. H. Marshall's famous tripartite division. T. H. Marshall, "Citizenship and Social Class," in *Class, Citizenship, and Social Development* (Chicago: University of Chicago Press, 1977).

25. Sidney Verba, Kay Schlozman, and Henry Brady, *Voice and Equality: Civic Voluntarism in American Politics* (Cambridge, MA: Harvard University Press, 1995); Andrea L. Campbell, *How Policies Make Citizens: Senior Political Activism and the American Welfare State* (Princeton, NJ: Princeton University Press, 2003); Suzanne Mettler, "Bringing the State Back into Civic Engagement: Policy Feedback Effects of the G.I. Bill for World War II Veterans," *American Political Science Review* 96 (June 2002): 351–365.

26. Verba, Schlozman, and Brady, *Voice and Equality*.

27. Ibid.

28. Kim Hill, Jan Leighley, and Angela Hinton-Anderson, "Lower-Class Mobilization and Policy Linkage in the U.S. States," *American Journal of Political Science* 39 (February 1995): 75–86; Edward Jennings, "Competition, Constituencies, and Welfare Policies in the American States," *American Political Science Review* 73 (1979): 414–430; Alexander Hicks and Duane Swank, "Politics, Institutions, and Welfare Spending in Industrialized Democracies, 1960–82," *American Political Science Review* 86 (1992): 658–674.

29. Campbell, *How Policies Make Citizens*. Valuable discussion of the important feedback effects of government policies on political rights can also be found in the following: Mettler, "Bringing the State Back"; Suzanne Mettler and Joe Soss, "Beyond Representation: Policy Feedback and the Political Roots of Citizenship," prepared for delivery at the Annual Meeting of the Midwestern Political Science Association, Chicago, IL, April 3–6, 2003; revised version, May 9, 2003.

30. Theda Skocpol, *Diminished Democracy: From Membership to Managed in American Civic Life* (Norman: University of Oklahoma Press, 2003).

31. Large majorities oppose not only redistribution but also the influence of interest groups over government policy, which growing numbers of Americans have perceived over the past three decades.

32. Benjamin I. Page and Robert Y. Shapiro, *The Rational Public: Fifty Years of Trends in American's Policy Preferences* (Chicago: University of Chicago Press, 1992); Mettler, "Bringing the State Back"; David Weakliem, Robert Andersen, and Anthony F. Heath, "The Directing Power? A Comparative Study of Public Opinion and Income Distribution," Center for Research into Elections and Social Trends, working paper no. 98 (September 2002), 1–54. The latter is also available at www.crest.ox.ac.uk/papers/p98.pdf.

33. Jennifer L. Hochschild, *What's Fair?: American Beliefs about Distributive Justice* (Cambridge, MA: Harvard University Press, 1981).

34. Marshall, "Citizenship and Social Class."

35. Lloyd Free and Hadley Cantril, *The Political Beliefs of Americans: A Study of Public Opinion* (New York: Simon & Schuster, 1968).

36. Lawrence R. Jacobs and Robert Y. Shapiro, "Pragmatic Liberalism Meets Philosophical Conservatism: Americans' Reactions to Managed Care," *Journal of Health Policy, Politics and Law* 24 (Fall 1999): 5–16; "Myths and Misunderstandings about Public Opinion toward Social Security," *Framing the Social Security Debate*, ed. R. Douglas Arnold, Michael Graetz, and Alicia Munnell (Washington, DC: Brookings Institution, 1998), 355–588; Fay Lomax Cook and Lawrence Jacobs, "Assessing Assumptions about Attitudes toward Social Security: Popular Claims Meet Hard Data," *The Future of Social Insurance: Incremental Action or Fundamental Reform*, ed. Peter Edelman, Dallas Salisbury, and Pamela Larson (Washington, DC: Brookings Institution, 2002), commentaries, 82–118; Page and Shapiro, *The Rational Public*.

37. Barbara Ehrenreich, *Nickel and Dimed: On (Not) Getting By in America* (New York: Metropolitan Books, 2001), 210–211; Richard Freeman, ed., *Working under Different Rules* (New York: Russell Sage Foundation, 1994).

38. Gosta Esping-Andersen, *The Three Worlds of Welfare Capitalism* (Princeton, NJ: Princeton University Press, 1990); Walter Korpi, "Power, Politics, and State Autonomy in the Development of Social Citizenship: Social Rights during Sickness in Eighteen OECD Countries since 1930," *American Sociological Review* 54 (1989): 309–328; *The Democratic Class Struggle* (London: Routledge & Kegan Paul, 1983); Hicks and Swank, "Politics, Institutions, and Welfare Spending."

39. Ann Shola Orloff, "Gender and the Social Rights of Citizenship: The Comparative Analysis of Gender Relations and Welfare States," *American Sociological Review* 58 (June 1993): 303–328; Diane Sainsbury, *Gender, Equality, and Welfare States* (New York: Cambridge University Press, 1996).

# Part II

# CORROSIVE MARKETS

Economic markets make formidable engines. They generate innovation, wealth, and freedom. However, there are many important things that free markets will not accomplish. They will not educate everyone's children, conquer segregation, or treat all the sick. They do not ensure that everyone gets the same chance at the American dream. That's because, left to themselves, markets are also powerful engines of inequality. The great question of modern American politics has been balancing free economic markets with government interventions designed to protect individuals and promote opportunity.

In the decades after World War II, an intricate public-private partnership built a formidable medical system alongside an extraordinary array of other collective projects—universities, highways, suburbs, a powerful military, a great attack on racial segregation, and the growth of Social Security's astonishingly successful antipoverty program.

However, in the past three decades, the great American balancing act—economic freedom versus broad opportunity—has decisively shifted back toward the former. The global economy quickens the trend. So do a host of other factors—dwindling unions, the decline of manufacturing, a new premium on specialized knowledge, rising suburbs unconnected to urban centers, and the intricacies of American racial politics. And while economic markets reach into—and transform—every corner of American life, the growing power of markets (and market thinking) has been most dramatic in the health care system.

Without countervailing forces, the silky claims about market efficiency obscure the real effects—hard times on the bottom, a rush of
resources to the top. Part II explores some of the reasons why. Deborah
Stone shows how markets, if left to themselves, exacerbate the sharp racial
disparities in health care. Mark Schlesinger traces the contested rise—and
broad corrosive consequences—of markets and health. Both chapters
offer the same warning: A health care system organized purely on market
principles will be deeply skewed. Meaningful reform has to begin by
frankly acknowledging the great social values—fairness, community, and
real opportunity for everyone—that markets brush aside in the race to
maximize investors' income.

# How Market Ideology Guarantees Racial Inequality

## DEBORAH STONE

*The Negroes of the South Are Free as Air to Vote for*
*the Republicans if They So Choose.* Thomas Nast,
*Harper's Weekly*, October 24, 1874.

Race has always fractured American politics. The United States never had the kind of strong class-based politics common to Western European nations in large part because the American working class was divided by race. Elites could exploit whites' racial fears to foment hostilities and quell any nascent working-class mobilization. At the same time, class differences and the prospect of upward social mobility hindered black political movements.[1] Black political equality has been stymied in no small measure by America's commitment to preserving economic differences—all in the name of liberty.

Just as American democracy aspires to a standard of full political equality ("one person, one vote"), the ideal standard of justice in health care should be "equal care for equal needs." But market ideology serves much the same role in health care as racism has served in the larger political economy. Market ideology turns the health care system into a competition between the rich and the poor instead of an orderly distribution of medical care according to medical need.

Of course, income and race are not the only sources of health care inequities. Disparities exist whenever some groups fail to receive the same clinically necessary and appropriate care that other groups receive, or when they suffer illness, disability, or death that could be prevented by appropriate medical care. The medical system is rife with disparities according to gender, state residence (some states are much more generous in social provision than others), regional and local residence, immigrant status, and type of illness (e.g., people with mental illness fare worse than those with physical illness). The "disadvantaged classes" in health care are thus divided by many fault lines other than race and income. At various times, different pieces of this identity puzzle mobilize themselves. As each group gains greater political salience, it draws attention away from the general problem of disparities in medical care. These cross-cutting divisions weaken any political support for reforms to make the system more just. Nevertheless, I argue, market ideology is the biggest obstacle to health care equity because in market theory, distribution is not supposed to follow need. It is supposed to follow economic demand.

The U.S. health care system is designed to produce disparities. Although physicians are trained to distribute medical care according to medical need, the larger health care system is organized to allocate medical care primarily by market criteria rather than by medical need. Market principles create, perpetuate, and intensify racial and ethnic disparities. Market ideology not only justifies racial and ethnic disparities in health care, it allows racism to continue under cover of economic justifications. Worse, market ideology organizes the financing and delivery of medical care in ways that reward physicians and hospitals for discriminatory practices and ensure that racial inequality will persist.

## A Standard for Judging Disparities

American political culture vacillates between two philosophic poles: egalitarianism and libertarianism. These poles provide our standards for distributive justice. Equality is homogenizing and centripetal. It holds people together by not letting anyone get too far away from the group norm. Under the egalitarian ideal, collective power is used to extract resources from those who get too far above to help those who fall too far below. Liberty is differentiating and centrifugal. It encourages people to innovate, take risks, and separate themselves from the masses. It rewards those who succeed but offers little comfort to those who fail. Liberty resists the very idea of collective governance. Medical care disparities are so intractable in part because the distribution of medical care is constantly pulled between these two poles, tugged by radically different standards of distributive justice.

As political philosopher Michael Walzer showed in *Spheres of Justice*, most societies, like the United States, operate with multiple standards of distributive justice.[2] Various goods, services, opportunities, and punishments are meted out according to standards the culture deems appropriate for each sphere of life. Walzer envisioned multiple spheres, each with its own criterion, legitimate in that sphere but not in others. In the United States, votes are distributed according to a standard of absolute equality: one person, one vote. Jobs and places in higher education are distributed according to merit (or at least, that's the ideal). Consumption goods are distributed according to ability to pay. To argue that any distributive outcome is inequitable and morally unacceptable, one has to make a convincing case that the distribution violates the standard that best applies to that sphere. Any political contest over distributive justice, therefore, begins by showing which standard, among several legitimate ones, ought to apply to the resource in question.

In contemporary American culture, the standard in the sphere of medical care is medical need. Everyone who needs cataract surgery to be able to see should have it; no one who does not need it should get it. Need-based distribution of medical care is something like custom tailoring—what each person gets should fit him or her to a T. Of course, this is the ideal standard, not the reality, but it is against philosophical ideals that we judge our practice.

Need occupies a small portion of the American distributive galaxy, and it partakes of elements of both the egalitarian and libertarian ideals. In one sense, distribution according to need is equality to the Nth—equality perfectly customized to the tiniest details of each person's situation. "To each according to his need" is a radically egalitarian standard. In another sense, though, distribution according to need is liberty to the Nth. Under a political system that maximizes liberty, each person should be able to follows his dreams, to do and give whatever he wants. Because, under a need standard, each person receives exactly what it takes to enable him to flourish as a free and independent person, distribution according to need is also radically libertarian. Libertarians object to government-organized redistribution primarily because it interferes with the individual's freedom to choose the recipients and amounts of his donations, but this objection doesn't resolve the curious paradox of the need standard: it is simultaneously egalitarian and libertarian.

There are three reasons (at least) why medical care ought to be distributed according to the standard of medical need. First, health is a prerequisite to everything else we value in life. Just as "equal starting resources" are necessary for the textbook ideal of free-market competition, basic health is necessary for a fair meritocracy. Health enables people to learn, work, contribute, and achieve; people cannot earn, merit, or deserve if they cannot function in the first place. If medical care were not distributed according to medical need, all merit-based distributions would be suspect—or should be.

Second, in our modern scientific culture, we do not believe health is primarily a matter of individual effort for which people deserve rewards. Sickness is not sin. Yes, smoking, drug and alcohol abuse, unsafe sex, overeating, and a "couch potato" lifestyle all cause health problems. The lifestyle theory of disease modified the earlier "germs and accidents" causal story and transformed at least some sickness into sin. But modern genetic research significantly diminishes the realms of illness where individual responsibility is a reasonable causal story. More important, the notion that people ought to receive medical care in accordance with their moral deservingness strikes most of us as wrong. Few of us would withhold medical care from sick people who smoked, lived on junk food, or got into an accident while driving and dialing.

Third, medicine is a science. We understand science to be a realm of expertise and objectivity where there are right and wrong answers and where remedies can be proven effective or not. This means that a standard of need can be arbitrated clearly and fairly. Each medical problem has a proper remedy; each person should get the remedy (or test, procedure, etc.) that is appropriate to his or her problem. Political and economic clout should have no bearing. To be sure, medicine is plagued by uncertainty, and the reigning cliché is that it is as much art as science. It is beset by internal disputes about the best treatments for a given disease. But if medicine lacks a correct answer for every individual situation, there are a great many diseases and problems for which there *are* proper standards of care. These are the standards we use to assess quality of care, and we use them this way precisely because they meet the test of scientific verifiability.

Disparity, as we now use the term in discussions of racial and ethnic patterns of care, has come to mean a deviation from a scientific standard of medically appropriate care. At first glance, the term seems to denote a comparison between groups, such as blacks and whites, without reference to an external scientific standard. However, public health advocates are really concerned about differences between racial and ethnic groups that cannot be explained by clinically relevant differences and that indicate that one group receives substandard care. For example, several studies demonstrated racial disparities in treatment of people who had heart attacks: whites received sophisticated diagnostic procedures and aggressive surgical treatments more frequently than blacks. Some researchers speculated that the disparities might be spurious. The differences, these critics said, might signify that whites (and their physicians) were overusing invasive cardiac procedures rather than that black patients were getting inadequate care. If that had been the case, the argument went, then black patients weren't disadvantaged by the disparities, and although the pattern of care might be wasteful, it wasn't particularly unjust. Further studies did not support this argument.[3] But the spat shows that the disparities issue is not about just any differences between groups, but only differences that reflect under-provision of clinically necessary and appropriate care.

The medical need concept of disparities provides a powerful moral justification for addressing all disparities, not only racial ones. If medical need is the right criterion for distribution of medical care, then any deviation from it is wrong and unjust. Disparities across regions, states, gender, age, race, ethnicity, and immigration are all troubling when they mean deviation from a medical need standard.

There are also several strategic reasons for addressing all medical disparities together. First, as the controversy over affirmative action has shown, remedying racial disadvantage directly provokes a profound backlash. We need solutions that apply the same standards to everybody—qualification and potential to succeed in the case of education, need, and potential effectiveness in the case of medical care. Second, race, income, education, gender, and region are overlapping categories, thoroughly interconnected and impossible to disentangle, so that disparities in one dimension will produce disparities in the others. We cannot hope to eliminate only racial disparities if other disparities are left intact. Third, multiple fault lines of privilege and disadvantage create a kind of identity politics in which reformist energies are divided and dissipated. Last, and perhaps most important, if the political culture permits some kinds of deviations from a need standard, this tolerance creates a climate of acceptability for deviations per se. When distributions according to some non-medical criteria are legitimate (say, income and state residence), the political system will not likely undertake to make medical need the sole criterion for distribution of medical care. It becomes much harder for those who are disadvantaged by the maldistribution to argue for change. The burden of proof falls on those who are disadvantaged to show why the particular form of deviation that harms them is morally and politically unacceptable.

And here the plot thickens.

## How American Pluralism Sanctions Medical Disparities

The U.S. health care system is self-consciously, deliberately pluralistic. It is designed to produce heterogeneous patterns of care rather than one monolithic standard.

For one thing, the U.S. health care system, like the rest of the political economy, is based on principles of federalism. Responsibility for "public welfare" is one of the constitutional prerogatives of the states, and that has come to mean state responsibility for public health. "States' rights," in turn, have been invoked fiercely and doggedly to maintain local race relations. Even our most centralized health insurance programs—Medicare, Medicaid, and Supplemental Security Income—are significantly decentralized. Medicare is the most federal of the three. Even though it was arguably made federal so that it *could* enforce black civil rights, and even though it succeeded in reducing racial disparities in access to care, enforcement of the civil rights component was selective and splotchy, and by providing lots of new revenue for hospitals, Medicare inadvertently enabled them to finance construction of private rooms, which in turn enabled de facto segregation.[4] Medicaid, though nominally a national program, is highly decentralized. States have authority to set and administer their own eligibility criteria; reimbursement rates; policies for participation of doctors, hospitals, and managed care plans; and to an ever larger extent, thanks to a flurry of waivers from federal standards, their own benefit packages and coverage policies. Supplemental Security Income, a major source of health insurance for low-income people with disabilities, uses federal guidelines to define disability but state agencies to examine applicants and decide who is eligible. Federalism means that citizens of different states who are "clinically identical"—that is, they have the same medical needs—may be legally entitled to different preventive, diagnostic, and therapeutic services.

In addition, the U.S. health care system is based on market principles. Markets cherish the distribution of goods and services according to consumer tastes and ability to pay. Markets also cherish multiplicity of producers, and they idealize the freedom of producers to provide goods and services as they see fit, as they imagine they might make the greatest profits. Freedom in the quest for profits is the key to innovation and productivity. Because the U.S. health care system is predicated on market principles, it will distribute medical care with great sensitivity to consumer income. Because it treats doctors and hospitals as economic suppliers, it will supply medical care with great sensitivity to provider profitability. Medical care will not flow only along channels of medical need, but some—maybe most—will be diverted through channels of economic demand and supply.

In at least two ways, then—federalism and free markets—American political culture tolerates and sustains a distribution of medical care that deviates from the scientific standard of medical need. Because American political culture endorses, indeed seeks, distribution according to standards other than medical need, deviations from medical need are *designed* into American medical care. The health care system is designed to allow deviations from the medical need standard because it is designed to foster other distributive criteria. This is a fundamental cultural and structural problem that goes far deeper than race.

The distinctive cultural and political pluralism of the United States creates the disparities that trouble us so much. This pluralism generates not only racial and ethnic disparities, but all the others as well—income, gender, geography, citizenship status, and medical status. The nation will not be able to ameliorate racial and ethnic disparities until political leaders are willing to face up to the consequences of their devotion to these pluralistic ideals in medicine.

Racial disparities in health care are also caused by the nation's profoundly racist heritage. David Barton Smith has shown that many features of the current health care system grew partly as "adaptations" by doctors and hospitals to political pressures to desegregate, especially the pressure of the 1964 Civil Rights Act. The virtually complete transformation of hospital accommodations from wards to private and semi-private rooms; the migration of hospitals out of center cities into suburbs; the migration of health care itself out of hospitals and into nursing homes, ambulatory clinics, and homes, where compliance with civil rights law was much, much harder to monitor, if it applied at all—each of these shifts in industrial organization was in part stimulated by a desire to evade the watchful eye of the Department of Health, Education, and Welfare's Office for Civil Rights. Physicians' practices were exempted from the Civil Rights Act from the start. Thus, physicians could go right on referring patients to specialists, hospitals, nursing homes, and other providers on the basis of race, and civil rights enforcement officers couldn't reach them. No wonder researchers still find racially patterned streams of physician referrals.[5]

Race has had a lasting influence on American health politics and policy, just as it has in every other sphere of American politics. My purpose here, however, is to show how one seemingly race-neutral ideal—free markets—helps to justify and enable racial divisions in health care. No doubt this ideal is so attractive and tenacious in part because it indirectly justifies racial division. But I do not address motives here. Rather, I simply show how certain principles of political organization and culture in the United States perpetuate racial disparities, no matter anybody's intent.

Over the last two decades, policy makers have pushed the health care system to conform more and more to market principles. Cost savings, the flip side of profit maximization, became the overriding goal for public payers as well as commercial insurers. Economic thinking became the dominant mode of analysis of health care systems. Legislators urged citizens to think of health insurance and medical care as consumption goods over which they should exercise their spending preferences. Insurers and health care providers were urged to think of themselves as producers—marketing goods, competing for customers, and producing the highest volume and quality at the lowest price. It is the consequences of this market thinking I want to explore.

## How the Ideal of Consumer Sovereignty
## Perpetuates Racial Disparities

In market theory, the only morally relevant standards of distributive justice are consumer preference and ability to pay. Deviations from a medical need standard are perfectly acceptable so long as the distribution of medical care (now treated as a consumption good) corresponds to the distribution of consumer preferences. Whatever distribution results from the free expression of consumer preferences is the morally right one. To the extent that medical care is organized according to market principles—in the United States, the trend is large and growing—there is little philosophical leverage for reforming distribution so that it accords more closely with any other standard.

Perhaps more disturbing, though, is the long-standing use of supposed consumer preferences to justify continued discrimination in health care (as well as other sectors). In 1966, as the Office of Economic Health Opportunity was trying to force southern hospitals into compliance with civil rights law, hospitals "adamantly refused to stop assigning patients on a segregated basis, insisting that Negroes and whites *preferred* to remain segregated."[6] Similarly, "freedom of choice" was a slogan commonly used by southern hospitals to justify segregation; the separation of white and black patients into different facilities, administrators claimed, was the natural result of patients freely choosing, and anyway, free choice of "assignment" was a right of hospital administrators.[7]

Justifying racial and ethnic disparities on grounds that they reflect consumer preferences is not merely a relic of the segregated past. In a 1990 civil rights case, Tennessee invoked patient preferences to defend its policy of allowing nursing homes to limit the number of beds certified for (that is, available to) Medicaid patients. Plaintiffs argued, and the court agreed, that the policy had a disparate impact on blacks, because black families are disproportionately reliant on Medicaid to pay for nursing homes. Indeed, according to the court, blacks comprised almost 40% of the Medicaid population but only 15.4% of those Medicaid patients who have been able to gain access to Medicaid-covered nursing homes. Tennessee claimed that "the 'self-selection preferences' of the minorities, based upon the minorities' reliance upon the extended family, lack of transportation, and fear of institutional care, adequately explain the disparate impact."[8] The court didn't swallow this one.

In a similar vein, a few researchers have recently suggested that at least some of the racial disparities in medical treatment are due to black patients' preferences. According to this theory, black patients choose to utilize certain procedures less often than white patients.[9] They are more prone to refuse invasive and high-tech procedures, even when a physician recommends them. Thus, for example, researchers looked for, and found, differences in the proportions of black and white patients who refused physician recommendations for invasive cardiac procedures or kidney transplants.[10]

In a culture of market distribution and consumer freedom of choice, any disparities due to patient preferences and choices are morally acceptable. They are not inequalities, not disadvantages, just different choices. In its recent report on racial and ethnic disparities, the Institute of Medicine showed little patience with the preference argument. There are still disparities in whether physicians recommend treatment to black and white patients in the first place, the report noted. Moreover, black and white patients' preferences are shaped by their very different experiences in the health care system.[11] Black and white preferences are simply not equally informed or similarly influenced. Nevertheless, the preference argument is still taken seriously in policy circles, seriously enough that there is a body of research on it and seriously enough that the prestigious Institute of Medicine felt compelled to consider it.

Because the market model legitimates disparities that are due to consumer preferences, it offers a powerful cultural excuse for allowing disparities to persist: "They prefer things that way." As in the civil rights era, reformers are forced to demonstrate that black people's apparent free choices are really coerced choices, or uninformed choices, or choices made in the context of distrust and fear and shaped by a legacy of mistreatment. Through the preference argument, market ideology dissipates the energies of those struggling to rectify racial inequalities, as they fight to prove the obvious—that blacks do not really prefer substandard care.

Faith in consumer sovereignty perpetuates racial disparities in another way. Most analyses of quality in health care point to having a "usual source of care" as a key ingredient. A stable relationship with a physician is essential for gaining access to medically appropriate tests and treatments, especially in an environment where insurers are seeking to cut costs by denying payment for care. In that kind of environment, having a physician who will advocate for your interests can make the difference between getting and not getting care. Minorities and people with low income are less likely than whites and people of higher income to have a regular physician and more likely to get their health care from a hospital or emergency room. This is true of minorities, even when insurance status is controlled.[12]

There are many reasons why some people have regular doctors and others don't, but market principles only exacerbate the problem. The market model of health care actually relies on instability for quality control. "Exit" is the main way consumers tell suppliers that they are unhappy with the quality of merchandise. They find a new supplier, buy a different brand, shop at a different market.[13] In markets, mobility is the engine of progress and quality control. In a health care system organized around market principles, patients are supposed to behave as active consumers. They are supposed to "shop around" for plans, diligently monitor quality, and vote with their feet. They are supposed to leave plans that aren't meeting their expectations or satisfying their preferences, whatever those preferences may be.

The theory of managed competition thus depends on the patient's willingness to sever his relationship with a provider in search of a better one. The market model fosters constant churning. Market ideology teaches patients that it's their responsibility to monitor the quality of their medical care and to rectify any problems by changing suppliers. It teaches them that they are suckers if they let loyalty override tough-minded critical scrutiny. If they receive poor quality care and don't change doctors, it's their own fault. When public policy relies on consumer sovereignty to police health care quality, it undermines one the key elements of quality—stable doctor-patient relationships. And it does nothing to correct racial (or any other) disparities in access to primary care physicians for their usual source of care.

## How the Ideal of Competitive Supply
## Creates Racial Disparities

Health insurance, a prerequisite to medical care, can be supplied as a public good or as a private, market good. As a market good, suppliers will supply it only if they can make a profit doing so. The United States has chosen to supply health insurance primarily through the market, using public programs only to cover those groups for whom the market fails.

Commercial health insurance operates on a different standard of distributive justice than the medical need standard. It is designed to be most expensive and least accessible to the people with the greatest medical needs. Insurers aim to price insurance so that people pay as closely as possible for the care they will eventually need and receive. This is called "experience rating." According to the principle of actuarial fairness at the heart of commercial insurance, premiums should be proportionate to risk.[14] Those who are sicker or have a higher risk of becoming sicker (and therefore needing more care) should pay more for their insurance than those who are healthier and at lower risk of illness. The ubiquitous preexisting condition clauses mean that people who are already sick when they purchase insurance will not have their care for those conditions covered. In the actuary's ideal world, insurance would be priced as if there *were* no insurance and policy holders were paying directly for their own care on the open market.

In the private market, insurers' pricing practices actually promote deviations from the standard of medical need. In fact, actuarial principles *reverse* the medical need standard; they make insurance, and therefore care, most accessible to those who least need it. The political choice to insure as many citizens as possible through private commercial insurance instead of public social insurance is a choice to promote a distribution of medical care that deviates substantially from medical need.

Advocates of organizing health insurance around market principles naturally do not argue for distribution of care according to financial status rather than need. But they do tend to justify competitive markets by portraying insurance as a "financial product" distinct from medical care itself. As a financial product, they say, it is not essential. Consumers should be allowed to exercise their "tastes" for different levels of risk, their "preferences" for different levels of quality, and their freedom to make their own budgetary trade-offs.[15] According to market principles, health care comes in a wide range of acceptable styles and quality. There is "Cadillac Care" and "Volkswagen Care" and lots in between. So long as everyone gets a car, variations in quality are not a problem. Within the range of clinically acceptable quality, care ought to be distributed according to consumer tastes and ability to pay.

In pursuit of this ideal of maximum consumer freedom, the market model encourages insurers to offer multiple plans with a variety of different covered services (some might cover reproductive and mental health, while others may not), different coverage limits (for example, unlimited mental health visits versus a lifetime limit of thirty visits), different limits on which doctors and hospitals members may use (ranging from small health maintenance organization panels to any qualified provider), and different provider reimbursement levels. Such variations in quality, according to the market model, are eminently desirable. They enhance consumer choice.

In theory, and certainly in fine print, all plans cover "medically necessary" care. When it comes to paying the bills, however, plans differ in how much money they can spend on their members in the name of medical necessity. They also have wide latitude in how they interpret medical necessity. Higher-end plans provide greater access to specialists, because they are more liberal about deeming referrals necessary and more generous in paying specialists. They are more liberal about allowing their members to be hospitalized, and about permitting longer stays. They pay for more expensive and (sometimes) more effective medications. They pay doctors and hospitals higher rates for treating their members than lower-end plans can pay for their members. Variations among insurance plans are often not matters of style, like tail fins and sunroofs. They are matters of essential mechanics and safety.

A highly diversified insurance market will stratify itself according to income. Racial and ethnic minorities, because they are more likely to have lower incomes, are more likely than whites to enroll in plans with more restricted benefits and more restricted access to providers.[16] Minorities are disproportionately covered by Medicaid. Once again, the market model knowingly accepts different levels of quality and predictably assigns racial and ethnic minorities to the lower tiers.

Many people argue that the high-end/low-end distinction is misleading. Medicaid, they say, may be a plan for poor people but it is not a poor plan. It offers a rich benefit package, more generous, in fact, than some commercial insurers and employer plans. For Medicaid beneficiaries, however, Medicaid's richness is paper wealth because Medicaid pays notoriously low rates to doctors and hospitals. If you were a bounty hunter and the going rate for wolves was higher than the going rate for squirrels, which would you hunt? Some states deliberately delay paying their Medicaid bills for weeks or months so they can capture interest on the money while it sits in their bank account instead of somebody else's. If you knew you were going to wait much longer to get paid for bringing in squirrels than wolves, would you waste much ammunition on squirrels?[17] A rich benefit package on paper is an empty promise to patients if they can't find anyone to make good on it.

## How Market-Inspired Cost Control
## Creates Racial Disparities

Starting in the 1970s, policy makers became obsessed with controlling health care costs and turned to economics to help them get a grip on expenditures. Market theory recommended two strategies, one aimed at consumers (patients) and one aimed at suppliers (doctors, hospitals, nursing homes, and anyone who provides medical care).

According to market theory, health costs were out of hand because people were consuming it with abandon. Health insurance was the culprit; it takes the brakes off medical consumption. People with insurance don't have to pay the full costs of their care. They pay only for insurance.

Insurance pays for whatever care they need and get. They have no incentive to hold back on enjoying medical care. Got an ache? Kids fussing? What the heck! See a doctor.

The market fix for this problem was obvious: cost sharing. Make patients pay at least a part of the cost of every doctor and hospital visit and they will think twice about consuming care. They will ask themselves, "Is it worth it to me? Do I really need a doctor visit or would I rather have a new coat?"

Cost sharing burdens some racial and ethnic groups more than others and increases the disparities in access to care.[18] First, because blacks and Hispanics have lower incomes than whites (on average), any cost sharing places a higher average burden on their budgets. Second, blacks and Hispanics are less healthy and at greater risk for illness than whites (again on average). They need more medical care, so cost sharing hits them extra hard. Third, to the extent that cost sharing deters people from getting early and preventive care, it exacerbates racial and ethnic gaps in health status. As economist Tom Rice puts it, "Cost sharing results in de facto discrimination."[19]

The cost explosion wasn't all the fault of consumers, though. Providers bore part of the blame, and again, insurance was the culprit. Typical insurance plans paid doctors, hospitals, and nursing homes on a fee-for-service basis. Providers determined what services a patient needed, rendered the services, and submitted the bills. Insurers paid up. Doctors and nurses had absolutely no incentive to be frugal with their care. They could prescribe any care they thought might help, and it would be paid for.

To deal with this problem, market thinking prescribed prospective reimbursement. Under prospective payment, payers set fees for different diagnoses. Providers are no longer paid for whatever care they think their patients need.[20] Instead, their fees are capped before any patients walk (or are wheeled) through the door. Prospective reimbursement is meant to dissociate reimbursement from the provider's judgment about the patient's need for care.

Prospective payment supposedly applies market principles to generate medical efficiencies. In theory, it entices providers to be efficient, because they may pocket the savings if they can treat a patient for less than the pre-arranged fee. In practice, providers can pocket more savings if they choose patients who are relatively healthy and don't need much—or much expensive—care to begin with. Thus, prospective payment gives providers incentives to direct their time and resources to the patients who need the least care. It is a system knowingly designed to direct medical resources according to provider profitability instead of patient medical need.

Race dovetails with this system in a particularly pernicious way. Racial and ethnic minority patients are disproportionately less healthy. They are disproportionately uninsured or underinsured, so they have erratic access to care. In turn, when they do finally seek care, their illnesses are more likely to be advanced and more severe.[21] At that point, they are very unattractive (economically speaking) to providers in a prospective payment system. Patients who are less healthy than average can't be treated for the full value of the fixed fee, let alone for less.

Because prospective pay encourages providers to avoid sicker patients, it stimulates and exacerbates racial discrimination. Physicians and hospital administrators learn from epidemiology, if not from firsthand experience,[22] that minority patients are likely to be less healthy than whites, to be less well insured, and to have had inadequate primary and preventive care. Race becomes a proxy for factors that make a patient detrimental to the bottom line: chronic illness, prior inadequate care, and no insurance or underinsurance. Prospective payment's financial incentives give providers a cruel choice: use race as a proxy or lose money. No wonder, then, as competitive pressures on hospitals increased in the 1980s, so did "financially motivated transfers of patients from private to public hospitals—up to 90 percent involving minority patients in some cities."[23]

Once again, market logic hides discrimination. Market thinking and market incentives allow doctors and hospitals to understand their own behavior as economically motivated and economically necessary—and it is—even as it is also racially discriminatory. Market thinking allows the larger polity to pretend racial discrimination isn't happening. Disparate patterns of care can easily be understood as efficiency playing itself out. Analysts can talk about "financially motivated transfers" when almost all the transferred patients are black.

Market pressures, besides pushing providers to avoid racial and ethnic minorities, also induce them to provide fewer services to those minority patients they do treat. Under pressures to be cost effective, providers need ways to judge when medical treatments are likely to be ineffective and therefore not worth offering. In addition to biomedical factors, doctors look for personal characteristics that might render treatment less effective. They look for things like not following medical advice (ominously dubbed "non-compliance" in the medical literature, as if we were talking about parolees), not filling prescriptions or not taking them as prescribed, missing appointments, inability to afford ancillary therapies, inability to take time to recuperate, and lack of caregiver support.

People who cannot easily afford medical care *are* less likely to "comply" with medical recommendations, since such compliance usually means spending money they don't have. They may not fill prescriptions, or fill only some of them, or take medicines less often than prescribed to make them last longer.[24] They may lack reliable transportation to get to a medical visit, or they may have difficulty getting time off from work during office hours. Simply knowing (or believing) that minority patients are less likely to be financially secure and well insured, physicians may assume they are also less likely to benefit from medical advice and treatment. At least one study found striking evidence of this: physicians believed that compared to whites, African-American patients were less intelligent and less educated, less likely to follow medical advice, more likely to abuse alcohol and drugs, and less likely to have caregiver support. Physicians often held these beliefs contrary to the written evidence in the patient's chart.[25]

Competitive pressures induce physicians to use lingering race and class stereotypes under cover of evaluating cost effectiveness. The stereotypes, in turn, make minority and low-income patients "less worthy" of treatment. Competitive pressures and the austerity of prospective payment thus induce physicians to offer fewer costly medical regimens to minority patients than to white patients. Under the old forthrightly racist health care system, minority patients were unworthy of the same care as whites. Now they are just less cost-effective—but don't call it discrimination.[26]

Prospective payment and its underlying cost-control impetus may fuel still another mechanism of racial inequalities. Under prospective payment, hospitals and managed care organizations succeed by keeping down their per capita costs. Black and Hispanic patients are (on average) sicker than white patients. Black physicians are likely to have a higher proportion of black patients in their practices than white physicians and are more likely to practice in minority, low-income, and medically underserved areas.[27] Latino physicians are more likely to have a higher proportion of Hispanic patients. Presto: Hospitals and managed care organizations have strong economic incentives to avoid minority *physicians* as well as minority patients.[28] So-called economic credentialing of physicians by managed care organizations thus fosters racial and ethnic profiling. Patterns of recruiting and retaining physicians that appear to be motivated by economics may disguise racial discrimination, or at least permit it to continue under cover of economic rationality.

## How Market Ideology Subverts Civil Rights Enforcement

As we have seen, because racial and ethnic minorities are dispropor-tionately low income, they are disproportionately harmed by market principles in health care. But as long as political culture countenances distribution of care at least partly by income, deviations from the medical need standard are not likely to generate much sympathy or impetus for reform. Market ideology forces people who come out behind to over-come a high political burden of proof. Why, they must answer, is the distributive outcome *not* morally acceptable? After all, we can't all live in mansions and drive Jaguars.

In American politics, racial discrimination is a trump (hence the expression "playing the race card"). Distributive outcomes that result from racial discrimination are not acceptable (at least not formally and openly.) If racial and ethnic minorities are disadvantaged by the distribu-tion of medical resources *and* they can show that their disadvantage results from racial discrimination, they can invoke the power of government to alter the distributive rules. The chief legal weapon for such claims is Title VI of the Civil Rights Act of 1964; it bans discrimination on the basis of race, color, or national origin by entities that receive federal public assistance. Almost all hospitals receive substantial revenues from Medicare and Medicaid.

As in other areas of civil rights law, Title VI recognizes not only intentional discrimination, but also discrimination that results from the disparate impact of race-neutral rules and policies. But here's the rub: As Sara Rosenbaum puts it, "Title VI bars racial, not economic, discrimina-tion."[29] Any disadvantages that result from economic factors—say, not being able to afford a hospital bed or not being a cost-effective patient—are not violations of civil rights law and will not be remedied by a court. Plaintiffs and their advocates face the difficult task of separating the effects of economic discrimination from those of race discrimination. Minorities are disproportionately poor and uninsured so they are doubly disadvan-taged; but it is extremely difficult to prove that only racial discrimination, not economic discrimination, is behind their poorer care.[30]

Essentially, civil rights law says, "Economic discrimination is not our department." From the perspective of civil rights enforcement, economic discrimination is not on the table. Economic discrimination is not on the table because like the larger political culture, civil rights policy accepts market principles for distributing medical care. Thus does market ideol-ogy hobble civil rights enforcement and protect racial discrimination in health care.

Market ideology hobbles civil rights and the fight for a racially just health care system in other ways. One might think the Title VI ban on racial discrimination would apply to physicians as well as hospitals, as they, too, receive federal reimbursement for treating Medicare and Medicaid patients. It does not. Physicians are exempt from Title VI because when Medicare was passed, they pressed for an interpretation of the law that deemed them not recipients of federal financial assistance, even though they would be receiving reimbursement from the federal government for treating patients insured through Medicare.[31] Physicians resisted the entire Medicare program out of a sense that government would interfere with their freedom as small businessmen. They jealously guarded their prerogatives to treat whomever they wanted and to select and exclude patients unimpeded by government rules.

This respect for doctors as independent entrepreneurs not only allowed frank racial discrimination to continue in medical offices, but it also prevented the Office for Civil Rights from fully desegregating hospitals. Long after 1966, admissions to southern hospitals continued to follow clear racial lines largely because physicians directed the traffic. They simply referred black and white patients to different hospitals. The Office for Civil Rights could not stop this practice because Title VI didn't apply to physicians. At one point, the Office for Civil Rights tried to get a ruling that hospitals, as employers of physicians, could be held responsible for physicians' referral patterns, but the argument went nowhere. Entrepreneurial freedom trumped racial discrimination.[32]

American health law has been very solicitous of doctors' entrepreneurial freedom. Malpractice law imposes a duty on physicians to render professionally competent and appropriate treatment to any and all patients they choose to treat, but no law requires them to accept patients in the first place. They have no legal obligations to provide care to anyone, no "affirmative duties" in legal parlance. This deference to doctors' freedom is not unique to the health arena; it is one of the core principles of capitalism.[33] Sellers have a right to sell to whomever they wish—and to *not* sell to anyone they don't wish to do business with. People in general have a right to choose whether or not to enter into contracts. If someone doesn't want to contract with you because they don't like the color of your fingernail polish, that's their prerogative.

The implications for civil rights enforcement are obvious. Physicians can be "too busy" to accept minority patients. They can refuse to accept Medicaid or any other insurance. They can locate their offices in places highly inaccessible to neighborhoods with high concentrations of minorities. They can do all these things even if their real motivations are racial rather than economic. They can fail to initiate a doctor-patient relationship with anybody for any reason and the law can say or do nothing about it. Even Title VI of the Civil Rights Act has no power, because physicians are exempt.

The market ideal protects hospitals' ability to discriminate on the basis of race almost as much as it protects physicians' discriminatory practices. Unlike physicians, hospitals *are* subject to Title VI, but as civil rights jurisprudence has evolved, courts have offered hospitals a very generous defense based on their role as market actors. Once plaintiffs have proven that a policy or practice has a disparate impact on racial or ethnic minorities, the defendant hospital will be permitted to continue the practice if it can show that the policy serves a legitimate business purpose. This is called the "business necessity defense."[34] Courts have interpreted this standard so leniently that hospitals may engage in behavior patently harmful to minorities under the protective coloration of entrepreneurship.[35] A multihospital system may shut down its hospital that serves a minority community; it may stop offering emergency or acute-care services in its hospital that serves primarily minorities; it may relocate to a white suburb. To satisfy a court, it need only show that its decision serves its business objectives.

When New York City decided to close Sydenham Hospital in Harlem, minority patients filed a class action suit.[36] The City argued that by closing the hospital, it could reduce its total health care expenditures and increase efficiency in the municipal hospital system as a whole. Never mind that the closure would *eliminate* care for many residents of Harlem, who were mostly black and Hispanic; as long as the hospital's global efficiency would increase, the court was satisfied. In a variety of similar hospital closure and relocation cases, courts have accepted the most superficial statements of "business objectives" as legitimate justifications. If hospitals argued the moves could accomplish financial savings, enable them to better compete in their markets, or improve the quality of their services (without saying "to whom"), courts tipped their hats and allowed the moves.[37] Here is how Sara Rosenbaum and colleagues summarize this aspect of civil rights enforcement: "Taken together, the cases suggest that where the issue at hand is a decision to move services away from a less generous market [read: poor or minority neighborhood] to one that is more amenable to the entity's financial situation, neither courts nor the enforcement agency will interfere. . . . "[38]

## What Is to Be Done?

The standard policy recommendations to address racial disparities fall into two broad categories: changing discriminatory attitudes and stereotypes, and changing structural features of the health care system that intensify or contribute to racial inequalities. My analysis suggests that neither of these approaches will work well in the absence of addressing the fundamental market principles at the heart of the health care system. Here I will sketch some examples of the most common policy recommendations.

Like a choral refrain, analysts of racial disparities typically conclude with a call for training in "cultural competence."[39] Somehow, such training is supposed to weed out stereotypes and re-educate health care providers, mainly physicians, to treat patients with objective clinical neutrality. Typically, "cultural competence" means speaking another language besides English or offering interpreters, providing information in languages other than English, becoming aware of one's own stereotypes, and being aware of alternative and spiritual healing traditions.[40] Sensitivity training and education in "cultural competence" may marginally influence providers' thinking about racial and ethnic stereotypes, but that will make very little difference in an economic system that rewards them for spending less money on patient care and a social system that makes racial and ethnic minorities more expensive to care for. Capitation payment presses physicians to minimize the time they spend with each patient. Managed care productivity quotas, meant to make physicians more efficient, do likewise. These market-inspired mechanisms fairly beg the physician to use group patterns of patient behavior to create shortcuts for themselves. Moreover, the reality is that minority patients are sicker and more costly to treat (on average) than white patients. Market incentives to treat a patient population for a fixed price (usually a very low price) push hospitals and physicians to avoid minority and low-income patients and to take race, ethnicity, and income into account as they make their clinical decisions.

Another standard recommendation is to rely more on scientific evidence for clinical decisions and cost-control policy. "Evidence-based medicine" is the buzz word. Distribution of care on the basis of medical need and appropriateness should indeed be the ideal and the standard of distributive justice for health care. However, evidence-based decision-making can improve care only for patients who are already in the system receiving care. When providers have to survive in a competitive market and do so by living within a prospective budget, they have powerful incentives to use all available evidence to avoid the sickest patients. The market model pushes insurers and providers to do evidence-based exclusion before they start doing evidence-based treatment. It pushes them to screen out patients according to need; it operates to keep those people who most need insurance from getting insurance and those people who most need care from getting care. Moreover, perfect, evidence-based medicine *inside* a hospital or an office cannot affect the distribution of care within the larger universe of people who don't get into hospitals and offices in the first place.

The Institute of Medicine report on racial and ethnic disparities recommends "de-fragmentation of health-care financing and delivery" in order to address the "disproportionate presence of racial and ethnic minorities in lower-end health plans."[41] It is an eminently sensible recommendation, but it runs counter to federal policy direction over the past 30 years. Federal policy makers have resisted consolidating insurance into large national pools. Instead, they have actively stimulated the proliferation of insurance options so there could be vigorous competition among them. Just as market theory considers that deviations from a need standard are good, it thinks that uniformity of insurance coverage is bad.

Similarly, well-meaning reformers call for policies to create stable doctor-patient relationships for minorities. The Institute of Medicine, for example, urges federal and state governments to set performance standards for managed care plans that include "guidelines for the stability of patients' assignments to primary-care providers."[42] This recommendation, too, ignores the entire rationale for competitive managed care. Why would any government require "stability of patient assignments" to doctors if it is trying to promote market competition in health care? In a health care market, patients are supposed to "shop around" for plans and diligently monitor quality. They are supposed to vote with their feet and leave plans that aren't meeting their expectations or satisfying their preferences, whatever those preferences may be. Consumer mobility is the engine of progress and quality control in markets.[43] The theory of managed competition depends on the patient's willingness to sever his relationship with a provider in search of a better one. The good consumer (oops, patient) is one who does not place a high priority on stability. The good policy maker who is overseeing a system predicated on the market model shouldn't overvalue stability of patient-provider relationships, either. He should foster high turnover in the name of aggressive consumer shopping and quality control. And the good evaluator, when he sees high turnover in patient-physician relationships, should judge the system to be working well: competition is doing its job. Without taking on the market model, recommendations such as these are whistling in the dark. Addressing racial and ethnic disparities in health care is difficult if not impossible when economic disparities are encouraged, when distributive standards other than medical need are considered legitimate, and when market mechanisms actually exacerbate racial disparities and give providers incentives to stereotype and discriminate. Cultural legitimacy of market distribution undercuts the moral legitimacy of the medical need standard and renders legal tools against discrimination impotent. There is only one cure for racial and ethnic disparities: health care rules and institutions that purposefully direct resources in accordance with medical need.

# Notes

1. The basic insight that one political fault line (such as race) disrupts and mutes conflict along another (such as class) was stated most forcefully by E. E. Schattschneider in *The Semi-Sovereign People* (Hinsdale, IL: Dryden Press, 1970), chapter 4. The application to race and class in American politics has been studied and sustained by many political scientists and historians. See David R. Roediger, *The Wages of Whiteness: Race and the Making of the American Working Class* (London: Verso, 1991).

2. *Spheres of Justice* (Cambridge, MA: Harvard University Press, 1986).

3. For a review of these studies and the conceptual question, see Institute of Medicine, *Unequal Treatment: Confronting Racial and Ethnic Disparities in Health Care,* ed. Brian D. Smedley, Adrienne Y. Stith, and Alan R. Nelson, Report of the Institute of Medicine Committee on Understanding and Eliminating Racial Differences in Health Care (Washington, DC: National Academy Press, 2003), 20–79.

4. See David Barton Smith, "Health Care's Hidden Civil Rights Legacy," *St. Louis University Law School Journal* 48 (2003): 37–60.

5. See David Barton Smith's extraordinary *Health Care Divided* (Ann Arbor: University of Michigan Press, 1999), especially 226–233 on system adaptation, and 145, 154, and 161–164 on physician referrals and the physician exemption.

6. Quotation from a memorandum to Joseph Califano, November 18, 1966, cited in Barton Smith, *Health Care Divided,* 146.

7. On the "freedom of choice" strategy to resist equality in health care, see Barton Smith, *Health Care Divided,* especially 148–153.

8. *Linton v. Carney* 779 F. Supp. 925 (M.D. Tenn 1990), in Rand Rosenblatt, Sylvia Law, and Sara Rosenbaum, *Law and the American Health Care System* (Westbury, NY: Foundation Press, 1997), 1197–1204, quotation on 1203.

9. See, for example, Jeff Whittle, Joseph Conigliaro, C. B. Good, and Monica Joswiak, "Do Patient Preferences Contribute to Racial Differences in Cardio-

vascular Procedure Use?" *Journal of General Internal Medicine* 12 (1997): 267–273, finding that "racial differences in revascularization rates may be due in part to differences in patient preferences." See Institute of Medicine, *Unequal Treatment*, 136–138, for a review of this line of research.

10. A. D. Schecter, P. J. Goldschmidt Clermont, G. McKee, D. Hoffeld, M. Myers, R. Velez, J. Duran, S. P. Schulman, N. G. Chandra, and D. E. Ford, "Influence of Gender, Race and Education on Patient Preferences and Receipt of Cardiac Catheterizations Among Coronary Care Unit Patients," *American Journal of Cardiology* 78.9 (1996): 996–1001; S. P. Sedlis, V. J. Fisher, D. Tice, R. Esposito, L. Madmon, and E. H. Steinberg, "Racial Differences in Performance of Invasive Cardiac Procedures in a Department of Veterans Affairs Medical Center," *Journal of Clinical Epidemiology* 50.8 (1997): 899–901; John Z. Ayanian et al., "The Effect of Patients' Preferences on Racial Differences in Access to Renal Transplantation," *New England Journal of Medicine* 341 (1999): 1661–1669.

11. Institute of Medicine, *Unequal Treatment*, especially 135–136. See also M. Gregg Bloche, "Race and Discretion in American Medicine," *Yale Journal of Health Policy, Law and Ethics* 1.1 (2001): 95–131, especially 104–105, arguing that prejudice and discrimination influence minority patients' attitudes toward medical care and that it is wrong to treat patient "preferences" as something distinct from and prior to experiences with the medical system. Bloche was a member of the Institute of Medicine committee that wrote *Unequal Treatment*. U.S. Civil Rights Commission, *The Health Care Challenge: Acknowledging Disparity, Confronting Discrimination, and Ensuring Equality*, vol. 1 (Washington, DC, September 1999), especially 78–82; Vanessa Gamble, "Under the Shadow of Tuskegee: African-Americans and Health Care," *American Journal of Public Health* 87.11 (1997): 1773–1778.

12. Marsha Lillie-Blanton, Rose Marie Martinez, and Alina Salganicoff, "Site of Medical Care: Do Racial and Ethnic Differences Persist?" *Yale Journal of Health Policy, Law and Ethics* 1.1 (2001): 1–17.

13. This is Albert Hirschman's "exit" strategy in his classic on quality control in markets, *Exit, Voice and Loyalty* (Cambridge, MA: Harvard University Press, 1970).

14. Deborah Stone, "The Struggle for the Soul of Health Insurance," *Journal of Health Politics, Policy and Law* 18.2 (1993): 267–317.

15. See Clark Havighurst, *Health Care Choices: Private Contracts as Instruments of Health Reform* (Washington, DC: American Enterprise Institute, 1995); Richard A. Epstein, *Mortal Peril: Our Inalienable Right to Health Care* (New York: Addison-Wesley, 1997).

16. Kathryn A. Phillips, Michelle L. Mayer, and Lu Ann Aday, "Barriers to Care among Racial/Ethnic Groups under Managed Care," *Health Affairs* 19 (2000): 65–75, cited in Institute of Medicine, *Unequal Treatment*, 13; see also 147–148, 182–184, and citations there.

17. Sidney D. Watson, "Medicaid Physician Participation Rates: Patients, Poverty and Physician Self Interest," *American Journal of Law and Medicine* 21 (1995): 191–220.

18. This paragraph draws on Tom Rice, "The Impact of Cost Containment Efforts on Racial and Ethnic Disparities in Health Care: A Conceptualization," in Institute of Medicine, *Unequal Treatment*, 699–721, especially 708–711.

19. Rice, Institute of Medicine, *Unequal Treatment*, 708.

20. The federal government now uses prospective payment to pay for hospital, nursing home, and home health care, and insofar as Medicare and Medicaid encourage or require beneficiaries to use managed care, prospective payment applies to their ambulatory care as well. Managed care, which is now the dominant form of private insurance, uses prospective reimbursement as well.

21. Institute of Medicine, *Unequal Treatment*, 38–64, 83–87.

22. Beverly Coleman-Miller, "A Physician's Perspective on Minority Health," *Health Care Financing Review* 21.4 (Summer 2000): 45–56, describes how one physician experienced this epidemiological pattern firsthand.

23. Mark Schlesinger, "Paying the Price: Medical Care, Minorities and the Newly Competitive Health Care System," *Milbank Quarterly* 65.2 (1987): 270–296, quotation on 279; citing R. L. Schiff, D. A. Ansell, J. E. Schlosser, A. H. Idriss, A. Morrison, and S. Whitman, "Transfers to a Public Hospital: A Prospective Study of 467 Patients," *New England Journal of Medicine* 314.9 (1986): 552–557.

24. Lucette Lagnado, "Uninsured and Ill, a Woman Is Forced to Ration Her Care," *Wall Street Journal* (12 November 2002): A1, describes how a young woman with glaucoma and no health insurance rations her own medical care, visiting doctors only when she is in severe pain and husbanding her eye drops.

25. Michelle van Ryn and Jane Burke, "The Effect of Patient Race and Socio-Economic Status on Physicians' Perceptions of Patients," *Social Science and Medicine* 50 (2000): 813–828.

26. See also Bloche, "Race and Discretion in American Medicine," especially 103–104.

27. Miriam Komaromy, Kevin Grubachm, Michael Drake, Karen Vranizan, Nicole Lurie, Dennis Keane, and Andrew B. Bindman, "The Role of Black and Hispanic Physicians in Providing Health Care for Underserved Populations," *New England Journal of Medicine* 334 (1996): 1305–1310.

28. This is a point made by Thomas Perez in "The Civil Rights Dimension of Racial and Ethnic Disparities in Health Status," in Institute of Medicine, *Unequal Treatment*, 626–663. Perez points to a survey showing that African-American physicians believe they are terminated from managed care networks because of their race. Risa Lavizzo-Mourey, L. Clayton, M. Boyd, G. Johnson III, and D. Richardson, "The Perceptions of African-American Physicians concerning Their Treatment by Managed Care Organizations," *Journal of the National Medical Association* 86 (1996): 191–199.

29. Sara Rosenbaum, Anne Markus, and Julie Darnell, "U.S. Civil Rights Policy and Access to Health Care by Minority Americans: Implications for a Changing Health Care System," *Medical Care Research and Review* 57.1 (2000): 236–259, quotation on 241.

30. Ibid.

31. Ibid., 238–239; the history of this fight is nicely rendered in Barton Smith, *Health Care Divided*, 161–164.

32. The story is told in Barton Smith, *Health Care Divided*, 173–176.

33. The lack of affirmative duties to treat or help someone is not unique to medicine. American law does not impose a duty on any citizen to "rescue" people who need help. There are few legal obligations to help another person, whether you are a layperson, a doctor, or someone with any kind of specialized rescue skills. For an explanation of the general principle of "no duty to care" in medicine, see Rosenblatt, Law, and Rosenbaum, *Law and the American Health Care System*, 42–63. For the lack of obligations to render assistance more generally in American law, see Mary Ann Glendon, *Rights Talk: The Impoverishment of Political Discourse* (New York: Free Press, 1991), chapter 4.

34. In theory, hospitals must overcome another hurdle. Plaintiffs may argue that the hospital could accomplish its business objectives with "less discriminatory means," and hospitals then must persuade the court that less discriminatory practices would not accomplish this objective. But as Sidney Watson has shown, courts rarely require this third step: "Reinvigorating Title VI: Defending Health Care Discrimination—It Shouldn't Be So Easy," *Fordham Law Review* 58 (1990): 939–978.

35. Watson, "Reinvigorating Title VI."

36. *Bryan v. Koch*, 627 F2d. 612 (2d. Cir. 1980). My description is from Watson, "Reinvigorating Title VI," 966–967.

37. Rosenbaum et al., "U.S. Civil Rights Policy," 247.

38. Ibid., 248, words in brackets added.

39. See U.S. Civil Rights Commission, *Health Care Challenge*, 42–55, 193–195; Institute of Medicine, *Unequal Treatment*, chapter 6.

40. See Joseph R. Betancourt, Alexander R. Green, and J. Emilio Carrillo, "Cultural Competence in Health Care," Field Report (New York: Commonwealth Fund, October 2002).

41. Institute of Medicine, *Unequal Treatment*, 13–14.

42. Ibid., chapter 5, 184–185.

43. Hirschman, *Exit, Voice and Loyalty*.

# 4

# The Dangers of the Market Panacea

## MARK SCHLESINGER

The art of being wise is the art of
knowing what to overlook.
—B. WILLIAM JAMES

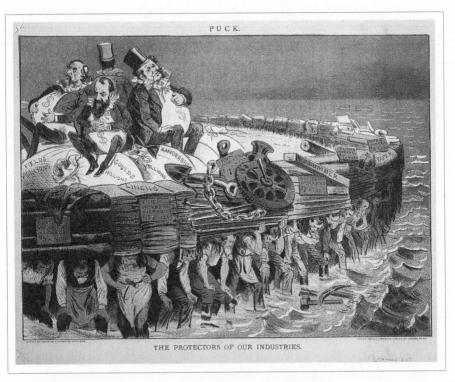

*The Protectors of Our Industries.* Bernhard Gillam,
*Puck*, date uncertain.

The familiar often becomes invisible. When you first move into a new residence, every creak of the building, every screech of tires from the street outside, seems to grab your attention. Within a week, you no longer pay these sounds any attention. It is as if they have totally disappeared. When something is a constant part of everyday life, it becomes so familiar that it vanishes from sight. It becomes something that you only really notice when it is gone.

Our perceptions of public affairs work in much the same way. Aspects of society that have become a constant in our lives get taken for granted, so much so that we may hardly even notice that they exist. This is true even for our most distressing social problems. Live long enough in a country beset by violence, distorted by racism, or contaminated by pollution, and citizens no longer see these circumstances as problems; they simply become a part of everyday life. It is only when things change, when circumstances worsen or improve, that we pay attention once more.

The same is true for our efforts to make sense of the social arrangements within which we live. The influence of important social institutions—the norms and practices that we share for interacting with one another—is often hard to understand, precisely because they have become such a constant in our lives that they effectively vanish from our conscious perceptions. The more pervasive a set of values, the more ubiquitous an accepted practice, the harder it is to judge their implications, because we have no ready standard of comparison.

It is precisely these circumstances that make it difficult to assess the impact of markets on American society, politics, and values. Markets are deeply rooted in our culture. There are few things that we don't see as "for sale," few situations which we wouldn't view as being improved by injecting a bit of competition.[1] We have come to perceive markets and democracy as closely linked, with the free market assuming the same sort of iconic status as freedom of religion, assembly, or speech.[2] Market ideas, principles, and practices play a vital role in shaping the goals and tools of public policy in this country. Ironically, it is precisely because this impact is so pervasive that it is difficult to fully appreciate and its implications are hard to discern.[3]

But contemporary health policy offers a striking exception to this rule. For much of the twentieth century, health care was an anomaly, a vital part of American society in which markets were not the norm. Most policy makers rejected market principles for medical care, arguing that the choices were too complex for consumers, that the circumstances of ill health left patients too much at risk of exploitation, that the social benefits of good health were too important to be left to self-regarding individual decisions. Over the past 25 years, however, policy makers' skepticism began to erode. A curious bipartisan coalition formed in favor of pro-market reforms. This new consensus was forged among liberals favoring patient empowerment and conservatives concerned with cost containment. Together, they promoted policy initiatives that introduced market practices into American medicine, to make individuals more responsible for the prudent purchasing of medical services and to make the system more responsive to consumer choice.

By the end of the twentieth century, market-oriented thinking had largely defined the terms in which American policy elites discussed health policy. Advocates of reform sought to introduce markets to both employer-based and government-administered health insurance arrangements.[4] New policies were developed to better inform consumers about the performance of competing health plans.[5] Long-standing government programs (Medicare and Medicaid) were redesigned to allow for (or, in some cases, require) beneficiary choice among plans. Proposals for newly expanded benefits, such as prescription drug coverage for the elderly, were almost entirely based on market models.[6]

It is my contention, however, that the apparent consensus favoring market-oriented medical care is more fragile than it appears. There are two sources of potential instability. The first involves cleavages among elites and advocates of the market, reflecting differences in the values thought to appropriately guide resource allocation in health care. The second source of instability involves cleavages between elite and public values. Despite a concerted effort by certain elite interests to convince the American public of the merits of markets for medical care, these efforts have not proven entirely persuasive. Most important, they have not recast some norms of fairness that conflict with the expected performance of market-oriented medicine As these hidden tensions are revealed over time, they may limit the application or effectiveness of market reforms. But other consequences of market thinking may persist, altering the ability of public policy to address disparate health outcomes.

It is precisely because the acceptance of markets in medical care is recent and still only partially complete that we can more readily examine its implications for the goals and practices of public policy. This chapter traces the emergence of market ideology and demonstrates how it has reshaped understanding of the nature and import of inequality within the American health care system. More specifically, I will argue that market thinking affects policy responses to inequality in four crucial ways.

First, the introduction of markets to medical care exacerbates unequal health outcomes. Long-standing differences in health care utilization and health outcomes related to socioeconomic status or race are likely to grow under market reforms, as will other less visible forms of inequality. Second, market arrangements have fostered the growth of large health care corporations. Their political power may circumscribe government policy making that could limit health inequalities, particularly at the state level. Third, market frames are associated, at least in the thinking of some policy elites, with different standards of fairness for assessing the performance of the health care system. This changes the sort of outcomes that are seen as inequitable, and hence suitable for government intervention. Fourth, market schemas have transformed prevailing discourse around a number of the other important perspectives on health policy, including the rights of citizens and the responsibilities of local communities. Although these conceptual side effects are subtle in nature, they can fundamentally reshape health policy.

Taken together, these four changes have dramatically altered the politics of inequality in medical care. These changes are likely to persist in the foreseeable future. They demand thoughtful responses, both from policy makers as well as the American public.

## Historical Perspectives: American Medicine Goes to Market

The institutional arrangements through which nations allocate and finance health services shape subsequent health policy in several ways. Different institutional arrangements produce different distributions of health outcomes. For example, when the United States adopted the Medicare program in 1965, it substituted a government-run health insurance program for private insurance purchased through the market. By so doing, policy makers increased overall access to health care for America's elderly and reduced the disparities in health care use and outcomes between high- and low-income elders.[7] Racial differences in health care use were also mitigated. These accomplishments recast the issues facing policy makers in the future. Once widely viewed as a disadvantaged group, older Americans subsequently were seen as well treated—perhaps even preferentially treated—compared to working-aged citizens.[8]

Equally important, institutional arrangements can transform the goals and expectations that policy makers and the general public have for the health system. Medical care and the health care system are complicated matters. Few citizens have the time or inclination to learn the details or

94

nuances relevant to health policy. Surprisingly few policy makers—either elected officials or their staffs—have much greater knowledge. So how do people decide what sort of goals are appropriate for health policy? Research in political psychology suggests that they do so by calling on simple stories that describe what the health care system ought to look like in ideal terms.[9] Political psychologists refer to these stories as frames or schemas. They can often be invoked by a single term or phrase that captures in a nutshell a set of expectations for how the system ought to operate and how government ought to go about reaching these goals.

Markets represent one such conceptual frame. When people think about a socially valued good or service as a "marketable commodity," that labeling carries with it a set of expectations. Goods that are allocated through the market are considered equitably distributed when they are appropriately matched to individuals' preferences. Those who have larger incomes or financial resources are assumed to deserve a larger share of the goods in question.[10] Within this frame, individuals have a responsibility for making wise choices about their medical care. The appropriate role of government within the market schema is to facilitate competition among medical practitioners and to ensure that consumers are sufficiently informed to be able to make reasoned decisions.[11]

But the market frame, with its attendant set of goals and expectations, is certainly not the only way of thinking about medical care. Historically, the acceptance of health care as a marketable commodity has waxed and waned. As the dominant frames for understanding health care and health policy have changed, so too have the goals and legitimate roles for government action. Changing expectations affect the extent to which unequal health outcomes are perceived as inequitable and the range of interventions that might be applied to address those inequities.

## The Historical Roots of Market Thinking

Medicine in nineteenth-century America was widely accepted as a market good. Competition among schools of medical thought was intense. During the first half of the century, "regular" physicians (who linked health to "capillary tension" and treated illness by letting blood, emptying stomachs, and purging bowels) were challenged by the doctrines of the Thomsonians (who believed cold to be the source of illness and heat to be the cure) along with practitioners of hydropathy (who, as their sobriquet suggests, favored various forms of water cures).[12] Entry to the medical profession was relatively open and required little training.[13] In the later half of the century, new understandings of medical care emerged.

But competition remained strong, with allopathic physicians vying with homeopaths, osteopaths, eclectics, and chiropractors to attract clientele.[14]

To promote a competitive marketplace, state officials either repealed state licensure laws or left them largely unenforced.[15] The "popular health" movement prominent in the 1830s and 1840s emphasized the consumers' role and encouraged the public to become more informed about the nature of medical care and the alternative schools of medical practice.[16] These expectations persisted through the late 1800s, spawning millions of popular medical advisories, pamphlets, and other guidebooks.[17]

## Alternatives Emerge to Medical Markets

During most of the twentieth century, however, the market frame was displaced by two alternative ways of thinking about medical care. The first involved forms of professionalism that largely rejected the role of the market and consumer decision making. By the end of the nineteenth century, the increasing technical complexity of medical practice was making it more difficult for consumers to effectively assess the merits of competing practitioners.[18] As the American Medical Association consolidated its professional authority, it restricted entry to the profession, limited the number of accredited medical schools, and adopted codes of practice that discouraged advertising to consumers.

By the 1930s, both clinicians and policy makers had grown skeptical of consumer choice in medical care. This sentiment was captured in a study conducted by the American Foundation in 1935–1936. Having collected and synthesized the sentiments of opinion leaders throughout the medical profession, researchers uncovered grave doubts about medical markets.

> Medical care is not a commodity. . . . Medical care is a very complex, uneven, and imperfect development. Commodity values, it is pointed out, cannot be attached to it and the attempt to do so will seriously distort the natural evolutionary tendencies toward improvement. . . . A number of our correspondents point out that a very large part of the public is quite incompetent to choose its physician and that the personal choice of the individual that belongs in this group is merely a recognition of the individual's right to be as foolish and ignorant as he pleases. That may be a great American right, but certainly there should be no implication that if an individual chooses his physician, adequate medical care will thereby have been made available.[19]

A second alternative frame for medical care began to emerge in American health policy after the Great Depression. Policy makers and the public began to think about medical care as a "societal right"—guaranteed by the national government for all of its citizens. Although this was a growing theme in congressional deliberations throughout the 1930s, this position was most famously enunciated by Franklin Roosevelt. In January 1944, he presented to the nation a call for a second Bill of Rights, including among these new economic rights the "right to medical care and the opportunity to achieve and enjoy good health."[20] Similar language was incorporated 4 years later into the United Nations' Universal Declaration of Human Rights (not coincidentally crafted under the direction of Eleanor Roosevelt).

Roosevelt asserted that his speech was simply a restatement of popular sentiment. Americans, he argued, "have accepted" exactly this sort of expanded notion of rights "under which a new basis of security and prosperity can be established for all." Polls from this period generally support this claim. In a survey conducted in 1942, 74% of the American public approved of tax financing for "medical care for everyone who needs it."[21] A poll fielded in July 1943 found that 58% of the public favored extending Social Security to cover medical expenses.[22]

Throughout much of the twentieth century, the framing of medical care as either a professional service or a societal right dominated the marketable commodity frame in the formulation of American health policy. Proponents of the professional paradigm contested with advocates of societal rights to shape public policy. The American Medical Association, for example, launched repeated campaigns against government-run medical insurance from the 1930s through the late 1960s.[23] In their efforts to fend off government involvement, physicians helped to keep market thinking alive in American health policy. For example, they frequently extolled the virtues of clinicians acting as small businessmen, comfortably nested in the heart of local communities.[24] In light of the threats that market-based reforms would later pose to the clinical autonomy of the medical profession, this embrace of the market was to prove most ironic.

Each of the dominant ways of thinking about medical care at midcentury emphasized different norms of equity and different roles for government in American medicine. Within the professional service frame, the dominant norm of equity shifted from deservingness to need, where need for medical care is defined in terms of professional norms, based on the scientific training and research base that informs clinical decision making.[25] Government's role within this paradigm is to strengthen that base of scientific knowledge and ensure that the public has equal access to medical professionals.

This frame provided the dominant standard for federal health policies in the middle of the twentieth century.[26] Federal funding of medical research increased exponentially after World War II, climbing from $4 million in 1947 to $400 million by 1960.[27] This laid the groundwork for a deepening commitment by policy makers to medical care as science, creating "a golden age of clinical research that lasted about two decades (the mid-1950s to the early 1970s). . . Enjoying immense prestige and resources, clinical research became a large-scale enterprise on which Americans placed their hopes for the conquest of disease."[28] When it was revealed that particular groups—defined by age, gender, or race—had been excluded from participation in clinical trials, this was seen as a crucial inequity that federal policy makers quickly worked to remedy.

The other primary inequity within this frame involved the uneven geographic distribution of medical professionals. To address these concerns, federal policy makers adopted the Hill-Burton program in 1948, which subsidized the construction of thousands of hospitals. Federal assistance was originally targeted to rural areas in which medical resources were scarcest, but was later expanded to include the underserved areas of inner cities.[29] During the 1950s, the Hill-Burton program was expanded to include support for the construction of nursing homes. During the 1960s, the federal government established a set of complementary programs subsidizing the construction of centers for outpatient services; one set of facilities to address physical illnesses, a second to address mental illnesses.[30]

The societal rights perspective, by contrast, emphasizes a standard of equality and the responsibility of the federal government in assuring equal access to medical services.[31] Although broadly endorsed by the public since the 1940s, this perspective was not translated into federal policy making until the mid-1960s in the form of the Medicare program, which provided equal health insurance coverage for (virtually) all elderly Americans.[32] Norms of rights-based equality remained a dominant theme throughout the 1970s, spawning half a dozen different proposals for national health insurance and a series of active debates in Congress on the topic.

In contrast to those federal initiatives that sought to address inequities in the supply of medical resources, programs embodying the societal rights paradigm emphasized equality of access and treatment. Following these norms, the Medicare program became a major tool for enforcing civil rights provisions related to medical care.[33] Within this frame, evidence of unequal treatment by race or income for program beneficiaries became an important concern for federal policy makers.[34]

## Markets Reborn in American Health Policy

Although largely displaced by the professional service and societal rights frames, notions of medical care as a marketable commodity remained a minor theme in political debates over health care reform after World War II.[35] The frequency with which the market frame was invoked began to increase in the early 1970s. Its rebirth reflected in part the increasingly conservative bent to American social policy generally during this era.[36] In addition, two different sets of elites sought to promote markets in medical care in particular. Each group of advocates had a distinctive political orientation and interpretation of how markets in medical care ought to behave.

The more predictable set of promarket reformers favored conservative ideologies. Their ideas were embodied in reform proposals developed by some of the more entrepreneurial of the policy-oriented economists drawn to public service during the 1960s. These proposals were intended to make the medical care system more market-like. They did this by introducing stronger financial incentives to make individuals more prudent in their purchase of either medical care or health insurance.[37] As public and policy makers' concerns about rapidly rising health care costs grew more intense, the benefits promised by these proposed reforms grew more alluring. Consequently, it was not until the late 1970s that these ideas were translated into policies that began to reshape medical care to be more commodity-like.[38]

The second group of advocates for market-oriented reforms was more surprising, since it was composed primarily of liberal politicians and political advocates. They were responding to growing evidence that medical professionals were insensitive to certain groups of patients. These concerns were first articulated by advocates in the women's health and disability rights movement.[39] The reformers sought primarily to give patients greater choice over their medical care. In order to accomplish this, however, it was deemed important that patients be aware of their options for switching among health care providers. Only if these options were known and could be readily exercised could patients be empowered to make demands of their physicians. Otherwise, they were trapped in relationships with unresponsive clinicians.[40]

The liberal version of market reform was the first to be translated into concrete policy, through a series of consent decrees negotiated by the Federal Trade Commission (FTC) with the medical professions in the late 1970s. These struck down professional prohibitions on advertising, building on an earlier Supreme Court ruling that made illegal advertising restrictions among lawyers. The rationale provided by the FTC for extending this doctrine to medical care was rather simplistic, treating all professions as identical for (antitrust) policy purposes. But under the Carter administration, the commissioner of the FTC clearly saw himself as a strong liberal advocate for consumers. He believed that the elimination of advertising restrictions would make the medical profession more responsive to consumer concerns, empowering individual patients.[41]

Procompetitive reforms aimed at reducing the growth of medical spending came soon after. The push toward a revitalized market in health care was furthered by Ronald Reagan's 1980 election. Reagan appointed a number of key policy advisers who had been proponents of market-based health care reforms while in Congress.[42] Although interest-group lobbying and other pressures limited their ability to impose significant changes, a number of more modest proposals were put into place, intended to stimulate competition among health care providers.[43]

The two camps favoring promarket reforms began to merge forces by the latter part of the 1980s, presaging a dramatic resurgence of the market paradigm in the policy debates of the 1990s. The common ground for this merger involved a new strategy for introducing markets to medical care, labeled by its proponents as "managed competition."[44] Rather than asking people to choose among health care providers at the time that they needed care, this approach emphasized choices among health plans. Because plan selection took place under less stressful circumstances, packaging services and providers together for easier comparison, managed competition was expected to lead to more effective consumer decision making. These choices were to be facilitated by "sponsors"—employers for the privately insured, public agencies for those covered by Medicare or Medicaid. Sponsors were charged with monitoring plan performance, providing consumers with unbiased information, and screening out those plans that performed poorly.

Managed competition seemed appealing to both liberal and conservative advocates of health care reform. In the role of the sponsors, the liberals saw the potential for transforming medical care, for displacing the entrenched interests of the medical profession, and for creating a powerful competitive dynamic for making the health system more responsive to consumers.[45] By contrast, conservatives saw managed competition as a more effective way to contain health care costs. By having employers and government programs cover the premium of only the cheapest of the competing health plans—and asking consumers who chose more expensive plans to make up the difference for their own pockets—managed competition could finally introduce prudent purchasing to American medicine. All government needed to do was to facilitate competition, then step back and watch the market perform.[46]

This sort of broad ideological appeal found a responsive audience in Bill Clinton.[47] Managed competition represented a seemingly perfect synthesis for the evolving paradigms of the New Democrats. It provided a platform for substantial social reform (through government subsidies for expanded private health insurance) while sidestepping the perennial charge that Democrats inevitably favored "big government." Indeed, by relying heavily on market forces and an active role for private employers, proponents of reform in the Clinton administration hoped to build a bipartisan coalition in favor of federal action.[48] Information describing the president's plan—termed the Health Security Act—continually invoked the importance of consumer choice. It became almost a mantra for reformers within the administration.[49] So it was that by the early 1990s, market-oriented approaches came to dominate debate over health care reform. The dramatic emergence of the market frame can be traced by the frequency with which it appeared in congressional hearings, where it was the single most commonly cited schema. [50] And market thinking was cited as frequently by Democrats as Republicans, used as often to bolster the case for health care reform as to argue against government action. Market terminology had, by the early 1990s, become the dominant vocabulary for politicians and interest groups engaged in health policy debates.

This embrace of the market persisted, despite the rather ignominious rejection of the Health Security Act. This shift in the dominant frame was reflected in subsequent proposals for reforming other government health programs. With substantial encouragement from Washington, state policy makers began incorporating the principles of managed competition into their Medicaid programs.[51] Republican plans for Medicare reform relied heavily on encouraging beneficiaries to choose among competing health plans. In their more extreme form, these proposals called for replacing the conventional Medicare program entirely with government-financed vouchers, which would be used by beneficiaries to purchase private insurance. Although this version of reform proved politically infeasible, Congress adopted a less aggressive set of changes in 1997 under the label of Medicare+Choice (and in 2003 under the guise of prescription drug benefits). These changes vastly increased the number of private insurance options available to Medicare beneficiaries, with the intent of enhancing choice and competition. Washington-based policy analysts across the political spectrum embraced these market-oriented models for Medicare reform.[52]

Although viewed with enthusiasm within the Beltway, the appeal of markets in medical care was less obvious to those outside of Washington. Many academic observers concluded that the track record of earlier competitive reforms was mixed at best, demonstrating little potential for cost containment and even less pressure for quality improvement.[53] The promise of patient empowerment proved equally elusive, given the limited willingness or ability of most patients to attend to the complexities of choosing carefully among health plans.[54]

Comparably mixed results emerged from efforts to incorporate market forces into programs like Medicare and Medicaid. It has proven difficult to restructure these programs to generate real competition.[55] Health plans were cautious about participating and quick to withdraw when conditions became unprofitable.[56] This ambivalent involvement left many parts of the country without effective competition. Plan withdrawals disrupted insurance and care-giving arrangements for millions of beneficiaries.[57] Numerous Medicare beneficiaries struggled to understand the choices they faced and the implications of their decisions. This experience left many policy analysts outside of Washington skeptical of market reforms for Medicare, questioning the bipartisan endorsement that seemed to exist within the Beltway.[58]

The American public was slower to embrace markets than were Washington elites. During the 1980s, between 30% and 40% of Americans questioned policies that promoted advertising by health care providers.[59] During the 1990s, while policy makers were enthusiastically expanding the role of the market in government health programs, they had difficulty convincing voters of the merit of these changes. When asked in July 1995 about Republican proposals to convert the Medicare program into a system of vouchers, a representative sample of the public soundly rejected the approach, 53% to 33% (the remainder weighed in as undecided).[60] Even among conservative respondents, 41% rejected the proposed changes. Nor did the appeal of this approach grow over time. Asked a comparable question in March 1999, public respondents again rejected vouchers, this time 52% to 34%.[61] A series of focus groups held in June 2001 found that while a majority of the public endorsed "more consumer choice in Medicare," these same individuals were strongly opposed to statements that "there needs to be more competition in the Medicare system" or that Medicare "should be privatized."[62]

Despite these doubts voiced from the hinterlands, the contemporary consensus within Washington favoring market-oriented reforms remains quite strong. This was exemplified by the report of the National Bipartisan Commission on the Future of Medicare. Established by Congress in the Balanced Budget Act of 1997, this Commission issued its report in the spring of 1999. The majority endorsed the replacement of the conventional Medicare program with a system of government premium subsidies to facilitate choice and competition among private insurance plans.[63] The strength of this elite consensus clearly comes more from the idea of the market in medical care than from the actual performance of market-based reforms, which was viewed as spotty even by market advocates.[64] It is thus essential for us to better understand the major dimensions of these market frames. This will help to predict the implications of market thinking for the extent of inequality in American medicine, the terms under which this inequality will be assessed, and the potential for effective policy responses.

## The Impact of Market Reforms on Inequality

As we saw in the preceding chapter, health services researchers have documented long-standing differences in health and health care use by Americans of different races, ethnicities, and differing socioeconomic status.[65] Managed competition can be expected to *worsen* these inequalities in health outcomes, even though there is less reason to expect that it would introduce inequalities to a system in which they had not previously existed.

### The Promise of Greater Equality

Proponents of markets see them as potentially reducing inequalities in health outcomes in two different ways. First, to the extent that particular groups face systematic discrimination or mistreatment, market reforms are seen as a means to allow members of these groups to seek out more sympathetic health care providers. To this end, many states have adopted managed competition models in order to allow Medicaid recipients to have more choice among "mainstream" medical practitioners. Second, many proponents of market-based reforms argue for providing vouchers or other subsidies to all citizens to ensure that they can participate effectively in markets for health care. Because those with limited incomes or from communities of color are currently less able to take advantage of the tax-based subsidies to purchase private insurance,[66] these voucher proposals would entail a substantial redistribution of government support to groups that have historically had worse health care outcomes.[67]

## The Reality of Expanding Inequalities

In practice, however, these promises appear insubstantial in the face of multiple sources of increasing inequality in health care use and health outcomes under competitive models. We can identify from this historical experience two distinct forms of growing inequality. We'll refer to the first as "observable inequalities." These are differences in health outcomes that are consistently associated with identifiable groups or subpopulations. The second form of inequality develops as "hidden inequalities"— that is, differences among groups that cannot be predicted by observable characteristics of those groups. Although the elimination of observable inequalities has been the primary focus of federal health policy emerging from the societal rights paradigm, hidden inequalities may prove at least as problematic in terms of exposing Americans to inadequate health care. And this second category of inequality may prove more difficult to remedy through public policy.

*Exacerbating Observable Inequalities.* Prior to the introduction of managed competition, market-oriented reforms emphasized charging patients for a share of the medical services that they used. The Health Insurance Experiment, funded by the federal government in the early 1970s, demonstrated that this sort of cost sharing would in fact reduce the use of medical services.[68] Not surprising, cost sharing of this sort had the largest impact on the health care use of lower income families. This threatened to produce more unequal health outcomes. Although the researchers who conducted the study found that cost sharing produced few deleterious effects on health in the short term, those problems that did emerge were concentrated among the lowest-income households.

Managed competition was intended to avoid these sorts of inequalities. By having participants choose among health plans, each having a budget for the medical care provided in the subsequent year, proponents expected cost-sharing arrangements to be largely eliminated in favor of other methods of controlling health care spending.[69] By introducing sponsors to oversee the choice among plans, advocates predicted that inequities would be more readily identified and addressed. If some plans remained unresponsive, the affected individuals could simply switch to another plan.

Practice has proven more problematic. Proposals for providing universal health insurance using vouchers appear to be no more politically feasible than those based on a government-operated insurance plan.[70] Nor have competitive arrangements provided much in the way of safeguards for potentially mistreated groups. Public and private sponsors have not proven very adept at monitoring the performance of health plans, leaving considerable potential for discriminatory or otherwise inadequate care.[71] Nor have individuals been provided with the sort of information that would allow them to identify unequal treatment. To do this, the track record of competing health plans would need to be presented separately for different groups of enrollees. In practice, this disaggregated information is rarely if ever provided to consumers, who must instead base their choices on how a plan purportedly performs for some mythical "average" enrollee. In addition to these problems of implementation, the basic structure of the managed competition model has proven ill equipped to address two crucial sources of unequal outcomes.

The first of these involves the ability of individuals to make informed decisions among health plans. Both advocates and critics of managed competition agreed that for this to occur, Americans had to become considerably better informed about how health plans operate and about what dimensions of their operation were most relevant to the individual's health needs. Sponsors have done their part to provide this information. A number of employers, a handful of states, and the Medicare program have all sought to compile data on health plan performance and disseminate that information to beneficiaries in the form of report cards or other easily understood documents. But individuals with greater education or more economic resources typically find it easier to make sense of this material. This creates a systematic bias in the ability to choose among health plans and respond to problems when they develop. It is not surprising to find that studies of outcomes under managed care plans find that low-income enrollees have significantly worse outcomes than enrollees with higher incomes enrolled in the same plans.[72]

The challenges of interpreting and responding to complex information have an important parallel in past efforts at health promotion. As we have learned more about the social and behavioral determinants of health, the media and public health officials have provided citizens with a growing body of information on healthy lifestyles. The response has been growing inequalities over time in healthy behaviors, use of preventive health services, and health outcomes, as those in higher socioeconomic strata respond more to this information than do other individuals.[73]

A second attribute of competition among health plans may prove to be an even more daunting source of unequal health outcomes. As a result of past differences in health care risks, access, and treatment, Americans from households that have limited income or that are composed of racial or ethnic minorities can be expected to be less healthy than are other citizens. But when a health plan enrolls a new member, the plan gets paid a premium intended to cover the costs of medical care for the average enrollee. Enrollees who are predictably sicker have predictably higher medical costs. They are, in short, enrollees on whom the plan can expect to lose money.

As health plans struggle to remain financially solvent in a competitive market, they have a strong incentive to avoid unprofitable enrollees. They can thus be expected to avoid marketing their services to neighborhoods in which there are high concentrations of minority or low-income residents. If the sponsor tries to prevent this by directly controlling the marketing process, plans can achieve the same end by locating their facilities and affiliated clinicians as far away as possible from these unprofitable neighborhoods. If all these efforts fail, and the plan inadvertently enrolls people for whom it will predictably lose money, it still has one more form of recourse. It can avoid treating them very well (short of overt discrimination, this could be accomplished by subtle differences in access to services). In a competitive market, dissatisfied enrollees can be expected to leave the health plan. This, of course, is exactly what is in the financial interests of the plan, since it eliminates enrollees who would have been predictable financial burdens.

There has long been evidence that health plans benefit from the selective enrollment of healthy populations and disenrollment by individuals in poor health.[74] Although people with chronic illnesses tend to be more dissatisfied then healthy enrollees under all forms of health insurance, the increase in dissatisfaction is markedly greater in plans under stronger financial pressures for cost containment.[75] Comparable patterns of dissatisfaction and disenrollment have been found when competitive models have been incorporated into Medicare and Medicaid.[76] A recent report by the federal panel overseeing the implementation of Medicare+Choice concluded that "whether the favorable selection into plans reflects intentional efforts to attract low-cost beneficiaries or simply that those beneficiaries find managed care more attractive than do higher-cost beneficiaries is not an issue; favorable selection in Medicare+Choice does occur."[77]

Under these circumstances, one would expect to find that health plan enrollees with limited incomes or from minority households are likely to be less satisfied with their medical care. Although information on this topic is limited, recent studies find exactly this pattern.[78] To reduce this potential for discrimination, advocates of managed competition have sought ways of adjusting the premium paid to plans to reflect the true "health risks" associated with their enrollees. Indeed, the quest for an effective risk-adjustment formula has become the "holy grail" in contemporary health services research. Unfortunately, it is proving equally elusive. Existing formulas can account for only a small portion of the variance in health care spending among individual enrollees, leaving plenty of incentive for exclusionary behavior on the part of health plans. Short of effective individual risk adjustment, one could address this same problem simply by paying plans' higher premiums for low-income or minority enrollees. But no existing managed competition scheme has shown an inclination to pay this sort of "bounty," perhaps out of a concern that the sponsors might be accused of reverse discrimination.

*Exacerbating Hidden Inequalities.* Under these circumstances, one would expect that promarket reforms based on managed competition would exacerbate differences in health outcomes associated with race, ethnicity, and socioeconomic status. These are visible disparities, in the sense that race or class can be measured and used to report on the performance of health plans. But managed competition may also introduce another important, but less visible, source of inequality. For this model to function effectively, sponsors must be willing and able to play their roles effectively. Experience to date suggests that employers and state governments vary considerably in their commitment to this task.[79] All else equal, people who are choosing health plans under an effective sponsor can be expected to make better choices and have better health outcomes than those whose sponsors are fully or partially abdicating their roles.

Some of the determinants of effective sponsor behavior are predictable. Larger employers are more likely to have the resources to be effective sponsors than are smaller firms. (Although the smaller firms have been encouraged to band together into purchasing cooperatives, these have had varying success, which introduces yet another source of inequality.) Similar patterns are replicated between large and small states in Medicaid oversight. Other factors that can affect the quality of sponsorship include the profitability of the firm, the extent of enrollee turnover, and the overall stability of the industry. Because low-income and minority workers are more likely to find employment in firms or industries that are marginally profitable or stable, varying performance by sponsors may exacerbate the sort of systematic inequalities that we identified above. Equally important, however, variation in effective sponsorship will add a more random aspect to the inequalities in question. Those who are fortunate enough to work for companies that are committed to the welfare of their employees, that operate in states with more robust economies, or that have been extensively unionized, can expect to have more effective choices among health plans. Their less fortunate peers can be expected to have a less positive experience with managed competition.

For all these reasons, one would expect that a health care system based on markets will in the first instance exhibit more extensive inequalities (visible or otherwise) than would a health care system organized around professional norms or societal rights. How this will eventually affect the health and welfare of individual citizens will largely depend on how policy makers interpret and respond to these emerging inequalities. In other words, the impact of market reforms can only be assessed if one has a clear sense of how government can be expected to respond to market outcomes.[80] This will depend in part on the norms applied to determine when inequalities are deemed inequitable and in part on the government's ability to respond to those circumstances perceived as inequitable.

## Market Frames and Norms of Fairness

As Deborah Stone discussed in chapter 3, there are different spheres of justice with different metrics for judging equity. Within the market frame, increasing disparities in health care might not be judged inequitable. The same thinking that leads decision makers to favor medical markets also provides a rationale for assessing the equity of the health care system in different terms than would be applied to health care rights or professionalized notions of health needs. Market norms emphasize the importance of individual responsibility and choice, assessing fairness in the distribution of medical care in terms of notions of deservingness, as measured by the productive contribution that individuals make to society.[81] Fairness defined in these terms legitimizes differences in health care and health outcomes by suggesting that individuals differ in the extent to which they merit these outcomes.

Does the coalition of elite and liberal support backing markets represent a true consensus around values, or does it mask differences in attitudes toward fairness in medical care? To the extent that market advocates have overcome the public's initial skepticism toward medical markets, have they also been able to transform the norms of fairness that the public applies in thinking about medical care? To address these questions, we turn to data from a recent study that explored how the American public and political elites think about complex social issues.[82]

## Consensus Frayed:
## Cleavages in Values among Policy Elites

Much of the political appeal of market-oriented reforms involves their ability to draw support from across the ideological spectrum. But this coalition may prove fragile when issues are raised about the fairness of market reforms or their implications. Market proponents with more liberal ideological leanings have very different expectations for fairness in medical care than do their conservative counterparts.

Conservatives tend to favor individual responsibility for health care. They prefer having medical care allocated on the basis of choice and productivity, rather than need or equality (see Table 4.1).

But liberal supporters of market-oriented policies judge fairness in strikingly different terms. They reject almost universally the notion that health care should be an individual responsibility. Although they share conservatives' endorsement of choice-based allocations as a fair way to distribute medical care, for the most part they reject the attendant emphasis on productivity and remain committed to the norms of need and equality. In other words, these elites see market-oriented policies such as vouchers as means to achieve more universalistic goals.[83]

## Consensus Torn Asunder:
## Cleavages between Elite and Public Attitudes

Additional cleavages emerge when one compares elite attitudes to those of the general public. Our findings reveal striking differences in the attitudes held by congressional staff and their constituents. Fifty-eight percent of the congressional health staffers endorsed the market frame for reform of social policies. By contrast, only 41% of the public endorsed this approach to social policy. This verifies the pattern revealed by our historical analysis—that the market has been more strongly embraced among elites in Washington than among the American public.

Table 4.1
Divided Beliefs about Fair Medical Care,
Liberal versus Conservative Market Advocates

| | Supporters of the Market | |
| Measures of Fairness | Conservatives | Liberals |
| --- | --- | --- |
| *Notions Involving Allocations of Responsibility* | | |
| Individuals should be responsible for physician and hospital services | 87.0% | 4.2% |
| Individuals should be responsible for nursing home and health care | 69.1% | 0% |
| Individuals should be responsible for treatment of substance abuse | 83.3% | 6.7% |
| *Particular Norms of Equity Applied to Health Care* | | |
| The health care system would be most fair if it allowed individuals to decide about the health insurance and health care that best matched what they want to pay for | 100% | 100% |
| People who are the most productive should make the most income and be offered the best fringe benefits | 40% | 11.1% |
| The most important aspect of a just health care system is that everyone be treated equally | 0% | 55.6% |
| People should get health care based on needs, as determined by medical experts, regardless of costs | 20% | 66.7% |

Our analysis of the relationship between market advocacy and ethical norms reveals a second striking difference between elite and public respondents. Among the modal elite respondent, embracing the market is associated with distinctive norms of equity and allocations of responsibility. Among the public, the minority who endorse the market do not embrace as distinctive a set of ethical principles for determining what is fair in American health care.

These findings are presented here in Table 4.2. Among congressional staff, proponents of the market are twice as likely to support individual responsibility, a pattern that is consistent (and statistically significant) across service domains. By contrast, market advocates among the public are slightly *less* likely to endorse individual responsibility for medical care. Again, this pattern is consistent across all three service domains.

In Table 4.3 we compare the norms of fairness applied to medical care. Not surprisingly, market advocates among both public and elite

**Table 4.2**
**Allocation of Responsibility Applied to Various Aspects of Health Care,**
**Supporters of Markets versus Other Respondents**

| | Respondent Group | | | |
| | Elites | | Public | |
| Percentage of Respondents Favoring Individual Responsibility over Collective Responsibility for: | Market Advocates | Other Respondents | Market Advocates | Other Respondents |
|---|---|---|---|---|
| Physician and hospital services | 58.5% | 28.8% | 29.0% | 33.9% |
| Nursing home and home health care | 48.9% | 30.0% | 25.6% | 35.9% |
| Treatment of substance abuse | 53.2% | 27.0% | 33.1% | 42.3% |

**Table 4.3**
**Norms of Equity Applied to Health Care,**
**Supporters of Markets versus Other Respondents**

| | Respondent Group | | | |
| | Elites | | Public | |
| Percent Agreeing with Each Norm: | Market Advocates | Other Respondents | Market Advocates | Other Respondents |
|---|---|---|---|---|
| The health care system would be fair if it allowed individuals to decide about the health insurance and health care that best matched what they want to pay for | 85.7% | 20.6% | 79.4% | 46.4% |
| People who are the most productive should make the most income and be offered the best fringe benefits | 23.8% | 12.9% | 31.8% | 27.8% |
| The most important aspect of a just health care system is that everyone be treated equally | 42.9% | 64.7% | 82.5% | 67.9% |
| People should get health care based on needs, as determined by medical experts, regardless of costs | 38.1% | 44.1% | 76.2% | 73.2% |

respondents were more supportive of choice. But that's where the agreement ends. Among elites, market advocates are more supportive of norms of deservingness, significantly less supportive of equality, and slightly less supportive of the norm of need. Among the public, in contrast, market advocates are only slightly more supportive of deservingness, but are substantially *more* supportive of equality as a norm for medical care and slightly more supportive of the need criteria.

## Some Consequences of Cleavages

These findings suggest that there are hidden tensions in the apparent hegemony of market thinking in contemporary American health policy. Among conservative policy makers, the embrace of market thinking inside the Beltway is likely to significantly reduce sensitivity to inequalities in health outcomes. Conservative market advocates simply aren't much concerned about equality in medical care. And they are significantly more likely to assign responsibility for medical outcomes to the individual, obviating any need for government to respond to unequal outcomes. These findings on elite opinion suggest a substantial recent shift in policy-relevant values. This change is not entirely surprising, given the Republican ascendancy in the 1994 congressional elections.

But elite support for the market may become unstable when policy debates focus on notions of equity. Almost half of all market advocates among congressional staff characterize themselves as moderates or liberals. These advocates embrace a very different set of values about just health care. They are unwilling to reject social responsibility for health care, and most of them have not yet abandoned norms of need or equality in medical care.

Perhaps more surprising are the gaps in values identified between elites and the general public. Republican efforts (supported by compatible thinking among New Democrats) to bring markets to medical care do not have a strong public mandate. Moreover, those among the public who do endorse the market model appear to be doing so in very different terms than is understood in Washington. Support for the market among the American public does not entail a reduced concern for equal treatment in the health care system, or an endorsement of greater individual responsibility. Indeed, the public seems to support market approaches largely out of a belief that voucher models will actually generate greater equality, a promise of market reformers that has been all but forgotten by contemporary policy makers.

## How Markets Affect Competing
## Prescriptions for Health Policy

The juxtaposition of the findings from the past two sections reveals an important emerging tension in contemporary American health policy. On the one hand, market reforms will almost certainly lead to greater inequalities in American medicine, both visible and hidden. These changing outcomes are compatible with changing goals among the majority of Washington-based elites. For these policy makers, acceptance of a market frame for public policy is associated with a reduced concern for equality and an increased willingness to assign responsibility for health care outcomes to the individual.

On the other hand, there are no comparable changes in the norms of the American public. The acceptance of the market in medical care is not only less complete among the public than among federal officials, but where there is public support for market-based reforms, it is *not* associated with a reduced concern for equality or collective responsibility for health care outcomes. One would thus expect the public to be far more aggrieved by the growing inequalities in American medicine that follow from market reforms. Although public concerns are likely to strike a responsive chord among liberal advocates of markets, the deep ideological divisions in values among market supporters will make it difficult to "fine-tune" market reforms to produce greater consensus around fairness.

Under these circumstances, one might expect to find a sort of policy paralysis at the federal level. This could be potentially overcome or circumvented through alternative policy approaches. But these alternative approaches have been weakened in various ways by the rise of market thinking. To see how, we'll consider two examples: first, the potential for state policy to supplement federal initiatives, and second, the potential for alternative policy frames to legitimize alternatives to market-oriented reforms.

### Market Reforms and the Concentration of Political Power

What happens when the public expects remedial policies, but their elected officials in Washington prove unwilling to comply? Federalism provides a safety valve that might relieve these political tensions. And that appears to be precisely the pattern observed through the latter half of the 1990s. While Congress dithered about various versions of federal regulation for managed care plans (failing to enact any of the alternative proposals), and while the Health Care Financing Administration lacked the will or resources to effectively regulate the new market mechanisms introduced into Medicare and Medicaid, state governments stepped into the breach.

Over the past 6 years, state regulatory oversight of managed care and managed competition has grown considerably.[84] Many of these regulations have focused primarily on the internal procedures found within managed care plans—by how they oversee physician practices, how they pay their clinicians, and what types of treatment they will consider "medically necessary." But a number of state initiatives are designed expressly to improve the performance of managed competition by assuring that enrollees are better informed or by protecting the interests of those individuals who have made less effective choices in the marketplace.

As of 1999, 17 states defined quality-of-care standards for health plans, 30 required that plans regularly file reports on quality with the state, 23 mandated participation in report-card systems that rated plan performance, 12 required that disputes between plans and enrollees be submitted to binding external review, and 18 established ombudsman offices to provide aggrieved enrollees with a source of external support. When health plans participating in Medicare threatened to drop participation or substantially reduce the services that they covered for beneficiaries, it was often state officials who responded most aggressively.

As the primary locus of health policy initiative shifted from federal to state governments, other consequences of market reforms became relevant. Market-enhancing public policies led to more intense competition among health plans during the 1990s. Growing competitive pressures, coupled with a long track record of financial instability among managed care plans, have led to significant consolidation of the industry.[85] The substitution of plans controlled by national firms for those with local ownership was particularly pronounced among investor-owned corporations, which controlled the majority of all managed care plans by the late 1990s. As one analyst noted, "Wall Street looks favorably at firms whose risks are diversified across markets with different business climates and across states with different regulatory climates."[86]

By the mid-1990s, over half of all managed care plans were affiliated with companies of national or regional scope. For some specific services, consolidation was even more advanced. In behavioral health care (covering the treatment of mental illness and substance abuse), for example, by the late 1990s, 69% of all enrollees were in plans affiliated with the five largest national corporations; 37% were covered by the single largest firm.[87]

Consequently, state regulators are increasingly faced with the task of overseeing the performance of large multistate corporations. A number of observers worry that state officials may be overmatched in this challenge.[88] The growing size of these large health care corporations gives them the capacity to engage large legal staffs. They may thus have a negotiating advantage over many state agencies. The interstate scope of these corporations adds to their bargaining power. If pressed too hard by state oversight, they can threaten to decamp from the state entirely. Finally, the size of these companies also gives them the capacity to be important political actors.

It may seem odd to worry about the capacity for states to address the distributional consequences of the market at a time when states are busy enacting a plethora of new regulations. But this flurry of activity masks several sources of possible concern. First, some states are far more active than others in their regulatory activity. For example, looking at the five forms of market-oriented regulation identified earlier, we find that through 1999, three states had enacted rules in all five categories; another four states had addressed four of the five. At the other extreme, nine states had taken no action in any of these areas. Another 14 states had acted in only one of the five dimensions of market regulation. There has been no research on the determinants of state regulatory involvement with managed care. Thus we have no means of determining whether political pressure from the industry has been an important deterrent of state action. Anecdotal reports do suggest that lobbying by managed care plans has been an obstacle for at least some regulatory initiatives.[89] At a minimum, it is clear that variation in state regulatory involvement has the potential to introduce yet another set of inequalities into American medicine, with residents of some states provided with much more extensive oversight than are citizens in other jurisdictions.

A second source of concern involves the focus of existing state initiatives. In order to determine whether market forces are exacerbating inequality in health care use or health care outcomes, the sorts of information provided in report cards needs to be disaggregated, reporting separately the experiences of the groups most at risk for systematic undertreatment. To date, information collected by the states is rarely disaggregated in this manner and is never conveyed to the public in this form.[90] It remains unknown whether this omission is simply an oversight, or the reflection of interests that have discouraged reporting plan performance in this manner.

Finally, the existence of regulations does not guarantee that they will be effectively enforced. Health plans may accept the enactment of man-

aged care regulation as a way to diffuse public anger about their policies and practices. If they are able to block effective enforcement, then
the actions of state legislatures are little more than symbolic, fooling the
public into believing that some real action has been taken to protect
their interests.[91] Here again, we have no systematic evidence about the
relationship between the political influence of the insurance industry
and states' propensity to effectively implement managed care regulations.
However, there are anecdotal reports that suggest that these concerns are
quite plausible.[92]

## The Corrosive Power of Market Thinking

The sorts of regulations discussed in the previous section were essentially minor repairs to the market model for medical care. These state
initiatives presume that the basic structure of managed competition is
sound. They address undesirable distributional consequences either by
providing consumers with more complete information or by offering
stronger safeguards on quality of care for those who are disadvantaged
in the market.

But these are not the only possible policy responses. To the extent
one views the inequities produced by medical markets as sufficiently pernicious and largely inherent in the basic structure of managed competition, it makes sense to consider other policy frames that represent alternatives to the market. A number of candidates exist. One need only to
look to other industrialized democracies to find numerous examples of
each. One alternative involves the societal rights frame described earlier.
Embodied in the sort of national health insurance programs found in
Canada or France, this approach would enroll all Americans into a single
health insurance plan (e.g., Medicare for all citizens), while still allowing them choices among health care providers. By so doing, it would
eliminate a number of the problematic distributional consequences of
unevenly informed choice or incentives for private insurers to select only
the healthiest enrollees.

Another alternative would provide universal health insurance coverage on a more decentralized basis. Instead of a single plan for the country
as a whole, all the residents of a community could be enrolled in a single
plan, but with different plans serving different communities. This more
localized version of universal insurance is similar in many respects to the
national health services operated by many of the Scandinavian countries.[93] It would introduce choice at the community level, but eliminate
incentives for selection at the level of the individual patient. We'll refer

to this alternative schema as the "community obligation model" of health care reform.

It is not far-fetched to imagine these alternative frames as guides to health policy reform. As we noted earlier, the societal rights frame was the dominant paradigm for federal health care reform as little as 15 years ago. The community-based model of health care reform has an even deeper historical pedigree, having dominated the thinking of policy makers for substantial parts of the nineteenth and early twentieth century. As late as the 1960s, it played an important role as a template for federal health policy, as embodied in the creation of community health and mental health centers.[94]

At least in principle, these other frames represent alternative directions for future health policy. In my assessment, however, the spreading influence of market thinking has done more than simply increase the salience of one of a variety of policy frames. Its influence has begun to permeate interpretations of these alternative frames. By so doing, the market paradigm is transforming its intellectual competitors into its own image. This may actually prove helpful for future transitions among policy paradigms, since it reduces the intellectual distance among these competing frames. But to advocates of older interpretations of societal rights or community obligation, contemporary transformations of these frames can be seen as corruptions of their original intent, a corrosive side effect of the acceptance of market thinking in medical care.

I am certainly not the first to argue that the norms of the market tend to permeate other aspects of society. Thomas Jefferson was among the first American political leaders to argue for a particular economic order to society (he opposed large-scale industrialization) in order to promote a particular conception of civic virtue.[95] Some economists have long warned against the propensity of market principles to undermine other valued social relationships,[96] or for particular concentrations of economic power to reshape America's political goals.[97] But I'm proposing that market thinking can also transform the nature of policy debate by reshaping other policy frames in a manner that I do not believe has been previously proposed or documented. Let me take the societal rights and community obligations frames as examples and illustrate the processes that I believe are at work.

*The Transformation from Political to Contractual Rights.*    In the early 1990s, the dominance of market-based models of health care reform in Washington debates was accompanied by a dramatic decline in the salience of conventional understandings of societal rights. The salience of the market frame gradually increased in congressional hearings between the mid-1960s and the late 1980s. By the early 1990s, references to the market paradigm doubled. We can also graph the frequency of references to the societal rights frame in elite discourse over this same time period (Figure 4.1). The conventional societal rights perspective, which had dominated political debate in Washington since the enactment of Medicare, collapsed in the 1990s, dropping from about 40% of all frame references to less than 15% during the debate over the Clinton administration's reform proposals.[98]

This sharp decline in salience cannot solely be attributed to elites' reactions to declining public confidence in the federal government, an inference that is often drawn.[99] Public confidence in national government had shown substantial decline since the 1960s, yet the salience of the societal rights frame remained strong in congressional hearings through the late 1980s.[100] Some other factor was clearly at work. My hypothesis is that this additional factor involved the transformation of the notion of rights into a version more compatible with market thinking. As the salience of the conventional societal rights frame declined, one could detect the growing endorsement of a notion of rights that was set in contractual relationships. This alternative frame was soon embodied in proposals for a so-called "patient bill of rights," intended to ensure that enrollees in

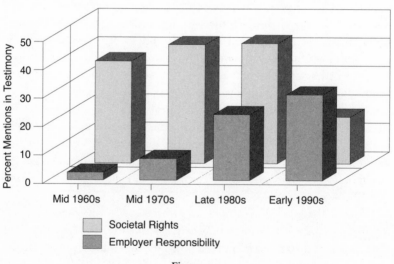

Figure 4.1
Changing frequency of other institutional frames.

private insurance received fair treatment in their dealings with managed care plans.[101]

This recasting of rights language was first proposed in 1997 by a presidential commission appointed to review threats to the quality of American medicine.[102] It was enthusiastically embraced by policy elites, spawning a number of congressional proposals and parallel initiatives among state governments.[103] The "rights" in these proposals involved issues of free access to providers, notification about financial payment arrangements, and assured mechanisms for appealing adverse review decisions. Although the American public enthusiastically endorsed a patient bill of rights,[104] congressional debate stalemated over the issue of whether such basic rights included the right to sue a health plan for malpractice.

This is a peculiarly privatized notion of rights to medical care. Compared to conventional understandings of societal rights, the Patient Bill of Rights debated in Congress clearly represented a very different understanding of what individuals can appropriately claim as citizens and what responsibilities the federal government should embrace. Rights in health care are no longer viewed as a matter of citizenship, but instead are an attribute of private contracts to provide medical care. Those without health insurance partake in none of these rights. Nor does government make any commitment to oversee the actual medical care being provided. In many ways, this is a reversion to a more natural rights understanding of collective responsibilities. Government is charged solely with protecting citizens from interference by insurance companies with their access to appropriate treatment.

Although it is a marked departure from the interpretation of rights to health care in the latter half of the twentieth century, this privatized understanding of rights is powerfully consistent with the notion of recasting medical care in a market model.[105] It asks the government to assure precisely those dimensions of access and treatment that are difficult to specify in a contract. And it addresses at least some of the inequalities that the managed competition model can be expected to generate. But it ignores many of the others. There is nothing in any version of the Patient Bill of Rights that assures equal treatment for enrollees with equal medical needs; no standard that calls for the least informed to be treated by the same standard as the best informed. Because the rights protected in this case are entirely procedural, there is no accommodation to the very different capabilities and resources that individuals have for exercising these rights. Consequently, they are likely to be subject to the same disparities in use that have previously emerged in treatment under managed care: differences associated with income, race, and educational attainment.

*Clashing Visions of Community: Geography and Employment.* American industries—in contrast to European ones—are organized around a division between workplace and home. As a result, American policy makers have long faced two very different visions of community: geography and employment. Programs organized around geography are more universal; those focused on employment are more targeted.

In chapter 5, Marie Gottschalk shows how organized labor became invested in employment-based health insurance during the late 1940s. American labor's self-interest helped subvert the universal health care ideals that inspired labor unions in other countries. More recently, the shift from geographic- to employment-based frames has spread.

As the market began to regain its salience among policy elites, the enthusiasm for connecting health policy to entire geographic communities began to fade. Arguably, this occurred in part because community-based policies were increasingly seen as conflicting with the market. As health care organizations began to face more competitive pressures, they began to abandon connections and obligations to community service that they had previously endorsed. Now those involvements seemed insufficiently businesslike.[106]

Support for community-level policy making was not entirely abandoned. It was instead transformed into a version that was more consistent with the market paradigm. Instead of linking citizens to geographic communities, policy makers began increasingly to see Americans as most appropriately connected their place of work.[107] Given the large number of American households in which all adults worked outside the home, and the long hours devoted to these work responsibilities, it was not far-fetched to see connections to one's coworkers as increasingly replacing those with one's neighbors.[108] We'll term this the employer responsibility frame.

Figure 4.1 shows the rising power of the employer responsibility frame. While government had encouraged employer health insurance (through tax and regulatory policies), in the 1980s and 1990s, the employer responsibility frame spread into publicly financed programs. This corresponded to the resurgence of interest in market models of health care reform, as well as to a decline in commitment to traditional notions of health care set within geographic communities. Employer-based communities are clearly more compatible with market principles.[109] Set in the workplace, they embody notions of deservingness based on productivity, closely akin to market norms of fairness. Employer-based communities allow for a greater role of choice in health care arrangements, since different work sites can be expected to provide different types of health benefits.[110]

Whatever their other merits, employment-based communities are in many ways rather weak forms of community. People switch jobs far more frequently than they change communities of residence. As a result, their ties to their coworkers tend to be weaker and less resilient than those that had traditionally been forged with their neighbors.[111] And peoples' sense of membership in employment-based communities is also weaker—there are few guarantees that they will not be fired or laid off if economic times are hard, even if they have been fully committed to their work and productive in their efforts. Work-site commitments will also vary with socioeconomic status. Those who work in routine jobs for relatively low pay are readily replaced by other workers. Better-educated members of the workforce, with more extensive training, are more difficult to replace, and hence more likely to be rewarded by employers with generous fringe benefits.[112]

## Limiting the Response to Market-Based Inequities in Health Care

The tendency of market thinking to transform (some might say "distort") other policy frames has important implications for the willingness and ability of policy makers to address the sorts of inequalities that are likely to emerge from market-based allocations of medical care. Expanding the role of markets in medical care is likely to exacerbate differences in health care use and health outcomes related to race, ethnicity, and socioeconomic status. Appeals to conventional notions of societal rights could highlight some potential remedies. But when rights are reinterpreted through the lens of contracts, they lose much of their applicability for addressing inequities in health care outcomes. Indeed, the sorts of procedural rights that are the embodiment of notions like a patient bill of rights are likely to be subject to the same sort of systematic disparities that would be generated by market-oriented reforms.

Similarly, appeals to traditional notions of community-based health care might broaden the protections for the most disadvantaged populations in those communities.[113] But when the relevant community is transformed from the place one lives to the place one works, it changes the terms under which membership is assessed and alters the array of policy responses that are seen as legitimate. Notions of community that rely on employers to exercise responsibility will again replicate the same sort of racial and socioeconomic differences that one would expect to be produced by the market. In short, market thinking renders impotent the alternative policy frames from which equity-enhancing policies might be derived or legitimated.

## Conclusions: Market Thinking
## and Health Care Inequality

It is easy to see the emergence of market thinking in medical care. Indeed, for anyone exposed to popular culture, it would be impossible to miss. One cannot drive down a major highway in any large American city without seeing billboards peddling local health plans and hospitals. One cannot watch commercial television for long without encountering an advertisement for some pharmaceutical product. Americans are increasingly being asked to make choices about their health insurance plans or their preferred forms of treatment.

The influence of market thinking on health policy in this country can be more readily overlooked. Although an apparently pan-ideological consensus in favor of markets has been forged among the Washington elite, this position is neither well recognized nor broadly supported outside of the Beltway. For example, although the Health Security Act was based on a model of managed competition, its market-based origins remained obscure for most of the American public.[114] And the results reported earlier suggest that the public thinks about markets in medical care in very different ethical terms than do Washington-based elites.

Despite these misperceptions—indeed, in part as a result of these misunderstandings—the emergence of the market frame among elites is having a crucial influence on the nature of inequality in American medicine, as well as the willingness and ability of policy makers to respond to those inequalities that are perceived as inequitable. The gap between elite and public interpretations of the market accounts for the growing role that state policy plays in addressing the distributional consequences of medical markets, filling a vacuum left by the persistent inaction of the federal government. I have argued that this seeming paralysis in federal policy making is in fact a reflection of divergences in the ethical criteria used by Washington elites to assess how medical care ought to be distributed among American citizens.

Policy stasis also has two other sources. Given the different understandings of market reforms held by elites and the general public, it is difficult for market advocates to even understand the circumstances troubling the public let alone effectively respond to them. And the options for effective policy response are further limited by the ways in which market thinking has undermined alternative frames for federal policy making. "Rights" lose much of their moral force when they apply only to those advantaged enough to be able to afford health insurance. Employment-based "communities" have little appeal for those with weak connections to particular employers or to the workforce generally.

I began this chapter by observing that markets are ubiquitous in American society. Much of our thinking—and that of our elected officials—is deeply stamped with the imprint of the market frame. This influence is so fundamental and so pervasive that we may fail to recognize its importance: In the words of a recent essay by Eric Patashnik, the market becomes "invisible."[115] In this sense, the contemporary health-policy debate provides us with a useful lens through which we can more clearly perceive processes that affect a much broader array of social policies. For example, many of the same issues raised here about the inequalities and inequities in medical care markets have been echoed in previous policy debates about public education and public housing policies.[116]

At the same time, it is important to not lose sight of the ways in which health care can be different from other social policy domains. Because there is such substantial redistribution between sick and healthy under health insurance, other forms of redistribution are masked in health policy to a much greater extent than is true for other forms of social policy. Because medical care is more complex, and the stakes of poor decisions are higher, it may prove more difficult to ensure that citizens feel reasonably secure in the choices they are making. Because health care costs vary so much among individuals, medical care markets are more prone to systematic disparities in treatment than would be true for services that are more standardized (e.g., public housing) or that have costs that vary less dramatically among individuals (e.g., public education, with the exception of students with learning disorders). Because the managed care industry has become more consolidated than is true for either education or housing, concentrations of political power may make it more difficult for state officials to appropriately oversee health policy and address any inequities that are produced by market reforms.

If we are to craft sound health policy, policy that is appropriately sensitive to inequalities of health care use or outcomes that we deem inequitable, we must be cognizant of the ways in which health care is and is not like other domains of social policy. The growing role of market thinking in medical care may help in this regard. Advocates for markets in medical care argue for a distinctive set of ethical standards that can and should be considered in any debate over health policy. Thoughtful citizens and political leaders can be expected to disagree about the merits of market-based norms and practices in medical care. The resulting debate ought to make us collectively wiser about the dimensions of health care that we most value and the forms of inequality that we will tolerate in American medicine.

In my assessment, however, the benefits of a more vibrant market frame in health policy fade to insignificance unless we guard against two types of problems identified earlier. The first involves the schism between public and elite interpretations of the meaning of market-based reforms in American medicine. In my experience, policy makers in Washington have no idea how strongly divergent their interpretations have become from those endorsed by the American public. That creates the potential for considerable political tension. It also foreshadows the creation of federal policies that will lack public legitimacy and, perhaps, the potential for grassroots rebellion.

The second relates to the transformative potential of market frames. It is desirable and healthy that the market frame be one of several policy paradigms considered in political debates. It becomes decidedly unhealthy for the body politic when the market frame so dominates thinking that it distorts the other policy frames that should serve as alternative policy ideals. It is in this manner that market thinking can corrupt political discourse, simply because it is so deeply rooted in American culture that it can powerfully reshape our interpretation of other frames. These changes in framing may be quite subtle, emerging only gradually over time. In this manner, the values of equality connected with older notions of societal rights, or the notions of social connections associated with community-based policies, may simply fade from contemporary discourse. And they'll only be noticed when their meaning and message has been lost.

If we lose the guidance offered by these other perspectives, we will have truly impoverished policy debate over the future of American medicine. Given evidence that this transformation is already under way, we need to find better ways of guarding against its effects and preserving a lively debate about truly distinctive directions for health policy. We can do this only by being self-conscious of our thinking about policy, both in political debates and public discussions. We must no longer overlook what markets mean, or what markets do.

## Notes

1. Martha Derthick and Paul Quirk, *The Politics of Deregulation* (Washington, DC: Brookings Institution, 1985).

2. Eric M. Patashnik, "Why Can't Politicians Think Straight about the Market?" Paper prepared for the Annual Meeting of the American Political Science Association, Washington, DC, August 31–September 3, 2000; Robert Kuttner, *Everything for Sale: The Virtues and Limits of Markets* (Chicago: University of Chicago Press, 1996).

3. Charles E. Lindblom, *Politics and Markets* (New York: Basic Books, 1977).

4. Mark Schlesinger, "Countervailing Agency: A Strategy of Principled Regulation under Managed Competition," *Milbank Quarterly* 75.1 (1997): 35–87.

5. Judith Hibbard, Lauren Harris-Kojetin, Paul Mullin, James Lubalin, and Steve Garfinkel, "Increasing the Impact of Health Plan Report Cards by Addressing Consumers' Concerns," *Health Affairs* 19.5 (2000): 138–143.

6. Mark McClellan, Ian Spatz, and Stacie Carney, "Designing a Medicare Prescription Drug Benefit: Issues, Obstacles and Opportunities," *Health Affairs* 19.2 (2000): 26–41.

7. Karen Davis and Cathy Schoen, *Health and the War on Poverty: A Ten-Year Appraisal* (Washington, DC: Brookings Institution, 1978).

8. Theodore Marmor, *The Politics of Medicare* (New York: Aldine de Gruyter, 1970/1973).

9. Mark Schlesinger and Richard R. Lau, "The Meaning and Measure of Policy Metaphors," *American Political Science Review* 94 (2000): 611–626; Grant Reeher, *Narratives of Justice: Legislators' Beliefs about Distributive Fairness* (Ann Arbor: University of Michigan Press, 1996).

10. For a general discussion of norms of equity associated with markets, see Jennifer L. Hochschild, *What's Fair?: American Beliefs about Distributive Justice* (Princeton, NJ: Princeton University Press, 1981). For an application to health care, see Theodore R. Marmor and David A. Boyum, "The Political Considerations of Pro-Competitive Reform," *Competitive Approaches to Health Care Reform*, ed. Richard Arnould, Robert Rich, and William White (Washington, DC: Urban Institute Press, 1993), 245–256.

11. George Annas, "Reframing the Debate on Health Care Reform by Replacing Our Metaphors," *New England Journal of Medicine* 332.11 (1995): 744–747.

12. Carol S. Weisman, *Women's Health Care: Activist Traditions and Institutional Change* (Baltimore: Johns Hopkins University Press, 1998), 42.

13. Charles Rosenberg, "Prologue, the Shape of Traditional Practice, 1800–1875," *The Structure of American Medical Practice: 1875–1941*, ed. George Rosen (Philadelphia: University of Pennsylvania Press, 1983), 3–4.

14. William Rothstein, *American Physicians in the Nineteenth Century* (Baltimore: Johns Hopkins University Press, 1972).

15. Paul Starr, *The Social Transformation of American Medicine* (New York: Basic Books, 1982), 58.

16. R. G. Walters, *American Reformers, 1815–1860* (New York: Hill and Wang, 1997).

17. Weisman, *Women's Health Care*; Ronald L. Caplan, "The Commodification of American Health Care: A Marxian Reappraisal," *Social Science and Medicine*

28.11 (1989): 39–48; James G. Burrow, *Organized Medicine in the Progressive Era: The Move toward Monopoly* (Baltimore: Johns Hopkins University Press, 1971).

18. This was reflected in a series of Supreme Court decisions in the 1890s upholding state laws requiring medical licensure. See Starr, *Social Transformation of American Medicine*. See also David Rothman, "The State as Parent: Social Policy in the Progressive Era," *Doing Good: The Limits of Benevolence*, ed. Willard Gaylin, Ira Glasser, Steven Marcus, and David Rothman (New York: Pantheon Books, 1978), 67–96.

19. Truman G. Schnabel, Esther E. Lape, and Elizabeth F. Read, *American Medicine: Expert Testimony Out of Court* (New York: The American Foundation, 1937), 218.

20. Cass R. Sunstein, *After the Rights Revolution: Reconceiving the Regulatory State* (Cambridge, MA: Harvard University Press, 1990), coverleaf.

21. Henry Cantrill, *Public Opinion: 1935–1946* (Princeton, NJ: Princeton University Press, 1951), 361.

22. Support waned somewhat when respondents were warned that this expansion would require a substantial increase in their payroll taxes. But even when confronted with the possibility of paying 6% of their salary for these benefits (a rather substantial overestimate, given medical costs at that time), 44% of the public supported the expansion. See Michael E. Schiltz, *Public Attitudes Towards Social Security, 1935–65* (Washington, DC: U.S. Department of Health, Education and Welfare, 1970), 131.

23. Starr, *Social Transformation of American Medicine*.

24. Deborah Stone, "The Doctor as Businessman: The Changing Politics of Cultural Icon," *Journal of Health Politics, Policy and Law* 22.2 (1997): 533–556.

25. Steven Brint, *In an Age of Experts: The Changing Role of Professionals in Politics and Public Life* (Princeton, NJ: Princeton University Press, 1994).

26. Starr, *Social Transformation of American Medicine*.

27. Eli Ginzberg and A. B. Dutka, *The Financing of Biomedical Research* (Baltimore: Johns Hopkins University Press, 1989).

28. Evan M. Melhado, "Innovation and Public Accountability in Clinical Research," *Milbank Quarterly* 77.1 (1999): 111–172.

29. William Rushing, "Public Policy, Community Constraints and the Distribution of Medical Resources," *Social Problems* 19.2 (1971): 21–36.

30. William Shonick, *Government and Health Services* (New York: Oxford University Press, 1995).

31. Charles Dougherty, *American Health Care: Realities, Rights and Reforms* (New York: Oxford University Press, 1988).

32. The invocation of the rights frame for elder health care was evident as early as 1958, when then-Senator John Kennedy proclaimed his support for a Bill of Rights for Our Elder Citizens. See Richard Harris, *A Sacred Trust* (New York: New American Library, 1966), 86.

33. David B. Smith, "Addressing Racial Inequities in Health Care: Civil Rights Monitoring and Report Cards," *Journal of Health Politics, Policy and Law* 23.1 (1998): 75–105.

34. K. L. Kahn, M. L. Pearson, E. R. Harrison, K. A. Desmond, W. H. Rogers, L. V. Rubenstein, R. H. Brook, and E. B. Keeler, "Health Care for Black and Poor Hospitalized Medicare Patients," *Journal of the American Medical Association* 271.15 (1994): 1169–74; P. J. Held, M. V. Pauly, R. R. Bovbjerg, J. Newmann, and O. Salvatiena, "Access to Kidney Transplantation: Has the United States Eliminated Income and Racial Differences?" *Archives of Internal Medicine* 148.12 (1988): 2594–2600. For a review of similar concerns in federal health programs for veterans, see J. Whittle, J. Conigliaro, C. B. Good, and R. P. Lofgren, "Racial Differences in Use of Invasive Cardiac Procedures in the Department of Veterans Affairs Medical System," *New England Journal of Medicine* 329.9 (1993): 621–627; E. D. Peterson, S. M. Wright, J. Daley, and G. E. Thibault, "Racial Variation in Cardiac Procedure Use and Survival following Acute Myocardial Infarction in the Department of Veterans Affairs," *Journal of the American Medical Association* 271 (1994): 1175–1180.

35. Starr, *Social Transformation of American Medicine*.

36. The support for markets more generally drew on the changing ideological climate in American politics and increasing concerns for efficiency in the delivery of government-financed services. See Derthick and Quirk, *The Politics of Deregulation*; Giandomenico Majone, "Public Policy and Administration," *A New Handbook for Political Science*, ed. Robert Goodin and Hans-Dieter Klingermann (New York: Oxford University Press, 1996).

37. Alain P. Enthoven, *Health Plan: The Only Practical Solution to the Soaring Cost of Health Care* (Cambridge, MA: Harvard University Press, 1973); Martin Feldstein, "A New Approach to National Health Insurance," *Public Interest* 23 (1971): 93–105; Laurence Seidman, "Reconsidering National Health Insurance," *Public Interest* 101 (1990): 78–89.

38. Eli Ginzberg, "Monetarization of Medical Care," *New England Journal of Medicine* 310 (1984): 1162–1165. If one looks with sufficient care, some aspects of a marketable commodity orientation can be discerned in the enthusiasm of the Nixon administration for prepaid health care plans, as embodied in the Health Maintenance Organization Act of 1973. See Lawrence Brown, *Politics and Health Care Organization: HMOs as Federal Policy* (Washington, DC: Brookings Institution, 1983). Proponents of the market also obtained federal funding for the Rand Health Insurance Experiment, which randomly assigned families to insurance policies with varying levels of copayment requirements to determine if cost-sharing would reduce use of medical services. See, for example, Joseph Newhouse and the Insurance Experiment Group, *Free for All? Lessons from the Rand Health Insurance Experiment* (Cambridge, MA: Harvard University Press, 1993).

39. Marc A. Rodwin, "Patient Accountability and Quality of Care: Lessons from Medical Consumerism and the Patients' Rights, Women's Health and Disability Rights Movement," *American Journal of Law & Medicine* 20 (1994): 147–174; Weisman, *Women's Health Care*.

40. Marie R. Haug, "The Erosion of Professional Authority: A Cross-Cultural Inquiry in the Case of the Physician," *Milbank Memorial Fund Quarterly* 54.4

(1976): 83–106. For a discussion of a similar embrace of the market by left-leaning policy analysts outside of health care, see Samuel Bowles and Herbet Gintis, *Recasting Egalitarianism: New Rules for Communities, States and Markets* (New York: Verson, 1998).

41. More conservative legal scholars have enunciated a similar viewpoint. See, for example, Clark Havighurst, "Competition in Health Service: Overview, Issues and Answers," *Vanderbilt Law Review* 34 (May 1981): 1117–1158.

42. Starr, *Social Transformation of American Medicine*, 419.

43. Mark Schlesinger and Pamela Brown-Drumheller, "Innovative Insurance Systems under the Medicare Program," *Renewing the Promise: Medicare and its Reform*, ed. D. Blumenthal, Mark Schlesinger, and Pamela Brown Drumheller (New York: Oxford University Press, 1988), 133–159.

44. Alain Enthoven, "The History and Principles of Managed Competition," *Health Affairs* 12 (Suppl. 1993): 24–48.

45. Jacob S. Hacker, *The Road to Nowhere: The Genesis of President Clinton's Plan for Health Security* (Princeton, NJ: Princeton University Press, 1997); Paul Starr, *The Logic of Health Care Reform* (New York: Penguin Books, 1994). The promise of choice-based empowerment would remain appealing to liberals, even after the failure of the Clinton administration's reform efforts. See, for example, Karen David, Katherine S. Collins, Cathy S. Schoen, and Cynthia Morris, "Choice Matters: Enrollees' Views of Their Health Care Plans," *Health Affairs* 14.2 (1995): 99–112.

46. Alain C. Enthoven and Sara J. Singer, "Market-Based Reform: What to Regulate and by Whom," *Health Affairs* 14.1 (1995): 105–119; Paul Ellwood, Alain C. Enthoven, and Lynn Etheridge, "The Jackson Hole Initiatives for a Twenty-First Century American Health Care System," *Health Economics* 1.3 (October 1992): 149–168.

47. Hacker, *The Road to Nowhere*.

48. Paul Starr, "Why the Clinton Plan Is Not the Enthoven Plan," *Inquiry* 31.2 (1994): 136–140; Walter Zelman, "The Rationale behind the Clinton Health Reform Plan," *Health Affairs* 13.1 (1994): 9–29.

49. Theda Skocpol, *Boomerang: Clinton's Health Security Effort and the Turn against Government in U.S. Politics* (New York: W. W. Norton, 1996).

50. As part of a larger study, I have had research assistants abstract testimony from hearings during five different episodes of health care reform in the postwar period.

51. Schlesinger, "Countervailing Agency."

52. Gail R. Wilensky and Joseph P. Newhouse, "Medicare: What's Right? What's Wrong? What's Next?" *Health Affairs* 18.1 (1999): 92–106; Henry Aaron and Robert Reischauer, "The Medicare Reform Debate: What Is the Next Step?" *Health Affairs* 14.4 (1995): 8–30.

53. M. Susan Marquis and Stephen Long, "Trends in Managed Care and Managed Competition, 1993–97," *Health Affairs* 18.6 (1999): 75–88; Robert H.

Miller, "Competition in the Health System: Good News and Bad News," *Health Affairs* 15.2 (1996): 107–120.

54. James Lubalin and Lauren Harris-Kojetin, "What Do Consumers Want and Need to Know in Making Health Care Choices?" *Medical Care Research and Review* 56 (Supplement 1, 1999): 67–102.

55. Bryan Dowd, Robert Coulam, and Roger Feldman, "A Tale of Four Cities: Medicare Reform and Competitive Pricing," *Health Affairs* 19.5 (2001): 9–29; Len Nichols and Robert Reischauer, "Who Really Wants Price Competition in Medicare Managed Care?" *Health Affairs* 19.5 (2000): 30–43.

56. Bradford Gray and Catherine Rowe, "Safety-Net Health Plans: A Status Report," *Health Affairs* 19.1 (2000): 185–193; Mary A. Laschober, Patricia Neuman, Michelle S. Kitchman, Laura Meyer, and Kathryn M. Langwell, "Medicare HMO Withdrawals: What Happens to Beneficiaries?" *Health Affairs* 18.6 (1999): 150–157.

57. Timothy McBride, "Disparities in Access to Medicare Managed Care Plans and Their Benefits," *Medicare and Managed Care*, ed. John Iglehart (Millwood, VA: Project Hope, 1999), 118–127; Laschober et al., "Medicare HMO Withdrawals."

58. Jonathan Oberlander, "Is Premium Support the Right Medicine for Medicare?" *Health Affairs* 19.5 (2000): 84–99; Jonathan B. Oberlander, "Managed Care and Medicare Reform," *Healthy Markets? The New Competition in Health Care*, ed. Mark A. Peterson (Durham, NC: Duke University Press, 1998), 254–283.

59. Mark Schlesinger, "A Loss of Faith: The Origins of Declining Political Legitimacy for the American Medical Profession," *Milbank Quarterly* 80.2 (September 2002).

60. Roper Center for Public Opinion, Internet-Based Access: Accession Number 0240187, Question No. 64. Survey fielded by Hart and Teeter Research, July 29–August 1, 1995.

61. Roper Center for Public Opinion, Internet-Based Access: Accession Number 0324807, Question No. 126. Survey fielded by Hart and Teeter Research, March 4–7, 1999.

62. Public Opinion Strategies and Peter D. Hart Research Associates, *Medicare and Prescription Drug Focus Groups: Summary Report* (Menlo Park, CA: Kaiser Family Foundation, 2001).

63. See Marilyn Moon, "Can Competition Improve Medicare?" *Can Competition Improve Medicare: A Look at Premium Support* (Washington, DC: Urban Institute, September, 1999), 5.

64. Marquis and Long, "Trends in Managed Care and Managed Competition."

65. Michael Marmot and Richard G. Wilkinson, eds., *Social Determinants of Health* (Oxford, UK: Oxford University Press, 1999); Michael Marmot, Martin Boback, and George Smith, "Explanations for Social Inequalities in Health," *Society and Health*, ed. B. Amick, S. Levine, A. Tarlov, and D. Chapman Walsh

(New York: Oxford University Press, 1995), 172–210; Gregory Pappas, Susan Queen, Wilbur Hadden, and Gail Fisher, "The Increasing Disparity in Mortality between Socioeconomic Groups in the United States, 1960 and 1986," *New England Journal of Medicine* 392.2 (1993): 103–109; Howard Greenwald et al., "Explaining Reduced Cancer Survival among the Disadvantaged," *Milbank Quarterly* 74.2 (1996): 215–238; Gary King and David Williams, "Race and Health: A Multidimensional Approach to African-American Health," in *Society and Health*, 93–130.

66. Catherine Hoffman and Alan Schlobom, *Uninsured in America* (Washington, DC: Kaiser Commission on Medicaid and the Uninsured, 2000).

67. Mark Schlesinger, "Paying the Price: Medical Care, Minorities and the Newly Competitive Health Care System," *Milbank Quarterly* 65 (Suppl. 1987): 270–296.

68. Newhouse et al., *Free for All*.

69. Alain Enthoven and Richard Kronick, "A Consumer-Choice Health Plan for the 1990s," *New England Journal of Medicine* 320.1–2 (1989): 29–37, 94–101.

70. At least in terms of public legitimacy, the two appear to be on par with one another. When given the choice among three reform proposals, one of which involved vouchers and the second a government-run national health insurance plan, public support divided evenly among the three reform options.

71. David Smith, *Health Care Divided: Race and Healing a Nation* (Ann Arbor: University of Michigan Press, 1999); Sara Rosenbaum, R. Serrano, M. Magar, and G. Stern, "Civil Rights in a Changing Health Care System," *Health Affairs* 16.1 (1997): 90–105.

72. Dana Gelb Safran, Alvin G. Tarlov, and William H. Rogers, "Primary Care Performance in Fee-for-Service and Prepaid Health Care Systems: Results from the Medical Outcomes Study," *Journal of the American Medical Association* 271 (1994): 1579–1586; Kip Sullivan, "Managed Care Plan Performance since 1980: Another Look at Two Literature Reviews," *American Journal of Public Health* 89.7 (1999): 1003–1008.

73. The impact of education-based differences in health knowledge has been identified as an important source of growing disparities in health outcomes. See, for example, Pappas et al., "Increasing Disparity in Mortality." For evidence of similar patterns for particular medical conditions, see S. Davis, M. Winkleby, and J. Farquar, "Increasing Disparity in Knowledge of Cardiovascular Disease Risk Factors and Risk-Reduction Strategies by Socioeconomic Status: Implications for Policymakers," *American Journal of Preventive Medicine* 11.5 (1995): 318–323; P. Katz, "Education and Self-Care Activities among Persons with Rheumatoid Arthritis," *Social Science and Medicine* 46.8 (1998): 1057–1066.

74. For a review of the early evidence, see Hal Luft and Robert Miller, "Patient Selection in a Competitive Health Care System," *Health Affairs* 7.3 (1988): 97–119. For later studies, see F. Sainfort and B. Booske, "Role of Information in Consumer Selection of Health Plans," *Health Care Financing Review* 18.1 (1996): 31–54.

75. Mark Schlesinger, Benjamin Druss, and Tracey Thomas, "No Exit? The Effect of Health Status on Dissatisfaction and Disenrollment from Health Plans," *Health Services Research* 34.2 (1999): 547–576.

76. Gerald Riley, Mary Ingber, and C. Tudor, "Disenrollment of Medicare Beneficiaries in HMOs," *Health Affairs* 16.5 (1997): 117–124; Gerald Riley, C. Tudor, Y. Chiang, and M. Ingber, "Health Status of Medicare Enrollees in HMOs and Fee-for-Service in 1994," *Health Care Financing Review* 17.4 (1996): 65–76; Susan DesHarnais, "Enrollment in and Disenrollment from Health Maintenance Organizations by Medicaid Recipients," *Health Care Financing Review* 6.3 (1985): 39–50.

77. Medicare Payment Advisory Commission, *Improving Risk Adjustment in Medicare: A Report to the Congress* (Washington, DC: MEDPAC, November, 2000), 6.

78. Kathryn Phillips, Michelle Mayer, and Lu Ann Aday, "Barriers to Care among Racial/Ethnic Groups under Managed Care," *Health Affairs* 19.4 (2000): 65–75.

79. James Fossett, Malcolm Goggin, John Hall, Jocelyn Johnston, Christopher Plein, Richard Roper, and Carol Weissert, "Managing Medicaid Managed Care: Are States Becoming Prudent Purchasers?" *Health Affairs* 19.4 (2000): 36–40; Pamela Peele, Judith Lave, Jeanne Black, and John Evans, "Employer-Sponsored Health Insurance: Are Employers Good Agents for Their Employees?" *Milbank Quarterly* 78.1 (2000): 5–21; Marquis and Long, "Trends in Managed Care and Managed Competition."

80. James Morone, "The Ironic Flaw in Health Care Competition: The Politics of Markets," *Competitive Approaches to Health Care Reform*, ed. Richard Arnould, Robert Rich, and William White (Washington, DC: Urban Institute Press, 1993), 207–222.

81. David Miller, *Distributive Justice: What the People Think* (Chicago: University of Chicago Press, 1992); James Kluegel and Eliot Smith, *Beliefs about Inequality: American's Views of What Is and What Ought to Be* (New York: Aldine de Gruyter, 1986); Hochschild, *What's Fair?*

82. Richard Lau and Mark Schlesinger, "The Impact of Metaphorical Reasoning on Support for Public Policies," *Political Behavior* (forthcoming); Schlesinger and Lau, "The Meaning and Measure of Policy Metaphors."

83. Bowles and Gintis, *Recasting Egalitarianism.*

84. Alice Noble and Troyen Brennan, "The Stages of Managed Care Regulation: Developing Better Rules," *Journal of Health Politics, Policy and Law* 24.6 (1999): 1275–1335; Nicole Tapay, Judith Feder, and Geri Dallek, *Protection for Consumers in Managed Care Plans: A Comparison of Medicare, Medicaid and the Private Insurance Market* (Menlo Park, CA: Kaiser Family Foundation, 1998); Tracy E. Miller, "Managed Care Regulation: In the Laboratory of the States," *Journal of the American Medical Association* 278.13 (1997): 1102–1109.

85. Jon Gabel, "Marketwatch: Ten Ways HMOs Have Changed during the 1990s," *Health Affairs* 16.3 (1997): 134–145.

86. James Robinson, "The Future of Managed Care Organizations," *Health Affairs* 18.2 (1999): 16.

87. Steven Findlay, "Managed Behavioral Health Care in 1999: An Industry at a Crossroads," *Health Affairs* 18.5 (1999): 118.

88. Robert Hackey, *Rethinking Health Policy: The New Politics of State Regulation* (Washington, DC: Georgetown University Press, 1998); Robert F. Rich and William D. White, eds., *Health Policy, Federalism and the American States* (Washington, DC: Urban Institute, 1996).

89. George Anders, *Health against Wealth: HMOs and the Breakdown of Medical Trust* (New York: Houghton Mifflin, 1996).

90. Mark Schlesinger, Benjamin Druss, and Tracey Thomas, "No Exit? The Effect of Health Status on Dissatisfaction and Disenrollment from Health Plans," *Health Services Research* 34.2 (1999): 547–576.

91. Murray Edelman, *Constructing the Political Spectacle* (Chicago: University of Chicago Press, 1988).

92. Anders, *Health against Wealth*.

93. Charles E. Andrain, *Public Health Policies and Social Inequality* (New York: New York University Press, 1998).

94. Schlesinger, "Paradigm Lost." See also James E. Rohrer, *Planning for Community-Oriented Health Systems* (Washington, DC: American Public Health Association, 1996); Karen K. Marczynski-Music, *Health Care Solutions: Designing Community-Based Systems That Work* (San Francisco: Jossey-Bass, 1994).

95. Michael Sandel, *Democracy's Discontent: America in Search of a Public Philosophy* (Cambridge, MA: Harvard University Press, 1996), 124.

96. Tibor Scitovsky, *The Joyless Economy: An Inquiry into Human Satisfaction and Consumer Dissatisfaction* (New York: Oxford University Press, 1976); Fred Hirsch, *Social Limits to Growth* (Cambridge, MA: Harvard University Press, 1976).

97. John Kenneth Galbraith, *The New Industrial State* (Boston: Houghton Mifflin, 1967).

98. This erosion can also be discerned in public opinion, though the absence of consistently worded questions over time makes it difficult to accurately measure the magnitude of the decline. Surveys archived at the Roper Center for Public Opinion indicate that at the time President Clinton is preparing to introduce the Health Security Act, popular support for health care rights is, at best, rather mixed. For example, a survey conducted between September 25 and September 28 asked respondents whether health care was "a right all Americans are entitled to receive from government" or "a privilege Americans should have to earn." Fifty-nine percent endorsed this definition of rights, thirty-six percent treating health care as a "privilege"; Roper Center for Public Opinion Research, Accession Number 0207137. Similarly worded questions fielded a decade earlier showed support for rights among 70%–75% of the population.

99. Robert Blendon, Mollyann Brody, and John Benson, "What Happened to Americans' Support of the Clinton Plan?" *Health Affairs* 14.2 (1995): 7–23.

100. There was, however, an increase in public distrust in the institutions of national government in the early 1990s, which may have exacerbated the decline in the societal rights frame. See Orlando Patterson, "Liberty against the Democratic State: On the Historical and Contemporary Sources of American Distrust," *Democracy and Trust*, ed. Mark E. Warren (New York: Cambridge University Press, 1999), 151–207.

101. Richard Sorian and Judith Feder, "Why We Need a Patients' Bill of Rights," *Journal of Health Politics, Policy and Law* 24.5 (1999): 1137–1144.

102. President's Advisory Commission on Consumer Protection and Quality, *Quality First: Better Health Care for All Americans* (Washington, DC: Government Printing Office, 1998).

103. Noble and Brennan, "Stages of Managed Care Regulation"; Daniel Fox, "Strengthening State Government through Managed Care Oversight," *Journal of Health Politics, Policy and Law* 24.5 (1999): 1185–1190.

104. When asked in March of 1999 how important "protecting patients' rights in the health care system" would be to their vote in the 2000 Presidential elections, 71% reported that it would be "very important," another 21% "somewhat important" (Roper Center on Public Opinion Research, Accession Number 0323542, Question No. 14, ABC News/*Washington Post*, fielded March 11–14, 1999).

105. Conversely, both political elites and the public see traditional notions of societal rights as being inconsistent with the market frame. See Schlesinger and Lau, "The Meaning and Measure of Policy Metaphors."

106. David Seay and Bruce Vladeck, eds., *In Sickness and in Health: The Mission of Voluntary Health Care Institutions* (New York: McGraw-Hill, 1988).

107. Sanford Jacoby, *Modern Manors: Welfare Capitalism since the New Deal* (Princeton, NJ: Princeton University Press, 1997).

108. Arlie Hochschild, *The Time Bind: When Work Becomes Home and Home Becomes Work* (New York: Metropolitan Books, 1997).

109. See Schlesinger and Lau, "The Meaning and Measure of Policy Metaphors."

110. The value of choice embodied in the employer responsibility frame was captured in surveys of public support for the Health Security Act. For example, one public opinion poll asked respondents to choose between health care arrangements that allows "the ability to shop for better health care coverage at another job" and those that would instead "guarantee that every job had the same health insurance coverage." Sixty-three percent of the public preferred the guaranteed coverage, thirty-five percent the choice to shop. See Roper Center Archives for Public Opinion, Accession Number 0203013, Question #5. Survey conducted by Gallup, July 1993.

111. Robert D. Putnam, *Bowling Alone* (New York: Simon and Schuster, 2000), 80–92.

112. Barbara Ehrenreich, *Nickel and Dimed: On (Not) Getting By in America* (New York: Metropolitan Books, 2001); Tom Rice, Kenneth Desmond, and Nady

Pourat, "Dark Clouds in Pleasantville: Trends in Job-Based Health Insurance, 1996–98." Paper presented at the 1999 Annual Meetings of the Association for Health Services Research; P. Yablonski, P. Fronstin, S. Snider, A. Reilly, D. Scheer, B. Custer, and S. Boyce, "Employment-Based Health Benefits: Analysis of the April 1993 Current Population Survey," *EBRI Issue Brief* No. 152 (Washington, DC: Employee Benefits Research Institute, 1994); Thomas Bodenheimer, "The Fruits of Empire Rot on the Vine: United States Policy in the Austerity Era," *Social Science and Medicine* 28.6 (1989): 531–538.

113. Mark Schlesinger, Bradford Gray, Gerard Carrino, Mary Duncan, Michael Gusmano, Vicent Antonelli, and Jennifer Stuber, "A Broadened Vision for Managed Care, Part 2: Toward a Typology of Community Benefits Provided by HMOs," *Health Affairs* 17.5 (1998): 26–49.

114. Skocpol, *Boomerang*.

115. Patashnik, "Why Can't Politicians Think Straight about the Market?"

116. See, for example, Jeffrey Henig, *Rethinking School Choice: Limits of the Market Metaphor* (Princeton, NJ: Princeton University Press, 1994).

# Part III

# SILENT GROUPS

Who might resist the markets and lead a charge for equity? In most countries, organized labor plays that role. Labor expresses social solidarity; it mobilizes an organizational check against the rush to profit at all (social) costs. The United States is the great exception, and Marie Gottschalk explains why in chapter 5. Many American social welfare benefits—especially health benefits—have long been provided by a kind of "shadow welfare state," by a public-private partnership. Government policies encourage private companies to offer workers things like health insurance. Since at least the 1940s, organized labor itself has been deeply invested in these arrangements. While labor in other countries pushes for universal policies, American labor has gotten entangled in our market-driven, employment-based social welfare policies. In the United States, the markets have bought off the union's reforming zeal. Here labor offers no institutional balance.

Chapter 6 focuses on another classic feature of the American political landscape—interest groups. Across time, groups with strong moral claims most successfully stand up to market thinking. Workers during the Depression, veterans returning from World War II, and African-Americans fighting segregation all made strong claims based on social justice. Each group successfully won programs that enhanced their opportunities for success.

In many other cases, however, even underprivileged groups fail to vigorously press their interests. Sometimes this is simply a question of power—they don't have the ability to shout over the American political din. But at other times, argues Constance Nathanson in chapter 6, groups face a whole range of different obstacles. The traditional solution—call for more effective representation—is nice, simple, and destined to fail. Our health care inequalities have much deeper roots.

In part III, we'll trace a contemporary American dilemma: the lack of any voice for community or solidarity. Many groups calculate their own self-interests, none stands for the collectivity or speaks up for the people's health.

# Organized Labor's Incredible Shrinking Social Vision

## MARIE GOTTSCHALK

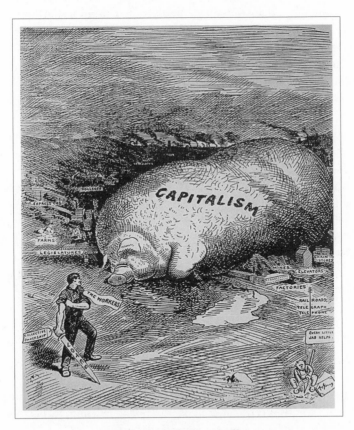

*The Workers Wield Their Votes.* Art Young,
date uncertain.

While talk of a growing health care crisis was widespread in the 1980s and early 1990s, a social movement or reform coalition to address widening inequities in health care and other areas never congealed in the United States. The political conditions seemed promising enough for a movement to emerge, given the economic dislocations associated with an employer quest for greater labor-market flexibility. Workers faced a dramatically new economic environment with the downsizing of the labor force, the retrenchment of the private-sector safety net of job-based benefits, growing income inequality, and a burgeoning contingent workforce. After President Clinton's Health Security Act was resoundingly defeated in 1994, interest in the nation's health care crisis receded, even as the number of uninsured Americans continued to rise steadily by about 1 million per year. At the close of the century, an estimated 44 million Americans, more than 16% of the population, had no health insurance.[1] Yet health care coverage was not a central issue in national elections after the turn of the century.

There are numerous reasons why health care inequalities failed to galvanize a social movement or a reform coalition.[2] One central reason has to do with the role of organized labor. In the past, unions had played a critical part in winning social welfare legislation, most notably Medicare. Now they were repeatedly unable to put together a winning coalition to secure universal health care and other measures to stem widening social and economic inequities. Indeed, in the 1993–1994 fight over President Clinton's Health Security Act, unions found themselves divided and on the defensive as they struggled to prevent any further erosion of the private-sector safety net.

The story of organized labor's role in addressing health care and other inequities in the postwar era is complex. It is more than a simple tale of unions charging into the fray with dwindling membership and sparse resources, only to be crushed again by opponents who are better organized, better financed, and better connected to the political establishment. As Douglas A. Fraser, the former president of the United Auto Workers, reminds us, "The strength and influence of the labor movement" is not based on size and resources alone. "It is also dependent on the agenda, the sense of commitment, and the manner in which the labor movement allocates resources."[3] Labor's political strategies, in turn, are influenced by the specific institutional context that entangles unions, notably the private welfare state of employment-based benefits.

Several institutions of the private welfare state, that patchwork of employment-linked social benefits sometimes called the "shadow welfare state,"[4] became a straitjacket for organized labor. This chapter focuses on two in particular: the Taft-Hartley health and welfare funds, which are a major source of health benefits for tens of millions of Americans, and a minor provision in the Employee Retirement Income Security Act (ERISA) of 1974 that allowed many large employers and unions to operate group health plans free of most state-level insurance regulations. Over time, these two institutions helped to reorient labor's interests, worldview, and political strategies, leading many unions to prefer private-sector solutions to public-sector ones. The institutional context brought the interests of the national leadership of organized labor more closely into line with those of large employers and the commercial insurers. All eschewed public-sector or state-led solutions to mitigate disparities in health care, such as creation of a national health insurance system loosely modeled after Canada's.[5] This, in turn, also aggravated divisions within organized labor and between labor and public interest groups. It made assembling an effective political coalition to address inequities in health care that much harder, even as the health care tab and the uninsured population continued to escalate.

The institutional context is only part of the story. Several political factors conspired to reinforce organized labor's tendency to stick to a policy path on health care issues that had been charted primarily by the business sector and leading Democrats. In 1978, organized labor formally abandoned its long-standing commitment to national health insurance. Over the next 15 years, it embraced private-sector solutions premised on a government mandate that would require employers to pay a portion of their employees' health insurance premiums.

This chapter focuses in particular on why organized labor adopted and then held fast to the idea of an employer mandate despite a drastically changing economic and political environment; it also examines some of the wider political consequences of that choice. It shows how the idea of an employer mandate took on a life of its own long before it was embraced by the Clinton administration, even prior to the spread of the antigovernment ideas that were the leitmotif of the Reagan era. Over time, this idea became embedded in a worldview closer to that of business and that was even at odds with the case organized labor was trying to make in other policy realms. The employer mandate played a critical role in defining the strategies and coalitions around which the health care debate would be waged and may have reduced the likelihood that labor could put together an alternate winning coalition to promote universal health care in the United States over the short or long run.

We begin by looking at labor's relative strengths and weaknesses to underscore the point that organized labor's capacity for political action depends on many factors besides the size of its rank and file. The second section examines two institutions of the private welfare state: the Taft-Hartley funds and ERISA, which were key in molding labor's stance on health care. The third section focuses on why organized labor adopted and then held fast to the idea of an employer-mandate solution and some of the wider political consequences of that choice. The fourth section examines how the institutions of the private welfare state and labor's commitment to the employer-mandate idea shaped the last major attempt to address health care inequities in the United States, the 1993–1994 battle over President Clinton's Health Security Act. The chapter concludes with a brief assessment of labor's potential in the future to address health care inequalities.

## Labor's Strengths and Weaknesses

A nalysts of contemporary health care politics generally dismiss the significance of organized labor. They view U.S. labor unions as too politically enfeebled by their dwindling membership base to shape health care policy and other issues associated with economic and social inequity in any meaningful way. Although labor's ranks have thinned considerably since the 1950s, on other fronts unions have acquired new political resources in recent years that complicate any simple picture of inexorable political decline. These resources include a swelling number of activist union retirees, important favorable shifts in public opinion regarding unions, labor's formidable financial resources, and closer institutional and financial ties between organized labor and the Democratic Party.

Except for a passing reference to a dying dinosaur or some such creature, union members are the missing millions in most analyses of contemporary social policy in the United States. This omission of labor is surprising in several respects. For over a century, labor has been instrumental in the development of the U.S. health care system. It established some of the first prepaid group practices and health maintenance organizations (HMOs); it was the leading voice for national health insurance until the 1970s; and it was decisive in the passage of Medicare.[6] The employment-based system of health benefits in the United States today is largely the product of a collective-bargaining regime established during and immediately after World War II.[7] By the 1980s, health benefits were a major arena of labor-management strife in the United States.[8] The neglect of labor in discussions of contemporary health policy is also surprising because labor was instrumental in shaping a number of major social programs, including Social Security and the Great Society.[9] Some scholars even credit labor with the creation of modern liberalism and the expansion of democracy in the United States.[10] In short, organized labor has been the primary defender of the interests of workers, the poor, and the disadvantaged.[11]

After a ritualistic recitation of the latest figures on labor's shrinking membership base, most analysts of health policy generally dismiss the political significance of organized labor and focus on other political actors, notably physicians and the corporate sector.[12] Yet the size of labor's membership base is a crude barometer by which to measure its political strength. That union membership in the United States plummeted from more than one-third of the workforce in the 1950s to barely 13.5% today—or just over 16 million members—is significant. The drop is even more perilous if one leaves out the public sector and considers just the private workforce. Today, barely 9% of the private sector is unionized—a figure comparable to the one on the eve of the Depression in 1929.[13] In most other industrialized countries, union membership remained reasonably constant over the past two decades or so, averaging about 45% of the employed workforce.[14] Though nearly all unions lost some ground since the 1970s, union density declined substantially in just a handful of advanced industrialized countries.[15]

The connection between union density, political mobilization, and political success is neither a simple nor a direct one in the United States, or elsewhere. For example, in France only about 10% of the workforce is unionized. Yet unions together with students carried out nearly a month-long series of strikes and demonstrations across the country in late 1995 that forced the Juppe government to reverse its austerity policies. Similarly, despite a small and declining membership, Spanish unions in the 1980s demonstrated a remarkable capacity for general worker mobilization, as did the ideologically splintered and organizationally weak Italian unions.[16]

Historically, the relationship between union density and political activism is not a direct one in the United States either. The desire to form legally recognized unions set off a wave of political activism in the mid-1930s at a time when labor's ranks were anorexic, in the wake of the "open shop" campaign and other antilabor measures of the 1920s and early 1930s. Union membership peaked in the United States in the mid-1950s, when the AFL-CIO (American Federation of Labor/Congress of Industrial Organizations) unions represented 40% of the private-sector labor force.[17] Despite record membership levels, U.S. labor unions generally were considered weak and quiescent in the 1950s.[18] Two of labor's most notorious legislative setbacks—passage of the Taft-Hartley Act in 1947 and the Landrum-Griffin Act in 1959—occurred when its membership rolls were flush. And the Landrum-Griffin Act was enacted despite the influx of a record number of liberal legislators into Congress after the 1958 elections.

For all the talk of membership decline, 16 million people belong to some type of union. More than 13 million of them are affiliated with the AFL-CIO, which remains the largest organization in the United States committed to defending the rights of working people.[19] The membership rolls and resources of the major unions dwarf those of many major public interest groups. For example, much was made in the early 1990s of the growth in membership of the Christian Coalition and that organization's central importance in shifting U.S. politics to the right. As of 1993, its dues-paying members (450,000) and affiliated activists (300,000) together totaled less than the combined active and retiree membership of just one union, the United Auto Workers.[20]

Concerns about labor's thinning ranks overshadowed several potentially more favorable developments for organized labor. First, retired unionists are a force to reckon with in local, state, and national politics in the United States. Over the past two decades, unions have attempted to revitalize their retiree roots by establishing retiree chapters in local unions and creating new retiree councils. Many retirees first became politically active during the early 1980s in response to the Reagan administration's assaults on Social Security. Organized labor's retirees have become significant political players in states like Nevada, Florida, and Arizona, which are home to large retirement communities.[21]

In another favorable development, public opinion has shifted significantly in favor of unions. In a 1999 Gallup poll, 65% of the public approved of unions, up from 55% in 1979 and 1981, the two lowest years for the American labor movement since the surveys began.[22]

Financial resources are another indicator of union strength—or potential strength. Despite a marked drop in membership, the financial resources available to unions remain virtually unaltered. Unions in the private sector softened the blow of falling membership by increasing fees, dues, and fines. Despite the loss of millions of members, union wealth (after adjusting for inflation) holds steady. Between 1979 and 1993, the total assets and wealth of the 28 major private-sector unions in the United States, as measured on a per-member basis, "actually increased by a significant amount."[23] Labor unions have $5 billion in annual resources.[24] Furthermore, the overall financial capacity to weather a strike or finance other major job actions has improved for most unions.[25] Similarly, labor's campaign war chest remained flush despite its waning membership. Eighteen of the twenty-eight major private-sector unions "actually raised more PAC [political action committee] money in real terms in 1994 than in 1980."[26]

The Democratic Party has been growing more dependent on labor money. The labor movement bestows substantial sums of "soft money" (contributions that are exempt from the limits and restrictions of federal campaign law) on the Democratic Party. In the early 1990s, organized labor accounted for slightly over 12% of the total "soft money" received by the Democrats, and its PACs contributed $40 million, on average, to Congressional elections in each campaign cycle. Almost all the PAC money went to Democratic candidates.[27] In 1996, contributions from labor PACs comprised 48% of all PAC donations to House Democrats, up from 33% in 1992.[28]

Since the 1980s, unions have strengthened their financial and institutional ties to the Democratic Party. In 1981, Douglas Fraser, president of the United Auto Workers, served as cochair of the Hunt Commission, which restructured the Democratic Party's nominating process to shore up the influence of party officeholders and union officials in the presidential nominating process.[29] As a result, labor has been well represented at the Democratic National Convention. In 1996, 28% of the delegates and alternates to the convention were members of the AFL-CIO or the National Education Association, one of the two leading teachers' unions.[30] Labor fortified its ties not only to party officials but also to leading officeholders. Coordination and cooperation between organized labor and congressional Democrats increased dramatically beginning in the second half of the 1980s, especially in the House, as a close alliance between labor and the Democrats was consolidated, thanks in large part to House Speaker Jim Wright (D-TX).[31] Labor's lobbying capacity also expanded dramatically as the AFL-CIO and individual unions invested more heavily in lobbyists, enlarged their research departments, and developed a grassroots lobbying network.[32]

Labor unions remain among the few organizations with power to reach straight into the pockets of their members as they channel dues directly from members' paychecks to union coffers. In the 1996 and 2000 elections, the AFL-CIO created massive electoral war chests that totaled $35 million and $40 million, respectively.[33] Although corporate financial contributions to campaigns dwarf labor contributions, unions, unlike other organizations with PACs, provide important "in-kind" contributions to political campaigns, such as labor-run phone banks and nonpartisan get-out-the-vote drives.[34]

In the 2000 elections, labor played a critical role. The AFL-CIO targeted its $40 million electoral war chest primarily at grassroots activity and created customized, state-by-state messages for the first time. Labor deployed 1,100 full-time staff members in 71 congressional districts in an effort to return the House of Representatives to Democratic control. Unionists, with their massive get-out-the vote drives, were the key to Al Gore's victories in battleground states like Michigan and Wisconsin where union households accounted for 43% and 32% of all voters, respectively. Nationally, union households accounted for one-quarter of the total vote.[35] Gore won 59% of the vote from union households, a figure that matched Clinton's margin in 1996.[36]

In short, labor's growing financial and institutional ties to the Democratic Party do not fit neatly into a story of inexorable political decline in the face of a hemorrhaging membership. Their political significance is more ambiguous. They represent a potential area of strength or weakness, dependent in part on how labor leaders interpret the political and economic environment and how they choose to respond to it; i.e., on labor's political strategies.

## The Private Welfare State

Two institutions of the private welfare state—the Taft-Hartley health and welfare funds and what became known as the ERISA preemption—powerfully and pervasively molded labor's political strategies in health care policy.

Among other things, the Taft-Hartley Act of 1947 established the institutional framework for collectively bargained health, welfare, and pension trust funds. These funds provide employers with a mechanism to contribute to benefit packages without assuming the administrative burden and expenses entailed in running their own benefit programs.[37] Today about 10 million American workers and 20 million of their dependents receive pension, health, and/or other benefits from joint labor-management plans established in accordance with the Taft-Hartley Act.[38] More than half of all union members covered by health plans receive their medical benefits through Taft-Hartley funds.[39]

Despite initial uneasiness on the part of legislators and labor officials, these funds began to proliferate in the 1950s as the movement for national health insurance sputtered.[40] Over the next two decades, the Taft-Hartley plans gradually took root, as did labor's attachment to them. The fact that this attachment was slow in coming is underlined by noting that when organized labor made its last major push for national health insurance in the early 1970s, labor officials were not unduly alarmed by legislative proposals that would have put the Taft-Hartley funds largely out of the health insurance business.[41] By the late 1980s, however, many national labor leaders, especially those of the building trades, were fighting tooth and nail to preserve the Taft-Hartley arrangements, even though many of these funds were under acute financial stress due to escalating health care costs and other factors.[42] They were cool by now to proposals for national health insurance, known as single-payer plans,[43] preferring instead private-sector solutions based on a government mandate requiring employers to pay for some portion of their employees' health insurance.

Some labor leaders were reluctant to eliminate the funds because they viewed them as an indispensable device to maintain important institutional ties and to preserve a sense of cohesiveness and identity for union locals whose members are scattered across numerous work sites and locales.[44] Moreover, the Taft-Hartley funds had created a potential conflict of interest for organized labor because they in effect catapulted some union officials into the lucrative insurance business and thus served to realign the interests of some labor leaders more closely with those of large employers and insurers.[45] For example, in 1991, Robert Georgine, head of the building and construction trades department of the AFL-CIO, began serving as chairman and chief executive officer of Union Labor Life Insurance Company, a private company that provides insurance for and manages the Taft-Hartley plans of hundreds of union locals.[46]

Finally, and most important, the funds, thanks to the enactment of ERISA, helped to spawn an important coincidence of interests between unions that operate health and welfare funds and large employers, both union and nonunion. Enacted in 1974, the year of labor's last big push for national health insurance, ERISA included a clause that the courts subsequently interpreted to mean that states are permitted to regulate employer-provided health insurance if the employer purchases it from an insurance company but not if the employer is self-insured.[47] Representatives of labor at the national level worked side by side with large employers to slip the preemption language into ERISA. Unions pushed hard for the ERISA preemption out of concern about possible taxation of Taft-Hartley funds, a fear that state-level mandates regarding health benefits would hamstring labor's efforts to negotiate national contracts, and a desire to avoid what labor saw as state interference in the private affairs of collective bargaining.[48] Over the years, large employers and unions with large Taft-Hartley funds became increasingly committed to retaining the ERISA preemption as more of them switched to self-insurance so as to circumvent state laws mandating that insurance policies cover certain specified medical services.[49] By the early 1990s, nearly 60% of Americans who were insured through their employers were covered by self-insured plans, and more than half of all Taft-Hartley funds had switched to self-insurance.[50]

The ERISA preemption and the Taft-Hartley funds pose sizable obstacles to state-level initiatives to address health care inequities.[51] Historically, state-level experimentation helped pave the way for the nationalization and quasi-nationalization of social welfare schemes, like old-age security and workers' compensation in the United States, and universal health care in Canada. Many health care plans run by employers and labor unions, inoculated from state-level mandates by the ERISA preemption, lie tantalizingly beyond the legislative and regulatory reach of individual states desiring to experiment with some kind of single-payer plan of their own.

Unions continued to stick by the ERISA preemption even though employers used it to perpetuate some highly discriminatory medical care practices. Thus, organized labor found itself in the early 1990s on the opposite side of the barricades from public interest groups that were battling the ERISA preemption and its discriminatory practices in the courts. For example, organized labor did not join public interest groups that mobilized on behalf of John McGann, whose health benefits for the treatment of AIDS were reduced from $1 million to $5,000 after his employer switched to a self-insured plan.[52] And in 1993, organized labor found itself on a collision course with advocates for the handicapped and AIDS activists when the Equal Employment Opportunity Commission under the Clinton administration enlisted the Americans with Disabilities Act of 1990 to challenge employers and unions that attempt to use the ERISA preemption to deny health insurance coverage to people with AIDS and other costly illnesses.[53]

In summary, the Taft-Hartley funds had several unintended consequences. They put unions in the insurance business and gave them a vested interest in maintaining the status quo—i.e., a system of social welfare provision rooted in the private sector and specifically based on job-related benefits. ERISA subsequently helped to fortify the coalition of unions and employers in favor of the status quo. These two institutions did not chain labor to the private welfare state overnight. Rather, they gradually pulled it in that direction. A vested interest in preserving the Taft-Hartley funds and the ERISA preemption molded labor's political preferences and behavior, predisposing it to private-sector alternatives.

The impact of these institutions was uneven, however, more so on some unions than others, and more so in some time periods than others.[54]

## The Employer-Mandate Idea

The Taft-Hartley funds and the ERISA preemption did not create the job-based system of health benefits. Rather, they helped lock it into place and solidify the commitment of organized labor to the private welfare state. It is important to keep in mind, however, that institutions are not destiny. Institutional factors alone do not explain labor's political strategies and political setbacks in its quest to mitigate health care inequities. We need to understand the role of ideas and, specifically, how labor helped to bolster a particular understanding of the U.S. political economy that took hold in the late 1970s and changed the debate over health care in subtle but important ways. Just as institutions can cause groups to rethink their interests and form new alliances, as we saw earlier, so can ideas. We will focus here on the political trajectory of one policy idea in particular—the employer mandate—that both complemented labor's institutional attachments and bolstered its commitment to private-sector solutions to health care problems.

Paradoxically, as the bond between employer and employee weakened beginning in the late 1970s with the growth of the contingent workforce, such that the very definition of what constitutes an "employee" would become a highly contested issue by the early 1990s, organized labor's commitment to an employment-based system of benefits rooted in the private welfare state became more intense. Despite significant misgivings among longtime supporters of national health insurance about the feasibility of an employer mandate, organized labor finally embraced this idea in 1978 after having spurned it since 1971, when President Richard Nixon first proposed an employer-mandate solution.[55] As key Democrats, notably President Jimmy Carter and Senator Edward M. Kennedy (D-MA), cooled to the idea of national health insurance, labor leaders hoped that a "rightward" compromise on labor's part would make unions part of a broad and a winning coalition—without foreclosing the possibility of achieving the ultimate goal of universal coverage.[56]

When it was initially adopted, labor viewed the employer-mandate idea as a way to reconcile temporarily the interests of state, labor, and business leaders such that they could forge a loose coalition on behalf of comprehensive health care reform. Over time, this policy idea took on a life of its own as it became embedded in a compelling causal story that *appeared* to explain some of the major shortcomings of the U.S. political economy. This causal story would have important consequences for the course of the debate over health policy, especially labor's political efficacy on health care reform and other matters.

"Appearances" are the bread and butter of politics. Political actors— be they labor leaders, business executives, public interest groups, or government officials—all compete to come up with convincing narratives that define the cause of a particular problem in such a way that certain policy proposals appear to be natural and obvious solutions.[57] Policy and political outcomes depend in part on how one particular definition and explanation of a problem wins out. New ideas often take flight on the wings of compelling causal stories that come to be accepted as fact, not interpretations.

Labor's fierce attachment to the employer-mandate idea over the years impeded its ability to come up with its own independent causal story about the relationship between the shortcomings of the U.S. political economy and the roots of the nation's health care dilemmas. As a consequence, organized labor was increasingly unable to develop a political strategy for universal health care that was independent of the perceived wishes and preferences of the business sector. Thus, labor was poorly situated to mobilize a wider constituency on behalf of universal health care, one that could outlast the political logic of the moment such that it could reshape health policy over the long run.

The Clinton administration's Health Security Act was developed and sold on the basis of several assumptions about the U.S. political economy and welfare state that had emerged during earlier debates over health care initiatives based on an employer mandate. In its eagerness to forge some kind of an alliance with business around the idea of an employer mandate, labor not only embraced but also even promoted these broader assumptions during the 1980s and 1990s. Among them was the assumption that the employer-mandate formula was not a radical or even new solution, but merely built on the well-established institution of employment-based benefits in the United States.

Furthermore, it was assumed that business bore most of the brunt of the private welfare state and thus the increasingly heavy burden of escalating medical costs, and that health care costs were imperiling the competitiveness of U.S. firms in the international marketplace. The administration and labor leaders contended that escalating health care costs were a major threat to the U.S. economy and were the root cause for most of the economic woes of the American worker. Taken together, these assumptions helped give shape to an alternative worldview, one that was quite sympathetic to business and that ultimately undermined labor's broader economic goals. These assumptions were just that—assumptions. Yet organized labor treated them as a set of uncontestable facts. A sustained and independent questioning of these ideas might have revealed their contingency and highlighted that they were "propositions" rather than "truths." Labor's tacit endorsement of these assumptions had important political consequences.

Despite widespread claims to the contrary, the burden of health care costs has weighed heaviest on the American public, not the business sector. In 1991, the United States was spending $6,535 per family on health care; about two-thirds of that was paid for by families and the rest by business.[58] In holding up the system of employment-based benefits as a model to be emulated and built upon, labor and other proponents of employer-mandate solutions ended up minimizing the enormous gaps and gross inequities on which the private welfare state was erected. Indeed, in certain important respects, it is a misnomer to refer to the health care system in the United States as an employment-based system at all. It is really more like a net through which a significant percentage of the population passes untouched.

Historically, labor market variables have been strong predictors of who receives benefits like health insurance coverage and pensions in the United States and who does not. Some of the critical labor-market variables include the racial, gender, and ethnic composition of occupations, how physically demanding a job is, and whether the workforce is unionized or not. For example, women are less likely to receive health insurance through their employers because they are more likely to work part time, to hold low-paying, nonunion jobs, and to experience greater job mobility.[59] In 1990, only 48% of Hispanics were covered by a private source of health insurance, compared with nearly 77% of whites and 52% of African-Americans.[60] For all the talk from the 1970s to the early 1990s about the need to build on the "employer/employee partnership," the fact is that only about 61% of the non-elderly population was receiving medical coverage through employment-based benefits when Clinton took office.[61] Indeed, most employers *did not* offer health insurance through the workplace, and many of those who did required employees to assume a large portion of the cost.[62]

The burden that health care costs pose for individual Americans has grown steadily since the 1970s in part because employers retain enormous capacity to engineer a retrenchment of the private welfare state in short order. As the social and political pressure to maintain the private-sector safety net eased up in the 1980s, employers were poised to shred significant pieces of it. They proved quite willing and capable of shifting more of the expense of medical care onto their employees through higher copayments, reduced coverage, the elimination of benefits, and drastic cuts in health benefits for retired workers.[63]

Organized labor's talk about the need to pursue a health care strategy that built on the existing job-based system of benefits obscured how that system was in the midst of a radical transformation as firms began to experiment widely with cutbacks in health and other benefits and with new ways of organizing the workforce—most notably a growing reliance on part-time and contingent workers.[64] From the 1970s onward, employment-based health coverage began to shrink as the initiative in industrial relations shifted radically from union to nonunion firms and from labor to management in ways that would threaten the entire private-sector safety net.[65] Despite the rapid increase in the number of temporary, part-time, and self-employed workers, the plight of contingent workers, who are more likely to be uninsured or underinsured,[66] remained marginal to most discussions of health reform during the 1970s and 1980s.[67]

To sum up, the employer mandate incorporated in the Clinton proposal and its legislative forerunners was pitched as a fundamentally conservative solution to the nation's health care woes. By making the case for an employer mandate based on the argument that most employers were already providing their employees with health benefits, labor unwittingly helped to draw public attention away from the enormous transformations that were taking place in the labor market and from employer culpability in these changes. It also downplayed the huge gaps and inequities on which the private welfare state was built. As a result, labor minimized the threat that shifting political and economic conditions posed for a system of job-based benefits. In practice, employers in many sectors of the economy had developed the muscle to retrench the private welfare state in quick order.

Organized labor left it largely to government actors—and then business—to decipher the shifts in the U.S. political economy and to define the nation's economic problems. Labor leaders eventually endorsed the idea of an employer mandate, acting more as passive transmitters of ideas rather than as active initiators. In contrast to the Canadian labor movement, which had advocated universal health care in the 1950s and 1960s, unions in the United States did not embed their health care strategy in a longer-term political strategy derived from a comprehensive and independent analysis of the rapidly changing political and economic context that addressed broader issues of equity.[68]

Labor's attachment to the institutions of the private welfare state and its embrace of a pro-business worldview, including a commitment to the employer mandate, spurred unions to pursue what turned out to be self-defeating political strategies. Organized labor was not, however, of a single mind about health care reform in the late 1980s and early 1990s. Just at the moment when single-payer proposals and the Canadian medical system were attracting wider attention and gaining respectability among policy makers and the general public, some labor unions were bitterly divided over this issue. Several AFL–CIO officials eventually succeeded in neutralizing the remaining support within organized labor for a single-payer system. John J. Sweeney, chairman of the federation's health care committee and president of the Service Employees International Union (SEIU), played a pivotal role here, as did Lane Kirkland, president of the AFL–CIO. While Kirkland and Sweeney were able to keep the AFL–CIO from officially straying down the single-payer path, they were unable to completely quell the growing sentiment for a Canadian-style solution in several unions. As a result, the AFL–CIO was forced to adopt a "wait-and-see" approach to health care reform that, not surprisingly, failed to inspire the rank and file and left labor fragmented and tentative, just as the health care issue lurched once again into the national spotlight with the November 1992 presidential election of Bill Clinton.

## Institutions, Ideas, and Clinton's Health Security Act

Despite the lack of any major legislative or political victories for labor in the months leading up to the official introduction of the Health Security Act in the fall of 1993, organized labor's commitment to President Clinton did not waver much, at least in public.[69] Labor leaders' close identification with Clinton's agenda ended up vexing unions with a serious case of political cognitive dissonance that undermined their stated quest for universal health care. This is most apparent in the drastically different approaches that the AFL–CIO and major unions took in their simultaneous fights against the North American Free Trade Agreement (NAFTA) and for the Health Security Act. At the same time that organized labor was engaged in a pitched battle with business and the White House over the free-trade agreement, it tried to make the case that both of them would be constructive partners on the health care issue. The political message was decidedly mixed and inconsistent. In the struggle over NAFTA, labor leaders faulted U.S. multinationals for what they characterized as a ruthless and unwarranted effort to shift production to low-wage countries with laxer environmental and labor standards at great cost to the American worker.[70] Unions sought to make the treaty a referendum on how corporate America was failing the average American worker and his or her family. Yet in discussions of health care, labor officials conceded, as they had for years, that U.S. corporations were under mounting and dire competitive pressures from low-wage, lower-benefit producers at home and abroad, and that escalating health care costs compounded those pressures.[71]

In the case of the free-trade agreement, unions sought to energize their grass roots for what they hoped would turn out to be a highly partisan fight that, simply put, would pit labor against capital. In doing so, organized labor forged some unprecedented alliances with consumer, environmental, farm, labor, and civil rights groups at home and abroad. In the case of health care, however, organized labor threw its lot in with an avowedly nonpartisan group composed of a loose-knit coalition of consumer, provider, business, and public interest groups called the Health Care Reform Project, which was slow to get off the ground.[72]

Despite the AFL-CIO leadership's steadfast commitment to the Clinton framework for health care reform, debilitating divisions simmered within organized labor. The single-payer activists among organized labor's rank and file remained reluctant to heed the leadership's call for a united front with the Clinton administration on health care. These rank-and-file activists were emboldened to stay the single-payer course in defiance of their national leadership by two related developments. First, public interest groups with whom organized labor had established closer ties during the NAFTA fight, notably Ralph Nader's Public Citizen, began making direct appeals to labor's rank and file on behalf of Canadian-style solutions.[73] Second, a new movement to establish a labor party as an alternative to the Democrats and Republicans emerged in the early 1990s and had singled out national health insurance as one of its top priorities. This movement represented no immediate threat to the Democratic Party, nor a serious challenge to the pro-Democratic Party line of the leadership of the AFL-CIO. However, it did provide a new venue for disgruntled labor activists to pursue an alternative political agenda and to link the single-payer issue to other broader social and economic concerns. It provided an opportunity for political activists to focus not just on the legislative battle of the moment but also on the development of long-range strategies to engineer a major and enduring political shift.[74]

The inherited institutional context compounded these divisions within organized labor over health care reform. Unions that depended heavily on Taft-Hartley funds for their health benefits remained reluctant to give them up. These unions fought long and hard to get a provision included in the Health Security Act that would permit Taft-Hartley funds with 5,000 or more members to opt out of the proposed health alliances if they so wished. This opt-out provision for the Taft-Hartley funds ended up strengthening the hand of large employers, many of whom had been lobbying hard for such a provision for themselves.[75] Some union officials went ballistic over organized labor's efforts to preserve the independence of large Taft-Hartley funds and to keep them out of the alliances. They contended that by doing so, labor was sanctioning the deleterious practice of carving up the health care market in a way that would essentially perpetuate the practice of experience rating, or pricing health insurance on the basis of how sick an individual is.[76] The health care alliances proposed in Clinton's Health Security Act would end up as the dumping grounds for less healthy people in need of greater—and more costly—medical care.

The divisions within organized labor, together with the distractions of the NAFTA fight, made it difficult for organized labor to take the offensive on health care reform in 1993–1994. Preoccupied with NAFTA until November 1993, organized labor left the field clear for opponents of the Health Security Act to define the terms of the public debate. Organized labor's efforts to mold the debate were sporadic at best. For the most part, the debate was conducted in a vacuum in which labor seldom raised broader issues about economic restructuring, the responsibilities of employers to their employees, and the role of insurance companies in the U.S. medical system. The harshest criticisms of the job-based system of benefits, the commercial health insurers, and the competitiveness argument wielded by business in its campaign against the administration's health care proposal came not from leading figures in organized labor, but from maverick legislators in the U.S. House of Representatives.[77]

## Labor's Role in the Future

The institutional context defined the coalitions, worldview, and strategies around which the fight for a more equitable health care system has been waged. Beginning in the early 1980s, organized labor sought to forge an alliance with business on health policy. In doing so, unions acquiesced to a redefinition of the terms of the health care debate. Whereas earlier struggles for universal health care, notably in the 1940s and early 1970s, were waged around issues of social justice, concerns about the economic competitiveness of U.S. companies predominated in the 1980s and 1990s as organized labor staked its strategy on working closely with business.

Unions were indeed highly constrained by the institutional contours of the private welfare state and broader shifts in the U.S. political economy. And certainly other features of the political and institutional environment constrained organized labor: its long-standing "barren marriage" or "abusive relationship" with the Democratic Party;[78] the formidable institutional barriers to creating a third party in the United States; the rise of a more forceful right flank in American politics; and the disproportionate resources that its opponents—notably the business sector—could muster. Although these obstacles are real and significant, they do not entirely explain why labor has not been more successful at addressing health care and other inequalities in the United States. A central argument here is that its own lack of political imagination constrained labor as well. On the health care issue, organized labor chose to concentrate most of its political activities and resources on what appeared to be achievable in the short term. But much of politics is about developing a new vision that transcends the given political environment; then using that vision as a tool or weapon to undermine, chip away at, delegitimize, and ultimately transform the existing political environment. For example, Representative Newt Gingrich (R-GA) did not accept his party's minority status in the U.S. House as a permanent feature of the political landscape. He developed a long-term strategy that by the early 1990s succeeded in mainstreaming what had been considered fringe political ideas two decades earlier.[79]

By comparison, organized labor was singularly unimaginative. It neglected to develop a long-term strategy to restructure a decidedly unfavorable political environment. It failed to seize the political opportunities that did present themselves. In the case of health policy, organized labor was unable to develop its own independent understanding of the U.S. political economy. As E. E. Schattschneider reminded us several decades ago: "The definition of the alternatives is the supreme instrument of power."[80] In the case of the most recent skirmishes over universal health care, organized labor, which was so central to earlier battles over health policy, failed to define meaningful alternatives. Instead, labor echoed business's view that escalating health care costs coupled with intensified economic competition at home and abroad put both the U.S. corporation and the U.S. worker in peril. This was a view at odds with many of the economic facts on the ground.

The preceding analysis demonstrates a broader point—that there really is no such thing as a politics of health policy per se.[81] Health care issues must be analyzed within a larger political and economic context that includes labor-management relations, electoral politics, and tax and regulatory policies. By taking this broader view of health policy, analysts are forced to reconcile the often competing and contradictory views of business and labor in social policy.

Inserting health policy into the larger debate over the U.S. political economy is also a way to wrest the issue of health policy away from the health care experts. In recent years, the debate over health policy increasingly operated "with the language, methodology, and mindset of bureaucratic actors."[82] Such a politically charged issue as health care is seemingly stripped of politics. Whether they intended to or not, many health care experts nonetheless succeeded in precluding wider public participation in the debate by treating health policy as if it somehow operates outside of the normal pushes and pulls of the political economy that shape other realms of social and economic policy.

Perhaps organized labor's repeated failures in securing universal health care signify its growing political impotence and waning relevance in struggles over issues of inequality in the United States. However, a closer look at the history of labor's triumphs and setbacks reveals that the seeds of renewal for organized labor may indeed come from within. And, furthermore, that failure may ironically serve as the soil that nurtures them.[83]

The emergence and spread of industrial unionism in the United States, which is associated with the birth of the CIO in the 1930s, fundamentally transformed the character of the U.S. labor movement and the character of American politics in important ways. Although the CIO was a new organization, it did not emerge out of political thin air. A vigorous debate over industrial unionism took place for many years within the more conservative AFL, long before the CIO was officially established.[84] The Canadian case also illustrates how the rebirth of labor can take place in the wake of major defeats at the bargaining table and in national politics. Canada's long history of strident social unionism can be traced back to Ottawa's failure to enact comparable New Deal–type legislation during the Depression in Canada in the 1930s. Unable to achieve a New Deal–style settlement until the 1940s, the Canadian labor movement harbored a deep mistrust of the two major political parties and subsequently set off on the path of social unionism rather than business unionism.[85] This deep-seated commitment to social unionism helped Canadian unions weather the massive economic restructuring of the past two decades and keep growing while the membership rolls of U.S. unions contracted.[86]

The foregoing analysis does at times put the national leadership of organized labor under a harsh light. This is not meant to suggest that the labor bureaucracy is so diseased from the head down that renewal can only come, as some critics have suggested, from the bottom up as workers develop new alliances with the wider community.[87] Success for organized labor in both the workplace and in the wider political arena must depend on a simultaneous revitalization at both the top and within the ranks. The grass roots just do not have the resources to do it on their own.

The 1993–1994 debacle over health care reform and the dismal performance of labor and the Democrats in the 1994 mid-term elections fueled an insurgent movement at the top and within the ranks of the AFL-CIO that toppled Kirkland's handpicked successor, AFL-CIO secretary-treasurer Thomas R. Donahue. The insurgent movement centered around SEIU president John J. Sweeney, the architect of organized labor's doomed health care strategy, and his "New Voice" ticket, which rode to victory in October 1995 in the federation's first contested election. After assuming the presidency of the AFL-CIO, Sweeney sought to sharpen the partisan edge of the federation's political activities and to reach out to the more disadvantaged members of U.S. society, both union and nonunion. He attempted to present a more comprehensive and multidimensional understanding of the U.S. political economy than the picture on which organized labor had staked its health care strategy. Instead of simply blaming escalating medical costs for pricing U.S. workers out of the international market and hurting their economic livelihoods, he castigated U.S. firms for taking the low road and for believing that "the best way to compete in the global economy was by driving down labor costs."[88] The federation became more committed to educating union members about broader economic issues and to developing its own independent understanding of the U.S. political economy. Among other things, it created a public policy department intended to take a long-range view of economic and social issues, including health care.[89]

In the years since the defeat of Clinton's Health Security Act in 1994, the AFL-CIO under Sweeney has racked up several impressive victories. In 1996, the federation waged a media-savvy grassroots campaign targeted at key congressional districts that secured a 90-cent increase in the minimum wage, the first hike since 1989.[90] That same year, the federation mounted a $35 million campaign to attack Republican members of the House who supported drastic cutbacks in Medicare and other social programs.[91] Although the AFL-CIO's electoral effort was insufficient to return the House and Senate to Democratic control, it did have a substantial effect on the 1996 elections.[92] And, as mentioned earlier, organized labor provided the margin of victory in a number of close and key races in the 1998 and 2000 elections.[93]

Unlike in the past, organized labor's electoral apparatus did not hibernate following each election, only to awaken 2 years later in the midst of another campaign. The most dramatic display of labor's strength and new stance on economic issues was the massive demonstrations it helped organize against the World Trade Organization in Seattle in late 1999 as a Teamster-turtle coalition of unionists and environmentalists began to coalesce.[94] In dozens of cities across the country, unions have been involved in successful "living-wage" campaigns to push for legislation that would require government contractors and businesses that receive government subsidies and tax breaks to pay their workers substantially more than the minimum wage. More than half the living-wage ordinances passed thus far also require or encourage tax-subsidized employers to provide health insurance. While local labor unions have been involved in many of the living-wage campaigns, the national leadership of the labor movement has not made these campaigns a top priority.[95]

U.S. unions are increasingly emphasizing the rights of workers around the world. In early 2000, the labor federation approved an expansive new plan to deepen its commitment to workers' rights in the new global economy and to improving the lives of workers both in the United States and abroad. The federation has been supportive of the Jubilee 2000 campaign to pressure developed countries, the World Bank, and the International Monetary Fund to offer extensive debt relief to poor countries.[96] Unions are using their "voice at work" campaign at home to underscore how workers in the United States are denied the right to organize because of flawed labor laws and aggressive corporate campaigns against workers. As part of its new effort to address the concerns of a broader spectrum of workers, the AFL-CIO dramatically reversed its long-standing position on immigration. In February 2000, its executive council called for granting immediate amnesty to undocumented immigrants and acknowledged that immigration laws for years have allowed employers to exploit undocumented workers.[97] In May 2001, unionists and immigrant activists organized rallies in several cities on behalf of undocumented workers. In Chicago, demonstrators rallied around the slogan "no human being is illegal" and made a human chain that stretched 181 blocks.[98]

Labor's new political activism and its greater willingness to embed its social and economic policies in a more comprehensive understanding of the political economy will not likely result in a more just American health care system any time soon. There are real limits to the Sweeney insurgency. He and other labor leaders continue to resist measures like direct election of labor officials. A more open internal political culture in unions is essential for developing an activist rank and file united by a coherent social vision and coherent political strategies.[99] After becoming president of the federation, Sweeney frequently railed against the growing income gap in the United States during the economic boom under Clinton. During the 2000 campaign, Sweeney and other labor leaders seldom brought up the widening income gap, however, for fear that focusing on it would embarrass Al Gore, their choice for president.[100] They did not publicly challenge the vice president's ever-so-modest proposals to increase health care coverage.[101] In his first major address on labor's stance toward the new Bush administration, Sweeney staked out a moderate, conciliatory position. Gone was talk of putting labor on a "war footing." Instead, Sweeney stressed the virtues of "bipartisanship" and failed to outline a broader social vision or an ambitious policy agenda.[102]

The AFL-CIO has yet to make a campaign for universal health care the centerpiece of its political activities. Its primary health policy focus lately has been a much more narrow one, the regulation of HMOs.[103] It is déjà vu all over again as the AFL-CIO works side by side with business and consumer groups to ensure that managed care insurance plans deliver quality health care.[104] The main focus of labor's health care efforts is legislation to establish a modest "patients' bill of rights" to curb the prerogatives of HMOs and other types of managed care. All the political brouhaha that this issue has generated obscures the fact that this measure amounts to little more than a Band-Aid on a health care system that remains in critical condition.

Some unionists and health care activists are pushing a more ambitious vision of health care reform. After the defeat of the Clinton proposal, the SEIU and other unions renewed their commitment to a Canadian-style, single-payer solution.[105] The Labor Party recently designated universal health care a top priority and won several ballot initiatives for its "Just Health Care" campaign in the 2000 elections.[106] However, the 1999 merger of the progressive Oil, Chemical, and Atomic Workers, a key Labor Party supporter and outspoken proponent of national health insurance, with the more conservative United Paperworkers has jeopardized a main pillar of support for the Labor Party.[107] On a more promising note, the revitalized National Association for the Advancement of Colored People has embraced national health care as a top priority.[108] And the country's largest physicians' groups launched a joint effort to make universal health care a leading issue as well.[109]

Labor's new political activism has ignited a fierce and concerted backlash from the Republican leadership. Shrewdly, the Bush administration has sought to divide labor unions and shred the emerging labor-environmental-social justice coalition by appealing to select unions on narrow bread-and-butter issues. The promise of more jobs for their members prompted the Teamsters and building trades to embrace drilling in the Arctic National Wildlife Refuge and the federation to take an ambiguous position on drilling in Alaska. Likewise, the United Auto Workers backed the weaker fuel efficiency standards included in the Bush energy package, and the Steelworkers were seduced by the administration's efforts to impose broad restrictions on imported steel.[110]

Unions remain highly constrained not only by the political context, but also by the institutional context. There are many indications that organized labor's attachment to the private welfare state is intensifying, and that the institutional context continues to be a severe impediment to the enactment of health care legislation that severs the tie between health benefits and employment status once and for all.

Organized labor is becoming a more significant health care provider in its own right. This will further strengthen its attachment to the private welfare state and to private-sector solutions for health care reform. As unions invest heavily in HMOs, seize opportunities to expand Taft-Hartley–style arrangements, and enter into the health insurance market in other ways, they will be less likely to embrace calls for an egalitarian overhaul of the health care system.

Labor's greatest victories in the battle to reduce health care inequities have come at the state and local level in recent years. In an important about-face, some union leaders, like Andy Stern, president of the SEIU, suggest that unions should focus their efforts on winning expansion of health care coverage at the state level and that this could provide the basis for eventual victory at the national level.[111]

The state-level activists have pushed the issue of universal health care onto the public agenda through ballot initiatives and new efforts to pass universal health care legislation. In Massachusetts, labor unions teamed up with doctors, nurses, and community groups to push for a sweeping measure on the November 2000 ballot that would require the legislature to enact a universal health care program and establish a stringent set of controls on HMOs. The measure almost passed despite the fact that its proponents were outspent $4.7 million to $65,000 or a ratio of 72 to 1.[112]

In Oregon, a ballot initiative that would have instituted universal health care in the state was resoundingly defeated in November 2002 after supporters were outspent 30 to 1 by a coalition of insurance companies and other health care interests who blanketed the state with negative ads.[113] While the Oregon AFL-CIO actively opposed the measure, elsewhere labor has been a key player in new pushes at the state level for publicly funded universal health care, notably in Ohio and California. Even John Sweeney is reportedly identifying himself, at least in private conversations with health care activists, as a single-payer advocate.[114]

Unions have won some major organizing victories the past couple of years. They have made inroads by targeting new sectors of the economy, including the high-tech and service sectors, and mounting some innovative organizing campaigns.[115] An August 2000 decision by the National Labor Relations Board recognizing the right of temps to join unions was a major victory for labor.[116] Two years ago, the SEIU succeeded in its 11-year campaign to organize tens of thousands of poorly paid home-care workers in Los Angeles County, many of them women and minorities. The unionization of these 74,000 service-sector workers was the largest organizing victory since 1937, when 112,000 General Motors workers joined the United Automobile Workers. Since unionizing, the home-care workers have received only a modest pay hike and have yet to receive a guarantee of health care coverage in their contracts.[117] Nationwide, an increasing number of doctors have joined unions or are trying to organize unions. The SEIU has pledged to spend $1 million annually to organize physicians.[118]

However, labor still faces a steep uphill battle to organize new workers. Job growth is fastest in those sectors of the economy where unions historically have been the weakest, notably the service and high-tech sectors. And job losses are mounting in industries where unions are strongest, such as manufacturing.[119] In 1999, the Bureau of Labor Statistics reported that labor had a net gain of 266,000 members. This kept the unionized share of the workforce constant after years of decline.[120] In 2000, union growth failed to match growth of the labor force. That year the percentage of organized workers dropped by 0.4% to a total of 13.5%.[121]

The battle to organize new workers got much tougher in the aftermath of September 11 and as a recession settled over the economy in late 2001. Labor organizers charged that employers were using the domestic war on terrorism as a pretext to selectively force out or lay off workers. "Employers are taking advantage of the situation. They're standing on the graves of 5,000 people to weaken unions," said one union member. An organizing campaign at the State Department had to be mothballed because security was so tight that it was impossible to get organizers in. Bomb scares, new security measures, and heightened paranoia disabled organizing campaigns elsewhere.[122]

The chillier political and economic climates were mutually reinforcing. Sustaining a commitment to organizing became that much harder in the face of devastating layoffs and cutbacks. The Hotel Employees and Restaurant Employees, one of labor's most dynamic organizers, saw at least a third of its members laid off. The airline industry laid off nearly 100,000 workers after September 11. Across the board, employers took a harder line at the bargaining table, demanding wage freezes and reduced benefits.[123]

The events of September 11 jeopardized key pieces of labor's new political agenda. The burgeoning movement against corporate-led globalization grappled with how to operate in a new political environment in which it no longer held the national or international spotlight. Labor and other activists involved in the campaign for the rights of undocumented workers were demoralized and demobilized as the debate suddenly shifted radically from loosening immigration controls to tightening them. The Republican Party attempted to use the pretext of September 11 and the recession to ram through bailouts and new tax provisions heavily skewed toward large corporations and the wealthiest individuals. Fearful of being tagged unpatriotic or pro-terrorist, the Democratic Party and AFL-CIO initially did not aggressively fight some of these giveaways.[124] Ultimately, the Democratic Party waged a somewhat spirited attack against the Republican Party's "economic stimulus" package in December 2001.[125]

Over the short term, the new economic and political environment does not bode well for the cause of universal health care in the United States. But, as in the late 1980s and early 1990s, growing inequities in health care coverage have the potential to ignite a broader debate about widening inequalities in other areas of U.S. society. In 2001, consumers faced the biggest surge in health care costs in a decade. Employers responded by eliminating coverage altogether or shifting more of the costs onto employees. Major employers are adopting new insurance schemes that financially discriminate in unprecedented ways against employees and their families who are sicker and require more medical care.[126] Health insurance companies have sought to restore their profitability by devising pricing and other strategies that drive away customers who are sicker (and therefore heavier users of medical services) and retaining a slimmed down, but healthier, membership base.[127]

The number of the uninsured is likely to grow as employers continue to reduce coverage and as low-income workers and the self-employed drop coverage in the face of escalating costs. The federal response remains wholly inadequate. President Bush's first budget proposed deep cuts in a range of programs for people without health insurance. Subsequent Republican proposals included only token gestures for workers who lost their jobs and insurance benefits following September 11.[128]

Though they continue to face significant obstacles, labor unions have the potential to galvanize the United States to achieve universal health care and other "practical utopias."[129] As one union organizer explained, the crisis in the wake of September 11 "exacerbates our issues but also offers an opportunity." He went on to say, "Ronald Reagan was the Osama bin Laden of the labor movement; we allowed the PATCO firings to convince us we could not organize. But we are dreamers. We dream of working conditions that are different than they are. Let us not stop dreaming."[130]

## Notes

1. Peter T. Kilborn, "Uninsured in U.S. Span Many Groups," *New York Times* (26 February 1999): A1. By all accounts, the uninsured problem worsened over the course of the 1980s and 1990s. In 1977, an estimated 26.2 million people (or about 14% of the non-aged population) did not have health insurance. See Lawrence D. Brown, "The Medically Uninsured: Problems, Policies, and Politics," *Journal of Health Politics, Policy and Law* 15.2 (Summer 1990): 413–414; and Emily Friedman, "The Threat of Time," *Frontiers of Health Services Management* 12.2 (Winter 1995): 35–39. These figures understate the extent of the uninsured problem. An estimated 20% of the nation (approximately 50 million Americans) is without health insurance for some portion of any given year. Healthline, "Health Insurance: Interruptions in Coverage Getting Shorter," *American Health Line* (24 June 1996), last accessed June 2004 at http://nationaljournal.com/pubs/healthline.

2. For more on the impediments to reform coalitions, see Margaret Weir, ed., *The Social Divide: Political Parties and the Future of Activist Government* (Washington, DC, and New York: Brookings Institution and Russell Sage Foundation, 1998).

3. Douglas A. Fraser, "Inside the 'Monolith,'" *The State of the Unions*, ed. George Strauss, Daniel G. Gallagher, and Jack Fiorito (Madison, WI: Industrial Relations Research Association, 1991), 413.

4. Cathie Jo Martin, "Inviting Business to the Party: The Corporate Response to Social Policy," *The Social Divide: Political Parties and the Future of Activist Government*, ed. Margaret Weir (Washington, DC, and New York: Brookings Institution and Russell Sage Foundation, 1998), 233.

5. The term "national health insurance" has many meanings. As used here, it refers to health care reform proposals modeled on the Canadian experience in

which the government replaces private insurance with its own public insurance system, thus eliminating the commercial health insurers. Commonly referred to as "single-payer" plans today, proposals for national health insurance can vary enormously on important details like financing, budgeting, taxation, and the role of individual states.

6. Monte M. Poen, *Harry S. Truman versus the Medical Lobby: The Genesis of Medicare* (Columbia: University of Missouri Press, 1979); Martha Derthick, *Policymaking for Social Security* (Washington, DC: Brookings Institution, 1979); Theodore R. Marmor, *The Politics of Medicare* (Chicago: Aldine Publishing, 1973); Lawrence D. Brown, *Politics and Health Care Organization: HMOs as Federal Policy* (Washington, DC: Brookings Institution, 1983); Ivana Krajcinovic, *From Company Doctors to Managed Care: The United Mine Workers' Noble Experiment* (Ithaca, NY: Cornell University Press, 1997); and Alan Derickson, *Workers' Health, Workers' Democracy: The Western Miners' Struggle, 1891–1925* (Ithaca, NY: Cornell University Press, 1988).

7. Donna Allen, *Fringe Benefits: Wages or Social Obligation?* (Ithaca, NY: Cornell University Press, 1964); Joseph W. Garbarino, *Health Plans and Collective Bargaining* (Berkeley: University of California Press, 1960); Raymond Munts, *Bargaining for Health: Labor Unions, Health Insurance, and Medical Care* (Madison: University of Wisconsin Press, 1967); Beth Stevens, "Labor Unions, Employee Benefits, and the Privatization of the American Welfare State," *Journal of Policy History* 2.3 (1990): 233–260; and David Rosner and Gerald Markowitz, "Hospitals, Insurance, and the American Labor Movement: The Case of New York in the Postwar Decades," *Journal of Policy History* 9.1 (1997): 74–95.

8. Cuts in medical benefits were the prime factor in nearly four out of five strikes by the late 1980s and were cited as a major issue for almost 70% of workers on strike who were "permanently replaced" by their employers. Polly Callaghan, "1990 Contract Innovations Address Family Security," *AFL-CIO News* (15 April 1991): 8; "News Brief," *Business and Health* (April 1990): 10; and Michael Byrne, "Health Care, Strikebreaker Ban: Ties That Bind" (10 June 1991): 1.

9. Graham K. Wilson, *Unions in American National Politics* (New York: St. Martin's Press, 1979); J. David Greenstone, *Labor in American Politics* (Chicago: Chicago University Press, 1977); Richard B. Freeman and James L. Medoff, *What Do Unions Do?* (New York: Basic Books, 1984); Dudley W. Buffa, *Union Power and American Democracy: The U.A.W. and the Democratic Party, 1935–72* (Ann Arbor: University of Michigan Press, 1984); Jill Quadagno, *The Transformation of Old Age Security: Class and Politics in the American Welfare State* (Chicago: University of Chicago Press, 1988); Kevin Boyle, "Little More Than Ashes: The UAW and American Reform in the 1960s," *Organized Labor and American Politics, 1894–1994: The Labor-Liberal Alliance*, ed. Kevin Boyle (Albany: SUNY Press, 1998); and Alex Hicks, Roger Friedlander, and Edwin Johnson, "Class Power and State Policy: The Case of Large Business Corporations, Labor Unions, and Governmental Redistribution in the American States," *American Sociological Review* 43 (June 1978): 302–315.

10. Karen Orren, "Union Politics and Postwar Liberalism in the United States," *Studies in American Political Development* 1 (1986); Orren, "Organized Labor and the Invention of Modern Liberalism in the United States," *Studies in American Political Development* 2 (1987); Joseph A. McCartin, *Labor's Great War: The Struggle for Industrial Democracy and the Origins of Modern American Labor Relations, 1912–1921* (Chapel Hill: University of North Carolina Press, 1997); and David Plotke, *Building a Democratic Political Order: Reshaping American Liberalism in the 1930s and 1940s* (Cambridge: Cambridge University Press, 1996), especially chapters 4–8.

11. Derek C. Bok and John T. Dunlop, *Labor and the American Community* (New York: Simon & Schuster, 1970), 465; Melvyn Dubofsky, *The State and Labor in Modern America* (Chapel Hill: University of North Carolina Press, 1994); and Vernon Coleman, "Labor Power and Social Equality: Union Politics in a Changing Economy," *Political Science Quarterly* 103.4 (1988). This is not to deny that labor's record on such issues as civil rights, feminism, and poverty alleviation has been uneven.

12. See, for example, Theda Skocpol, *Boomerang: Clinton's Health Security Effort and the Turn against Government in U.S. Politics* (New York: W. W. Norton, 1996), chapter 3, especially 84–88; John B. Judis, "Abandoned Surgery: Business and the Failure of Health Reform," *The American Prospect* 6.21 (Spring 1995): 71–72; and Cathie Jo Martin, "Stuck in Neutral: Big Business and the Politics of National Health Reform," *Journal of Health Politics, Policy and Law* 20.2 (Summer 1995): 433.

13. For the current figures, see Steven Greenhouse, "Unions Hit Lowest Point in 6 Decades," *New York Times* (21 January 2001): 20. For the eve of the Depression, see Irving Bernstein, *The Lean Years* (Boston: Houghton Mifflin, 1960), 84.

14. Calculated from Jelle Visser, "The Strength of Union Movements in Advanced Capitalist Democracies: Social and Organizational Variations," *The Future of Labour Movements*, ed. Marino Regini (London: Sage, 1992), 19.

15. Michael Shalev, "The Resurgence of Labor Quiescence," *The Future of Labour Movements*, ed. Marino Regini (London: Sage, 1992); and Bruce Western, *Between Class and Market: Postwar Unionization in the Capitalist Democracies* (Princeton, NJ: Princeton University Press, 1997), 21, 145. See also Miriam A. Golden, Michael Wallerstein, and Peter Lange, "Postwar Trade-Union Organization and Industrial Relations," *Continuity and Change in Contemporary Capitalism*, ed. Herbert Kitschelt, Peter Lange, Gary Marks, and John D. Stephens (Cambridge: Cambridge University Press, 1999), 194–230.

16. Visser, "The Strength of Union Movements," 237; and Richard M. Locke, *Remaking the Italian Economy* (Ithaca, NY: Cornell University Press, 1995), 99–102.

17. Richard Freeman, ed., *Working under Different Rules* (New York: Russell Sage Foundation, 1994), 16.

18. Many union officials deliberately sought to politically demobilize their rank and file in the aftermath of the massive strike wave of the late 1940s and to

bureaucratize labor-management relations so as to tame the radicals and insurgents within their swollen ranks at the time. Nelson Lichtenstein, *Labor's War at Home: The C.I.O. in World War II* (Cambridge: Cambridge University Press, 1982); Martin Halpern, *U.A.W. Politics in the Cold War Era* (Albany: State University of New York Press, 1988); Judith Stepan-Norris and Maurice Zeitlin, "Insurgency, Radicalism, and Democracy in America's Industrial Unions," *Social Forces* 75.1 (September 1996); and Howell John Harris, *The Right to Manage: Industrial Relations Policies of American Business in the 1940s* (Madison: University of Wisconsin Press, 1982).

19. Herbert Asher, Eric S. Heberlig, Randall B. Ripley, and Karen Snyder, *American Labor Unions in the Electoral Arena* (Lanham, MD: Rowman & Littlefield, 2001), 9.

20. As of 1990, the United Auto Workers had 868,000 active dues–paying members and 450,000 retirees, or about one retiree for every two working members. "U.A.W. Finances, 1990," *Solidarity* (November–December 1991): 20. These membership figures for the Christian Coalition come from Skocpol, *Boomerang*, 154–155.

21. "Partners for Life: The UAW and Retired Workers," *Solidarity* (December 1987): 12–16; and Dave Elsila, "Retirees Who Won't Quit," *Solidarity* (September 1990): 9–14.

22. The Gallup Organization, "Labor Day Finds Continued Strong Support for Unions," September 2, 1999, last accessed June 2004 at http://www.gallup.com/poll/releases/pr990902.asp; "More Americans Say Yes to Unions," *AFL-CIO News* (27 August 1988): 1; and Seymour Martin Lipset, "Labor Unions in the Public Mind," *Unions in Transition: Entering the Second Century*, ed. Seymour Martin Lipset (San Francisco: ILR Press, 1986).

23. It is important to note that five of the major unions held almost two-thirds of that wealth, and that public-sector unions generally do not hold wealth comparable to private-sectors ones. Moreover, even though organized labor's wealth has held steady, operating income has plummeted in many unions, compelling significant reductions in their expenditures. Marick F. Masters, "Unions at the Crossroads," *WorkingUSA* (January/February 1998): 14–15.

24. Katrina Vanden Heuvel, "Building to Win," *The Nation* 9 (July 2001): 25. See also Marick F. Masters, *Unions at the Crossroads: Strategic Membership, Financial, and Political Perspectives* (Westport, CT: Quorum Books, 1997), 73.

25. Richard Rothstein, "Toward a More Perfect Union: New Labor's Hard Road," *The American Prospect* (May–June 1996): 51; and Masters, *Unions at the Crossroads*, 15.

26. Masters, *Unions at the Crossroads*, 16, 121–124. See also Jonathan Tasini, *The Edifice Complex: Rebuilding the American Labor Movement to Face the Global Economy* (New York: Labor Research Association, 1995), 19.

27. Tasini, *The Edifice Complex*, 21; and Larry Makinson and Joshua Goldstein, *Open Secrets: The Encyclopedia of Congressional Money and Politics*, 4th ed. (Washington, DC: Congressional Quarterly, 1996), 84–85.

28. Jill Abramson and Steven Greenhouse, "Labor Victory on Trade Bill Reveals Power," *New York Times* (12 November 1997): A-1.

29. Mike Davis, *Prisoners of the American Dream: Politics and Economy in the History of the US Working Class* (London: Verso, 1986), 265–266.

30. Kevin Sack, "Differences Aside, Labor Embraces the Democrats," *New York Times* (26 August 1996): A-9.

31. Taylor E. Dark, "Organized Labor and the Congressional Democrats: Reconsidering the 1980s," *Political Science Quarterly* 111.1 (1996): 90.

32. Dark, "Organized Labor and the Congressional Democrats," 91–92.

33. Robin Toner, "Battered by Labor's Ads, Republicans Strike Back," *New York Times* (15 July 1996): A-1; and Glenn Burkins, "Labor's Bid to Aid Democrats Faces One Hurdle: Many of Its Members Often Vote for Republicans," *Wall Street Journal* (9 April 1996): A-20. On the 2000 election, see Tom Infield, "Big Push to Get Out the Union Vote: Organizers Will Urge the Rank and File to Flock to the Polls," *Philadelphia Inquirer* (2 November 2000): A-1.

34. James T. Bennett, "Private Sector Unions: The Myth of Decline," *Journal of Labor Research* 12.1 (Winter 1991). In the 1995–1996 campaign cycle, corporate PAC, individual, and "soft money" contributions totaled $653.4 million compared to $58.1 million in labor contributions, or a ratio of 11:1, up from 10:1 in 1994 and 9:1 in 1992. Figures from Center for Responsive Politics, "The Big Picture," last accessed June 14, 2004, at http://www.opensecrets.org/pubs/bigpicture1998/index.htm and http://www.opensecrets.org/pubs/bigpicture2000/bli/index.ihtml. See also Makinson and Goldstein, *Open Secrets*, 24–26.

35. Kim Moody, "In Other Election News," *Labor Notes* (February 2001): 5.

36. Infield, "Big Push to Get Out the Union Vote"; Steven Greenhouse, "The 2000 Campaign: The Unions; Labor Tailors Its Vote-for-Gore Message, State by State," *New York Times* (2 November 2000): A-27; Majorie Connelly, "Who Voted: A Portrait of American Politics, 1976–2000," *New York Times* (12 November 2000), sec 4: 4.

37. In the typical Taft-Hartley plan, employers contribute some negotiated amount to a pension, health, and/or welfare fund. Employers usually are not actively involved in either the administration of the plan or the design of benefits.

38. "Multiemployer Trust Funds," *Employee Benefits Basics* (International Foundation of Employee Benefit Plans), July 1988: 1; National Coordinating Committee for Multiemployer Plans (NCCMP), "Taft-Hartley, Multiemployer Health & Welfare Plans and National Health Care Reform, report (Washington, DC: NCCMP, n.d.); and NCCMP, "Multiemployer Plans: A Basic Guide," pamphlet (Washington, DC: NCCMP, n.d.).

39. John T. Dunlop, "Health Care Coalitions," *Private Sector Coalitions: A Fourth Party in Health Care*, ed. Jon B. Jaeger (Durham, NC: Department of Health Administration, 1983), 10.

40. See, for example, George Meany to National and International Unions, State Federations, City Central Bodies, Federal Labor Unions, and Regional

Organizers, January 7, 1953, AFL, AFL-CIO Department of Legislation Collection, George Meany Memorial Archives, Silver Spring, MD, Box 24, Folder 39, "Health"; and Harry A. Millis and Emily Clark Brown, *From the Wagner Act to Taft-Hartley: A Study of National Labor Policy and Labor Relations* (Chicago: Chicago University Press, 1950), chapter 15.

41. See also Bert Seidman to Al Barkan et al., May 21, 1970, re. Health and Welfare Trusts and National Health Insurance, attachment, 2, AFL-CIO Department of Legislation Collection, Box 25, Folder 24, "Health Insurance."

42. Leo J. Purcell, letter to Robert Georgine, January 28, 1991, personal files of Robert McGarrah, American Federation of State, County and Municipal Employees (AFSCME) headquarters, Washington, DC; Laborers' Health & Security Fund of America, "Cost Shifting: Who Shoulders the Burden of the Health Care Crisis," report (Washington, DC: Laborers' Health & Safety Fund, n.d.); and Howard S. Berliner, "Payment for Uncompensated Hospital Care in New Jersey: Impact on Union Health and Welfare Funds," report (Washington, DC: Laborers' National Health and Safety Fund, March 1989), 5.

43. See note 5.

44. James S. Ray, legislative representative, NCCMP, interview, Washington, DC, June 13, 1996; J. Peter Nixon, senior policy analyst, SEIU, interview, Washington, DC, June 3, 1996; Claudia Bradbury St. John, former senior health policy specialist, AFL-CIO, interview, Washington, DC, June 7, 1996. See also J. Peter Nixon, memo to Hal Alpert, president of Local 531 of the Service Employees International Union, re. health care reform, March 2, 1994, personal files of J. Peter Nixon, SEIU Headquarters, Washington, DC.

45. Merrill Goozner, "Health Care Debate Splits Union Ranks," *Chicago Tribune* (18 February 1991): 1.

46. Albert B. Crenshaw, "The Aim to Be Letter Perfect; ULLICO Repositions for Growth and 'A' Insurance Rating," *Washington Post* (11 July 1994): 1; and "Ullico Inc.," *Washington Post* (18 April 1995). Richard Trumka, president of the United Mine Workers, reportedly tried, but failed, to have Georgine disqualified from voting on the critical issue of whether or not the AFL-CIO should endorse a single-payer plan when it came before the federation's health care committee in the 1990–1991 period, charging that the head of ULLICO had a conflict of interest. Robert McGarrah, director of public policy, AFSCME, interview, Washington, DC, June 5, 1996; and Ray interview (see note 44).

47. Firms that self-insure use their own assets to fund their health benefit programs and typically hire outside companies to administer the plans.

48. Daniel M. Fox and Daniel C. Schaffer, "Health Policy and E.R.I.S.A.: Interest Groups and Semipreemption," *Journal of Health Politics, Policy, and Law* 14.2 (Summer 1989).

49. Gail A. Jensen, Michael A. Morrisey, and John W. Marcus, "Cost Sharing and the Changing Pattern of Employer-Sponsored Health Benefits," *Milbank Quarterly* 65.4 (1987); and Joseph B. Treaster, "Protecting against the Little Risks," *New York Times* (31 December 1996): D-1.

50. Malcolm Gladwell, "When Health Plan Changes Leave Employees Vulnerable; AIDS Case Targets Federal Self-Insurance Law," *Washington Post* (20 August 1992): A-1; and testimony of Robert Georgine, "Health Care Reform," Part 5, Subcommittee on Health and the Environment of the Committee on Energy and Commerce, U.S. House of Representatives, 103rd Congress, 1st Session: 103–105.

51. Mary Ann Chirba-Martin and Troyen A. Brennan, "The Critical Role of ERISA in State Health Reform," *Health Affairs* (Spring 1994): 142–156; and Wendy Parmet, "Regulation and Federalism: Legal Impediments to State Health Care Reform," *American Journal of Laws and Medicine* 19.1–2 (1993): 132–140.

52. Robert Pear, "Court Approves Cuts in Benefits in Costly Illness," *New York Times* (27 November 1991): A-1; "U.S. to Argue Employers Can Cut Health Coverage," *New York Times* (16 October 1992): A-18; and Thomas D. Stoddard, "Now You're Insured, Now You're Not," *New York Times* (23 May 1992): 23.

53. Richard A. Oppel, Jr., "Health-Benefits Ruling Poses Risk for Small Firms; EEOC Decision Would Not Allow Discriminatory Coverage," *Dallas Morning News* (11 June 1993): D-1; and Alex Michelini, "Unions $1M AIDS Penalty," *New York Daily News* (15 December 1995): 16.

54. For a development of this point, see Marie Gottschalk, *The Shadow Welfare State: Labor, Business, and the Politics of Health Care in the United States* (Ithaca, NY: Cornell University Press, 2000).

55. James C. Corman to Douglas A. Fraser, December 20, 1978, UAW President's Office: Douglas A. Fraser Collection, Walter P. Reuther Library, Wayne State University, Detroit, Mich., Box 2, Folder 23, "CNHI, 1978"; and Keith W. Johnson to Douglas A. Fraser, January 17, 1979, UAW Fraser Collection, Box 2, Folder 21, "CNHI, 1982–83."

56. Tom Wicker, "The Health Insurance Minefield," *New York Times* (20 December 1977); "New Kennedy Bill Signals Retreat on National Health Insurance," *Labor Notes* (24 April 1979): 10. See also Max W. Fine to George Hardy, May 30, 1978, UAW Washington Office: Stephen Schlossberg Collection, Walter P. Reuther Library, Wayne State University, Detroit, Mich., Box 56, Folder 43; and CNHI, report sent to members of the technical committee, April 13, 1978, Committee for National Health Insurance (CNHI) Collection, Walter P. Reuther Library, Wayne State University, Box 15, Folder 20, "Technical Committee, memos, 1975–79."

57. Deborah Stone, "Causal Stories and the Formulation of Agendas," *Political Science Quarterly* 104 (1989): 282.

58. Families USA, "Health Spending: The Growing Threat to the Family Budget" (Washington, DC: Families USA Foundation, December 1991).

59. When wages are controlled for, the difference in pension, health, and disability coverage for men and women disappears. Janet Currie, "Gender Gaps in Benefit Coverage," NBER working paper no. 4265 (Cambridge, MA: National Bureau of Economic Research, January 1983). See also Angela M. O'Rand, "The Hidden Payroll: Employee Benefits and the Structure of Workplace Inequality,"

*Sociological Forum* 1.4 (Fall 1986): 657–683; Lawrence S. Root, "Employee Benefits and Social Welfare: Complement and Conflict," *Annals of the American Academy of Political and Social Science* 479 (1985): 101–118; Laurie Perman and Beth Stevens, "Industrial Segregation and the Gender Distribution of Fringe Benefits," *Gender and Society* 3.3 (September 1988): 388–404; and Nancy S. Jecker, "Can an Employer-Based Health Insurance System Be Just?" *The Politics of Health Care Reform: Lessons from the Past, Prospects for the Future*, ed. James A. Morone and Gary S. Belkin (Durham, NC: Duke University Press, 1994).

60. "Health Inequities Put Hispanic Workers at Risk," *AFL-CIO News* (25 May 1992); and *Wall Street Journal* (9 January 1991): B-4. See also Peter T. Kilborn, "Denver's Hispanic Residents Point to Ills of the Uninsured," *New York Times* (9 April 1999): A-1.

61. Carolyn Pemberton and Deborah Holmes, eds., *EBRI Databook on Employee Benefits*, 3rd ed. (Washington, DC: Employee Benefit Research Institute, 1995), 237.

62. John J. Motley, vice president for federal-governmental relations of the National Federation of Independent Business, estimated that only 42% to 45% of U.S. employers provide employment-based health benefits. See U.S. House, Subcommittee on Small Business, "The Small Business Community's Recommendations for National Health Care Reform," 103rd Cong., 1st Session, August 4, 1993: 17.

63. Congressional Research Service, "Health Insurance and the Uninsured: Background Data and Analysis" (Washington, DC: Government Printing Office, May 1988), 3; Ida Hellander, J. Moloo, David Himmelstein, Steffie Woolhandler, and Sidney M. Wolfe, "The Growing Epidemic of Uninsurance: New Data on the Health Insurance Coverage of Americans," *International Journal of Health Services* 25.3 (1995): 377–392; Richard Kronick, "Health Insurance, 1979–1989: The Frayed Connection between Employment and Insurance," *Inquiry* 28.4 (Winter 1991); Laura A. Scofea, "The Development and Growth of Employer-Provided Health Insurance," *Monthly Labor Review* (March 1994): 3–10; SEIU, Department of Public Policy, "Employer-Paid Health Insurance Is Disappearing" (Washington, DC: SEIU, July 1989); Clifford Staples, "The Politics of Employment-Based Insurance in the United States," *International Journal of Health Services* 19.3 (1989): 415–431; Gail A. Jensen, Michael A. Morrisey, and John W. Marcus, "Cost Sharing and the Changing Pattern of Employer-Sponsored Health Benefits," *Milbank Quarterly* 65.4 (1987); and Mark J. Warshawsky, *The Uncertain Promise of Retiree Health Benefits: An Evaluation of Corporate Obligations* (Washington, DC: AEI Press, 1992).

64. Anne E. Polivka and Thomas Nardone, "On the Definition of 'Contingent' Work," *Monthly Labor Review* (December 1989): 13–14; and David M. Gordon, *Fat and Mean: The Corporate Squeeze of Working Americans and the Myth of Managerial "Downsizing"* (New York: Martin Kessler Books, Free Press, 1996), 226–227.

65. Karen Swartz, *The Medically Uninsured: Special Focus on Workers* (Washington, DC: Urban Institute Press, July 1989); and Thomas A. Kochan, Harry C.

Katz, and Robert B. McKersie, *The Transformation of American Industrial Relations* (New York: Basic Books, 1986), 9 and chapter 3; Sanford M. Jacoby, ed., *Masters to Managers: Historical and Comparative Perspectives on American Employers* (New York: Columbia University Press, 1991), 283; and George Strauss, "Industrial Relations: Time of Change," *Industrial Relations* 23.1 (Winter 1984): 3.

66. Sar A. Levitan and Elizabeth Conway, *Part-Time Employment: Living on Half-Rations* (Center for Social Policy Studies, George Washington University, 1988), working paper no. 101, as cited in Richard S. Belous, "How Human Resource Systems Adjust to the Shift toward Contingent Workers," *Monthly Labor Review* (March 1989): 7–12; and Pemberton and Holmes, *EBRI Databook*, 263.

67. See, for example, the deliberations surrounding the 1987–1988 Minimal Health Benefits for All Workers Act, which was based on an employer mandate, and the final report of the bipartisan Pepper Commission, which endorsed a modified employer-mandate solution by a bare majority in 1991.

68. For more on labor and the Canadian case, see Malcolm G. Taylor, *Health Insurance and Canadian Public Policy: The Seven Decisions that Created the Canadian Health Insurance System* (Montreal: McGill-Queen's University Press, 1978); Antonia Maioni, *Parting at the Crossroads: The Emergence of Health Insurance in the United States and Canada* (Princeton, NJ: Princeton University Press, 1998); and William M. Chandler, "Canadian Socialism and Policy Impact: Contagion from the Left?" *Canadian Journal of Political Science* 10.4 (December 1977): 755–780.

69. Kim Moody, "Is There a Future for Unions in the Clinton Administration's Plans?" *Labor Notes* (October 1993): 13; "Labor in the Clinton Era: New Opportunities, New Problems," *Labor Notes* (February 1993): 1; Keith Brooks, "Clinton's 'Economic Stimulus Package': Much Ado about Not Too Much," *Labor Notes* (June 1993): 12; and Christina Del Valle, "Labor Didn't Expect Much from Bill and Is Getting Even Less," *Business Week* (21 June 1993): 51.

70. David Moberg, "The Morning NAFTA," *In These Times* (13 December 1993): 20–21; and Louis S. Richman, "Why Labor Hates NAFTA," *Fortune* (15 November 1993): 28.

71. The resolutions adopted by the UAW at its 1992 convention epitomized this mixed message. On the one hand, the UAW attacked NAFTA, charging that the "main beneficiaries of these policies are the multinational corporations who are searching out the lowest costs and the highest profits over the short term, all at the expense of workers." Yet in the next breath, the union appeared acutely sensitive to corporations and how the "skyrocketing costs of health care adversely affect the international competitiveness of many businesses and threaten the job security of millions of Americans." UAW, "Proceedings of the 30th Constitutional Convention," June 14–18, 1992, San Diego, CA, 123–142. See also SEIU, "Out of Control, Into Decline" (Washington, DC: SEIU, 1992), 1–10.

72. Dana Priest and Michael Weisskopf, "Health Care Reform: The Collapse of a Quest," *Washington Post* (11 October 1994): A-6.

73. Sara Nichols, former staff attorney, Public Citizen, interview, Washington, DC, June 13, 1996.

74. Kim Moody, "Activists Signing Up to Build a Labor Party," *Labor Notes* (May 1991): 8; Jane Slaughter, "Labor Party Advocates Plan to Organize Founding Convention in 1995," *Labor Notes* (November 1993): 5; and "Advocates to Launch Labor Party," *Labor Notes* (March 1995): 7.

75. James B. Parks, "Kirkland: Undaunted Unionists 'Agents of Change,'" *AFL-CIO News* (18 October 1993): 5.

76. Under experience rating, health insurance is priced on the basis of how sick an individual is, or is likely to be. The alternative is community rating, whereby the entire community assumes the risk for those who might become ill and therefore insurance rates do not vary much from one individual to the next in a given community.

77. See, for example, Rep. Jim McDermott's (D-WA) remarks in "Hearings on Health Care Reform," vol. 2, Committee on Education and Labor, U.S. House, 103rd Cong., 2nd Session, January 31, 1994, and February 7, 1994: 205, 212, and 219; and Rep. Pete Stark's (D-CA) remarks in "Financing Provisions of the Administration's Health Security Act and Other Health Reform Proposals," Committee on Ways and Means, U.S. House, 103rd Cong., 1st Session, November 16, 18, and 19, 1993: 119.

78. Davis, *Prisoners of the American Dream,* 52; and Joel Rogers, "The Folks Who Brought You the Weekend: Labor and Independent Politics," *Audacious Democracy: Labor, Intellectuals, and the Social Reconstruction of America,* ed. Steven Fraser and Joshua B. Freeman (Boston: Mariner, 1997), 255.

79. Dan Balz and Ronald Brownstein, *Storming the Gates: Protest Politics and the Republican Revival* (Boston: Little, Brown, 1996), 116–117, 142–143; and Dale Russakoff, Dan Balz, Charles R. Babcock, and Serge F. Kovaleski, "Mr. Speaker: The Rise of Newt Gingrich," four-part series, *Washington Post* (18–21 December 1994): A-1.

80. E. E. Schattschneider, *The Semi-Sovereign People: A Realist's View of Democracy in America* (New York: Holt, Rinehart, and Winston, 1960), 68.

81. For a development of this point, see Theodore R. Marmor, "Introduction," *Political Analysis and American Medical Care: Essays* (Cambridge: Cambridge University Press, 1983).

82. James A. Morone, "The Bureaucracy Empowered," *The Politics of Health Care Reform: Lessons from the Past, Prospects for the Future,* ed. James A. Morone and Gary S. Belkin (Durham, NC: Duke University Press, 1994), 149.

83. See Solomon Barkin, "Pure and Simple Unionism: An Adequate Base for Union Growth?" in Strauss et al., *The State of the Unions.* On the Canadian case, see Edward Ian Robinson, "Organizing Labour: Explaining Canada–U.S. Union Diversity in the Post-War Period" (Ph.D. dissertation, Yale University, 1992).

84. Moreover, the founders of the CIO hailed from the AFL, and some of them had even served on its executive council. Barkin, "Pure and Simple Unionism," in Strauss et al., *The State of the Unions.*

85. Robinson, "Organizing Labour."

86. Between the early 1960s and the early 1980s, Canadian unions more than doubled their membership. By the early 1980s, the unionized sector of the Canadian workforce approached 40%, more than double the figure for the United States. David Brody, *Workers in Industrial America: Essays on the Twentieth Century Struggle* (New York: Oxford University Press, 1993), 245–246. For a more pessimistic view of the recent political prospects for organized labor in Canada, see Leo Panitch and Donald Swartz, *The Assault on Trade Union Freedom: From Wage Controls to Social Contract* (Toronto: Garamond Press, 1993); and Miriam Catherine Smith, "Labour without Allies: The Canadian Labour Congress in Politics, 1956–1988" (Ph.D. dissertation, Yale University, 1990).

87. See, for example, Jeremy Brecher and Tim Costello, eds., *Building Bridges: The Emerging Grassroots Coalition of Labor and Community* (New York: Monthly Review Press, 1990). For a critical view of this perspective, see Kim Scipes, "Labor-Community Coalitions: Not All They're Cracked Up to Be," *Monthly Review Press* 43.7 (December 1991): 34–46; and the response by Brecher and Costello, 47–51.

88. "Sweeney's Wake-Up Call to Business," *Economic Notes* (January 1996): 3.

89. Gerald M. Shea, assistant to the president for governmental affairs, AFL-CIO, interview, Washington, DC, June 13, 1996; John J. Sweeney, with David Kusnet, *America Needs a Raise: Fighting for Economic Security and Social Justice* (Boston: Houghton Mifflin, 1996); "AFL-CIO Is Planning to Focus Anew on Social Issues" in Glenn Burkins, "A Special News Report about Life on the Job—And Trends Taking Shape There," *Wall Street Journal* (18 February 1997): 1; David Moberg, "Union Pension Power," *The Nation* (1 June 1998): 16–20; and Jo-Ann Mort, ed., *Not Your Father's Union Movement: Inside the AFL-CIO* (London and New York: Verso, 1998).

90. One needs to be careful not to overstate the significance of this victory. Republicans were able to tack onto the minimum wage legislation billions of dollars in tax breaks and subsidies that had been on the wish lists of the Fortune 500 and the small business sector for years. Elizabeth Lee, "The Minimum Wage Increase Act of 1996: Minimum Wage Increase, Maximum Benefits for Business" (Senior Essay, Yale University, April 1997).

91. Estimates vary enormously on just how much organized labor spent. The oft-cited figure of $35 million actually was a supplement to other spending for political purposes that did not have to be reported to the Federal Election Commission because it was not spent on advertisements that specifically advocated the election of a Democratic candidate. Morton M. Kondracke, "Payback Time: GOP Plots Attack on Labor Unions," *Roll Call* (21 November 1996): 6.

92. By Gary C. Jacobson's calculations, "targeted incumbents, freshmen or otherwise, lost much more frequently than those who were not targeted" by organized labor. Jacobson, "The 105th Congress: Unprecedented and Unsurprising," *The Elections of 1996*, ed. Michael Nelson (Washington, DC: Congressional Quarterly, 1997), 156–157.

93. See note 39. See also "A Few Good Victories," *The Nation* (23 November 1998): 3–4; and Steven Greenhouse, "Republicans Credit Labor for Success by Democrats," *New York Times* (6 November 1998): A-28.

94. Sarah Luthens, "Labor to Join the 'Protest of the Century' against World Trade Organization," *Labor Notes* (October 1999): 16.

95. David Moberg, "Martha Jernegons' New Shoes," *The American Prospect* 11.15 (June 19–July 3, 2000); Leah Samuel, "Living Wage Campaigns Become a Movement," *Labor Notes* (July 1999): 1; Steve Cagan, "Cleveland Activists Win Living Wage," *Labor Notes* (August 2000): 1; Robert Pollin and Stephanie Luce, *The Living Wage: Building a Fair Economy* (New York: Free Press, 1998), 178; and Bobbi Murray, "Living Wage Comes of Age," *The Nation* 23/30 (2001): 24–28.

96. David Moberg, "Labor Goes Global," *In These Times* (20 March 2000): 12–13; Tim Shorrock, "Creating a New Internationalism for Labor," *In These Times* (September/October 1999): 36–40; and "Labor and Protest in DC," *The Nation* (1 May 2000): 3.

97. Teo'filo Reyes, "In Dramatic Turnaround, AFL-CIO Endorses Amnesty for Undocumented Immigrants," *Labor Notes* (April 2000): 1.

98. Sonia Pinto-Torres, "With Linked Arms and Fates, Immigrants and Unions United in Fight for Amnesty," *Labor Notes* (June 2001): 1, 10.

99. Kim Moody, Reply to "Changing to Organize," *The Nation* 3/10 (September 2001): 22–23.

100. Steven Greenhouse, "A Rising Tide, but Some Boats Rise Higher Than Others," *New York Times* (3 September 2000): 4-3.

101. Robert Pear, "Health Care Proposals Help Define Democrats," *New York Times* (December 20, 1999): A-32.

102. Steven Greenhouse, "Labor Looks for Common Ground with Bush," *New York Times* (6 February 2001): A-14.

103. The one major exception here is the OCAW and other unionists associated with the fledgling Labor Party, which kicked off a national campaign for a single-payer health care system at the party's constitutional convention in late 1998. Kim Moody, "Labor Party's Convention Clears the Way to Run Candidates, Sets Health Care Campaign," *Labor Notes* (December 1998): 3.

104. See Lisa Belkin, "The Ellwoods; but What about Quality?" *New York Times Magazine* (8 December 1996): 68; SEIU, "Demanding Quality: SEIU Principles for Quality Care" (Washington, DC: SEIU, 1996); and the home page for FACCT, last accessed June 2004 at http://www.facct.org. See also David Bacon, "Whose Side Are You On?" *In These Times* (11 August 1997): 28–29; and Marc Cooper, "Labor's Hardest Drive: Organizing a New Politics," *The Nation* (24 November 1997): 18.

105. At the SEIU's April 1996 convention, delegates passed a resolution proposed from the floor by the reform faction that committed the union to a Canadian-style, single-payer system. J. Peter Nixon, senior policy analyst, SEIU, interview, Washington, DC, June 3, 1996.

106. Moody, "In Other Election News," 5. For more on the Labor Party's "Just Health Care" proposal, see http://www.igc.apc.org/lpa/documents/jhc_financing.html, last accessed June 2004.

107. Leah Samuel, "Business Unionism Triumphs in OCAW-Paperworkers Merger," *Labor Notes* (March 2001): 1, 11.

108. Robert Dreyfuss, "Till Earth and Heaven Ring: The NAACP Is Back," *The Nation* 23/30 (July 2001): 16.

109. "Nation's Largest Medical Societies Launch Campaign for Universal Health Coverage," last accessed June 2004 at http://medicalreporter.health.org/tmr0699/universal_health.html.

110. Joseph Kahn, "Bush Moves Against Steel Imports; Trade Tensions Likely to Rise," *New York Times* (6 June 2001): A-1; Greenhouse, "Labor Looks for Common Ground with Bush"; Moberg, "The Six-Year Itch: John Sweeney Sees the AFL-CIO through Some Growing Pains," *The Nation* 3/10 (September 2001): 15–16.

111. Moberg, "Do or Die," *In These Times* (19 March 2001): 12–13.

112. Raphael Lewis, "Initiative Tallies Show Conservative Bent in Some Cases, Spending Not Deciding Factor," *Boston Globe* (9 November 2000): B-2; and Raja Mishra, "Election 2000/Question 5; Health Care Initiative Apparently Defeated; Ad Drive Erodes Initial Support," *Boston Globe* (8 November 2000): B-3.

113. Christopher Marquis, "Education and Lottery Measures Prove Popular, but Health Care Fares Poorly," *New York Times* (7 November 2002): B-3; and Fairness and Accuracy in Reporting, "NBC Slams Universal Health Care," November 12, 2002, last accessed June 2004 at http://www.fair.org.

114. Health Care for All-Oregon asked the AFL-CIO in Oregon to remain neutral if it could not bring itself to endorse Measure 23. For years, Health Care for All-Oregon had reportedly attempted to get the AFL-CIO involved in drafting the measure. The labor organization did help to draft a Taft-Hartley exemption, but that was the extent of its involvement in formulating the measure, which the labor group ended up actively opposing. Mark Lindgren, Chairperson, Health Care for All-Oregon, personal communications, June 10, 2002, and November 14, 2002; Daniel Marshall Hodges, Health Care for All-California, personal communication, October 1, 2002; and Jerry Gordon, "Conversation with Sweeney about National Health Care," October 1, 2002. Available at http://www.laborstandard.org/New_Postings/Labor_Tues_Oct1_02.html.

115. Steven Greenhouse, "The Most Innovative Figure in Silicon Valley? Maybe This Labor Organizer," *New York Times* (19 November 1999): B-26.

116. Frank Swoboda, "Temporary Workers Win Benefits Ruling," *Washington Post* (31 August 2000): A-1; and Steven Greenhouse, "Labor Board Makes Joining Union Easier for Temp Staff," *New York Times* (31 August 2000): A-16.

117. Steven Greenhouse, "In Biggest Drive since 1937, Union Gains Victory," *New York Times* (26 February 1999): A-1; Nancy Cleeland and Nicholas Riccardi, "L.A. County Home-Care Aides Still Seek 'Fair Share,'" *Los Angeles Times* (14 March 2000): A-1; Hugo Martin, "Home-Care Workers Get Raise, Call It Too

Small," *Los Angeles Times* (13 September 2000): B-1; and Nicholas Riccardi and Gina Piccalo, "Home-Care Worker Pay Mired in Dispute," *Los Angeles Times* (11 September 2000): B-1.

118. Annette Fuentes, "White Coats with Blue Collars," *In These Times* (3 March 1997): 17–19; and Sharon Bernstein, Nancy Cleeland, and Nicholas Riccardi, "Union Plans Drive to Organize Doctors," *Philadelphia Inquirer* (3 March 1999): A-3.

119. Steven Greenhouse, "Union Leaders See Grim News in Labor Study," *New York Times* (13 October 1999): A-23.

120. David Moberg, "Labor Goes Global," *In These Times* (20 March 2000): 12–13.

121. Greenhouse, "Unions Hit Lowest Point in 6 Decades."

122. Chris Garlock, "After September 11, New Organizing Challenges," *Labor Notes* (December 2001): 5, 7.

123. "Labor and the War," *Labor Notes* (November 2001): 9; and Steven Greenhouse, "Labor Runs into Hard Times as It Negotiates for Raises," *New York Times* (9 December 2001): A-49.

124. Doug Henwood, "In Time of War, Who Pays?" *Labor Notes* (December 2001): 1; and John Nichols, "The Democrats' Dilemma: In Trying to Avoid Being Seen as Unpatriotic, They Risk Looking Like Lapdogs," *The Nation* (29 October 2001): 15.

125. Richard W. Stevenson, "Congress Gives Up on Deal this Year to Help Economy," *New York Times* (20 December 2001): A-1; and Robin Toner, "A Stubborn Fight Revived," *New York Times* (20 December 2001): A-34.

126. Milt Freudenheim, "A New Health Plan May Raise Expenses for Sickest Workers," *New York Times* (5 December 2001): A-1.

127. Joseph B. Treaster, "Aetna's Strategy Results in Tenfold Jump in Quarterly Profit," *New York Times* (2 August 2002): C-10.

128. Robert Pear, "Bush Budget on Health Care Would Cut Aid to the Uninsured," *New York Times* (4 April 2001): A-1.

129. The phrase "practical utopias" comes from Adolph Reed, Jr., reply to "Changing to Organize," *The Nation* 3/10 (September): 22.

130. In 1981, Reagan fired striking members of PATCO, the air-traffic controllers' union. Garlock, "After September 11," 7.

# Interest Groups and the Reproduction of Inequality

## CONSTANCE A. NATHANSON

*He Is After the Little Ones, Now. The Ram's Horn,*
April 24, 1897.

" At the close of this century, we have a brief window of opportunity to eliminate one of the public health threats we've been battling the longest. But if we don't take the opportunity now, we'll lose our chance."[1] Jeffrey Koplan, Director of the Centers for Disease Control and Prevention (CDC), made this statement in the fall of 1999. The public health threat to which he referred was syphilis. The "window of opportunity" is presented by the fact that syphilis—a disease that rises and falls in a 7- to 10-year cycle—is at an all-time low and is concentrated in 1% (28) of U.S. counties. Syphilis seriously compromises women's reproductive health and increases the likelihood of HIV transmission. Syphilis is preventable, and it is curable with a single shot of penicillin. The CDC's proposed strategy—an aggressive program of free diagnosis and treatment—is classic in public health. The problem is that this strategy costs significantly more money—approximately $22 million more—than Congress was willing to appropriate for this purpose.

In an article recently published in *The New Yorker*, Malcolm Gladwell attributes what he sees as congressional penny-pinching to "the ways in which disease has become steadily politicized."[2] Gladwell argues that the example set by the AIDS and breast cancer constituencies—they took their case "directly to Capitol Hill, bypassing the medical establishment entirely"—has "given Congress an excuse to treat public health as another form of interest-group politics, in which the most deserving constituencies are those that shout the loudest." The constituency most directly affected by syphilis—African-Americans living in poverty—Gladwell characterizes as one that "cannot shout at all."[3] Worse, syphilis is a sexually transmitted disease, and sex, race, and poverty are "words that the present Congress has difficulty pronouncing individually, let alone in combination."

These observations raise a series of questions. First, is the politicization of disease something new? Is policy makers' treatment of public health as a form of interest-group politics a recent phenomenon, or is what we observe simply the old politics in new forms? More fundamentally, how do public health issues reach the American political agenda? If, indeed, public health in the United States is largely driven by lay interest–group pressures and ideological commitments, what are the consequences of this policy regime for the reproduction of inequalities in health?

Second, are poor African-Americans and other disadvantaged groups truly unable to shout, are they perhaps unwilling to shout, or do they shout in languages that policy makers have trouble understanding or would prefer to ignore? I will argue that the barriers to representation of disadvantaged minority voices in the realm of public health are socially structured, that they arise from within these groups themselves as well as from without, and that external and internal barriers are inextricably intertwined. An inability to shout is the least of these barriers.

Finally, do the moral connotations of a public health problem and the perceived respectability of its victims influence that problem's ability to command public and policy attention? The answer to this question may seem a self-evident "yes" but the implications of moral disrepute go far beyond the construction of boundaries between the deserving "us" and the undeserving "them." The capacity for mobilization on behalf of public health, as well as the nature and influence of collective action, are profoundly affected by whether the disease in question, along with its advocates, are on the right, or the wrong, side of these moral boundaries.

I base my answers to the questions I have posed on analysis of three dramatic public health stories: (1) tuberculosis at the turn of the last century and (2) HIV/AIDS and (3) cigarette smoking at the turn of this one. My focus in telling these stories is on this society's recognition of and response to the emergence of systematic inequalities in the risk of disease and death. In a political system powered by contending interests, the unequal distribution of resources for collective action plays a major role in the reproduction of these inequalities. For disadvantaged groups, the political barriers to good health are deeper and more subtle than an inability to shout.

## Public Health Story I: Tuberculosis

In 1815, Thomas Young, an English physician, wrote, "Of all hectic affections, by far the most important is pulmonary consumption, a disease so frequent as to carry off prematurely about one-fourth part of the inhabitants of Europe, and so fatal as often to deter the practitioner from attempting a cure."[4] A recent medical textbook on tuberculosis offers the estimate that "at the turn of the nineteenth century, one in every five people developed TB [tuberculosis] during their lifetime, making TB the number-one killer, the 'captain of all these men of death.'"[5] The U.S. Census Bureau called tuberculosis "easily first in importance among all causes of death."[6] These estimates are not particularly reliable.[7] They convey, nonetheless, the overall importance of tuberculosis as a cause of death in nineteenth-century Europe and America, its emotional impact, and its medical intractability.

Tuberculosis is a chronic infectious disease that manifests itself in different forms. Respiratory (pulmonary) tuberculosis, also known as phthisis or consumption, is the form we most commonly think of. In addition to being chronic—the time from the disease's first appearance until death was counted in years rather than days or months–tuberculosis was severely debilitating. Nevertheless, despite its prominence as a cause of death, tuberculosis commanded little in the way of public attention until late in the nineteenth century. There was no cure until the discovery of antibiotics in the 1940s, and for much of the nineteenth century, there was no agreement on its cause. Public recognition that tuberculosis was a serious health problem came about as a result of Koch's isolation of the tuberculosis bacterium in 1882 and of his uncomfortable pronouncement that tuberculosis was a contagious disease.[8]

Throughout much of the nineteenth century, the ravages of tuberculosis were greatest among young adults; historians uniformly emphasize its romantic association with promising youth cut off in its prime.[9] However, by 1900, these perceptions had shifted dramatically in the United States, and the "contagious consumptive" was "most often pictured as a menial laborer or a domestic servant, usually a recent immigrant or African-American newly arrived in a city."[10] While early twentieth-century data on residence, race, and class differences in tuberculosis were even less reliable than estimates of disease rates overall, such data as are available portray tuberculosis as a disease of cities and of the poor.[11] The tuberculosis mortality rate for New York in 1900 was somewhere between 200 and 300/100,000.[12] (To provide some perspective, the estimated crude death rate for tuberculosis in the United States in 2000 was 51/100,000.[13]) Multiple generations, packed together in "huge grimy tenements," were discovered by settlement workers to have sickened and died of tuberculosis. These observations were supported by data from the New York City Health Department, newly enthusiastic about the value of maps and statistics in its efforts to develop a rational basis for disease control. Dots on the Health Department's maps showed heavy concentrations of reported "consumption" in the worst tenement blocks.[14]

Black mortality from tuberculosis at the turn of the century was anywhere from three to four times the mortality of whites. While the precise magnitude of the difference may be in doubt, authorities recognized the enormity of the gap at the time.[15] In the death "registration area," which excluded the South where nearly 80% of the black population lived, the rate for blacks was 485/100,000 compared to 174/100,000 for whites.[16] An Alabama county health officer (white), writing in the *Journal of the American Medical Association* in 1903, stated that "the Negro death rate from tuberculosis is more than three times that of the whites from the same disease." In 1912, a black physician wrote somewhat more cautiously

that "the death rate of American Negroes from tuberculosis is undoubtedly large, and larger than that of American whites."[17]

Katherine Ott has titled one of the chapters in her recent book,
*Fevered Lives: Tuberculosis in American Culture since 1870*, "Race-ing Illness
at the Turn of the Century." In the 1890s, she observes, "Tuberculosis
became a primary site of meaning for the middle-class white psyche as it
objectified a racial and ethnic Other."[18] Race rather than (as in England,
for example) social class became the defining demographic identifier, regularly attached to patient records and to public health reports of mortality
and morbidity. Throughout the Progressive Era, the trappings of science
were used by white physicians, public health officers, statisticians, and
social reformers to portray African-Americans either as "savages" inherently more susceptible to tuberculosis or as rendered more susceptible
by ignorance, improvidence, and immorality: "Possibly the most fruitful source of disease among these people is found in their excessive and
corrupt immorality, giving lodgment for the germs of tuberculosis . . ."[19]
(The writer was not a physician, but a former governor of Georgia. His
comments were read before a meeting of the Southern Medical Association and given space in its journal.) While leaders among the black
medical profession did not accept this analysis, their voices went largely
unheard, in part because they were confined to black publications and in
part because these physicians believed the debate itself was pointless:

> [W]hether there is some racial inherency productive of its high
> mortality, or whether it is due to environment, the race is real-
> izing that its death-rate is high; that certain diseases are taking
> more than their toll of human life from its ranks, and that many
> of these diseases are preventable. With this realization, many
> Negroes have set to work to improve their living conditions and
> reduce mortality.[20]

Fear of contagion and knowledge that contagion was preventable generated substantial voluntary as well as professional mobilization
against tuberculosis among both blacks and whites. The political, social,
and demographic as well as the ideological contexts in which mobilization occurred were, however, quite different. The vast majority of blacks
at the turn of the century lived in the South, where they were excluded
from political power and from social interaction with whites except as
domestic servants. White mobilization against tuberculosis was centered
in the northern cities of Philadelphia and New York and took two forms:
aggressive measures of surveillance, disinfection, and quarantine under
municipal supervision; and large-scale voluntary organization.

The earliest chapters of the tuberculosis story in the United States are dominated by the rapid and enthusiastic welcome given to the idea of contagion by physicians of the New York City Health Department. Under the forceful direction of Herman Biggs (a pathologist who went on to become a major figure in early twentieth-century public health), the department instituted mandatory tuberculosis reporting, surveillance (including home visiting) of reported cases, and "forcible detention" of "willfully careless consumptives."[21] The identification of "consumptives" with poor, largely immigrant tenement dwellers living in atrocious conditions no doubt contributed to the relative ease with which these draconian measures were accepted by Progressive elites: the Health Department's zeal was unlikely to target them.[22] Commenting on this phenomenon, Ott observes that "[t]he common Progressive perception was that foreigners were a potential menace and the best policy was one that efficiently assimilated and controlled them." Black assimilation, by contrast, was thought to be impossible: "the Progressive expectation was for control."[23]

A second highlight of white response to tuberculosis was its incorporation in a series of crusades bordering on the religious.[24] Organization began in 1892 under the leadership of a Philadelphia physician, Dr. Lawrence F. Flick. By 1904, when the National Association for the Study and Prevention of Tuberculosis (later the National Tuberculosis Association [NTA]) was formed, there were already 23 state and local societies primarily dedicated to mass public education to prevent tuberculosis. The organizers of the movement against tuberculosis were members of the Progressive Era's socially conscious professional and business elite.[25] The NTA had three presidents of the United States as honorary officers, along with the "backing of prominent physicians, philanthropists, and politicians."

> At the peak of its influence in the late 1910s, the NTA and its approximately 1,300 affiliates enlisted thousands of American men, women, and children in the work of preventing tuberculosis. Their methods were so spectacularly successful that they were imitated by subsequent groups organized to combat mental illness, cancer, diabetes, and infantile paralysis.[26]

"Spectacularly successful" as it may have been, the NTA paid little or no attention to the ravages of tuberculosis among blacks. While some among the northern medical establishment were aware of the facts, David McBride argues that they accepted "the authority of the South's medical elite on the issue of blacks and disease," effectively shrouding the black health crisis from nationwide public view until after the massive migration of blacks to northern cities that followed the First World War.[27]

Marginalized by the dominant society, southern blacks in the early twentieth century launched a parallel campaign: "[F]rom within the lay black community and black medical profession, a largely voluntary public health movement emerged to curtail the spread of TB and other contagious health threats."[28] Grassroots organizing before the First World War was largely the work of black women.[29] Its roots were in the black church and in the newly formed women's clubs:

> High morbidity and mortality rates in black communities led black women to integrate health education and health care into the activities of local chapters of such organizations as the National Association of Colored Women (NACW), a national organization founded in 1896 to represent black club women. Public health work was important in black communities because racism led to a shortage of health professions and medical institutions willing to serve African-Americans.[30]

The movement was promoted by lay leaders such as Booker T. Washington, as well as by prominent black physicians and by the National Medical Association (the black counterpart to the American Medical Association). It was consistent with and, indeed, an expression of the "self-help" philosophy articulated by John A. Kenney and others. The movement had other motives as well, however. As Smith observes, "Black middle-class women felt a personal stake in the 'improvement' of the poor because of the potential effects on their own status."[31] White America did not recognize class differences among blacks and judged all African-Americans by "the impoverished condition of the majority and not by the noble achievements of the ever increasing few."[32]

In the course of the 1920s and 1930s, black voluntarism centered on the neighborhood, and the church was displaced by "social welfare and medical professionals working in the black community, along with their white supporters in philanthropy and private health agencies."[33] This shift was associated with the wholesale movement of blacks out of the South into the industrial cities of the North, with the gradual development of a black professional class, and with a social philosophy among white liberal philanthropists that saw the training of black medical and public health professionals and the support of separate black medical institutions as the solution to black health problems. A serious critique of this approach on the part of black professionals and advocacy groups did not develop until the end of the 1930s, and it was not until the 1960s that it began to have any effect on government policies.

During much of the twentieth century, Smith argues, "Without community activism, much of it carried out by black women, public health work simply would not have reached most black communities."[34] The white medical establishment (including public health officials as well as private physicians) in the South where most blacks lived in the early part of the twentieth century was supportive neither of separate black medical institutions nor of sharing their own resources with the black community.

> Public health officials occasionally endorsed ceremonial activities ... but not any sort of build-up of a permanent health-care infrastructure for black communities; that is, an infrastructure with substantial revenues, ongoing screening and treatment programs and institutions, and capable black administrative leadership.[35]

At the same time, these officials' commitment to Jim Crow prevented the integration of black professionals (not to speak of the black laity) into the dominant group's medical institutions and decision-making structures. A black physician, professor of public health at Howard University in 1923, wrote of his frustration: "Theoretically, the Public Health movement in America stands for the health preservation of all the people and really seems so to function. But actually—with very few exceptions—the various state, county, and city boards of health erect a political and social barrier, which prevents the cooperation of the Negro profession . . ."[36]

The main thrust of black professional activism in the 1920s and 1930s was to generate support from the federal government, as well as from white philanthropists (principally the Julius Rosenwald Fund) for the development of separate black medical schools and hospitals and for the training of black nurses. Among the principal arguments for this support, advanced by prominent black spokespersons such as Booker T. Washington, as well as by liberal whites, was that "germs know no color line." This slogan was adopted by Provident Hospital, a black hospital in Chicago, because it "served to remind potential white donors that, if not for humanitarian reasons, then at least for self-protection, the improvement of black health deserved their financial support."[37] White support for black health campaigns was explained by an aide to Washington on the grounds that "if we die, they die; if we get diseased, they will get diseased, and they know it."[38] This rhetoric must be understood in context of the socially and politically legitimate racism and institutional segregation of the inter-war period; in exploiting the construction of blacks as a danger to the white community, however, these arguments contributed to the medical marginalization of African-Americans.

The federal government under the New Deal was somewhat more responsive to pressure, largely from black health professionals, for attention to the health problems of blacks. From the perspective of present knowledge and present values, that attention may have done as much, if not more, harm than good. It was, in the first place, more token than reality:

> African-Americans were not a political priority for government officials. If federal activity reached black communities, it invariably rested on a foundation of black health programs put into place by middle-class black activists well before the New Deal. Although inroads were made, the USPHS [U.S. Public Health Service] and local health departments failed to demonstrate a serious commitment to black health improvement and black rights.[39]

An underfunded and understaffed Office of Negro Health was established within the USPHS during the 1930s, effectively isolating the health problems of African-Americans from the rest of the Public Health Service. Second, among the consequences of the government's increased attention was the Tuskegee syphilis experiment, following the disease progression of black men with untreated syphilis. Much like the rhetoric employed in the Provident Hospital fundraising campaign, what we now see as unconscionable was at that time not only accepted by, but actively involved, black as well as white medical professionals.

During much of the twentieth century, medical and public health attention to the high rates of tuberculosis (and other diseases) among blacks only came about as the result of shouting by lay club women and black professionals. Their shouts were muffled by a caste system that shaped the forums within which shouting could occur and the language that could be employed. In what became a self-fulfilling prophecy, those forms and that language reinforced the very inequalities they were intended to address. I will return to these points in the chapter's concluding discussion. From a cross-national comparative perspective, among the most striking things about African-Americans' response to their condition was the virtually total absence of politicization until very late in the century: "Although black physicians and activists recognized the adverse effect of a segregated medical care system, most did not call for its dismantlement as a solution to the health problems of African-Americans."[40] While, for example, French socialists and union organizers used the disproportionate impact of tuberculosis on the working class to advocate social insurance or, more radically, the overthrow of capitalism itself, American blacks largely accepted the caste system and attempted to work within it and around it. These facts are, in themselves, testimony to that system's power.

## Public Health Story II: HIV/AIDS

The early epidemiology of HIV/AIDS was dominated by white gay men. Whether or not this dominance was exaggerated from the beginning, there is no question that it no longer exists today. Close to two-thirds of AIDS cases diagnosed in 1985 were among whites; of cases diagnosed in 1996, 63.8% were among blacks and Hispanics. In 1999, the annual rate of AIDS cases among African-American men was 125/100,000, eight times that among white men. The comparable rate among African-American women was 49/100,000, 21 times the rate for white women. Cases among black men are about evenly divided among injection drug users and "men who have sex with men"; two-thirds of the cases among black women are attributed to heterosexual contact and about one-third to injecting drug use.[41] Despite their magnitude, these race differences in HIV/AIDS have remained largely invisible to the public.[42]

AIDS prevention and treatment in the United States has been heavily dependent on the organizational resources and capacities of the affected groups, defined on the basis of their exposure category. For a number of reasons, the earliest to mobilize were white gay men, and their interests have dominated the AIDS agenda. The social position of many gay men increased the likelihood that their symptoms would come to medical attention: "Gay men, some of them affluent and relatively privileged, found their way into private doctors' offices and prominent teaching hospitals—and from there into the pages of medical journals—while drug users often sickened and died with little fanfare."[43] The government agency primarily responsible for disseminating information about the epidemic, the CDC, was familiar with the gay community as a result of prior research on sexually transmitted diseases (STDs) using gay participants. By contrast, "the marginalized status of poor people and injection drug users, who had limited access to the health care system, rendered them invisible to the CDC."[44] If, as Cathy Cohen indicates, AIDS deaths among injection drug users were invisible to the CDC, then these deaths were equally invisible to their own—largely minority—communities.

Gay men's resources included not only wealth and privilege, but also experience in political organization on behalf of the gay community: Within 6 months of the first report of AIDS in the *New York Times*, gay and lesbian organizations that would prove pivotal in confronting the epidemic had been formed in New York City and San Francisco. The gay community's early mobilization beat local public health officials to the punch, forcing them into negotiation with gay spokespersons and allowing these officials to emphasize coordination rather than direct service. "With the white homosexual community left to raise its own funds and mount its own education campaign, the IVDUs (intravenous drug users) and the gay men and bisexuals in the minority community were virtually ignored."[45]

Perhaps the most striking aspect of both public health and social scientific commentary on HIV/AIDS in minority communities is its heavy emphasis on the absence and/or ineffectiveness of mobilization by these communities in response to the epidemic. For example, "In spite of the long history of black mobilization, there has been little mobilization around AIDS."[46]

> AIDS program efforts in African-American communities and in other communities of color have suffered because there has not been a united effort within the community to pressure public health authorities and other governmental agencies to provide resources and services.[47]

The implications of these comments are twofold. First, that absent a "united effort within the community" governmental agencies not only will not, but cannot be expected to, "provide resources and services"; and, second, that the responsibility for lack of a "united effort" lies with the affected communities themselves. If services and resources are insufficient, then it is the African-American (and other minority) communities that are at fault. The first of these implications is central to my thesis: In the American political system only squeaky wheels get greased. The second contains a modicum of truth, but oversimplifies the complex circumstances associated with the African-American response to AIDS.[48]

The African-American community is not altogether powerless, as Cohen points out. While gay men may be better off in wealth and privilege, a number of urban communities where AIDS was (and is) concentrated had black mayors and black city council members who controlled city resources. During the period when Congress was most heavily focused on AIDS (in the late 1980s and early 1990s), Democrats were in control, and some black members of the House of Representatives (e.g., Rep. Charles Rangel, D-NY) held important committee positions. National black organizations play a major and influential role in legislative and legal battles affecting civil rights. Nevertheless,

> Most indigenous black institutions . . . provided a mixed, limited, and often reluctant response to (the AIDS) epidemic. The AIDS programs initiated by these organizations were designed not only to provide needed services to segments of black communities, but also to fit within a constrained moral and political framework, where anything from a lack of expertise on this issue or the word of God were offered (the former by the NAACP, the latter by black clergy) as reasons for doing less.[49]

Cohen advances three types of explanation for the black establishment's uneven response to AIDS. First, the absence of mainstream white (as well as black) media attention to AIDS among African-Americans "supported the denial of black community leaders, who viewed AIDS as a disease they did not have to own."[50] Second, injection drug use and homosexuality are highly stigmatized identities in black (as in white) communities: community leaders and politicians moved quickly to distance themselves from any implication that these behaviors were inherent among blacks.[51] Cohen comments on the hierarchy of stigma employed by black politicians:

> Many black legislators instituted a two-tier system of recognition whereby black women and children were used to distract attention from black injection drug users, and black injection drug users were used to distract attention from black gay men and black men who have sex with other men . . . subgroups were promoted selectively, based on their perceived respectability and empathetic value.[52]

Third, Cohen suggests that the black establishment has, to some degree, been co-opted by dominant white institutions, and that many leaders may not see it as in their interest to shout too loudly on behalf of groups stigmatized even within their own communities.

AIDS activism exists among blacks, more highly developed among gays than among injection drug users and their partners. These activists have encountered multiple obstacles, both in their interaction with white institutions in control of AIDS funds and with mainstream black community organizations. The former gaze with suspicion on small militant groups, regarding them as unreliable grantees, and the latter distance themselves from subgroups whose existence in their communities they would prefer not to acknowledge. In comparing the AIDS mobilization potential of blacks with gays, it is important to keep in mind that while gay activists could persuasively represent themselves as speaking for the entire gay community, black AIDS activists not only cannot claim to represent the black community as a whole but were they to make such a claim, it would be summarily rejected.

## Public Health Story III: Cigarette Smoking

Tobacco use, particularly cigarette smoking, remains the leading cause of preventable illness and death in this country," wrote Donna E. Shalala, the Secretary of Health and Human Services, in her introduction to the most recent Surgeon General's report on smoking and health. The elimination of "health disparities among different segments of the U.S. population" has been identified as one of the department's two major goals for the next 10 years.[53] Among the most marked disparities in health-related behavior documented in this country are social class differences in cigarette smoking. Based on Shalala's initial statement, we might reasonably anticipate that these disparities would be urgently addressed. They are not. Except in statistical tables where smoking prevalence is reported by education, these differences have been largely invisible. They are never mentioned in the 462-page Surgeon General's report issued in 2000, and in the 1998 report they appear only as statistical controls to determine whether race/ethnic differences in smoking are "explained" by differences in education. (They are.) Yet these differences are profound, and they are increasing.

Currently, about 25% of Americans smoke, down from close to half in 1965.[54] In 1965, however, smoking was an equal opportunity habit: around 45% of American adults smoked cigarettes irrespective of education or race. In the course of subsequent years, this pattern has markedly changed. While only around 15% of college graduates currently smoke, the percentage of smokers among individuals with no more than a high school education is more than double, or about 32% higher than the percentage of college graduates who smoked in 1970. The evidence for social class differences in smoking is particularly striking among women of reproductive age: Among women with less than a high school education, half are smokers. This percentage drops to one-third among high school graduates, and to 15% among college graduates. These distributions are essentially the same among African-Americans as they are among whites.

The foregoing observations raise two questions. First, how are these differences to be explained? Second, why are they ignored by public health authorities in the United States? The pattern of social class differences I have described is not unique to this country; similar patterns emerged over the same period in other industrialized countries, most strongly in those with the longest history of cigarette smoking.[55] The uniqueness of the United States lies not in the fact of differences but that in this country, the differences are ignored.

Corresponding to its invisibility in the realm of public health policy, there has been little or no research conducted in the United States on social class and smoking. Based on their investigation of class differences in Britain, Alan Marsh and Stephen McKay comment on possible explanations for these differences:

> Unlike most people, the lowest income families really do have ... strong reasons for wanting to smoke. They alone in our society are under the greatest pressure, experience the greatest inequality of choice and opportunity in their lives. Some of them, especially the lone parents, feel they exist solely to service their children's daily needs. They to do so at a level so basic, it removes them entirely from the "real" world of people who have comfortable homes, cars, and holidays. ... Smoking is their only luxury. They defend it, aggressively sometimes. In a world of many luxuries for others, one luxury for oneself becomes a necessity.[56]

"Aggressive defense" is not limited to Great Britain. In justifying that organization's opposition to federal regulation of smoking in the workplace, an official of the AFL-CIO (American Federation of Labor/Congress of Industrial Organizations) invoked the smoking "culture" of union members: "There has been a change in the culture, but there are still a lot of people who smoke who think that they should be able to smoke in workplaces. They think they should be able to smoke in bars and restaurants...There are a lot of places in this country where the culture is not the same as it is in Washington, DC, or in southern California."[57] The word "culture" in this context does little more than restate the fact of difference. It is nonetheless true that in its origins, its style, its rhetoric, and its modes of organization, the tobacco control movement was thoroughly middle class. It appealed to the same constituency as the environmental movement, the gun control movement, the breast cancer movement, and other advocates for "lifestyle" reform.[58] While this was, in the United

States, a "grassroots" movement in many respects, its roots did not go very far down the social scale.

For most of the 35 years since the dangers of smoking were widely acknowledged by the scientific community, the principal warriors in the battle against smoking were the three large health voluntaries (American Cancer Society [ACS], American Lung Association, American Heart Association), Action on Smoking and Health (ASH), and nonsmokers' rights groups, principally GASP (Group Against Smokers' Pollution). These groups have varied in relative importance over time and have played complementary roles in advancing the overall tobacco control agenda.[59]

The major player among the health voluntaries, the ACS, had its greatest influence during the 1950s and 1960s, using its substantial resources and authority to help create and then to promote the problem of smoking and health within and outside the government. The ACS is, however, a large national association with multiple interests and a substantial budget (by far the largest among the health voluntaries) and is dependent on the enthusiasm of its local chapters for members and contributions. The ACS is led by prominent physicians and business executives. Its conservative leadership and an unwillingness to risk other interests for the sake of the smoking/tobacco control movement prevented the society from going much beyond its self-defined role as health educator until the early 1980s. When in the 1970s the ACS virtually disappeared as a public advocate on behalf of smoking and health, the banner was taken up by a proliferation of single-issue groups, resource-poor relative to the ACS but unburdened by its conservative baggage.

ASH was founded in 1967 with the sole purpose of engaging in legal action against smoking at the federal level. ASH was in no sense a grassroots organization. It was a small professionally operated public interest group with a paid staff and no organization or activities at the local and state level. At the other end of the spectrum of collective action was the nonsmokers' rights movement. GASP was founded in early 1971 by a young mother, the wife of a university professor, working out of her living room. She used her experience and connections in the environmental movement and with the American Lung Association to spread the word, urging the "involuntary victims of tobacco smoke" to rise up and assert their "right to breathe clean air (that) is superior to the right of the smoker to enjoy a harmful habit."[60] These early nonsmokers' rights activists were well-educated members of relatively affluent (often university) communities; their rhetoric was highly effective among people like themselves.[61]

In its origins, the tobacco control movement was white as well as middle class. Emergence of a tobacco-control infrastructure within the African-American community has been a relatively recent development.[62] The authors of the 1998 Surgeon General's report on tobacco use among U.S. racial/ethnic minority groups describe in some detail a history of close and positive relationships between the tobacco industry and the black community: "The tobacco industry has often been the only source of funds for community initiatives" leading to a reticence among "some leaders and organizations" to take action on behalf of tobacco control.[63] As I noted earlier, however, both the percentage of smokers and the pattern of social class differences in smoking among blacks and whites are essentially identical, suggesting that whatever the explanation for these differences may be, it is unlikely to differ substantially by race.

Why, then, are social class differences in smoking ignored by policy makers and the public? A brief digression overseas may help to account for this phenomenon. In 1990, prominent physicians confronted the French government with tobacco control legislation that the government was—for economic and political reasons—reluctant to support. The key argument in convincing the newly elected socialists of the need for legislation was the social inequality of sickness and death; inequality, these physicians argued, created by diseases associated with tobacco (and alcohol, which was included in the legislation as well). For a "government of the left," this inequality was an argument impossible to ignore.[64] Solidarity—understood as the minimization of inequalities among different segments of the population—is in France a primary responsibility of government and a central principle by which public policies are judged. In the United States, while the sustained efforts of organized racial and ethnic minorities have forced political attention to inequalities of race and ethnicity, inequalities of class have no organized constituency and are not framed in terms of discrimination and civil "rights." While some might have disagreed with him, no one questioned the appropriateness of a black, nonsmoking Secretary of Health and Human Services excoriating the tobacco industry for targeting black consumers.[65] A similar attack on the industry by a nonsmoking Secretary of Labor for targeting blue-collar consumers would more than likely be received by these consumers and their allies as arrogant paternalism.

Rather than question the invisibility of social-class differences in smoking, we might better ask why organization on behalf of smokers' rights has been so relatively weak and ineffective in this country.[66] There is no National Rifle Association for smokers. Smoking and the cigarette have been transformed from symbols of "modernity, autonomy, power, and sexuality" to symbols of weakness, irrationality, and addiction, little better than addiction to heroin or cocaine.[67] Snow, rain, or shine, smokers are relegated to doorsteps and sidewalks. Thus, not only is there little political pressure for attention to the health of low-income smokers from those—like the AFL-CIO—who might speak for this constituency, there is equally little incentive for smokers to organize around a stigmatized identity. In these circumstances, and in the absence of a government mandate to address inequalities of illness and death, the path of least resistance is for social class differences in smoking to be ignored.

## Discussion

Tuberculosis, HIV/AIDS, and smoking have each been described as the most significant public health problem of the time. The forms of action and ideological beliefs that surround these conditions fairly represent how Americans manage the public's health. Based on the evidence of these examples, I now return to the questions posed at the beginning of this chapter.

First, is any of this new? Clearly not. Organization around health interests emerged during the Progressive Era hard on the heels of organization around farmers', women's, and labor interests. The same circumstances that led these latter groups to organize around their specific interests and engage in lobbying activities outside the established political parties led health interest groups to do the same. Confronted by rapid social and economic change and supremely dissatisfied with the two-party system's capacity to respond, reformers adapted existing forms of organization (religious, fraternal, social) to new political purposes, including the purpose of advancing the public's health.[68] And, just as forms of civic engagement more generally have changed over time, so also the forms of advocacy on behalf of health interests have changed.[69] While the large and relatively conservative health voluntaries founded early in the twentieth century continue alive and well, they have been supplemented by more agile, more specialized, and often more militant advocacy groups.

There is a further important distinction to be made between organization on behalf of and by affected populations. Historically, most health-related mobilization has fallen into the former category. Among the more striking shifts that have occurred over the decades since the 1960s is the move toward organization by affected groups. The nonsmokers' rights movement was among the earliest of such groups, modeling itself on and adapting the rhetoric of the civil rights movement. Over time, as other disenfranchised groups—the disabled, breast cancer survivors, persons with AIDS—adopted this same model, mobilization by affected groups was transformed from an innovation to an expectation. This expectation is clearly reflected in the comments cited earlier decrying the absence of black mobilization around AIDS. More recently, the expectation has further evolved into a mandate—embodied, for example, in the Ryan White Act for the care and treatment of AIDS patients—requiring that representatives of affected communities be included on boards or as advisory groups as a condition for external funding. Mandated mobilization—like the Office of Negro Health established by the USPHS in the 1930s—undoubtedly brings formerly excluded groups into the mainstream organizational fold. However, it may also depoliticize them, blunting their struggle for meaningful health policy change.

"Americans of all ages, all conditions, and all dispositions, constantly form associations."[70] This propensity was, in 1835, and continues to be among this country's most distinctive characteristics, and Tocqueville believed it to be essential for the preservation of democracy in a society that had abolished aristocratic distinctions. What Tocqueville did not observe was that the capacity to form associations and to realize their power is itself unevenly distributed.

Second, is it true that disadvantaged groups are unable to shout? While the evidence I have unearthed is uneven, in large part due to the conflation in virtually all writing on this topic of "disadvantage" with race and ethnicity, the answer I would argue is a resounding no. The barriers to politically effective collective action confronted by disadvantaged groups are far more complex than a simple inability to shout. There is ample evidence of early twentieth-century black community and professional organization in response to tuberculosis. And while the labor unions, social service organizations, and churches that principally represent low-income workers and minority communities today may have been relatively unresponsive to the dangers of cigarette smoking and HIV/AIDS, there has been a substantial amount of small-scale, locally based AIDS-related organization in and on behalf of minority communities and users of narcotic drugs.[71] Organizations exist. Their ability and willingness to be politically effective on behalf of public health goals is limited not only by organizational weaknesses, but also by substantial ambivalence and suspicion within disadvantaged communities about the goals themselves. Early twentieth-century black community and professional organizations were committed to the goals of preventing tuberculosis (and other health problems) and created organizations parallel to those of the white community. These early entrepreneurs were limited by their inability to attract mainstream sponsorship and by the racially segregated social structures within which they were constrained to work. Contemporary advocacy groups that have sprung up around problems specific to HIV/AIDS in minority communities confront the same sponsorship barriers, imposed not only by the dominant community, but also by some elites in their own community.[72] At the same time, a preference for non-hierarchical, non-bureaucratic forms of organization may limit these groups' ability to apply for and attract the government and/or foundation support that would enable them to carry on independently.

Third, how do the moral connotations of a public health problem influence that problem's claim on public and policy attention? Americans have been remarkably consistent in their predilections, first, for the attribution of responsibility for disease to that disease's victims and, second, for the drawing of boundaries between those victims ("them") and the rest of society ("us"). Historically, populations already marginalized by poverty, race, and ethnicity have been particularly vulnerable to these predilections, triply stigmatized by illness, race, and class. Not only does the presence of stigma inhibit popular concern, it is an additional barrier to collective action. Mainstream groups have difficulty in garnering support for action on behalf of individuals perceived as responsible for their own condition. Potential leaders within the affected communities are understandably averse to actions they may perceive as adding to rather than mitigating the marginalization of populations they represent. Sustainable and politically effective organization by stigmatized individuals demands that the stigma itself be transformed into the basis for a legitimate identity.[73] Given these obstacles, it is unsurprising that a condition for the claim on public attention of health problems that primarily affect the disadvantaged and for their ability to attract organizational resources is that these problems threaten (or can be portrayed as threatening) the larger society. In the absence of a credible threat (e.g., both HIV/AIDS and smoking are now "contained" in subgroups largely invisible to much of the population), these problems are likely to remain unaddressed.

In the United States, we are subject to periodic debates about the legitimacy of interest-group politics. This form of political representation is, nevertheless, well established in our system of government and is unlikely to disappear, however much hand wringing it generates (and was, indeed, celebrated by James Madison in the 10th *Federalist* as a necessary buffer against the tyranny of the majority.)[74] Public health is perhaps in principle the province of the "medical establishment" (e.g., CDC, National Institutes of Health, the Institute of Medicine, *Journal of the American Medical Association*). Nevertheless, within the American political system, while the power and respect accorded to "experts" in medicine and public health have varied over time, their authority in matters of public policy has never been comparable to the authority of elite physicians in many European countries. In health as in other policy arenas, the voices of medicine and science must compete with the voices of other powerful interests with very different ideological agendas. The inequities that result are unlikely to be resolved by a newfound deference to accredited experts.

## Conclusion

This country's social and political structure creates a range of obstacles to representation of the interests of marginalized groups, as I have demonstrated. At the same time, virtually every commentator on the public health problems of poor and minority groups assumes, first, that interest-group representation is a prerequisite for government action on behalf of these groups and, second, that lack of representation is a weakness of these groups themselves, rather than of a structure in which they are systematically disadvantaged. From the earliest days of our republic, constitutional scholars and judges have been concerned with how minority interests may be represented in a system of majority rule (most explicitly in Madison's 10th *Federalist*). Insofar as these interests are not represented by the structures of civil society, then it is the responsibility of government to speak and act on the behalf of those whose voices would otherwise be unheard. Our present political system is one in which both government and civil society appear equally incapable of effective action. This system skews government benefits in favor of the powerful, contributing directly to the reproduction of inequalities in health.

## Notes

1. Centers for Disease Control and Prevention, *Syphilis Continues to Retreat: Nation Sets Sights on Elimination* (October 9, 1999).

2. "Cheap and Easy," *New Yorker* (10 July 2000): 21–22.

3. According to the CDC, syphilis "disproportionately affects African-Americans living in poverty." While this disproportion has declined in recent years, in 1998 the syphilis rate for blacks was 34 times greater than the rate for whites.

4. Rene Dubos and Jean Dubos, *The White Plague: Tuberculosis, Man, and Society* (New Brunswick, NJ: Rutgers University Press, 1987).

5. Christopher R. Braden, Ida M. Onorato, and Joseph H. Kent, "Tuberculosis–United States," *Tuberculosis*, 1st ed., ed. William N. Rom and Stuart M. Garay (Boston: Little, Brown, 1996), 85–97.

6. U.S. Bureau of the Census, *Mortality Statistics 1907* (Washington, DC: Department of Commerce and Labor, 1909).

7. Kevin White has recently argued that data on tuberculosis death rates are relatively reliable compared to data for other causes of death: "Its symptoms had long been recognized, making TB a dreaded and carefully identified disease by the turn of the century, less apt to be confused with other diseases than most causes of death at the time." "Cardiovascular and Tuberculosis Mortality: The Contrasting Effects of Changes in Two Causes of Death," *Population and Development Review* 25.2 (1999): 292.

8. In fact, Jean-Antoine Villemin established the contagious nature of tuberculosis in 1865, almost 20 years in advance of Koch, but his findings were rejected by the French Academy of Medicine and ignored by the medical establishments of most countries, in large part because of their disturbing nature.

9. Dubos and Dubos, *The White Plague*; Pierre Guillaume, *Du Desespoir Au Salut: Les Tuberculeux Aux 19e Et 20e Siecles* (Paris: Aubier, 1986); F. B. Smith, *The Retreat of Tuberculosis 1850–1919* (London: Croom-Helm, 1988).

10. Katherine Ott, *Fevered Lives: Tuberculosis in American Culture since 1870* (Cambridge, MA: Harvard University Press, 1996), 101.

11. Lillian Brandt, a social reformer and statistician with the New York Charity Organization Society, suggested that data for the "registration area," which included many of the country's largest cities, while relatively more reliable than for the country as a whole, may have underestimated death rates from tuberculosis. Committee on the Prevention of Tuberculosis, "The Social Aspects of Tuberculosis Based on a Study of Statistics," *A Handbook on the Prevention of Tuberculosis* (New York: Charity Organization Society, 1903), 31–115.

12. Barron H. Lerner, "New York City's Tuberculosis Control Efforts: The Historical Limitations of the War on Consumption," *American Journal of Public Health* 83 (1993): 758.

13. White, "Cardiovascular and Tuberculosis Mortality."

14. Ott, *Fevered Lives*. Tuberculosis among the more affluent members of society is likely to have been seriously underreported, both because health department workers were less likely to visit middle-class homes and because the physicians who attended middle-class tuberculosis patients were less likely to report the disease to the health department, given the stigma attached to this diagnosis. Nevertheless, the overcrowded conditions that characterized city slums in the early twentieth century were ideally suited for tuberculosis transmission.

15. Brandt, "The Social Aspects of Tuberculosis"; Ott, *Fevered Lives*; Susan L. Smith, *Sick and Tired of Being Sick and Tired: Black Women's Health Activism in America, 1890–1950* (Philadelphia: University of Pennsylvania Press, 1995); Vanessa N. Gamble, *Germs Have No Color Line: Blacks and American Medicine, 1900–1940* (New York: Garland Publishing, 1989); David McBride, *From TB to AIDS: Epi-*

*demics among Urban Blacks since 1900* (Albany: State University of New York Press, 1991).

16. As noted previously, these figures are likely to underestimate the actual rates. Whether there was a differential underestimate for blacks and whites is impossible to know.

17. E. M. Boyle, "The Negro and Tuberculosis," *Journal of the National Medical Association* 4 (1912): 344–348.

18. Ott, *Fevered Lives*, 101.

19. W. J. Northern, "Tuberculosis among Negroes," *Journal of the Southern Medical Association* 6 (1909): 407–419.

20. These comments were made in 1911 by John A. Kenney, the medical director of Tuskegee Institute and editor of the *Journal of the National Medical Association*. They are cited in McBride, *From TB to AIDS*, 23.

21. Lerner, "New York City's Tuberculosis Control Efforts," 760.

22. Emily K. Abel, "Taking the Cure to the Poor: Patients' Responses to New York City's Tuberculosis Program, 1894 to 1918," *American Journal of Public Health* 87.11 (1997): 1808–1815.

23. Ott, *Fevered Lives*, 3.

24. Nancy Tomes, *The Gospel of Germs: Men, Women, and the Microbe in American Life* (Cambridge, MA: Harvard University Press, 1998). Tomes quotes from a physician's 1909 address on tuberculosis prevention to a group in Pennsylvania: "The antituberculosis campaign has in it much of the fervor of a new religion," 114.

25. Michael E. Teller, *The Tuberculosis Movement: A Public Health Campaign in the Progressive Era* (New York: Greenwood Press, 1987), 40.

26. Tomes, *The Gospel of Germs*, 114.

27. McBride, *From TB to AIDS*, 31. To what extent, by whom, and for how long excess death rates among blacks were recognized as a problem even after the war is unclear. In 1937, the prominent statistician Louis Dublin wrote that tuberculosis among blacks in New York City was "for the most part . . . overlooked," and as late as 1946, a Harlem physician observed that "City health authorities were 'all but oblivious' to the tuberculosis problem among Blacks." Lerner, "New York City's Tuberculosis Control Efforts," 760.

28. McBride, *From TB to AIDS*, 10.

29. "Black health reform was gendered to the extent that men held most of the formal leadership positions and women did most of the grass roots organizing," Smith, *Sick and Tired of Being Sick and Tired*, 1.

30. Ibid., 17–18.

31. Ibid., 18.

32. Ibid.; the comments are those of Mary Church Terrell, first president of the NACW, speaking in 1904.

33. McBride, *From TB to AIDS*, 31.

34. Smith, *Sick and Tired of Being Sick and Tired*, 59.

35. McBride, *From TB to AIDS*, 27.

36. Algernon Brashear Jackson, reprinted in Gamble, *Germs Have No Color Line*, 81.

37. Gamble, *Germs Have No Color Line*, Introduction.

38. Smith, *Sick and Tired of Being Sick and Tired*, 41.

39. Ibid., 59.

40. Gamble, *Germs Have No Color Line*, Introduction.

41. The data in this paragraph are from the AIDS surveillance program of CDC, reported on July 31, 2000, available at http://www.cdc.gov/hiv/stats; *Surveillance Report* 11.2: Tables 7–24.

42. Cathy J. Cohen, *The Boundaries of Blackness: AIDS and the Breakdown of Black Politics* (Chicago: University of Chicago Press, 1997); Bob Herbert, "The Quiet Scourge," *New York Times* (11 January 2001): A-25:5.

43. Steven Epstein, *Impure Science: AIDS, Activism, and the Politics of Knowledge* (Berkeley and Los Angeles: University of California Press, 1996), 49–50.

44. Cohen, *Boundaries of Blackness*, 130.

45. Charles Perrow and Mauro F. Guillén, *The AIDS Disaster: The Failure of Organizations in New York and the Nation* (New Haven: Yale University Press, 1990), 83.

46. Ernest Quimby and Samuel R. Friedman, "Dynamics of Black Mobilization against AIDS in New York City," *Social Problems* 36 (October 1989): 403.

47. National Commission on AIDS, *The Challenge of HIV/AIDS in Communities of Color* (Washington, DC: National Commission on AIDS, 1992), 33.

48. I am much indebted to Cohen's *Boundaries of Blackness* for the following highly abbreviated version of her detailed account of AIDS politics among African-Americans.

49. Cohen, *Boundaries of Blackness*, 256.

50. Ibid., 182.

51. Perrow and Guillén, *The AIDS Disaster*.

52. Cohen, *Boundaries of Blackness*, 324.

53. U.S. Department of Health and Human Services, *Reducing Tobacco Use: A Report of the Surgeon General* (Atlanta, GA: U.S. Department of Health and Human Services, Centers for Disease Control and Prevention, National Center for Chronic Disease Prevention and Health Promotion, Office on Smoking and Health, 2000), 11.

54. U.S. Department of Health and Human Services, *Tobacco Use among U.S. Racial/Ethnic Minority Groups—African Americans, American Indians and Alaska Natives, Asian Americans and Pacific Islanders, and Hispanics: A Report of the Surgeon General* (Atlanta, GA: U.S. Department of Health and Human Services, Centers for Disease Control and Prevention, National Center for Chronic Disease Prevention and Health Promotion, Office on Smoking and Health, 1998).

55. Constance A. Nathanson, *Disease Prevention as Social Change: The State, Society, and Public Health in the U.S., Canada, Britain, and France*, n.d.

56. Alan Marsh and Stephen McKay, *Poor Smokers* (London: Policy Studies Institute, 1994), 82–83.

57. Constance A. Nathanson, "Social Movements as Catalysts for Policy Change: The Case of Smoking and Guns," *Journal of Health Politics, Policy and Law* 24.3 (1999): 450.

58. Tobacco control constituencies in other industrialized countries have a somewhat narrower base than in the United States (e.g., in Britain and France they were driven initially by physicians rather than by lay advocates as in this country) but are no less middle-class in approach and organization. It is tempting here to refer to Michael Foucault's analysis of how the nineteenth-century bourgeoisie "cultivated" its own body—its "strength, vigor, health, and life"—as a strategy for affirming its political and social supremacy. Michel Foucault, *The History of Sexuality* (New York: Vintage Books, 1976), 125.

59. For a detailed account of the social movement for smoking/tobacco control in the United States, see Nathanson, "Social Movements as Catalysts for Policy Change."

60. Ibid., 448.

61. Analysis of the timing of smoking control ordinance adoption in relation to aggregate family income among California counties demonstrates a highly significant association between counties' aggregate wealth and early adoption; ibid., 462.

62. U.S. Department of Health and Human Services, *Tobacco Use among U.S. Racial/Ethnic Minority Groups*.

63. Ibid., 213.

64. Albert Hirsch and Serge Karsenty, *Le Prix De La Fumée* (Paris: Editions Odile Jacob, 1992).

65. Children are, of course, an equally if not more acceptable constituency around which to rally the troops and frame attacks on the industry.

66. The National Smokers' Alliance claims to be "a nonprofit, grass-roots membership organization with more than 3 million members." However, its receipts from membership dues in 1996 were only $74,000. The bulk of its budget as well as infrastructure support for its activities appear to come from the tobacco industry. U.S. Department of Health and Human Services, *Reducing Tobacco Use: A Report of the Surgeon General*, 254.

67. Alan Brandt, "The Rise and Fall of the Cigarette: A Brief History of the Anti-Smoking Movement in the United States," *Advancing Health in Developing Countries*, ed. L. C. Chen, A. Kleinman, and N. C. Ware (New York: Auburn House, 1992), 70.

68. Elizabeth S. Clemens, *The People's Lobby: Organizational Innovation and the Rise of Interest Group Politics in the United States, 1890–1925* (Chicago: University of Chicago Press, 1997).

69. Theda Skocpol, "Advocates without Members: The Recent Transformation of American Civic Life," in *Civic Engagement in American Democracy*, ed. Theda Skocpol and Morris P. Fiorina (Washington, DC, and New York: Brookings Institution/Russell Sage Foundation, 1999), 461–509.

70. Alexis de Tocqueville, *Democracy in America*, Mentor Book ed. (New York: New American Library, 1956), 198.

71. Nathanson, "Social Movements as Catalysts for Policy Change," 462; Cohen, *Boundaries of Blackness*, 324.

72. Don Des Jarlais, who has worked with minority communities on initiatives to prevent HIV/AIDS in injection drug users for many years, states in a recent article that some racial/ethnic minority community leaders have moved from opposition to support of needle exchange programs "as a result of the accumulated data.""Research, Politics, and Needle Exchange," *American Journal of Public Health* 90.9 (2000): 1392–1394. Writing in 1997, Cohen stated that "a lack of leadership, particularly transformative leadership, best characterizes the response to AIDS from traditional black organizations and elites." Cohen, *Boundaries of Blackness*, 341.

73. See, for example, A. R. Henman, D. Paone, D. C. Des Jarlais, L. M. Kochems, and S. R. Friedman, "Injection Drug Users as Social Actors: A Stigmatized Community's Participation in the Syringe Exchange Programmes of New York City," *AIDS CARE* 10.4 (1998): 397–408.

74. James Madison, Alexander Hamilton, and John Jay, *The Federalist Papers*, Penguin Books ed. (London: Penguin Group, 1987).

# Part IV

# CHAOTIC INSTITUTIONS

In *Mr. Smith Goes to Washington*, Jimmy Stewart leaves his small New England town, heads down to Washington, fights off the selfish political barons, and single-handedly filibusters Congress into doing the right thing. The movie serves up a full helping of all-American idealism: The common man stands up to the cynical politicians and wins the day for the people.

Alas, the real political world operates on less inspiring principles. Even if public health reformers stood up and roused Americans into action against inequality, political institutions with a very distinct set of operating rules would shape the results. The institutional rules inevitably tilt the politics. That tilt—organized deep in the political machinery— makes egalitarian reform extremely hard to win. Our political apparatus is geared to defer to market winners. Part IV shows how and why.

Any major American reform must pass through Congress. And Congress, as Mark Peterson tells us in chapter 7, might be called the graveyard of major health reforms. Peterson takes us on panoramic tour of the congressional process. What we see is the daunting number of organizational levers that have to click into place for legislation—any big-scale legislation—to win. And yet, Congress is always changing, always evolving. Peterson shows us how and why attacking inequality is difficult—and how those difficulties might be overcome.

The judiciary offers an alternative political path. Could we imagine courts nudging the United States toward a more egalitarian society? Or discovering a broad American right to health care? In chapter 8, Peter Jacobson and Elizabeth Selvin explore the answers. They examine the courts' role in creating rights (very rare) and reviewing legislation (the wild card); they show us how the courts balance philosophical, political, and practical considerations. And they remind us that all the great debates about wealth and poverty, health and illness, turn into far more narrow, often technical, questions as they pass through the judicial eye of the needle.

Both chapters reach the same conclusion. Neither Congress nor the courts are designed to address big and systematic problems—like inequality and its impact on health. Rather, these institutions defer to market winners (and, perhaps, the prevailing political mood). Only a powerful, sustained, grassroots movement—one that jars the entire American political frame—will push these institutions into championing large-scale health reforms. That's precisely how it happened in the past. Accumulating inequalities triggered forceful populist surges that led, eventually, to Progressive reforms, the New Deal, and the Great Society.

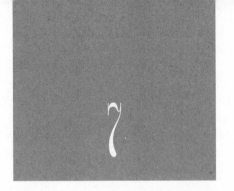

# The Congressional Graveyard for Health Care Reform

## MARK A. PETERSON

*The Bosses of the Senate.* Joseph Keppler, *Puck*, 1889.

A simple but poignant underlying normative question motivates this volume: How should we, can we, motivate the political process to nurture a society with fewer and less-pronounced health disparities across social and economic groups? Reducing the disparities will require action by Congress, the ultimate and often unresponsive linchpin in asserting public authority. Without the collaboration of our national legislature, there can be no public-sector endeavor of suitable scale to allay the sources of health inequality.

Sources of inequality operate on three levels, and Congress has resisted action on every one. First, as Ichiro Kawachi shows in chapter 1, there is evidence that yawning gaps in income contribute to adverse health. The effects of income disparities may either directly harm individual health or encumber the least well off by threatening the social capital—the networks of civic engagement—needed to cement collective bonds within their communities. These conclusions, however, are controversial.[1] Furthermore, acting on them would require a profound reorientation of American popular attitudes, elite commitments, and public policy. It is no surprise that Congress has not traveled down this road in a long time.

For a second source of health inequality, however, the evidence is more difficult to ignore. Poorer people suffer higher rates of illness. Income is simply instrumental to obtaining food, housing, education, transportation, clean environments, and public safety—contextual factors linked with health status. Lower income is also associated with behavioral patterns, such as tobacco use, that undermine good health. Redistribution could play a role here, too. We can help poor people and communities secure suitable nutrition, adequate shelter, effective education, appropriate transportation, an unsoiled environment, and safe streets as well as mitigate incentives for risky behavior. For this type of policy, Congress has been more active, albeit with comparatively anemic social policies like the food stamp program, restricted housing assistance, public transportation subsidies, cash assistance for some categories of the "deserving" poor, the earned income tax credit, environmental initiatives, and some explicit public health strategies. However, with nearly the lowest rate of overall taxation of all nations in the Organization of Economic Cooperation and Development (OECD), and with so much of its public revenues devoted to investments in national defense, the United States has built one of the least mature welfare states among industrialized nations. And rarely outside the public health cognoscente are the non-medical predicates to health even discussed as part of an overt *health* strategy.[2]

Health status does come to the fore, however, when we talk about explicit medical conditions and health insurance. Forget, for a moment, all of the ways in which levels or disparities in income, wealth, and position influence the incidence of disease and poor health more generally. What happens when a person gets sick? Almost everyone agrees that access to medical care (and, more broadly defined, health care) is relevant to averting illness, reestablishing good health once ill, and managing the effects of chronic conditions that cannot be cured. We know, too, that individuals with insurance coverage—not just ad hoc access to health care providers through public clinics, charity, and goodwill—receive the most extensive and intensive treatment, often with better outcomes.[3] As other chapters have argued, research on the social determinants of health has made us well aware that even guaranteed access to medicine is far from being the panacea for sustained good health. Indeed, excess utilization can be as harmful as deficient care. Even when everyone in a firm or a country has nominally comparable insurance benefits, the pernicious effects on health of variations in income and status still reveal themselves. Nonetheless, the consensus about the significant role of insurance is so apparent that every one of the other 29 member states of the OECD, and all advanced and even less developed industrial societies worldwide, endow their citizens with some form of universal health insurance coverage. And if there is trepidation about potential disincentives for work, productivity, and responsibility created by dramatic efforts to reduce income inequality or by programs to provide the less affluent with nutritional, housing, educational, and other resources—a reason for the widely disparate policies across nations—such concerns have decidedly not thwarted the emergence of a near universal and reasonably consistent "international standard" of coverage and financing for medical services.[4] Even the Anglo countries with the most pronounced traditions of individual liberty and responsibility, from England itself to its former Canadian and Australian colonies, recognize the degree to which ill health has to do with genetic and experiential bad luck, and grant universal care.

The United States is the one startling exception. In this chapter, I take a more direct look at why this is the case by focusing on Congress where, when all is said and done, national public policy of this scope either succeeds or fails. I will also concentrate on the specific issue of universal health insurance coverage, which has the least contentious association with health status and is the indisputable norm for all other advanced industrial democracies. When it comes to national proposals for comprehensive health care reform, including ensuring universal coverage, Congress has been an unrelenting graveyard.

I start with the overall institutional setting of U.S. governance in which Congress is embedded and highlight the challenges it generally poses for large-scale policy making compared with those of other countries. Next, I turn to the general problem of coalition building in legislatures, using that foundation to illustrate the challenges and opportunities engendered by Congress in the twentieth century. From there, I zero in on how reform advocates, from organized interests, prominent members of Congress, and in particular selected presidents have pursued universal coverage in the congressional context. In the process, I will also highlight the manner in which our system's institutional features and health care politics have changed over time, creating different opportunities for coalition building. With that comes an explanation as to why those opportunities have been missed or ineffectively pursued. The health care reform debates of the early 1990s offer the most telling illustration of these dynamics. Finally, I close with some ideas for enhancing future opportunities to enact universal coverage.

## Not Coming to Our Consensus

The lack of insurance coverage of some kind for all is not for want of general support. Large public majorities consistently affirm that individuals ought to have access to medical services regardless of their income and social standing. Even in the context of the 2000 elections, which produced the first conservative, unified Republican government in nearly a half century, 64% of the public agreed that "it is the responsibility of the federal government to make sure all American have health care coverage." Significant majorities—in the range of 70% to 90% for the last 20 years—have found fault with the existing arrangements for financing and delivering health care and called, in some fashion, for major changes. Typically that support comes with the understanding that government would have to play an important role.[5] Though universal health care had strong advocates by the 1910s, it was not until 1939, when New York Senator Robert Wagner introduced a relatively modest, state-based health care reform bill, that something resembling national health insurance entered the congressional arena. That set the ball rolling. In 1943, Senator James Murray and Representative John Dingell joined Wagner to introduce the first bill to develop a national, comprehensive, universal health insurance program, this one tied to Social Security. (Dingell's son replaced his father in 1955 and has reintroduced the national health insurance bill in every Congress since.) In the fall of 1945, shortly after he assumed the presidency, Harry Truman became the first sitting president to launch a national, compulsory health insurance plan. He granted it a prominent place on his legislative agenda throughout the late 1940s. As part of the Great Society legislation of the 89th Congress in 1965–1966, President Lyndon Johnson successfully enacted Medicare and Medicaid, but did not press for universal coverage. In the next decade, politicians like Democratic Senator Ted Kennedy and Republican President Richard Nixon returned national health insurance to the political agenda. By early 1974, President Nixon offered an expansive Comprehensive Health Insurance Program (CHIP), designed to use employer mandates and public coverage for the working poor and unemployed to yield universal coverage. Nixon's plan, along with the competing Democratic plans, was the first health care reform proposal to engender serious congressional attention. In 1979, President Jimmy Carter proposed universal coverage provided by competing private health care plans financed by both employers and government. Although President Ronald Reagan avoided the issue, President George H.W. Bush made legislative overtures to expand insurance coverage, a defensive posture stimulated by rapidly escalating calls for health care reform and the introduction of major proposals by both Democratic and Republican leaders in the House and Senate. Finally, Bill Clinton campaigned in 1992 with health care reform and universal coverage as a centerpiece of his platform. He made his Health Security Act a lead issue on his subsequent presidential agenda.

Despite all of this attention to the issue at multiple times in the previous century, and notwithstanding the hundreds of plans formed and bills introduced, some offered by presidents and a few given the full weight of their administrations, *not a single health care reform initiative has ever come to a vote on the floor of either chamber of the U.S. Congress.* They have all been deflected by wanton congressional inaction. The first floor *debate*, held in the Senate, did not even ensue until the 103rd Congress and the presentation of Clinton's plan. How is it possible that Congress has proven so incapable of joining, or so unwilling to join, the international standard of universal coverage—the one strategy for mitigating health care disparities for which there is widespread support among the public and public officials? Sven Steinmo and Jon Watts, students of cross-national politics and social policy making, have a simple answer: "It's the Institutions, Stupid!"[6] First drafted before the failure of Clinton's health care reform effort, their article, subtitled "Why Comprehensive National Health Insurance Always Fails in America," argues that the design of our governing arrangements, especially Congress and its relationship with other institutions, has made and will always make it impossible to enact such sweeping reform.

At one level, this assertion is reasonable. James Madison and the other founders constructed a constitutional system conventionally termed "separation of powers." It is more accurately captured by Richard Neustadt's phrase, "separated institutions *sharing* powers."[7] Because of both explicit provisions of the Constitution and institutional arrangements that developed later, enacting legislation requires assembling a daunting series of like-minded coalitions in multiple venues—the House, the Senate, committees and subcommittees in each of those chambers—while also promoting or maintaining collaboration with the White House. Everything about American politics, such as the separate constituencies and election timetables for the president, the House and the Senate, makes that difficult to do.

The comparative context illustrates the point. Arend Lijphart identified a number of essential attributes of constitutional design that distinguish between two "ideal types" of democratic government: "majoritarian" and "consensus."[8] Thoroughly majoritarian systems simplify the burdens of decision making and concentrate power in the hands of the political party that won the most recent election. They have a single executive leader; executive and legislative authority is fused in a parliament from which the prime minister's cabinet is formed. The legislature has only one body with policy-making authority. Only two parties compete meaningfully in elections and on issues that clearly divide the parties; in those elections a legislative district is represented by the candidate who won a plurality of the vote. Lower-level governments are under the authority of the national government. And the constitution is unwritten, interpreted by the parliament instead of an independent branch of government.

New Zealand's political system is an example that fits this image nearly perfectly. As a result, with extraordinarily little difficulty, the government enacted a "radical health sector restructuring" in 1993 predicated on a major infusion of market-like arrangements. With similar institutional arrangements, including a disciplined unicameral parliament at the focal point, the United Kingdom and Canada had earlier built quite different publicly financed systems of universal coverage.[9]

Alternatively, nations that comport with Lijphart's "consensus" arrangements have governing systems in which taking action is challenging and requires the nurturing of pervasive agreement among myriad policy makers with authority in multiple venues. Everything about these systems fragments power where majoritarian systems concentrate it. They invite the interests with the largest stakes in any policy question to work the institutional crevices of dispersed policy making in order to veto those provisions they dislike.[10] While the United States possesses a number of majoritarian attributes (executive power concentrated in a single president, a two-party system, and plurality elections for Congress and the president), core features like the separation of powers, shared authority between the House and Senate, a federal system with semi-autonomous states (reflected back in the Senate and tensions between the House and Senate), and a written constitution with the independent judiciary as the final interpreter tilts our system heavily in the direction of the consensus model. That is one significant reason why Canada and the United States could have strikingly similar intense national debates about establishing a program of universal coverage and effective health care cost control in the 1940s and 1970s, but only Canada would eventually put such a system into place.[11] In addition, the United States has few of the other social institutions, such as muscular political parties, a tradition of strong government and effective administrative performance, and a widely organized and influential labor movement, that bridge remaining institutional divides in other countries. Elsewhere, these institutional arrangements contributed to the development of the advanced welfare state, including social insurance for health care.[12]

To end the story here, though, would be premature. However profound the differences between the governing structures of the United States and the other industrial nations, American institutional arrangements and health care politics have actually varied considerably. They have dramatically altered the prospects of reform from one period to the next. There have been times when we could have—indeed, perhaps came close to having—enacted universal coverage. The consistency of the policy outcome in the United States has obscured the substantial variability of the policy process. Steinmo and Watts have simply drawn too bright a line. Rather than accepting the notion that health care disparities are immutable even at the level of insurance and access to medical care, we have to ask ourselves what real opportunities for policy innovation in Congress have emerged in the past, what policy makers did with those opportunities, and exactly why health care reform met repeatedly with congressional inaction.

## Barriers to Coalition Building in Congress

Opportunities emerge in the legislative setting when a changed context makes it newly possible to pull together winning coalitions. What is required for that to happen? Three dimensions come to mind. Let us call them "party" (the percentage of seats held by the political party that generally favors the policy change), "cohesion" (the level of agreement or unity among the members of that party), and "structural coherence" (the degree to which the legislature's decision-making authority is concentrated rather than dispersed, and thus can be coordinated by the majority party).

The first dimension represents the proportion of the legislative chamber's membership that has a predisposition to support a particular policy approach. On many issues, including health care reform, a reasonable surrogate is the relative stature of the political party most likely to endorse the policy innovation. Although many Republicans in Congress have worked earnestly for health care reforms (the late Senator John Chafee of Rhode Island comes to mind), the most ardent advocates of universal coverage have consistently been Democrats. And they have been a fairly numerous bunch. Between 1933 and 1994 (during which the most important health care reform debates transpired), Democrats held majorities in the House for all but 4 years (1947–1948 and 1953–1954) and in the Senate for all but 10 years (the addition of 1981–1986). Sometimes those majorities were quite large. During Franklin D. Roosevelt's Second New Deal, Johnson's Great Society, and Jimmy Carter's first 2 years in office, Democrats controlled 77%, 68%, and 67% of the House, respectively, and roughly the same proportions of the Senate. When in the majority since 1932, Democrats have held on average approximately six of ten House and Senate seats. These are fairly healthy margins, and with majority control the Democrats have held the House speakership, leadership positions, considerable leverage over the floor agenda, the chairs of all committees and subcommittees, the bulk of the staff, and other legislative resources. Universal coverage should have had a leg up in Congress.

However, the second dimension of relevance to coalition building—cohesion—draws attention to how limited the utility of legislative majorities can be, especially in the American context. Let us stay with political party as a proxy for the potential coalition base. A deeply divided party, even if nominally in the majority, will not be able to deliver reliable votes for significant policy initiatives like health care reform. In many parliamentary systems, on such core votes the majority party has to hang together or, in the extreme case, the government falls. In Lijphart's "majoritarian" systems, rarely is a "government" (the prime minister and cabinet drawn from the parliamentary majority party) unable to hold the ranks together and secure a legislative victory, even for the most sweeping and controversial legislation. U.S. political parties at the national level could hardly be more different. For a host of reasons—such as relatively weak national party organizations; the use of primaries to select nominees for legislative office; the rise of campaign funding and operational resources independent of the parties; and significant differences between urban and rural, northern and southern constituency values—most members of the House and Senate most of the time have established a base in their constituencies that is not dependent on their party's electoral organizations or its legislative leadership.

As a result, both Democratic and Republican leaders have often had trouble getting large numbers of their representatives and senators to support the position adopted by most members of the party's caucus.[13] These difficulties are reflected in average "party unity scores"—the percentage of a party's members who voted with a majority of their compatriots when, on a recorded roll-call vote, a majority of one party voted against the majority of the other party. From 1954 to 1996, for example, Democratic Party unity on all such votes in the House ranged from a low of 70% during the Nixon administration to an 88% high in Clinton's first term (Republicans followed a similar pattern, and the Senate closely matched the House).[14]

The data for 1955 to 1994, during which Democrats enjoyed continuous control of the House of Representatives, illustrate the potential problem of achieving what might be called a *reliable* majority (one that would be of sufficient size *and* unity to produce an expected majority vote in favor of policy approaches presented on the floor). If one multiplies the percentage of seats controlled by the Democrats (the starting base in the calculation) times the average percentage of Democrats that voted with their party on party unity votes (a measure of how likely it was at that time for individual Democratic members to vote with their party), in only 18 out of the 40 years does the result produce on average at least a slim expected majority. Most of the time, therefore, having a majority in seats did not translate into mustering a majority of votes on contentious issues.

Of those 18 years, only 5 had a Democratic president (thus, a chief executive who would have endorsed Democratic health care reform efforts): Kennedy's third year, the 89th Congress during Johnson's Great Society, and Clinton's first 2 years in office. For reasons that have never been well explored, Johnson led the passage of Medicare and Medicaid when the combined size and unity of the Democratic majority in the House was at its postwar zenith, but chose not to offer a more expansive health care reform agenda. The situation in the Senate is even worse. Because of the filibuster, which allows any individual senator or small group of senators to block floor action by conducting endless debate, legislation can be thwarted unless a supermajority of 60 votes is available to enforce cloture on debate. Even during Johnson's heyday in the 89th Congress, the combined Democratic seats and unity nudged a bare majority in the Senate, well short of a sustained effective coalition that would be needed in the face of serious opposition on the floor. In short, if enactment of universal coverage depended on the Democratic Party in Congress alone, there have been precious few obvious windows of opportunity.

The reformers' task becomes even more complicated—and daunting—when we introduce the third dimension of coalition building: the structural coherence of the legislature itself. Put bluntly, are institutional power and resources concentrated in the hands of the majority and its leadership, or are they more widely dispersed? We start with the knowledge that congressional authority is evenly divided between two houses with very different organizational characteristics, constituencies, electoral schedules, and incentives. But we can go further. One can imagine three possible organizational arrangements in each chamber. The first would be a centralized structure, with the majority party leadership in command of decision-making—agenda control, staff, legislative mark-up, and so on. The most pristine form is the Westminster-style parliament found in New Zealand or the United Kingdom. When the majority party leadership wishes to act, it can act. The second form of legislative organization would be a decentralized institution in which power and resources are distributed beyond the majority party's leadership. For example, considerable authority is often granted to the chairs (or the members) of legislative committees. The consequences are most pronounced when committee chairs differ from the rest of the party members. In this setting, the committees might effectively veto reforms by not reporting out the relevant bills for consideration by the whole chamber; for example, the House Ways and Means Committee blocked Medicare throughout the Kennedy administration. However, when a committee favors legislation, it can move the initiative forward and build support for it on the floor. The final organizational form fragments power even further, perhaps granting most individual legislators the opportunity to influence the course of legislation. Working coalitions are difficult to orchestrate and maintain when so many individuals have a claim on the legislative process. Such dispersed power offers multiple paths to overcome one committee's opposition.

In reality, the House or Senate can display attributes associated with all three structural patterns, but at different moments some features become more pronounced than others. I have developed indices to represent these three patterns of power—centralization, decentralization, and fragmentation—in the House and Senate from 1909 to 2000.[15] The House of Truman's day, for example, ranked low in centralization and fragmentation, but high on the second dimension, decentralization; that is, the committee chairs wielded significant power. In addition, the committees that had jurisdiction over health care reform legislation were more conservative than the House as a whole, and their chairs opposed Truman's national health insurance plan. Veto they could and veto they did.

Fly forward to Carter's administration and one discovers a fundamentally changed legislative institution. The Democratic majority in the House was much larger, but also much more divided within itself. The power of the committee chairs (decentralization) had been supplanted by widespread fragmentation. Rank-and-file members had more staff and more influence. (The House came to look a lot more like the Senate, which has always been a more fragmented institution.[16]) The Carter years did not offer an opportune context for putting together a coalition on an issue as significant, complicated, and threatening to so many stakeholders as health care reform and universal coverage.

The congresses during which Bill Clinton ran for president and took office, however, showed more promising signs.[17] Many features of fragmentation remained. However, the committees of jurisdiction—all with chairs supportive of reform and members more liberal than the House as a whole—had regained some of their influence (the decentralization index was higher), and there were more rules that enhanced the influence of the Speaker to coordinate the legislative process. There were still plenty of institutional barriers, but at the start of the Clinton administration the 103rd Congress combined attributes—Democratic majority, unity, and institutional coherence—that gave reform-minded coalition builders a better organizational chance than they had had in any previous national health insurance round.

## Congress in the Web of Interests

Congressional deliberations do not, of course, occur in a vacuum. Indeed, health care policy has often been characterized as the natural result of interest group politics.[18] Mobilizing large memberships, leveraging skilled and well-endowed lobbying organizations, fertilizing congressional access with hefty campaign contributions, and sometimes financing sophisticated public relations drives, physicians, hospitals, insurers, and employers are thought to channel their way into the open legislative process, preserve their own interests, and fend off health care reform and universal coverage.[19]

For a long time, that imagery was consistent with the observable patterns of policy making on issues both small and large. When Franklin

Roosevelt contemplated health care coverage next to Social Security and Truman proposed national health insurance, the American Medical Association (AMA) led a powerful antireform alliance that included medicine, insurance, and business. It dominated the interest group scene and out-influenced what we might term the "stake challengers"—mainly labor unions who endorsed national health insurance. For the most part, in the highly decentralized Congress of the time, this antireform alliance found ready partners among the chairs and members of the committees of juris-diction. As presidents for the first time were moving universal coverage to their programmatic agendas, reform did not stand a chance in Congress. Anticipating the result, Roosevelt pulled back from even launching an initiative, and Truman's proposal could garner no more than a single, brief committee hearing.[20]

By the time that Richard Nixon and Jimmy Carter were engaged in their own health care reform efforts, the interest group world had begun to change. The rise of social movements in the 1960s and 1970s had given birth to new organizations representing consumers, women, environmentalists, and other segments of the population dedicated to social change. New "patrons of political action," including foundations and wealthy individuals, had emerged to help these organizations acquire the resources they needed to maintain themselves by overcoming the inherent difficulty of mobilizing large, dispersed groups of individuals for collective action.[21] Many of these "citizen" organizations would join with labor in challenging the stakeholder interests and promoting uni-versal coverage.[22] However, the antireform alliance remained unified in its opposition to such large-scale government intervention. Although the reform debates of the 1970s remained largely "inside-the-Beltway" con-tests, reformers faced significant challenges in the idiosyncratic features of presidential politics at the time (e.g., the ramifications of Nixon's Water-gate scandal), the general divisions among congressional Democrats, and the chaotic setting of the increasingly fragmented House and Senate.[23] However, Congress did more than hold brief perfunctory committee hearings. There had been one possible path to compromise on health care reform that could have emerged, and almost did.[24] More on that story in a moment.

Between Jimmy Carter's return home to Plains, Georgia, in 1981, and Bill Clinton's bus trip from Thomas Jefferson's Monticello to his inauguration in 1993, a metamorphosis took place in the community of organized interests focused on health care reform. More than a decade of sharply rising health care costs, huge disparities in coverage provided by large and small employers, and increased medical specialization splintered the old antireform alliance. The divisions emerged both across and within the domains of medicine, insurance, and business. In the meantime, more citizen groups arrived on the scene; most were sympathetic to universal coverage but some, such as the Christian Coalition, reflected a conservative countermobilization against greater government taxation and economic regulation.[25] Ironically, the two leading antagonists in the health care reform wars of the past—the AMA and organized labor—had each diminished considerably in strength. Instead of including nearly all practicing physicians, as in the past, the AMA's membership slipped to just four in ten doctors by the early 1990s. Labor's ranks had declined from representing better than a third of the labor force at its 1950s zenith to just under 15%.[26] By the late 1980s, these "peak associations" that once spoke for whole sectors of the economy had become "just another interest group" or "just one more PAC [political action committee]."[27] The AMA, for all intents and purposes, dropped entirely from the relevant set of organized interests on health care reform. Labor remained a player, but, as Marie Gottschalk describes in chapter 5, became weakened on this issue by its diminished base and its commitment to employer-based insurance.

New organizational leaders would emerge on both sides of the reform debate. The National Association of Independent Business (NFIB), the hard-right point organization for small business; the Health Insurance Association of America (HIAA), the trade association for commercial insurers; and the Pharmaceutical Research and Manufacturing Association (PhRMA), representing the drug companies, took up the charge against government reform. On the other side, the AARP (formerly known as the American Association of Retired Persons), Families USA, and Citizen Action—all either relatively recently founded or revitalized groups—provided much of the organizational wherewithal for the proreform forces.[28] The Democratic Congress of the early 1990s offered opportunities for each side of the debate. Which interest group coalition would coalesce most effectively, succeed in the court of public opinion, and demonstrate efficacious use of the legislative levers of influence? The gates to the congressional graveyard were unlocked, but would they open?

## Presidents in the Legislative Arena

The legislative dictum of the modern era is that the president proposes and Congress disposes. Like most maxims, that one is too simplistic. Even with the postwar enlargement of the presidency's aura in all matters of policy, foreign and domestic, Congress has continued to be the source of much legislative energy and policy innovation.[29] Nonetheless, it would be difficult to envision the enactment of a reform as expansive as universal health care coverage without the collaboration—indeed, the leadership—of the chief executive.[30] The only times that health care reform has been seriously on the agenda, regardless of the trends in the ranks of the uninsured or the costs of the health care system, has been when presidents have been formally engaged as initiators of formal proposals. That is not to say that their involvement has always been purely voluntary. Both Richard Nixon, with his comprehensive plan carried forward a bit by Gerald Ford, and George H. W. Bush, with his more incremental approach, were in some manner responding to the Democrats' potential advantage on this issue. Many presidents, of course, have also used their influence to thwart any reform impulses by simply ignoring the issue. Still, if one wants to assess those moments when something substantive about reform was in the air, one has to look to the actions of particular presidents.

Three possible strategies have been available for presidents interested in health care reform: combat, collaboration, and co-optation. And all three have been tried. Perhaps befitting his personality, and clearly linked to the context in which he served, Harry Truman chose combat. His plan for compulsory national health insurance, publicly financed, and linked to Social Security, was favorably received by the public but ran entirely counter to the constellation of organized interests and the preferences of members of Congress who dominated health care legislation, especially during the Republican Congress of 1947–1948. This was no effort to engage the stakeholder interests or skeptics in Congress. He sought to "give 'em hell," to attack the "do nothing Republican Congress," and to mobilize public opinion (although far too casually to be effective). No matter what he might have tried, however, an institutional analysis reveals that no strategy was available that could break the lock against health care reform. Defeat was ensured by the partnership of the antireform alliance's policy monopoly with the relevant committee chairs and members in Congress who were antagonistic to major government intervention in health care financing.

A second strategy is collaboration. To a large extent, that was the theme of the 1970s. Both Nixon and Carter sought to build universal coverage on the existing system of employer-sponsored insurance, filling in the gaps with a publicly financed program. Private insurers would not be put out of business, and employers (along with labor) would continue to have a primary role in offering coverage. By collaborating with both stakeholders and opposition members of Congress, each president envisioned a grand compromise.

A collaborative, bipartisan process might have had a chance. Flint Wainess argues, in fact, that in August 1974 we came very close to enacting universal coverage predicated on employer mandates and some public financing. A compromise appeared to be in motion among President Nixon (and then Ford), Senator Ted Kennedy (who had earlier advocated full public funding), Senator Russell Long (fairly conservative Democratic chair of the Senate Finance Committee), and Wilbur Mills, the chair of the House Ways and Means Committee who was always seeking ways to control the agenda as much as possible on his terms. Losing some southern Democrats but picking up a few Republicans, as well as holding onto all of the liberal Democrats on the Committee, Mills came within a vote or two of reporting out a bill that would have given universal coverage some momentum.[31] One can only speculate whether such a Ways and Means bill sent to the floor on a deeply split vote would have survived in the full House and then the Senate. Several Democrats, for example, were anticipating a huge Democratic pick-up in the fall elections following Nixon's resignation. Many were further convinced that 1976 would bring the election of a Democratic president committed to more expansive health care reform. They might have thwarted Mills's efforts in preparation for a better package in the future.[32] Two things remain clear, however. First, congressional committees (including Senate Finance) actually marked up legislation for the first time, suggesting that some version of reform appeared to emerge into the realm of the possible. But, second, universal coverage died again, never making it out of committee, never coming to the floor of either chamber.

I would argue that the Clinton period is the most intriguing, and beguiling, of all. In the early 1990s, the indicators of problems in the health care system were more pronounced than ever before. Health care costs continued to escalate rapidly. For the first time, the United States became a remarkable outlier, spending far more than any other nation on health care per capita and as a percentage of the gross domestic product. In addition, commencing around the mid-1980s, health care coverage started to shrink, reversing decades of broadening employer-based insurance and the enormous coverage gains achieved by Medicare and Medicaid. In another first, the AMA was hardly relevant as a health care power any longer, and to the extent it was involved in the debate, it had even endorsed universal coverage. The interest group politics of health care reform were up for grabs. As I noted earlier, too, Clinton could work with a Congress in which the size of the Democratic majorities and the general unity within them offered an unusual window of opportunity. The institutional character of the House, at least, afforded coalition-building advantages not found in previous periods. Taken together, by 1993 almost all the participants in health care reform politics and policy making, even the stakeholders vehemently opposed to the idea, had concluded that some version of reform would soon be enacted.[33]

Obvious risks remained, however. President Clinton was pursuing a popular idea—health care reform—but with no particular electoral mandate generated by his feeble plurality win of just 43% in the 1992 presidential election. Both the House and Senate still yielded opportunities for many members to delay or thwart legislative action, if they chose to do so. The Republicans in Congress had, in opposition, become just as unified in their ranks, as had the Democrats. Finally, all other advanced democracies had enacted and implemented their systems for universal coverage *before* the stakes in the status quo arrangements had grown so enormous for providers of all kinds, private insurers, and employers.[34]

Both during the presidential campaign and once in office, Clinton chose a strategy of co-optation to develop his approach to health care reform and universal coverage. The more combative approaches taken by Democrats in the past had led to defeat. Their proposals for publicly financed programs fed Republican rhetoric about Democrats as the "tax-and-spend" party. Several initially collaborative bipartisan efforts had also come up short, losing the support of both conservatives and liberals.[35]

Clinton's approach, reflected in the "managed competition under a budget" rubric of the Health Security Act, was to co-opt the left and right simultaneously, and along the way capture the voters, interest groups, and centrist members of Congress. Liberals would be energized by his commitment to universal coverage, achieved through a combination of employer mandates and an expanded public program that replaced Medicaid for the poor and unemployed; the cost-control discipline ensured by imposing a form of budget on health care expenditures backed up by insurance premium caps; and the standardization of basic coverage for people regardless of their socioeconomic standing. Conservatives would resonate with the "private," market-oriented features of the initiative—the primary use of private insurance carriers, the role of competition among insurance plans participating in "health alliances" to discipline costs and give people, as consumers, choices over insurance products, and the movement of Medicaid beneficiaries into private insurance.[36] Other provisions and subsidies would mitigate concerns about the employer mandate's impact on small businesses. With the left and right joined, health provider organizations, business groups, insurance carriers, and other moderate stakeholders would enlist in the coalition.

To avoid the pitfalls of previous bipartisan efforts, however, the *process* toward enacting legislation would follow the pattern Charles Jones describes as "co-partisanship."[37] Clinton and the Democrats would initially craft their version of health care reform; the Republicans would pursue their own. Then—each plan falling somewhere in the general domain of managed competition among private health insurance plans—a final compromise could be struck that was more expensive and regulatory than Republicans favored and launched more slowly, with greater variability in insurance arrangements, than Democrats preferred.

That was the projection. In reality, Congress was once again the graveyard of reform. Despite full engagement by several House and Senate committees, intense ongoing negotiations over alternatives and possible compromises, and even formal debate in the Senate chamber, universal coverage died once again without a single vote being taken on the floor of either the House or Senate. The full story, of course, is nuanced and complicated, the subject of numerous books.[38] For our purposes, let me highlight a few issues of particular relevance to Congress. To start, bicameralism became a major barrier. Because the Senate was more institutionally fragmented and more conservative than the House, the White House and Democratic leaders in Congress expected to pass legislation in the House first. That success would create the impetus needed to leverage favorable action in the Senate. But this strategy was stymied by the residual politics of Clinton's budget and economic program, enacted in the summer of 1993. That initiative had originally included a tax on energy consumption, calibrated using British thermal units (BTUs), a standard measure of energy. House Democrats stuck with the president in support of this controversial provision because he promised not to drop it in the Senate, where energy producers are more effectively represented. To get the Senate's agreement on the economic program, however, Clinton ultimately felt compelled to sacrifice the energy tax (Vice President Al Gore had to cast a tiebreaking final vote on the package). House members, not wanting to be "BTUed" again, insisted that the Senate move first on health care reform, which had equally controversial elements. Action in the Senate, though, was much harder to achieve. After intense and lengthy efforts behind closed doors and in open session, the Senate Finance Committee was not able to report out an acceptable compromise.

Passage of health care reform in either the Senate or the House was stymied by an intense, highly mobilized opposition that brought together most Republicans, including much of their leadership, with the "No-

Name Coalition," the new antireform alliance that emerged under the leadership of small business (the NFIB), health insurers (HIAA), and the pharmaceutical industry (PhRMA). Clinton's method of drafting the Health Security Act, and the byzantine substantive policy requirements of achieving universal coverage and cost control using disparate private institutions, also gave the opponents of health care reform the ammunition they needed to defeat the proposed legislation.

Because of the complexities involved in designing a fresh take on health care reform, and the emergence of issues like the budget fight, NAFTA ratification, and unexpected foreign policy setbacks, it took much longer to develop the president's initiative than expected (Clinton announced the plan in a major speech to the public from a joint session of Congress in September 1993, but the actual proposal was not available to Congress until the start of 1994). That gave the opposition time to find allies, marshal resources, develop a strategy, and hone a message. The Health Security Act itself, an intricate plan articulated in 1,342 pages of legislative language, provided keys to that message. Clinton's opponents unrelentingly declared the president's plan a "government takeover of health care"—a bureaucrat's dream for government intervention into every nook and cranny of one's relationship with doctors, hospitals, and insurers. In the meantime, the liberal groups, and liberal members of Congress, frequently refused to sign on.

The co-optation of left and right failed. Mike Lux, the White House liaison to health care groups, wrote in a May 3, 1993, confidential memorandum to Hillary Clinton, who was leading the President's health care reform effort: "I'm beginning to grow a little concerned that in our health care decision making, we may end up with a reform package that excites no one except our opposition—in other words, we could end up with a bill that generates intense opposition from several powerful special interests, but only lukewarm support from the people we've counted on to be our base."

In a survey I conducted of 120 health care interest groups after the end of the reform debate, the results were exactly as Lux predicted. Among groups that held positions and had resources that made them likely allies of Republican opponents to reform, almost 60% actively fought to defeat the Health Security Act. Among those organized interests that should have been targeted by Democrats and been fully mobilized advocates of reform, only about one quarter endorsed the president's plan. Another quarter favored it but did not formally lend their endorsement. Fully one half of these groups liked some features of the plan and but actually opposed others, thus preventing them from becoming active members of a coalition favorable to reform. These interest group results, I believe, closely parallel the reactions of both the public and members of Congress.[39]

Had Clinton chosen differently, would the results have been different? Congress may have been the graveyard, but did the president commit involuntary manslaughter? One answer is that Clinton, choosing another strategy, could hardly have done worse. Given the new opportunities I have discussed throughout this chapter, it seems hard to believe that more could not have been won. But it is impossible to know to whether an alternative approach might have shifted the outcome from one that saw no floor action in either house of Congress to enactment by both chambers.

Instead of managed competition under a budget, an entirely new idea, Clinton could have selected one of at least four other options. First, he could have launched reform with a bipartisan process designed to draft a method of obtaining universal coverage that would have attracted sufficient numbers of adherents from both parties. Such approaches in the past, however, had never attracted enough Republican support for the kind of provisions required to reach universal coverage.

Second, Clinton could simply have endorsed the "pay-or-play" plans already drafted by Democratic leaders in the Senate and House in the early 1990s. They would require employers to either provide insurance coverage to employees (play) or finance the coverage by contributing to a public program (pay).[40] Republicans, however, had not signed onto this approach; the 1992 campaign showed it vulnerable to their "tax-and-spend" criticism; and much of the interest group opposition would have been just as unyielding.

Third, rather than attempting sweeping reform, Clinton could have charted a long-term course for achieving universal coverage by signing onto proposals to expand insurance coverage. These approaches used either tax credits and deductions (the Bush approach) or targeted particular populations, such as children or the near elderly. But even if this kind of reform were enacted into law, it offered no guarantees of reaching anything remotely close to universal coverage. It would also ensure that the levels and quality of coverage would vary enormously across groups (and for individuals through different economic circumstances). In addition, it provided no mechanisms for addressing the central issue on the agenda in the 1990—the rising cost of health care. That was also a primary source of increases in federal deficits and thus constrained all social policy initiatives.[41]

Finally, the president could have taken the far bolder step of following in the footsteps of Truman and other past Democratic initiatives, adopting a "single-payer" approach of public national health insurance, perhaps a version of "Medicare for All."[42] The liberals in Congress would have been pleased—and mobilized. During the 102nd Congress, before Clinton took office, nearly 80 House Democrats had sponsored or cosponsored H.R. 1300, a single-payer bill. Many in the Senate had also drafted legislation along roughly those lines. The core progressive groups in the interest group community that Clinton had so ineffectively courted would have cheered and lent their strong grassroots support. Tied to Medicare, an enormously popular program, the public message would have been far simpler to convey. Most important, it would have anchored the initiative in symbols that resonate with the public (I recall Harvard's Robert Blendon, an analyst of public opinion on health care, telling the Senate Finance Committee in 1991 that no matter what approach to reform the Senate enacts, it should call the plan "Medicare").

Given all of the parameters I have surveyed in this chapter, I believe that the 103rd Congress offered the best opportunity in the twentieth century to fight for public financing of universal coverage. Interest group liaison Mike Lux, instead of lamenting the situation being produced by the Health Security Act, could have written memos about the enthusiasm, not the reticence, of "the base"; but he would also have been writing about the even more strenuous opposition. The No-Name Coalition would have initiated an intensified scorched-earth campaign about the government takeover of one's health care (with the very existence of private insurance directly threatened, the stakes could be not more stark). Republicans would have been in high dungeon about an attack on the very fabric of American liberties. In the midst of rising federal deficits, concerns about increased government spending and the problem of raising taxes in an antitax society would have been brought unavoidably front and center. A variety of provider and business organizations sympathetic to universal coverage, and even government involvement, would have balked at having the public sector assume such influence. It is anyone's guess how this high-stakes scenario would have played out, but it does offer some clues to future strategies.

## Making the System Work

Short of redesigning the constitutional architecture of American government to conform with the majoritarian model—a most unlikely proposition—any future efforts to get Congress to adopt a program of universal coverage will have to be responsive to the particular institutional dynamics I have discussed in this chapter, as well as the more encompassing roles played by values, socioeconomic classes, organized labor, and social movements examined by other contributors to this volume. Let me here identify a set of contextual factors that reform advocates must understand and be strategic about, if universal coverage is ever to be enacted.

The history of health care reform debates, and in particular the course of American politics in the last 25 years, confirm that addressing health care inequalities through government action and establishing a mechanism for providing universal coverage for health care services, will depend on the election of a Democratic president and Democratic majorities in Congress. These are clearly not sufficient conditions, but they are necessary. Richard Nixon stands alone as the only Republican president to have ventured so far toward systematic health care reform, and, indeed, expansions of social policy occurred under his watch. It is unlikely that a future Republican chief executive will play a similar role anytime in the foreseeable future.

Instead, the antagonism of Republican elected officials to an enhanced role for government has become all the more pronounced. Since roughly the early 1980s, the first years of the Reagan administration, the presidential and congressional wings of the GOP have become increasingly conservative. Roll-call data from the House and Senate reveal how far the Republican caucuses in Congress have shifted away from ideological moderation, and in the process have become more homogenous within their ranks.[43] Leading the opposition to health care reform of any kind, Newt Gingrich viewed such a proposed expansion of the social welfare state as a direct threat to the future growth and potential majority of a conservative Republican Party. Reform, therefore, had to be stopped in its tracks. In the 1994 congressional elections, he exploited the foibles of the Clinton administration, thwarted the Health Security Act, and helped engineer the election of the first Republican (and decided hard-right) majorities to control both houses of Congress in four decades.[44]

Today, with George W. Bush's ascension to the White House, we have the first fully unified Republican government in two generations, strikingly dominated by conservative forces. Although the language of his first campaign was moderate in tone, underscored by his commitment to be a "compassionate conservative," Bush in office has presided over the most conservative presidential agenda since early in the twentieth century. He continues to support extremely modest tax credits as a way to entice lower-income families into purchasing private health insurance, to be sure, but his proposed massive cuts in programs to assist the uninsured, among many other forms of redistribution of resources from the poor to the wealthy, leave little question that the prospects for universal coverage are all but nonexistent during Republican government.

For years one of the core challenges to proposals for expanded coverage was the federal deficit and the lack of resources to pay for it without raising taxes. As Theda Skocpol has pointed out, even with the unprecedented federal surpluses we were experiencing prior to the looming recession and terrorist attacks of 2001, which had been projected to persist over several years, covering the uninsured was off the table: "Ten years ago we were saying, 'Gee, we'd like to do it if we could afford it.' We don't even mention that anymore."[45]

More to the point, in pursuing the biggest ticket item on their own agenda, tax cuts, President George W. Bush and Republican leaders in Congress were extraordinarily effective in precisely the terms suggested by the analysis in this chapter. Despite being the first president since the election of 1876 to have lost the popular vote, thus entering office with a most questionable mandate, Bush has demonstrated the utility of political assets other than simple election returns. Seizing the opportunity of unified government (its significance reinforced by its novelty for the GOP), recognizing the relative unity within their House and Senate majorities, utilizing the congressional leadership's instruments for coalition building in the legislature, identifying a set of policy choices and thematic messages that would mobilize their base among organized interests (from business enterprises to the social movement politics on the right), and tapping effectively into the public's concerns about big government with a simple media message, Republicans were able to enact a program of enormous tax reductions that serve well their constituency and threaten to deny any future Democratic government the resources necessary for future program development, such as universal health care coverage. Not a single Republican member of the House or Senate broke ranks on the votes for the overall bill.[46]

Eventually the partisan winds will change. Future elections could once again grant Democrats the reins of unified government. When a new opportunity emerges for pursuing an agenda that includes universal health insurance coverage, those leading the reform vanguard will have to demonstrate unusual savvy in what I call the art of political entrepreneurship.[47] As demonstrated in recent years by Republican successes and Democratic failures, that demands the ability to recognize when more favorable political and institutional conditions have arisen, and precisely what approaches to health care reform are most suited to the new setting. For example, a serious opportunity was missed during the Nixon/Ford administrations because reform advocates both expected too much from waiting for a new president and were blind to the political virtues of a bipartisan approach given the institutional characteristics of the time (including the peak of fragmented power in the House and rather deep divisions within the causes of both parties). A careful reading of Congress, the parties in Congress, and changes in the interest group system would have highlighted what could be achieved with greater accommodation.

Bill and Hillary Clinton, on the other hand, fully and appropriately recognized the unusual window of opportunity created in the early 1990s, but, in my view, profoundly misread *how* to best exploit the new situation in Congress and the community of organized interests. Although there were a few Republican moderates willing to play, the Republicans in Congress by this time—in contrast to the 1970s—were mostly unified in opposition to major government initiatives. The Democrats, too, were far more united than in the past, but the benefits of that comity had to be grasped quickly.

Most important, compared to previous reform eras, many new citizen groups were available for the kind of grassroots mobilization that lends resiliency to the congressional Democratic majorities. The Clintons, however, chose a policy strategy and process that only solidified the Republican and interest group opposition and kept the "natural base" in Congress and among organized interests from coming together. At the same time, once Clinton, during the campaign and then in office, chose his policy direction on health care reform, the leaders of liberal groups were too rigid to adapt adequately to the new nexus of politics and program.

Another essential message of the more recent health care reform debates, and the politics of tobacco, among other areas, is the instrumental value of not just garnering the support of conventional organized interests, but also profiting from the whole social movement that lies behind many of these organizations.[48] Commercial trade associations, nonprofit outfits, and citizen groups all now use a form of public mobilization. For many large-scale policy debates, quiet inside lobbying is no longer sufficient to influence the legislative process, even for commercial interests.[49] The No-Name Coalition was successful in contributing to the death of Clinton's Health Security Act because of its close ties to Republican health care reform opponents in Congress, to be sure, but also as a result of its extensive media campaign to shift public opinion and its capacity to mobilize political action at the grass roots, from small businesses throughout the nation to individuals in the Christian Right.[50] One U.S. senator active in the health care reform battles of the 103rd Congress lamented to me that a major cause of defeat was the failure to reach the public effectively through broad-based social movement–like mobilization by progressives.

Without the rise of citizen engagement of this scope and level of intensity, the proponents of major changes in social policy lack the necessary political leverage to overcome the influence of stakeholder interests and their politician allies who can lay claim to vital institutional niches of American policy making.

Is this kind of progressive grassroots politics possible in the United States? One supportive of policies that would mitigate the challenging politics of health care inequality? The disquieting answer is that 1992 may have presented the best shot in the modern era, had there been attuned political leadership to capture the moment. The presidential election that year was all about the call for change and making things work. Nearly two out of three voters "wanted to put an end to business as usual."[51] Ross Perot rode (and helped inspire) the tidal wave of discontent that gave him the largest vote share for a third-party candidate in presidential elections since 1912. People were alienated. Nearly one half of Americans responding to surveys said that government would be improved if *every* elected official were replaced in this election. Among Perot supporters, the figure was 57%.[52] Perot's main focus was on the weak economy, insecure jobs, and the mounting federal debt, but his campaign, including a commitment to universal health insurance coverage, also had a populist impulse to enhance the economic and social security of average Americans by giving them active and competent government.[53]

The first 2 years of the Clinton presidency ended up in part being a battle between the Democratic administration and congressional Republicans to enlist the army of alienated, distrustful citizens energized by Perot in order to take decisive control of the future contours of American politics. Clinton's effort at health care reform and sudden emphasis on fiscal discipline tapped this vein, but Republicans proved to be far more successful in mining the discontent and the anger at government. Clinton's impenetrable Health Security Act and his failure to solve the problems plaguing health care seemed to feed the perception that activist government was at once too intrusive and all thumbs.

Finally, one must carefully consider what symbols and rhetoric a particular policy approach permits. Because American governance requires the holding together of coalitions in multiple venues and grants access to opposition forces in many institutional fissures within the system, health care reform is more likely to succeed when the structure of the policy approach and the associated message adhere to relatively simple principles consistent with values Americans already hold dear. Clinton's novel method for bridging the left-right divisions turned out to be too clever by half. The complexity of the Health Security Act, and its inability to connect to well-established positive symbols of government action, made it impossible to explain quickly, parsimoniously, and adequately. It confused the public and hobbled the groups that could have orchestrated grassroots support. Yet it afforded adversaries an uncomplicated line of attack—"a government takeover of medical care"—that proved difficult to challenge. Employer mandates (devoid of the Health Security Act superstructure) or "Medicare for All" play to common experience and understandable themes.

For all the apparent consistency of the congressional graveyard and the undeniable barriers that continue to threaten efforts at reform, the American political process is not ever cast in stone. Nor are the policy outcomes. The path of policy deliberation and decision is affected by the rich, intertwined texture of contemporaneous politics. Only an astonishingly astute practitioner of congressional politics could have fully anticipated the ramifications for health care reform of the BTU experience. The antennae of reform advocates and President Clinton, however, should have picked up some signals.

Long ago, Richard Neustadt argued that the successful application of presidential power hinges on making good judgments about how decisions made today, whatever the issue, will affect the future power stakes surrounding a decision to be made in the future.[54] A strategy for enacting universal coverage, therefore, not only rests on the partisan composition of Congress (and the partisan orientation of the president); a sophisticated recognition and interpretation of the ever changing political landscape specifically relevant to health care policy; a sustained project of social movement mobilization; and a well-honed, accessible synthesis of policy approach and message. It also demands a full appreciation of, and adaptability to, the complex interdependencies of the politics of the moment.

## Notes

1. Jennifer M. Mellor and Jeffrey Milyo, "Reexamining the Evidence of an Ecological Association between Income Inequality and Health," *Journal of Health Politics, Policy and Law* 26 (June 2001): 487–522.

2. *OECD Health Data 1996* (CD-Rom).

3. Institute of Medicine, National Academy of Sciences (Washington, DC: National Academy Press, 14 January 2004).

4. Joseph White, *Competing Solutions: American Health Care Proposals and International Experience* (Washington, DC: Brookings Institution, 1995).

5. Lawrence R. Jacobs and Robert Y. Shapiro, "Don't Blame the Public for Failed Health Care Reform," *Journal of Health Politics, Policy and Law* 20 (Summer 1995): 416–417; Gallup Poll, September 2001; poll data from 1982 to 2000.

6. Sven Steinmo and Jon Watts, "It's the Institutions, Stupid! Why Comprehensive National Health Insurance Always Fails in America," *Journal of Health Politics, Policy and Law* 20 (Summer 1995): 329–372.

7. Richard E. Neustadt, *Presidential Power* (New York: John Wiley & Sons, 1960), 42, italics in the original.

8. Arend Lijphart, *Democracies: Patterns of Majoritarian and Consensus Government in Twenty-One Countries* (New Haven, CT: Yale University Press, 1984).

9. Robin D. C. Gauld, "Big Bang and the Policy Prescription: Health Care Meets the Market in New Zealand," *Journal of Health Politics, Policy and Law* 25 (October 2000): 815; White, *Competing Solutions*.

10. Ellen M. Immergut, *Health Politics: Interests and Institutions in Western Europe* (New York: Cambridge University Press, 1990); Charles H. Blake and Jessica R. Adolino, "The Enactment of National Health Insurance: A Boolean Analysis of Twenty Advanced Industrial Countries," *Journal of Health Politics, Policy and Law* 26 (August 2001): 679–708.

11. Antonia Maioni, "Nothing Succeeds Like the Right Kind of Failure: Postwar National Health Insurance Initiatives in Canada and the United States," *Journal of Health Politics, Policy and Law* 20 (Spring 1995): 5–30.

12. Lawrence Jacobs, "Health Disparities in the Land of Equality," chapter 2 in this volume; Blake and Adolino, "The Enactment of National Health Insurance"; Immergut, *Health Politics*; Sven Steinmo, Kathleen Thelen, and Frank Longstreth, eds., *Structuring Politics: Historical Institutionalism in Comparative Analysis* (New York: Cambridge University Press, 1992).

13. Roger H. Davidson, ed., *The Postreform Congress* (New York: St. Martin's Press, 1992); Allen D. Hertzke and Ronald M. Peters, Jr., eds., *The Atomistic Congress: An Interpretation of Congressional Change* (New York: M. E. Sharpe, 1992); Lawrence R. Jacobs and Robert Y. Shapiro, *Politicians Don't Pander: Political Manipulation and the Loss of Democratic Responsiveness* (Chicago: University of Chicago Press, 2000); Thomas E. Mann and Norman J. Ornstein, eds., *The New Congress* (Washington, DC: American Enterprise Institute, 1981); David W. Rhode, *Parties and Leaders in the Postreform House* (Chicago: University of Chicago Press, 1991); Barbara Sinclair, *Legislators, Leaders, and Lawmaking: The U.S. House of Representatives in the Post-Reform Era* (Baltimore: Johns Hopkins University Press, 1982); Barbara Sinclair, *Majority Leadership in the U.S. House* (Baltimore: Johns Hopkins University Press, 1983); and Barbara Sinclair, *The Transformation of the U.S. Senate* (Baltimore: Johns Hopkins University Press, 1989).

14. Norman J. Ornstein, Thomas E. Mann, and Michael J. Malbin, *Vital Statistics on Congress, 1997–1998* (Washington, DC: Congressional Quarterly, 1998), 200–201, 213.

15. Mark A. Peterson, "Stalemate: Opportunities, Gambles, and Miscalculations in U.S. Health Policy Innovation," book manuscript. My measures include the characteristics and allocation of staff resources, legislative mark-up and hearing activities, the process of selecting committee chairs, and the availability of rules that empower leadership.

16. Davidson, ed., *The Postreform Congress*; Hertzke and Peters, Jr., eds., *The Atomistic Congress*; Mann and Ornstein, eds., *The New Congress*; Rhode, *Parties and Leaders in the Postreform House*; Barbara Sinclair, *Legislators, Leaders, and Lawmaking*; Sinclair, *Majority Leadership in the U.S. House*; Sinclair, *The Transformation of the U.S. Senate*; Steven S. Smith and Christopher J. Deering, *Committees in Congress* (Washington, DC: CQ Press, 1984).

17. Peterson, "Stalemate."

18. Robert R. Alford, *Health Care Politics: Ideological and Interest Group Barriers to Reform* (Chicago: University of Chicago Press, 1975); Paul J. Feldstein, *Health Associations and the Demand for Legislation: The Political Economy of Health* (Cambridge: Ballinger Publishing, 1977); Starr, *The Social Transformation of American Medicine* (New York: Basic Books, 1982); Carol S. Weissert and William G. Weissert, *Governing Health: The Politics of Health Policy* (Baltimore: John Hopkins University Press, 1996).

19. Mark A. Peterson, "From Trust to Political Power: Interest Groups, Public Choice, and Health Care Markets," *Journal of Health Politics, Policy and Law* 26 (October 2001): 1145–1163.

20. Frank D. Campion, *The A.M.A. and U.S. Health Policy Since 1940* (Chicago: Chicago Review Press, 1984); Peterson, "Stalemate"; Mark A. Peterson, "Congress in the 1990s: From Iron Triangles to Policy Networks," James A. Morone and Gary S. Belkin, eds., *The Politics of Health Care Reform: Lessons from the Past, Prospects for the Future* (Durham: Duke University Press, 1994), 103–147; Monte M. Poen, *Harry S. Truman versus the Medical Lobby* (Columbia: University of Missouri Press, 1979).

21. Mancur Olson, *The Logic of Collective Action* (Cambridge, MA: Harvard University Press, 1965); and Jack L. Walker, Jr., *Mobilizing Interest Groups in America: Patrons, Professions, and Social Movements* (Ann Arbor: University of Michigan Press, 1991).

22. Peterson, "Congress in the 1990s."

23. Peterson, "Stalemate"; Flint J. Wainess, "The Ways and Means of National Health Care Reform, 1974 and Beyond," *Journal of Health Politics, Policy and Law* 24 (April 1999): 305–333.

24. Wainess, "The Ways and Means of National Health Care Reform."

25. Peterson, "Stalemate"; Theda Skocpol, *Boomerang: Clinton's Health Security Effort and the Turn against Government in U.S. Politics* (New York: W. W. Norton, 1996).

26. Barnaby J. Feder, "Medical Group Battles to Be Heard over Others on Health-Care Changes," *New York Times* (11 June 1993): A-22; Michael Goldfield, *The Decline of Organized Labor in the United States* (Chicago: University of Chi-

cago Press, 1987); Marie Gottschalk, *The Shadow Welfare State: Labor, Business, and the Politics of Health Care in the United States* (Ithaca, NY: Cornell University Press, 2000).

27. John P. Heinz, Edward O. Laumann, Robert L. Nelson, and Robert H. Salisbury, *The Hollow Core: Private Interests in National Policy Making* (Cambridge, MA: Harvard University Press, 1993); Peterson, "From Trust to Political Power;" Peterson, "Stalemate"; Richard Sammon, "Fall of Striker Bill Spotlights Doubts about Labor Lobby," *Congressional Quarterly Weekly Report* (20 June 1992): 1810.

28. Haynes Johnson and David S. Broder, *The System: The American Way of Politics at the Breaking Point* (Boston: Little, Brown, 1996); Peterson, "Stalemate."

29. Charles O. Jones, *The Presidency in a Separated System* (Washington, DC: Brookings Institution, 1994).

30. Mark A. Peterson, *Legislating Together: The White House and Capitol Hill from Eisenhower to Reagan* (Cambridge, MA: Harvard University Press, 1990).

31. Wainess, "The Ways and Means of National Health Care Reform."

32. Starr, *The Social Transformation of American Medicine.*

33. Mark A. Peterson, "Report from Congress: Momentum toward Health Care Reform in the U.S. Senate," *Journal of Health Politics, Policy and Law* 17 (Fall 1992): 553–573; Mark A. Peterson, "The Politics of Health Care Policy: Overreaching in an Age of Polarization," *The Social Divide: Political Parties and the Future of Activist Government*, ed. Margaret Weir (Washington, DC, and New York: Brookings Institution and Russell Sage Foundation, 1998), 181–229.

34. Lawrence R. Jacobs, "The Politics of America's Supply State: Health Reform and Technology," *Health Affairs* 14 (Summer 1995): 143–157.

35. Peterson, "The Politics of Health Care Policy."

36. Jacob Hacker, *The Road to Nowhere: The Genesis of President Clinton's Plan for Health Security* (Princeton, NJ: Princeton University Press, 1997); Paul Starr, *The Logic of Health Care Reform: Why and How the President's Plan Will Work* (New York: Whittle, 1994).

37. Jones, *The Presidency in a Separated System.*

38. See, for example, Gottschalk, *The Shadow Welfare State*; Hacker, *The Road to Nowhere*; Jacobs and Shapiro, *Politicians Don't Pander*; Johnson and Broder, *The System*; Cathie Jo Martin, *Stuck in Neutral: Business and the Politics of Human Capital Investment Policy* (Princeton, NJ: Princeton University Press, 2000); Peterson, "Stalemate"; and Skocpol, *Boomerang.*

39. Mollyann Brodie and Robert J. Blendon, "The Public's Contribution to Congressional Gridlock on Health Care Reform," *Journal of Health Politics, Policy and Law* 20 (Summer 1995): 403–410; Hacker, *The Road to Nowhere*; Jacobs and Shapiro, *Politicians Don't Pander*; and David W. Brady and Kara M. Buckley, "Health Care Reform in the 103rd Congress: A Predictable Failure," *Journal of Health Politics, Policy and Law* 20 (Summer 1995): 447–454.

40. Skocpol, *Boomerang.*

41. Peterson, "The Politics of Health Care Policy."

42. Skocpol, *Boomerang.*

43. Jacobson, "Party Polarization in National Politics"; Jacobs and Shapiro, *Politicians Don't Pander.*

44. Peterson, "The Politics of Health Care Policy."

45. Robin Toner, "The World: Capitalist Tools; Cutting a Rightward Path," *New York Times* (4 March 2001): 4-1.

46. Such unity and support for the president was not ensured on all issues, however. See, for example, Janet Hook, "The Nation: GOP Moderates Willing to Defy Party, Politics," *Los Angeles Times* (23 July 2001): 13.

47. Peterson, "Stalemate."

48. Constance A. Nathanson, "Social Movements as Catalysts for Policy Change: The Case of Smoking and Guns," *Journal of Health Politics, Policy and Law* 24 (June 1999): 421–488.

49. Ken Kollman, *Outside Lobbying: Public Opinion & Interest Group Strategies* (Princeton, NJ: Princeton University Press, 1998).

50. Raymond L. Goldsteen, Karen Goldsteen, James H. Swan, and Wendy Clemens, "Harry and Louise and Health Care Reform: Romancing Public Opinion," *Journal of Health Politics, Policy and Law* 26 (December 2001): 1325–1352; Jacobs and Shapiro, *Politicians Don't Pander;* Johnson and Broder, *The System;* Peterson, "The Politics of Health Care Policy"; and Skocpol, *Boomerang.*

51. R. W. Apple, Jr., "The 1992 Elections: New Analysis," *New York Times* (4 November 1992): 1.

52. Steven A. Holmes, "The 1992 Elections: Disappointment—New Analysis," *New York Times* (5 November 1992): 1.

53. Ross Perot, *United We Stand: How We Can Take Back Our Country* (New York: Hyperion, 1992).

54. Neustadt, *Presidential Power.*

# 8

# Courts, Inequality, and Health Care

## PETER D. JACOBSON AND ELIZABETH SELVIN

*On a Populistic Basis. Harper's Weekly,*
September 12, 1896.

Within recent memory, there was a time when the judiciary eagerly accepted the challenges of economic and social inequality. Invited by a welcoming Supreme Court under Chief Justice Earl Warren, liberals used litigation to achieve social goals when other policy solutions, particularly legislative, were blocked by a more conservative establishment. For a relatively brief period in the 1960s, it seemed as though litigation was the answer to society's most pressing and intractable social policy dilemmas. All it took to remedy racial segregation was to issue a Supreme Court opinion declaring an odious practice unconstitutional, such as the refusal to serve blacks in a restaurant, and social justice would prevail.

As a young attorney in the early 1970s, Peter Jacobson (coauthor of this chapter) began a legal career with the fervent conviction that the courts were instruments of social change. The remnants of the Warren Court permitted the dream that when other social institutions ignored or abandoned social and economic disparities, the courts would surely act differently. Now, 30 years later, that legal world no longer exists. A nearly 25-year retrenchment against so-called judicial social activism has been transformed into a judicial approach to social and economic disparities that can at best be described as indifferent and at worst as hostile. The conservative judicial counterreformation has taken hold, resulting in a shift of power back to the legislative branch of government.

Where courts once protected those without power and influence, they now genuflect to the powerful and influential. Where courts once offered expansive interpretations of congressional legislation to reduce social inequalities, they now interpret congressional intent narrowly to preserve the status quo. Where courts once perceived inequalities to be evidence of governmental failure, they now take the distribution of goods and services as a given. This chapter reflects on these changes as they apply to health care inequalities.

## The Courts as Policy Makers: The Historical Context

Like it or not, the judiciary plays an important role in social policy. At a minimum, the Supreme Court's role in interpreting the Constitution assures it a central place in deciding some of the most contentious social policy issues. Beyond that, courts have traditionally reviewed and interpreted state and federal legislation. Judicial review therefore provides the courts with a unique role in the American legal system.

Prior to the New Deal in the 1930s, the U.S. Supreme Court routinely blocked states from regulating economic and social activity and decided that most of the early New Deal legislation was unconstitutional. After Franklin Roosevelt's landslide election in 1936, the Court removed its objections and allowed the New Deal legislation to be implemented. But it wasn't until the 1960s that the Supreme Court became actively involved in changing social policy. Most of the public attention (and antipathy) to the judiciary's social policy advocacy emanated from the Warren Court's constitutional rulings expanding civil rights and criminal rights, as well as the Court's subsequent protection of abortion rights. Yet an equally important set of Warren Court rulings aggressively attacked social problems through broad interpretation of legislation that pushed social problems to the forefront of the Court's agenda and forced the government and country to confront social and economic inequality.

Whatever one may think of the Warren Court's vigorous social policy advocacy, we currently inhabit a fundamentally different legal universe than the one Warren and his supporters helped create. Social policy questions aggressively attacked by the Warren Court are equally aggressively avoided by the current Rehnquist Court. Consider, for example, the case of *Pegram v. Herdrich*.[1] Speaking for a unanimous Supreme Court, Justice David Souter deflected one of today's most pressing health policy questions to Congress: Do managed care's financial incentives interfere with patient care? Today, that's not for the courts to say. Imagine Chief Justice Earl Warren, also speaking for a unanimous Supreme Court in 1954, saying that Congress should impose school desegregation, not the courts. It's hard to envision what might have emerged absent the Court's leadership in civil rights.[2]

Aside from the generally conservative nature of today's judiciary, factors intrinsic to health care contribute to limited prospects that the courts will redress health care inequalities any time soon. More often than not, courts defer to the will of the majority (as expressed by the legislative branch) or to the market, rather than attempting to lead social change. In a market-driven health care system, remedying disparities in access to health care seems a distant afterthought. Courts may not be barriers to reducing health care inequalities, but they are unlikely to lead the attack. In essence, courts maintain the status quo. Despite occasional bursts of expansive decisions that help shape social policy, courts are generally reactive institutions that protect existing social and economic arrangements. Taking into consideration the courts' current reluctance to establish new rights or usurp legislative functions, it is unlikely that the judiciary will use their available tools to fundamentally challenge health care inequalities in the near future.

## Inequality and the Courts: Is Anyone Listening?

### Framing the Judicial Inquiry

The historical development of health care delivery in the United States shapes the way in which inequalities might be framed if challenged in court. Health care is different from other aspects of social policy. Unlike welfare, which is a governmental entitlement program, or education, which is a legal requirement, health care is provided by the private sector based on voluntary contractual arrangements. Until the mid-1960s, most hospitals provided large amounts of charity care, thus minimizing the disparities in access to medical care seen today. But the advent of technologically sophisticated and expensive health care services, growing governmental reimbursement for Medicare and Medicaid, and sharpening competition among health care payers (who respond by working hard to control their costs) has made it difficult for hospitals to provide the same level of charity care. When combined with increasingly expensive health insurance, the result is substantial growth in the number of people without access to health care services.

Despite differences with other areas of social policy, the courts still have adequate mechanisms for addressing health care inequalities. If it so desired, the Supreme Court could interpret the Constitution broadly to mandate a right to health care. Courts could also address disparities in health care services through creative statutory interpretations that expand access to particular services or by broadly interpreting insurance contracts to expand the meaning of what constitutes a medically necessary service. The distinction between creating new rights and a broad interpretation of legislation designed to reduce health care inequalities is important for understanding how the courts will frame the judicial inquiry into health inequality.

### Ducking Inequalities—The Absence of Judicial Leadership

When interpreting legislation, courts are often presented with opportunities to address health care inequalities. Among the many possible examples, we will describe four instances showing the judiciary's reluctance to confront health care inequalities. The results are not promising for those looking to the courts for leadership. These examples are selected either for their direct applicability to the disparities just described or for a general potential to reduce disparities. A number of other illustrations could be included, but we are not aware of any case that would produce a different result.

*Medicare and Medicaid.* The Medicare program provides health coverage for virtually all persons aged 65 and over in the United States. Medicaid is a state-federal program that provides health coverage for poor persons who meet certain eligibility requirements, mostly defined by each state. Individuals who are poor and are also blind, disabled, or have dependent children are generally eligible for Medicaid. Both programs have increased the availability of medical care for certain groups of people.

By their very nature, these programs are characterized by economic inequalities. Medicare, for example, did not provide coverage for prescription drugs until 2005, and recipients must purchase supplemental insurance for certain services. Medicaid benefits vary across states and are much less generous than Medicare, offering particular opportunities for judicial intervention. As illustrated by Colleen Grogan and Eric Patashnik in chapter 9, the Medicaid program is rife with equity concerns, particularly with regard to differential benefits for poor families and the elderly, blind, and disabled. Indeed, Grogan and Patashnik suggest that Medicaid has actually exacerbated existing health care inequalities. Repeatedly, however, the courts have refused to redress inequalities in government health care programs.

In a landmark case, *Alexander v. Choate*,[3] Medicaid beneficiaries challenged the Tennessee Medicaid program's 14-day limitation on annual inpatient days as a violation of Section 504 of the Rehabilitation Act of 1973. The beneficiaries argued that the limitation disproportionately affected persons with disabilities who would require more inpatient care. In rejecting the challenge, the Supreme Court suggested that Congress did not intend to require the state to provide specific levels of care and that the state retained considerable discretion in how to structure its program. Significantly, the Court signaled its unwillingness to address any resulting inequalities by stating that "to require that the sort of broad-based redistributive decision . . . always be made in the way most favorable, or least disadvantageous, to the handicapped . . . would be to impose a virtually unworkable requirement on state Medicaid administrators" (p. 308).

*Alexander v. Choate* characterizes the prevailing judicial attitude toward addressing deficiencies in state and federal programs. It is hard to imagine a more explicit statement opposing an expansive role in redressing social inequalities. Since this case, the courts have only rarely taken affirmative steps to address inequalities in governmental health care programs, despite increasing evidence of widening racial and socioeconomic disparities in Medicare and Medicaid.

As an example of how the legal landscape has changed, Warren-era courts applied robust due process requirements before permitting the government to terminate benefits (as discussed later). Those due process requirements have not been pursued in the Rehnquist era. For instance, in a case involving a challenge to denial of Medicare benefits, the beneficiary alleged a denial of due process for failure to provide a hearing before denying benefits. Despite a favorable ruling from the Ninth Circuit Court of Appeals, the Supreme Court reversed, stating that the Medicare carrier was a private entity and not subject to due process requirements.[4]

*Emergency Medical Treatment and Active Labor Act.* Congress enacted the Emergency Medical Treatment and Active Labor Act of 1986 (EMTALA) in response to concerns about "patient dumping." This occurs when patients who are unable to pay are refused emergency medical treatment or are transferred from one hospital to another before their condition has been diagnosed and stabilized. Underlying the EMTALA statute is the assumption that people have a right to at least basic emergency medical attention regardless of insurance status or ability to pay. EMTALA requires that a patient be diagnosed and stabilized before being transferred to another facility. Most states have more stringent requirements for emergency departments to provide care of last resort.

The original legislative intent of EMTALA was to reduce discriminatory practices in emergency rooms and prohibit socioeconomic inequalities in access to emergency medical treatment. From its inception, however, the legislative goals of EMTALA were not well defined, allowing considerable room for judicial interpretation. The Supreme Court first addressed EMTALA in *Roberts v. Galen* of Virginia,[5] holding that a plaintiff does not need to prove that the failure to provide emergency treatment resulted from an improper motive. But the courts have generally held that EMTALA's requirements are limited in scope: EMTALA's duty to stabilize a patient only applies to emergency medical conditions that are diagnosed at the time of the patient's initial screening in the emergency room. Once those emergency medical conditions have been stabilized, the requirements of EMTALA are wholly satisfied and the statute does not impose any obligations with respect to further conditions or complications that may arise after the hospital admits the patient for treatment. After initial screening and stabilizing treatment, the hospital's duty is solely governed by state law.

EMTALA does not establish a federal standard of emergency medical care, and the courts have refused to broaden EMTALA to address inequalities in access to basic medical services. As a general proposition, courts have deferred to Congress for any such expansion. Under current law, where no emergency situation (or other exception) exists, physicians in a fee-for-service arrangement retain the authority to refuse treatment to any individual without facing legal liability.[6]

To be sure, some opinions have expanded EMTALA's scope. For example, courts have held that EMTALA applies to all patients in the hospital who have an emergency condition, not just those who arrive for treatment in the emergency room. Courts have also applied EMTALA to all parts of a hospital or health care system. Nonetheless, most judicial interpretations of EMTALA have been restrictive, holding that the courts should not address the efficacy or appropriateness of medical procedures performed under the statute. Most courts have ruled that EMTALA ensures only that the hospital's protocol is uniformly followed regardless of a patient's ability to pay.[7]

*Hill-Burton Act.* The 1947 Hill-Burton Act was passed in response to a perceived national shortage of hospitals and provided federal monies for the unprecedented expansion of the U.S. hospital sector. The primary intent of the Hill-Burton Act was to provide federal financial assistance to states to "provide for adequate hospitals and other facilities" and "to furnish needed services for persons unable to pay." To this end, the act required that the facilities receiving assistance must (1) make the facility available to all persons residing in the territorial area, and (2) provide a "reasonable volume of services" to persons unable to pay. Unfortunately, these two stipulations—the "community service obligation" and the "reasonable volume" (or "uncompensated care") assurances—were not well defined and initially not widely enforced.

The Hill-Burton obligations were at best a vague and limited legislative attempt to address economic and social inequalities in the provision of health care services. From 1946 to 1976, the Hill-Burton program supported the construction of 40% of hospital beds in the United States.[8] But the community service and reasonable volume requirements were largely ignored by hospitals receiving Hill-Burton funds. It was not until the late 1970s when federally funded legal service lawyers persuaded the federal courts to enforce these requirements of the Hill-Burton statute.[9] During this time, advocacy groups for indigent patients unsuccessfully sought to use Hill–Burton to establish a right to health care for the indigent.

In 1979, primarily in response to Hill–Burton litigation, the Department of Health and Human Services (DHHS) issued regulations interpreting the community service and uncompensated care requirements. These requirements placed severe time limits on the uncompensated care provision, but did not place any time limits on the community service requirement. For most Hill–Burton hospitals, the uncompensated care requirement expired more than 10 years ago, having had only a limited effect on the quantity of uncompensated services provided to indigent patients. The courts have consistently rejected the opportunity to expand Hill–Burton's community service requirement, which remains in place, beyond the DHHS regulatory provisions.

The community service obligation of the Hill–Burton Act is one of the clearest opportunities for courts to interpret legislation to reduce inequalities in access to health care services. Even though the regulation permits denial of care based on ability to pay, there is wide latitude in the regulation for interpretations that could dramatically increase the availability of health care services to indigents. But the judiciary has declined this opportunity. Courts have not taken advantage of the community service provisions to require Hill–Burton facilities to address inequalities. There are few (if any) reported cases that have used the community service requirement to reduce disparities in health care services.[10] Indeed, in a recent volume devoted entirely to U.S. health care inequality, Hill–Burton is not even mentioned as a potential legal remedy.[11]

*Employee Retirement Income Security Act.* The Employee Retirement Income Security Act (ERISA) offers an interesting study in the doctrine of unintended consequences. Originally enacted to prevent recurring pension plan abuses, Congress included employee health benefits within its coverage. The act is widely regarded as having contributed to the growth of managed care by limiting the ability of state law to regulate ERISA-covered benefit plans. In doing so, however, ERISA unwittingly created a managed care regulatory vacuum since the act preempts (that is, precludes) state regulatory oversight of managed care delivery or state tort litigation against managed care organizations for an ERISA-covered patient. There is no countervailing federal regulation of employee health benefits.

The effect of ERISA preemption is to separate patients into two mutually exclusive categories—those covered by ERISA and those not covered. (Approximately 125 million Americans receive health insurance under an ERISA-covered benefit plan.) Suppose that two patients have health care denied for similar medical problems. An ERISA-covered patient essentially is without legal recourse, while a non-ERISA patient can sue for damages in state court. This situation is symptomatic of the courts' current reluctance to usurp legislative choices, despite vociferous complaints about unjust results.

After a series of judicial decisions that expanded preemption beyond congressional intent, the Supreme Court began to backtrack in 1996, allowing some litigation against managed care organizations to go forward in state courts and some states laws to be implemented. In general, however, courts have rejected challenges to the inequalities brought about by the operation of managed care's financial incentives, ruling that public policy has encouraged the use of financial incentives to reduce health care costs. The courts have stated that Congress, not the courts, should make any changes to managed care policy.[12]

In strongly deferring to Congress, the Supreme Court has sent an unmistakable signal that it does not view its mandate as alleviating market deficiencies or inequalities. For those concerned with inequalities in health care, the *Pegram v. Herdrich* case is a striking example of market deference. In this case, the patient challenged the operation of managed care's financial incentives in delaying needed health care. The Supreme Court ruled that Congress, not the judiciary, should evaluate whether financial incentives are appropriate. What is particularly troublesome about the *Pegram* opinion is that the Court went further than necessary to resolve this case. The Court easily could (and should) have retained an institutional oversight role to ensure that incentives operate fairly. That the Court voluntarily abjured its traditional oversight role means that it is unlikely to use its existing powers to alleviate health care inequalities. Any attempt to redress inequalities in health care through litigation in federal court must therefore overcome the courts' institutional constraints and concerns. For reasons we will explain later, it will be difficult, if not insurmountable, to convince the judiciary that its over-reliance on institutional reasons to ignore policy issues leaves patients vulnerable and inequalities festering.

## Doing Better in Other Areas of Social Policy?

To provide a broader perspective on the health care case examples, it is useful to compare how the courts have ruled in other areas of social policy. The Warren Court often seemed willing to expand congressional efforts to address social and economic disparities in social policy areas other than health care, such as education and welfare. The conventional wisdom is that courts have aggressively acted to alleviate social inequalities in education and welfare cases. If so, shouldn't the same apply to health care?

The conventional wisdom confuses two separate issues: interpreting legislation broadly to expand services and using the Constitution to create rights. Courts in the 1960s, led by the Supreme Court, often expanded congressional intent and required government to provide more services. At the same time, however, the Warren Court was hesitant to create new rights and resisted numerous opportunities to do so:

> Almost thirty years ago, the Supreme Court refused to find a right to welfare in the Federal Constitution, contending that the "administration of public welfare assistance" raises "intractable economic, social, and even philosophical problems" that "are not the business" of the Court. Since then, the Court has rejected constitutional claims to housing, to public education, and to medical services, on the view that the government does not owe its citizens any affirmative duty of care.... [T]he Court has resisted acknowledging any "affirmative right to government aid, even where such aid may be necessary to secure life, liberty, or property interests of which the government itself may not deprive the individual."[13]

The actions of courts in three particular areas—education, welfare rights, and judicial takeovers of certain institutions—will clarify what might be characterized as the outer range of judicial policy involvement.

*Education.* The area of social policy most directly analogous to health care is education. Since the mid-nineteenth century, education has been established as an obligation in the United States. All children are required to attend school up to the age of 16. The country's commitment to public education is unparalleled. One might assume, therefore, that the courts have been assiduous in protecting and expanding the right to public education. At the state level, this seems accurate; but at the federal level, it is not correct.

In 1973, the Supreme Court clearly held that public education is not a fundamental right under the Constitution. In *San Antonio Independent School District v. Rodriguez*,[14] the Court rejected a challenge to the Texas system of relying on property taxes to finance public education. *Rodriguez* claimed that the system's reliance on local property taxes favored wealthy communities and violated the equal protection clause of the Fourteenth Amendment because of resulting disparities in per-pupil expenditures. In a 5–4 decision, the Court held that education is not a fundamental right, even though it is one of the most important services provided by the government. The Court ruled instead that the state has considerable latitude in how education is financed and delivered. In short, a federal constitutional right to education has been restricted to the equal provision of the educational resources already being provided. At least at the federal level, therefore, it will be difficult to use education cases as a model for a right to health care.

If such a model is to emerge in education, it will be at the state level. Courts usually defer to the states in setting education policy. To the extent that courts have imposed what might be considered a right to education, it has been under state constitutions, most of which describe the state's duty to educate.[15] For example, state courts have relied on state constitutions to declare school funding systems unconstitutional. Judges have also required state legislatures to create tax equalization mechanisms for school funding. In response to recent public pressure for educational reform, there has been a flood of state judicial activity addressing inequalities in educational opportunity, financing, and quality. Judicial rulings may not amount to a right to education, but the opinions certainly have forced state after state to reconsider inequalities in school funding, opportunities, and quality of education. Whether this will stimulate radical change in school financing remains to be seen.

*Welfare Rights.* Another area of social policy where the courts are considered to have been influential has been in welfare rights. In the 1970s, when the Supreme Court decided several important welfare cases, it seemed to many that the Court was on its way to creating a constitutional right to welfare. In *Shapiro v. Thompson,*[16] the Court invalidated state residency requirements for welfare benefits, preventing states from denying benefits to persons on welfare if they moved from one state to another. While the 6–3 decision was justified under the auspices of the fundamental right to interstate travel, some scholars have argued that the Court came extremely close to creating a constitutional right to welfare assistance.

But in *Goldberg v. Kelly*[17]—generally considered one of the landmark cases in welfare rights—the Court failed to establish a right to welfare benefits. Instead, the Court focused on assuring that welfare recipients were granted due process before welfare benefits were terminated, ruling that welfare grants were legal entitlements that could only be withheld or terminated according to due process of law. The Court reasoned that any piece of welfare legislation could not override the constitutionally guaranteed right to due process under law; thus welfare benefits could neither be granted nor denied without due process for recipients.

Despite active debate over welfare rights in the 1970s, the courts ultimately did not establish a fundamental right to welfare. The legacy of the Warren Court was one of due process rights, not of rights to welfare benefits. And while the courts have the institutional capacity to create a right to welfare, it is clear that this outcome would not be politically feasible. A federal constitutional welfare right would be difficult to enforce judicially because of concerns about federalism, separation of powers, and institutional capabilities,[18] problems equally applicable to health care.

Growing political antipathy to welfare rights cases culminated in 1996 when Congress quelled any discussion of entitlement to welfare with the enactment of the Personal Responsibility and Work Opportunity Reconciliation Act. The act explicitly eliminated entitlements by imposing time limits, work requirements, and other conditions of eligibility for welfare benefits.

*Agency Takeovers.* On rare occasions, courts will find the operation of governmental programs so deficient that they will take judicial control over social policy. For instance, courts have on occasion assumed supervisory responsibilities over prisons, social welfare agencies, and desegregation practices (e.g., busing). Judicial takeovers of this kind have occurred primarily at the local level, but occasionally at the state level as well, and only where governmental programs are at issue.

When a court is convinced that the local government is incapable of providing an adequate level of the services it is obligated to offer, a master will be appointed to operate the system. The master reports to the court, which supervises the entire process. In one recent case, a federal judge in Texas ruled that child health care programs provided by the state Medicaid program were "badly flawed." The judge found that appropriate health care under federal law had not been provided to over 1 million children in the state.[19]

In recent years, appellate courts have been reluctant to allow the lower courts to exercise such authority. The judicial retreat from affirmative action is one example. Even aside from the appellate courts' retrenchment, the takeover theory is only applicable to services that government is obligated to provide and only arises under dire circumstances. In limited circumstances, advocates could use this approach to reduce health care inequalities, but judicial takeovers of large governmental health programs are highly unlikely.

## Markets over Equity

Despite precedent for judicial intervention to change social policy in public education, welfare rights, and judicial takeovers of certain institutions, there has been considerable judicial reluctance to do so in health care. The courts have systematically chosen markets over equity. Taken together, Medicare/Medicaid, EMTALA, Hill-Burton, and ERISA are examples that suggest several trends advocates should consider in devising strategies for reducing health care inequalities.

First, the case examples have presented the judiciary with tremendous opportunities to interpret legislation to reduce inequalities in the provision of health services (what we discuss later as a "rights enforcing" approach, which would presume that Congress intended to enhance access to health care). Our analysis suggests that there have been no breakthroughs in interpreting health care legislation in a manner that could be considered rights-enforcing. To the extent that these statutes have reduced inequalities in health care, it has largely been without assistance from the courts.

Second, the courts now consistently defer to Congress to address health care inequalities. Absent more explicit congressional action, the courts are unwilling to impose broader access requirements and unfunded mandates on the health care system. If change is to occur, it must be through the political process. Essentially, this means that the courts have simply reinforced the status quo. While the courts have shown no inclination to block congressional health care initiatives, they are, for now, unlikely to interpret legislation expansively.

Third, courts send signals as to how active they will be in using their powers to establish social policy. By interpreting legislation expansively or by indicating a willingness to create new rights, courts would be inviting further litigation to reduce health care inequalities. Likewise, by narrowly interpreting legislation and by refusing to consider new rights, courts signal that further litigation is unlikely to achieve the desired objectives. In the current climate, the signal in opposition to redressing health care inequalities is clear. Litigants have gotten the message, as there is virtually no current litigation to expand the scope of health care legislation. If anything, the signal from the Rehnquist Court is for conservative legal organizations to bring cases that will challenge federal legislation and regulation.

The Hill-Burton and EMTALA litigation best demonstrates these principles. Both statutes were originally designed, at least in part, to reduce inequities in health care. They afforded the courts tremendous opportunity to increase access to resources and health care services for those most in need. But the legacy of these two statutes has largely been one of judicial non-expansion. The statutes became casualties of a conservative judiciary more concerned with protecting the market's distribution of goods and services than reducing social and economic inequalities in health. In short, the courts have signaled an unwillingness to take affirmative steps to address inequalities within government health programs.

Fourth, while the courts have uniformly refused to create new rights to social services, they have been somewhat more aggressive in alleviating inequalities in education and welfare programs.[20] At the very least, the due process protections imposed in welfare litigation provide important protections for welfare beneficiaries. By contrast, the courts have been far less active in addressing inequalities in health. Judicial involvement in education and welfare has focused on the expansion of established rights in reviewing existing legislation, or state constitutional provisions guaranteeing the right to education. In these other areas, courts have also been more aggressive in establishing and protecting due process rights. But when the market or the political system has set limits on the provision of health services, as is the case with insurance limits for AIDS patients, the courts have consistently deferred, upholding the current distribution of goods and services.

Fifth, because the most profound inequality in health care services in the United States reflects socioeconomic disparities, the courts have limited ability to fundamentally affect health care inequality. Short of declaring a violation of equal protection if health care access is denied, the courts have little ability to affect inequalities that are *external* to the health care system. External inequalities apply to those without insurance or current access to the health care system, creating disparities in the availability of health care services that courts cannot easily address. The courts do, however, have the ability to fill in gaps in legislation designed to reduce inequalities that are *internal* to the health care system. Internal inequalities apply to those individuals who are entitled to receive health care services, either through specified governmental programs or through private health insurance. Regardless of their ability to reduce some types of health care inequalities, the courts have not done so. The judiciary has consistently deferred to the market, under the premise that there is no constitutionally held right to health care.

## The Judiciary's Role in Social Policy

Now that we have described how courts have actually ruled in litigation affecting health care inequalities, a reader might well assume that these trends were simply preordained or resulted from the absence of appropriate judicial mechanisms for redressing social policy inequities. This assumption is incorrect. We now turn our attention to the tools available to courts to develop different legal doctrine.

If they so desire, the courts have various means to redress health care inequalities. These are constitutional interpretations, statutory interpretations, and common law development (contract and tort standards). Legislatures can always override statutory and common law decisions, though only a constitutional amendment could overturn a constitutional interpretation.

### Judicial Activism, Judicial Restraint

Not surprisingly, there is considerable political and scholarly controversy over the appropriateness and capacity of the judiciary to resolve social problems.[21] For example, one author has applied a systematic conceptual approach to the analysis of the social change implications of judicial decisions in civil rights and abortion cases and has produced a useful model for examining the role of the courts in reducing health care inequities.[22] This model describes two very different versions of judicial involvement in social policy disputes: a dynamic model and a constrained model.[23]

The dynamic view holds that the courts are effective in generating social change. Proponents of the dynamic view argue that as independent institutions, courts can issue rulings (especially constitutional interpretations) that directly induce policy change when other institutions are politically stymied. The dynamic view postulates that courts can also induce policy change indirectly by educating the public, stimulating public debate, and serving as a catalyst for change.[24] In this way, the dynamic view takes into account the courts' ability to directly influence the nature of the policy agenda, if not its outcome.

In contrast, the constrained view holds that inherent constraints inhibit courts from leading social change. In the constrained view, courts face three structural limitations: (1) constitutional limits on creating rights; (2) the lack of independence from other branches of government; and (3) the inability to establish, implement, and enforce policies. This view is quite skeptical about courts as policy makers, arguing that judicial policy-making is undesirable, primarily because "the judicial process is a poor format for the weighing of alternatives and the calculation of costs."[25] Judicial capacity to make policy is limited relative to other institutions, especially given judicial limitations on implementation and enforcement, the problem of case-by-case decision making, and constraints on agenda-setting. Nevertheless, this view still recognizes that judicial decisions on statutory interpretation indeed help shape public policy.

Under almost any circumstances, the policy agenda is rarely determined exclusively by the courts. The courts engage in a dialogue with the other branches of government, and the instances in which the judiciary can unilaterally determine policy are likely to be few in number. In health care, the executive and legislative branches usually set the agenda.[26] Thus, courts must be sensitive to how other institutions respond to its decisions, particularly the market and the political process (i.e., the legislative and regulatory branches).

Yet the notion that the system specifically designed to address policy issues—the legislative and regulatory institutions—is sufficient in and of itself fails to account for the well-known phenomenon of regulatory capture, that agencies might be dominated by the interests of the regulated industry.[27] For example, the American Medical Association has successfully opposed national health insurance and the managed care industry has successfully avoided serious regulation.

### Establishing Rights—Still Reluctant after All These Years

The first mechanism for courts to respond to health care inequalities is by ruling that the Constitution includes a right to health care. It would then be congressional responsibility to implement and enforce that right. As with the right to privacy created by the Supreme Court out of a broad "penumbra of rights,"[28] the Court could determine that various constitutional provisions, such as the Fourteenth Amendment's right to liberty, imply a constitutional right to health care for all citizens. Given the Court's current distaste for broad constitutional interpretations, this seems unlikely any time in the immediate future, and few scholars have supported a judicially created right to health care.[29]

The dominant position, one now common to libertarians and conservative scholars, is that it is inappropriate for courts to create rights that are not directly in the Constitution.[30] Aside from a very few rights that the Supreme Court considers to be fundamental to the concept of ordered liberty (such as procreation, marriage, travel) or those that fall under the penumbra of rights inherent in the constitution (such as privacy), the Court has not ventured very far to create rights to health, food, or housing.[31]

Some might argue that the right to health care (or, for that matter, to food and housing) is no less fundamental than the few fundamental rights already recognized. Repeatedly, however, the Supreme Court has deferred to the political process to address these problems. If rights, such as the right to health care, are to be created, the courts have ruled, with only rare exception, that the legislative branch should make that determination, not the courts through expansive constitutional interpretations. The right to privacy (and with it, the right to contraception and abortion) is an uncommon departure. But in the long run, the constitutional rights strategy is one that we ought to bear in mind—at least to help stretch the reforming imagination.

## Statutory Interpretation

A more promising approach would be to provide expansive interpretations of legislation and regulations and broadly interpret congressional intent to give meaning to congressional desires to reduce inequalities. For example, the courts might have taken the opening phrase of the National Health Planning and Resources Development Act of 1974, which said that access shall be a priority of this act, to require state health planning agencies to address access issues in all decisions. Health planning collapsed politically before courts ruled on this provision. Likewise, the courts could have interpreted the ambiguous community services requirements in the Hill-Burton Act to require recipients to take affirmative steps to reduce disparities in the provision of health care services. As we have already seen, courts have not done so in recent years.

As noted earlier, one legal scholar argues that courts should adopt a rights-enforcing approach in reviewing legislation.[32] In the rights-enforcing approach, a court "recognizes important rights implicit in the modern welfare state"[33] and enforces those rights. Legislation in the welfare state would then be read broadly to create enforceable rights (that is, a binding obligation to provide services to beneficiaries), as opposed to a narrow interpretation that presumes no binding obligations absent specific congressional intent. The courts would block regulatory agency actions that failed to enforce these rights and require that the agency explain its actions in implementing legislation. In sum, the courts could potentially fill in the inevitable gaps in legislation to favor reducing health care inequities. Arguably, this is exactly the legacy of the Warren Court from the mid-1960s until its reversal by the Rehnquist Court beginning in the 1980s.

## Common Law

Courts, particularly state courts, can also use their common law jurisdiction governing torts (civil wrongs) and contracts to impose certain costs on stakeholders whose actions create or exacerbate health care inequalities. For instance, if a managed care organization consistently provides lower quality of care to minorities or to Medicaid recipients, they could be sued for breach of contract or for damages under medical liability law. To address disparities within the existing health care system, courts could require providers to ignore resource constraints or require greater justification for implementing cost containment. The common law, however, develops slowly and incrementally. While it has an important place in accountability, the common law is unlikely to play more than a marginal role in reducing health care inequalities.

A related but highly unlikely common law strategy would be to treat health care as a public utility. Doing so would force the health care system to be more responsive to the entire community, especially those without health insurance (external inequalities), much like the telephone industry has been. This model posits that because of the importance of the health care industry to the general public, the body politic should have power to influence the industry's practices. For example, the courts could extend the antitrust doctrine of essential facilities to mandate that hospitals be more responsive to medically underserved communities or individuals.[34] Under a public utility model, the courts have imposed two particular duties that could dramatically address health care inequalities: all regulated public utilities have a duty to serve—they must serve all who apply for service; and a utility may not discriminate in providing service. Generally, courts are reluctant to declare that an industry should be regulated as a public utility, leaving that decision to the political branch, but nothing in principle prevents the courts from imposing similar requirements.

## Barriers to Judicial Participation in Social Policy

While courts are very good at stopping odious practices, they are less willing to order change. For example, courts will not hesitate to issue injunctions against certain behavior, such as excessive or violent picketing, but rarely issue mandatory injunctions compelling governmental officials to exercise their responsibilities. In addition, courts will protect against an invasion of constitutionally granted rights, but, as we have seen, are averse to creating new rights.

A recurrent problem with judicial intervention to reduce health care inequalities is that courts are in a weak strategic position to order social policy changes, especially when compelling a state legislature to spend money or raise taxes. Reducing health care inequalities would require exactly the kinds of affirmative steps that the courts are least willing to provide. As we discuss later, this reluctance is not simply based on political ideology, but reflects legitimate concerns about judicial capacity to order social change. Courts can stop some practices that foster health care inequalities, but are unlikely to compel governmental officials to undertake policy measures to reduce them.

Those who retain an idealistic view of judicial policy making need to consider another barrier. Courts might not always reach the desired result. Conservative scholars are fond of saying that the Rehnquist Court has simply restored the proper judicial function after an overly activist Warren Court. The reality is much different. The Rehnquist Court is no less activist that the Warren Court—it is just activist in a conservative direction. Thus, advocates of a judicial strategy to address health care inequalities need to be concerned that the courts will now take action that will directly undermine the desired result.

## Institutional Concerns—Judicial Capacity

Any effort to use or rely on the courts to redress health care inequalities must confront and overcome the stark reality that the courts' own institutional considerations impose substantial impediments. These institutional concerns are conceptual, practical, and political. Scholars and other observers too often overlook the judiciary's institutional considerations when commenting on what the courts do or should have done.

*Conceptual.* Under Chief Justice William Rehnquist's leadership, the current Supreme Court has emphasized two constitutional theories that surely limit federal judicial responsiveness to health care inequalities: separation of powers and federalism. Taken together, these two theories advocate a powerful restraint on the Court's willingness to use its powers to "legislate" from the bench.

For our purposes, two aspects of the Supreme Court's opinion in *Pegram v. Herdrich* characterize the difficulty of using the courts to reduce health care inequalities at this time. First, the Court strongly and directly deflected any questions of changing public policy to Congress. As a philosophical matter, the Court based its unanimous opinion on the doctrine of separation of powers. Second, the Court cited institutional considerations beyond separation of powers for rejecting *Herdrich's* challenge. Although the opinion does not fully detail the Court's institutional concerns, and may not necessarily be applicable in constitutional decisions, the language used indicates the Court's underlying concern for avoiding policy debates.

For example, the Court noted that if it were to permit *Herdrich* to challenge how managed care's financial incentives operate, it would open the courts to endless litigation in trying to fine-tune market mechanisms. We quote at length from the opinion because the institutional concerns expressed are critical to understanding the Court's approach.

> [A]ny legal principle purporting to draw a line between good and bad HMOs [health maintenance organizations] would embody, in effect, a judgment about socially acceptable medical risk. A valid conclusion of this sort would, however, necessarily turn on facts to which courts would probably not have ready access.... But such complicated fact-finding and such a debatable social judgment are not wisely required of courts unless for some reason resort cannot be had to the legislative process, with its preferable forum for comprehensive investigations and judgments of social value, such as optimum treatment levels and health care expenditure.... The very difficulty of these policy considerations, and Congress' superior institutional competence to pursue this debate, suggest that legislative not judicial solutions are preferable.[35]

One of the principal interpretive tenets or norms repeatedly stated by the current Supreme Court is that social policy should be made by the elected representatives, not by the courts. Many similar decisions support that proposition; for example, the Court refused to interpret the Food, Drug, and Cosmetic Act as providing authority for the Food and Drug Administration to regulate tobacco products.[36] If a right to health care is to be imposed, it should emanate from Congress, not from the courts. The separation of powers doctrine was much less important to the Warren Court, which was willing to take and decide cases that altered social policy.[37]

An important corollary doctrine about the structure of government is federalism—the question of whether power resides with the states or with the federal government. This debate goes back to the earliest days of the republic, with the federalists (led by Alexander Hamilton) arguing for a strong central government, while the Jeffersonians argued for greater state sovereignty. Under the Warren Court, the rulings generally favored the federal government and expanded the reach of federal legislation. But that has been reversed under the Rehnquist Court, which generally defers to the states within the federalist structure. Recently, the Court has restricted the reach of the federal government by constricting Congress's legislative authority under the commerce clause. The importance of the Court's changing federalism doctrine is that congressional actions will now be more closely scrutinized, but states will be given greater latitude to redress health care inequalities. Nevertheless, it is unlikely that the Court, as currently comprised, would overturn national health insurance or similar congressional action based on federalism doctrine. What's important about the federalist system is that state and federal courts may reach different conclusions on the same issue, particularly when a state court relies on state constitutional provisions. State constitutions may impose different requirements than the federal constitution, providing state courts with the opportunity to go far beyond what the federal courts would do in responding to perceived social inequalities. Thus, a state court could rule that a particular state's constitution mandates universal health insurance, even though such a ruling under the federal constitution is implausible. This suggests that any litigation strategy to attack health care inequalities should be at the state, rather than the federal, level.[38]

*Practical.* Even if the conceptual concerns could be surmounted, proponents of a judicial solution must still confront several practical considerations. Judges have repeatedly expressed concerns about court congestion resulting from increased litigation and the costs to the judicial system.[39] As a result, judges approve plea bargains in criminal cases and sealed settlements in civil litigation even when the public is not informed of serious public safety hazards.[40] Judicial resources do not necessarily increase along with expanding caseloads. In this regard, the federal courts are like any other agency petitioning Congress for funds. Supreme Court justices must take into account the volume of litigation likely to emerge if the Court were to rule in favor of a constitutionally determined right to health care. This is one reason why the federal judiciary advises Congress against creating new rights that would result in extensive federal court litigation.[41]

Another practical institutional consideration is that the courts have become increasingly reluctant to require unfunded mandates. Any ruling that requires the expenditure of funds would need to be securely located within the Constitution. Since the Court has recently overturned congressional statutes that impose unfunded mandates on states, it is highly unlikely that the Court would in turn impose such funding requirements on Congress.

To the Court's credit, it was quite explicit about some of these practical concerns, especially the potential explosion of litigation, in the *Pegram* decision. The guiding philosophy now is in part a response to "the institutional stresses brought on by the [Warren] era's most expansive...decisions."[42]

*Political.* Consistent with judicial concerns about separation of powers and legitimacy, courts are likely to be apprehensive about the political realities that confront them. When the courts aggressively attack social inequalities, the public reaction can be furious. Many readers may remember the "Impeach Earl Warren" signs that became a staple seen when driving along southern highways in the 1960s. Part of Richard Nixon's presidential campaign strategy in 1968 and 1972, the so-called "southern strategy," was to take advantage of popular dissatisfaction with the perceived intrusion of the judiciary into the South's segregated way of life. Since then, the Supreme Court has become an increasingly conservative social institution, fearful of losing its public legitimacy if it intrudes too aggressively into social policy.

Far more than the other branches of government, the judiciary relies on its legitimacy as a co-equal branch of government to secure public compliance with judicial decisions. Aside from its political and social legitimacy, the courts have very little ability to enforce their decisions. As Andrew Jackson said after a Supreme Court decision that he opposed, "John Marshall has made his decision, now let him enforce it."[43] When Chief Justice Warren was assembling his unanimous opinion in *Brown v. Board of Education*, he had to confront two aspects of the legitimacy issue.[44] On the one hand, he had to deal with recalcitrant colleagues who felt that the decision to integrate the schools should be made by Congress and that the Court's constitutional mandate would be publicly viewed as illegitimate (at least in the South). On the other hand, to gain legitimacy, Warren needed unanimity. In the end, he got both—a unanimous decision that sparked repeated calls to "Impeach Earl Warren." The danger to the Court of not obtaining unanimity in controversial cases was palpable in the furious reaction to the 5–4 decision in *Bush v. Gore*.[45]

Courts function as an integral part of the American political system and are hardly immune from political and social influences, even as they attempt to minimize their political role. For example, the Supreme Court has long espoused the political question doctrine to avoid involvement in directly political questions. According to this doctrine, political questions, such as whether a declaration of war is appropriate, should be left to elected representatives, not the courts. The results of departing from that doctrine have not been beneficial for the judiciary. The news headlines that followed the Supreme Court's intervention into the 2000 presidential election were a stark reminder that the Court's political legitimacy can be threatened if the public perceives its decisions to be politically motivated rather than being grounded in robust legal or constitutional analysis.[46]

Unexpected support for this concern comes from a reinterpretation of the Warren Court, which argues that the Court's opinions were not in fact ahead of public opinion. Instead, the Court "reached results that conformed to the values that enjoyed significant national support in the 1960s."[47] If that's an accurate reflection of how the Supreme Court reflects political values, the broad creation of rights must await a sea change in the current political environment—a conclusion that echoes many of the chapters in this volume.

From policy decisions and judicial appointments to the courts' decisions on which cases to accept or reject, politics is an inherent part of the judicial enterprise. Partisan politics has sharply intensified in recent years. Examples include the debate over *Roe v. Wade*,[48] the controversial Supreme Court nominations of Robert Bork (during the Reagan administration), and the conflict over Clarence Thomas's Supreme Court appointment (during the first Bush administration). Both the Bork and Thomas nominations involved an unprecedented number of organized interest groups:

> The trend toward institutionalization of the role of interest groups in the selection of federal judges reflected in part a growing recognition of the Court's role in facilitating the agendas of such groups. This trend accelerated during the Reagan–Bush era, when liberal groups became alarmed over Republican attempts to pack the courts with so-called conservative judges.[49]

Public opinion and organized interest groups have come to play an increasingly influential role in the appointment of federal judges and in how cases are presented and argued, ultimately shaping judicial selection of cases and legislative interpretation. The same phenomena have also occurred at the state level where partisan rancor and political groups are increasingly influencing judicial elections. For example, conservative activists in the 1980s led a successful political assault on three California Supreme Court judges for their opposition to the death penalty. A similar battle occurred in Texas in the late 1990s over tort reform, and a Republican group announced its intention to oppose the re-election of three Florida Supreme Court judges in retaliation for their role in the Florida 2000 election recount.

Such issue-based judicial campaigns threaten the judiciary's political insulation and its legitimacy as being above partisan politics. It is also likely to affect judicial attitudes toward redressing health care inequalities—in a way that will most likely encourage reluctance to intervene. In a socially and politically conservative era, an activist judiciary will be a target.

Aside from the high political stakes, one reason for the increased political pressure on the judiciary is a scholarly literature suggesting that judges are no longer viewed as neutral arbitrators of the law (if, indeed, they ever were). Numerous legal scholars have asserted that judges seek to influence and realize certain policy goals.[50] In fact, one school of thought, the "attitudinal model," states that "the Court's decisions are based on the facts of a case in light of the ideological attitudes and values of the participating justices; in other words, on the basis of the individual justice's policy preferences."[51] This view of judges as "policy maximizers" has fueled interest group participation and political advocacy as part of the judicial process.

> [J]udges with liberal inclinations seek to push case outcomes in that direction, whereas their conservative counterparts wish to move it the other way. If federal judges did not pursue ideological agendas, organized interests on both sides of the spectrum would show less concern about who sits on the federal courts than they do.[52]

The ability of the courts to accept cases and interpret legislation allows them to influence policy outcomes. This was clearly true for the Warren Court's activism in civil rights cases. The Warren Court was highly responsive and encouraged liberal interest groups to use the judiciary to protect and expand their rights as an alternative to the failure of other branches of government.[53] The reverse is now true. When the Republicans took control of the White House in 1969, members of the Warren Court were replaced with more conservative justices. Since then, liberal organizations have had a hard time mounting campaigns to expand and enforce rights in a generally more conservative political climate and in the face of a conservative judiciary. By contrast, conservative groups have had relatively more success in influencing the judicial agenda and the courts have been more rewarding of conservative interest group activity.

Through *amiucus curiae* (friend of the court) legal briefs, conservative groups have been able to articulate new theories of the law that litigants themselves may be reluctant to advance. In many instances, federal courts have quoted verbatim language from these briefs in adopting legal positions that will essentially foreclose the use of the courts in reducing health care inequalities.[54] A conservative political climate and a shift in judicial attitude have combined to deal a devastating blow to the ability of the courts to effectively address social and health care inequalities. Only a powerful political change rising up from the grass roots could (possibly) swing the courts back in a more egalitarian direction.

## Conclusion

The courts have tremendous ability to redress social and economic inequalities. But advocates of social change need to weigh the benefits of a judicial approach to social policy against the efficacy of pursuing social change through other political institutions.

### Relying on the Courts

There are snares in relying on the courts to address social inequalities, particularly in the current political climate. Proponents of pursuing policy objectives through litigation must be wary; there are no political guarantees that litigation would indeed remedy the types of social inequalities confronted today. In a conservative social era with a generally conservative judiciary, courts will be most reluctant to usurp the legislative branch in changing social policy. But can additional litigation do any damage? Yes. Since our case examples show that the courts have not attempted to reduce health care inequalities, it is likely that further litigation could do much harm.

Litigation plays an important role in policy making and implementation, but with respect to health care inequalities, the judicial capacity to stimulate policy change can be severely constrained. Advocates of social change ought to rely on social and political movements. This can be as direct as electing politicians who will appoint judges more sympathetic to using the full panoply of judicial mechanisms to redress health care inequalities. Indeed, the power of judicial appointments is often an important reason to support a particular presidential candidate or political party. Social movements can result in significant changes in policy and social attitudes.

## A Political Response

Today, relying on the federal courts to systematically reduce inequalities in the health care sector seems illusory:

> For those enamored with "The Federal Courts" because they assume that inherent in the charter of life-tenured judges is a commitment to guarding, it may well be time to leave behind that romance. As an educational and rulemaking organization, the federal judiciary has adopted an anti-adjudication and pro-settlement agenda. As a lobbying organization, the federal judiciary has chosen to oppose creation of new federal rights.[55]

The abdication of the federal judiciary as a powerful force for social change does not eliminate the potential for better results in state courts based on state constitutions, but it suggests that the remedy to health care inequalities will be political, not judicial.

Of course, a political solution will not be easy during a time when governmental solutions are viewed skeptically and the dominant political philosophy favors markets and individualism. In this environment, collective solutions to social problems will be difficult to achieve. In addition, the Supreme Court's current doctrine toward federalism (which essentially shifts power from the federal to the state governments) presents both opportunity and challenge. As opportunity, it suggests that state legislatures and courts will be given considerable flexibility in defining and responding to social problems. Thus, we suggest that any litigation strategy be developed based on state law and state constitutional provisions. But as challenge, it suggests that the federal government may not be much help. The increasing politicization of the judicial process and changes in the composition of the appellate courts can have a dramatic effect on the judiciary's willingness to engage in social change.

For those who look to the judicial branch to alleviate health care inequalities, our review is likely to be disappointing. At best, the courts have deferred to the political branch and have simply reaffirmed the status quo. Although our case examples found no evidence that courts systematically block attempts to alleviate inequalities, as it stands now, advocates will need to focus on the political system for social change. To some, this conclusion will be as it should be. But to those who remember fondly the excitement of the Warren Court's engagement in social policy, it will be another reminder of how far away we are from that era.

# Notes

1. 530 U.S. 211 (2000).

2. True, Warren operated under a constitutional challenge while Souter was interpreting legislation, but as we shall see, that only accounts for part of the difference.

3. 469 U.S. 287 (1985).

4. *Shalala v. Grijalva*, 526 U.S. 1096 (1999).

5. 525 U.S. 249 (1999).

6. S. Rosenbaum, A. Markus, and J. Darnell, "U.S. Civil Rights Policy and Access to Health Care by Minority Americans: Implications for a Changing Health Care System," *Medical Care Research and Review* 57 (Supp. 2000): 236–259.

7. Michael J. Frank, "Tailoring EMTALA to Better Protect the Indigent: The Supreme Court Precludes One Method of Salvaging a Statute Gone Awry," *DePaul Journal of Health Care Law* 3 (2000): 195–244.

8. R. E. Rosenblatt, S. E. Law, and S. Rosenbaum, *Law and the American Health Care System* (Westbury, NY: Foundation Press, 1997).

9. Ibid.; James F. Blumstein, "Court Action, Agency Reaction: The Hill-Burton Act as a Case Study," *Iowa Law Review* 69 (1984): 1227–1261; In *Newsom v. Vanderbilt University*, 453 F. Supp. 401 (M.D. Tenn. 1978), the court declared that indigent patients had a "constitutionally protected right . . . to needed uncompensated services under the Hill-Burton Act."

10. In fairness to the judiciary, the absence of federal regulatory enforcement of the community service provision is a substantial reason why courts have not been more involved.

11. M. Lilli-Blanton, M. Brodie, D. Rowland, D. Altman, and M. McIntosh, "Race, Ethnicity, and the Health Care System: Public Perceptions and Experiences," *Medical Care Research and Review* 57 (Supp. 2000): 218–235; Rosenbaum, Markus, and Darnell, "U.S. Civil Rights Policy and Access to Health Care by Minority Americans: Implications for a Changing Health Care System."

12. *Pegram v. Herdrich*, 530 U.S. 211 (2000). For a more detailed analysis, see P. D. Jacobson, *Strangers in the Night: Law and Medicine in the Managed Care Era* (New York: Oxford University Press, 2002).

13. Helen Hershkoff, "Postive Rights and State Constitutions: The Limits of Federal Rationality Review" *Harvard Law Review* 112 (1999): 1132–1133.

14. 411 U.S. 1 (1973).

15. P. L. Lundberg, "State Courts and School Funding: A Fifty State Analysis," *Albany Law Review* 63 (2000): 1101–1146.

16. 394 U.S. 618 (1969).

17. 397 U.S. 254 (1970).

18. Hershkoff, "Positive Rights and State Constitutions."

19. R. A. Oppel, "Judge Orders Texas to Improve Children's Medicaid Programs," *New York Times* (30 August 2000): A-1, 14.

20. It is, perhaps, somewhat strange that courts have been more expansive in welfare and education than in health care. But it is beyond the scope of this chapter to explore the comparison in greater depth.

21. This analysis borrows liberally from P. D. Jacobson and K. E. Warner, "Litigation and Public Health Policy: The Case of Tobacco Control," *Journal of Health Politics, Policy and Law* 24 (1999): 769–804. See also P. D. Jacobson and S. Soliman, "Litigation as Public Health Policy: Theory or Reality?" *Journal of Law, Medicine, and Ethics* 30 (2002): 224–238.

22. G. N. Rosenberg, *The Hollow Hope: Can Courts Bring about Social Change?* (Chicago: University of Chicago Press, 1991); G. N. Rosenberg, "The Real World of Constitutional Rights: The Supreme Court and the Implementation of the Abortion Decisions," *Contemplating Courts*, ed. L. Epstein (Washington, DC: Congressional Quarterly, 1995).

23. Rosenberg, *The Hollow Hope*, a proponent of the constrained view, argues that the presumed political and social changes stemming from civil rights, abortion, and environmental litigation have been illusory. Instead, Rosenberg (*The Hollow Hope*, "Real World of Constitutional Rights") concludes that changes in public opinion and action by elected officials, rather than court decisions, are required to engender significant social change. Rosenberg's conclusions and model remain controversial. For example, McCann criticizes the approach for ignoring "the many more subtle, variable ways that legal norms, institutions, actors and the like do matter in social life" (472). For our purposes, Rosenberg's framework simply provides a useful starting point. M. McCann, "Causal versus Constitutive Explanations (or, On the Difficulty of Being So Positive)," *Law and Social Inquiry* 21 (1996): 457–482.

24. R. S. Melnick, *Regulation and the Courts: The Case of the Clean Air Act* (Washington, DC: Brookings Institution, 1983).

25. D. L. Horowitz, *The Courts and Social Policy* (Washington, DC: Brookings Institution, 1977), 357; Melnick, *Regulation and the Courts*; Melnick, *Between the Lines: Interpreting Welfare Rights* (Washington, DC: Brookings Institution, 1994). Rosenberg studied the effects of judicial decisions in civil rights, abortion, and environmental cases. Horowitz reached similar results in studying the effects of leading cases in police practices, education, juvenile justice, and the Model Cities program. Melnick studied environmental litigation (*Clean Air Act*), and welfare, education for handicapped persons, and the food stamp program (*Between the Lines*).

26. N. K. Komesar, *Imperfect Alternatives: Choosing Institutions in Law, Economics, and Public Policy* (Chicago: University of Chicago Press, 1994).

27. J. Q. Wilson, *Bureaucracy: What Government Agencies Do and Why They Do It* (New York: Basic Books, 1989).

28. *Griswold v. Connecticut,* 381 U.S. 479 (1965).

29. For an interesting analysis comparing constitutional interpretive trends over the past 100 years, see Judge Wilkinson's concurring opinion in *Brzonkala v. Virginia Polytechnic Institute and State University,* 132 F.3d 949 (4th Cir. 1997).

30. J. F. Blumstein, "Rationing Medical Resources: A Constitutional, Legal, and Policy Analysis," *University of Texas Law Review* 59 (1981): 1345–1400; P. H. Schuck, "Malpractice Liability and the Rationing of Health Care," *University of Texas Law Review* 59 (1981): 1421.

31. For a general discussion of these issues, see L. O. Gostin, *Public Health Law: Power, Duty, Restraint* (Berkeley: University of California Press, 2000).

32. R. E. Rosenblatt, "The Courts, Health Care Reform, and the Reconstruction of American Social Legislation," *Journal of Health Politics, Policy and Law* 18.2 (1993): 439–476.

33. Rosenblatt, "The Courts," 440.

34. Under the essential facilities doctrine, a health care facility must provide services where there is no realistic alternative. The court in *Blue Shield Blue Cross of Wisconsin v. Marshfield Clinic,* 65 F.3d 1406 (7th Cir. 1995) rejected this approach.

35. *Pegram v. Herdrich* (98–1949) 530 U.S. 211 (2000) 154 F. 3d 362, reversed.

36. *Food and Drug Administration v. Brown & Williamson Tobacco Corporation,* 529 U.S. 120 (2000).

37. See, e.g., Judge Wilkinson's concurring opinion in *Brzonkala v. Virginia Polytechnic Institute and State University,* 132 F.3d 949 (4th Cir. 1997): "Finally, our role in this modern era is not as substantive adjudicators, but as structural referees. The due process decisions of the *Lochner* and Warren eras, as well as the individual rights rulings of the latter, attempted to remove the subject matter of those cases from the political debate altogether."

38. A complication, well beyond the scope of this chapter, is ERISA preemption. The adverse effects of ERISA preemption on alleviating internal inequalities are clear. Altering ERISA preemption would require congressional action. See, e.g., Jacobson, *Strangers in the Night: Law and Medicine in the Managed Care Era.*

39. See, e.g., Mark A. Peterson and M. Selvin, "Mass Justice: The Limited and Unlimited Power of Courts," *Law and Contemporary Problems* 54 (1991): 227–247.

40. See, e.g., M. France, "Commentary—The Hidden Culprit: The U.S. Legal System," *Business Week* (18 September 2000): 42.

41. J. Resnik, "Trial as Error, Jurisdiction as Injury: Transforming the Meaning of Article III," *Harvard Law Review* 113 (2000): 924–1037.

42. Judge Wilkinson's concurring opinion in *Brzonkala v. Virginia Polytechnic Institute and State University.*

43. C. Sellers, *The Market Revolution: Jacksonian America, 1815–1846* (New York: Oxford University Press, 1991), 311.

44. R. Kluger, *Simple Justice: The History of Brown v. Board of Education and Black America's Struggle for Equality* (New York: Random House, 1977).

45. 121 S. Ct. 525 (2000).

46. See M. Tushnet, "The Politics of Constitutional Law," *Texas Law Review* 79 (November 2000): 163–187, 186.

47. L. A. Powe, *The Warren Court in American Politics* (Cambridge, MA: Harvard University Press, 2000).

48. 410 U.S. 113 (1973).

49. W. G. Ross, "The Supreme Court Appointment Process: A Search for a Synthesis," *Albany Law Review* 57 (1994): 993–1042.

50. G. A. Caldeira and J. R. Wright, "Lobbying for Justice: The Rise of Organized Conflict in the Politics of Federal Judgeships," *Contemplating Courts*, ed. L. Epstein (Washington, DC: Congressional Quarterly, 1995), 44–71; W. F. Murphy, *Elements of Judicial Strategy* (Chicago: University of Chicago Press, 1964).

51. H. J. Spaeth, "The Attitudinal Model," *Contemplating Courts*, ed. L. Epstein (Washington, DC: Congressional Quarterly, 1995), 296–314.

52. Caldeira and Wright, "Lobbying for Justice."

53. R. L. Pacelle, "The Dynamics and Determinants of Agenda Change in the Rehnquist Court," *Contemplating Courts*, ed. L. Epstein (Washington, DC: Congressional Quarterly, 1995).

54. This occurred in *Pegram v. Herdrich* (note 1).

55. J. Resnik, "Trial as Error, Jurisdiction as Injury," 995. Randall Kennedy puts it more bluntly: "Because of progressive Court decisions from the 1940s through the 1960s, many liberals have come to believe that there is something peculiarly virtuous about the third branch of government. . . . A reconsideration of that particular dogma is long overdue." Kennedy, "Contempt of Court," *The American Prospect* (1–15 January 2001): 16.

# Part V

# THE TERRITORY AHEAD

## Little Victories

What next? What should Americans do about inequality and health? How do we build a nation that is healthy, wealthy, and fair?

First, consider some small steps. Conventional political wisdom suggests making the easy moves—build incrementally and, over time, incrementalism might just add up to a better society.

Chapter 9 turns to one partial success story. Medicaid began as welfare medicine designed—quite explicitly—to arrest universal health insurance. Over time the program expanded, attracted unexpected champions, and developed new clients. Today, it stands poised between the middle class (mainstream) program and welfare medicine. In the past 15 years, Medicaid has repeatedly expanded health care services—to mothers, children, seniors, and others. In the process, Medicaid negotiated every barrier laid out in previous chapters: interest group politics, market ideology, the courts, and the congressional graveyard. Of course, Medicaid's future remains up for political grabs. But for cautious incrementalists, expanding this program offers an alluring option. It is a small, manageable step, quite within the pragmatic reformer's grasp.

Not all the breakthroughs take place in big programs or on a national stage. In chapter 10, Elizabeth Kilbreth and James Morone explore a quiet success. Far below the media radar screen, reform-minded public health officials—state bureaucrats—organized local coalitions that won and maintained school health centers. The local groups—Democrats and

Republicans, rich and poor—overcame an extraordinary array of political obstacles to win their little victories from Maine to Texas.

Still, it will take much bolder breakthroughs to squarely address the problems we posed at the start of the book. As Lawrence Brown suggests in chapter 11, incrementalism is a long, slow, often helpful, and ultimately inadequate response to American inequality. In the end, we will have to think big. In chapter 12, Benjamin Page breaks out of the usual box and suggests what a strong, committed national government could do—and how to think about getting there. Our conclusion continues the discussion of ambitious reforms.

What drives our new Gilded Age? We suggest that a great economic transformation is remaking the worlds' economies. How do we resist its worst consequences? We propose a series of bold programs: national health care (Medicare for all), a living wage, a lifelong educational system, and new ways of thinking about taxation. Today these are not likely reforms—none of them are focus-group ready. Nor do we propose them naively. The preceding chapters lay out the many barriers they face.

However, our shared problems—our eroding communal lives—push fresh ways of thinking toward the American agenda. Constructing a better society begins with building a grassroots, social movement. And for that we need proposals that fire the reforming imagination, ideas that touch (as Abraham Lincoln put it) the better angels of our nature.

At the turn of the last century, industrial capitalism transformed the American economy, opened up fabulous opportunities for many, and fostered a great gap between rich and poor. Today, global capitalism creates precisely the same conditions—great opportunities for the successful, terrible troubles for those who are left behind. A century ago, American populists won reforms that created a far more equitable nation; in part VI, we call for a new egalitarian surge. A good society protects all Americans from the market storms blowing across the world economy, it offers every family genuine opportunity, and it lends a hand (perhaps repeatedly) to neighbors who have fallen on hard times and need help getting back up.

# Medicaid at the Crossroads

## COLLEEN GROGAN AND ERIC PATASHNIK

A pauper family appears before a juvenile
delinquency board. 1886.

Medicaid is often described as America's "health care program for the poor." In reality, Medicaid covers only some of the poor and it extends coverage to many non-poor persons. Medicaid's complexity defies any simple definition of the program's mission. Indeed, an accurate understanding of Medicaid's role in the American welfare state has never been more elusive. Whom should Medicaid serve, and what type of coverage should eligible beneficiaries receive? What should be the role of Medicaid in future health care reform efforts? These questions about Medicaid—and implicitly about the social policy designs best equipped to promote more equal access to health care in America—remain unanswered.

Medicaid has reached a critical juncture in its political development. Two distinct paths for its future evolution lie in view, and they lead in opposite directions. If policy makers decide to continue taking incremental steps toward coverage expansion—as they did in the 1980s and 1990s—Medicaid could serve as the path to a more universal health care system for millions of Americans. Alternatively, if policy makers opt for the second path, Medicaid could revert back to "welfare medicine." Conceivably, the program might offer health coverage only to the most indigent.[1]

A surprisingly diverse coalition presses Medicaid policy makers to take the first path. Indeed, proposals for significant Medicaid coverage expansions have elicited support from across the ideological spectrum. The Health Insurance Association of America and Families USA—bitter opponents during the battle over the Clinton health reform bill in 1993–1994—have both endorsed a compromise reform proposal that calls for Medicaid to serve as the cornerstone for expanding health access. Under this plan, Medicaid expansions would cover all persons with incomes below 133% of poverty.[2] Although it would preserve a means test (that is, it would be restricted to people with low income), the plan would eliminate the arcane categorical requirements that now prevent single persons and couples without children from gaining Medicaid eligibility. The National Governors' Association has also proposed "radical changes in Medicaid."[3] The governors' plan would allow states to extend a restricted benefit package to millions of additional citizens. In short, a new politics of Medicaid is discernable today. Exciting new opportunities for health care reformers have arisen.

Yet if Medicaid is increasingly viewed as a plausible vehicle for health care expansion, the program has been threatened repeatedly with policy retrenchment.[4] While Medicaid has been delinked from Aid to Families with Dependent Children (AFDC) as a result of the 1996 welfare reform legislation, Medicaid remains a means-tested program that still carries the moral stigma of welfare in some eyes. Given its means-tested design and prior history, whether Medicaid can be *permanently* transformed into a relatively broad-based health care program acceptable to "mainstream" citizens remains an open question.

In this chapter, we scrutinize Medicaid's future possibilities by probing its political and administrative evolution over the past 35 years. Only against this historical background can Medicaid's future prospects be appraised. We argue that decisions made at the time of Medicaid's enactment in 1965 have set the matrix for struggles over the program's development. Two crucial technical concepts embedded in the 1965 legislation—medical indigency and comprehensive benefits—left Medicaid's relationship to the cash welfare system ambiguous. The effect of such political ambiguity has been twofold. First, it has permitted actors with different ideological orientations to contest Medicaid's generosity, public reputation, and budget status as a mandatory entitlement program. These political contests over Medicaid's defining attributes would arguably have been less frequent and intense if Medicaid's place in the American welfare state had been more secure—or less so. Second, the ambiguity of Medicaid's status vis-à-vis other social welfare programs has allowed, and in certain respects invited, policy makers to reinforce or create divisions *among* Medicaid's beneficiaries in order to promote their particular political projects and substantive policy goals.

The first section of the chapter examines the key provisions of the 1965 Social Security Act that have influenced the program's development since its original adoption. Next, it examines policy decisions made at two critical junctures in Medicaid's early political history. These early decisions had the practical effect of inhibiting efforts to construct a broad coalition in support of generous Medicaid benefits and program expansions. The third section elaborates on the character of social policy-making that emerged during the 1980s as a result of Medicaid's initial trajectory. We discuss, for example, how elderly recipients of Medicaid were isolated politically from poor mothers and children who obtained Medicaid eligibility as a result of their status as AFDC recipients. The fourth section examines the incremental (but cumulatively substantial) Medicaid expansions that were adopted during the 1980s. We claim that these expansions gave rise to a new political dynamic in the 1990s. As policy makers fought over proposed program liberalizations, as well as over conservative retrenchment initiatives, Medicaid's inherited image as a residual welfare program became newly contested political terrain. By the decade's end, Medicaid's political framing as a program for the poor had been substantially recast in elite rhetoric, although the basic political conflict over Medicaid's status in the American welfare state had not been wholly resolved. Finally, we conclude with a brief assessment of Medicaid's potential to expand health care access and reduce health inequalities in the future.

## Medicaid's Origins

Medicaid's adoption in 1965 must be understood in the context of the long struggle to adopt universal health insurance in the United States. By the late 1950s, liberal proponents of health care reform were focusing their attention on senior citizens, a clientele group that was viewed sympathetically and was already tied to the state through the Social Security system. In 1964, most political observers thought Congress would adopt one of three alternative approaches to improve access to health care for the elderly: (1) a universal hospital insurance program based on Social Security (the King-Anderson bills of 1963 and 1964); (2) a voluntary physician services program supported by beneficiary premiums; or (3) an expansion of the means-tested Kerr-Mills program, which offered a wide range of health care benefits to the low-income elderly. Under the influence of Ways and Means Committee chairman Wilbur Mills, the Social Security amendments of 1965 combined all of these approaches into a single package. By all accounts, the creation of this massive "three-layer" cake took nearly everyone by surprise.[5] The first layer was Medicare Part A, a hospital insurance program based on the Social Security contributory model. The second layer was Medicare Part B, a voluntary supplementary medical insurance program funded through beneficiary premiums and federal general revenues. The third and final layer was the Medicaid program (originally called Part C), which broadened the protections offered to the poor under Kerr-Mills. The Kerr-Mills means-test was liberalized in order to cover additional elderly citizens, and eligibility among the indigent was broadened to include dependent children, the blind, and the permanently disabled.

Medicaid carried over two crucial provisions from Kerr-Mills that would profoundly influence its subsequent policy evolution: the concept of medical indigency and comprehensive benefits. Kerr-Mills had originally been drafted in 1959 as an alternative to the Forand Bill, which proposed universal coverage for the elderly with a restricted benefit package.[6] Proponents of the Kerr-Mills approach argued that a means-tested program would be more efficient than a universal program because it offered help to the most needy. At the same time, this approach offered the truly needy more security than the Forand Bill, because it covered both hospital and physicians services. Although Kerr-Mills was a targeted program, it was designed to be distinct from welfare. Eligibility for benefits under Kerr-Mills was restricted to the "medically indigent." These were older persons who needed assistance when they became sick because they had large medical expenses relative to their current income. Proponents emphasized that the "medically indigent should not be equated with the totally indigent" (the latter term referring to those who receive cash assistance).[7]

While unexpected, the adoption of Kerr-Mills in combination with Medicare makes sense given the incentives of key political actors at the time. By 1965, forty states had already implemented a Kerr-Mills program. A majority of these state programs provided nursing home coverage and/or prescription drugs. Withdrawing such benefits from existing Kerr-Mills recipients would be politically unpopular, since their inclusion under Medicare was essentially ruled out. At the same, Medicaid's creation promoted Mills's goal of forestalling the enactment of national health insurance—which he feared would be massively expensive and could endanger the actuarial soundness of the Social Security system—by giving health benefits to the poor, a potentially vocal constituency for universal coverage.[8]

The motivation of its political architects aside, Medicaid's adoption was perceived to be a minor piece of the 1965 Social Security legislation, certainly of far less significance than the creation of Medicare. Government estimates of Medicaid's future budgetary needs assumed the program would not lead to dramatic expansion of health care coverage.[9] For example, even assuming that all 50 states would implement the new program, the federal government projected Medicaid expenditures to be no more than $238 million per year above what was already being spent on medical welfare programs. As it turned out, this level was reached after only six states had implemented their Medicaid programs. By 1967, 37 states were implementing Medicaid programs, and annual spending was rising by 57% to an annual expenditure of about $1.3 billion. This was about $500 to $600 million more than the cost of pre-Medicaid programs (medical welfare payments and Kerr-Mills combined).[10]

A key factor that explains Medicaid's early expenditure growth was the establishment of generous eligibility standards under various state "Medically Needy" programs. Known as Kerr-Mills extensions, the Medically Needy programs allowed states to extend Medicaid eligibility to persons with income levels above the regular Medicaid income eligibility established in each state. A number of states initially set a very high medically needy eligibility level. For example, New York enrolled families with incomes up to $6,000 per year (for four persons) in 1966. As a point of comparison, by July 1991—25 years later—13 states with medically needy programs set income eligibility levels below $6,000 in current dollars. Under New York's generous enrollment standards, almost half of the state's population in 1966 could have potentially qualified for Medicaid's comprehensive medical coverage, including access to prescription drugs and long-term care facilities.[11] In sum, New York state policy makers clearly envisioned Medicaid as the stepping-stone to universal health care for citizens within its borders.

## Medicaid's Early Critical Junctures

This view of Medicaid as a potential lead-in to national health insurance created a branching point in Medicaid's political evolution. The federal government had to decide whether it should embrace this expansive vision of Medicaid or, instead, restrict program eligibility to a narrow clientele. The federal government chose the latter course, clamping down hard on New York's attempted liberalization. In 1967, only a year after the New York expansion began, Congress passed legislation lowering the medically needy eligibility level to 133.33%[12] of a state's AFDC means-tested level. New York's generous $6,000 eligibility level for a family of four was thereby reduced to $3,900. As a result of this federal intervention, about 600,000 potentially eligible persons were denied medical benefits in 1967. The number of potential Medicaid recipients was reduced by 750,000 in 1968 and 900,000 persons in 1969.[13]

The federal government's decision to crack down on New York was influenced in part by interstate rivalry. In 1967, New York accounted for almost 35% of total Medicaid expenditures in the nation. The next two biggest-spending states, California and Massachusetts, accounted for only 14% and 6%, respectively.[14] Members of Congress from states other than New York, including a number of liberal Democrats, feared that New York's budgetary demands would directly or indirectly siphon resources from their states. A political race to the top might leave citizens of states with less generous Medicaid programs on the floor. As Senator Albert Gore, Sr. (D-TN), stated:

[I question] the justice of taxing a person in Nebraska who has earnings of $4,000 a year to pay the medical expenses of a citizen in New York who earns $6,000 a year ... [W]hile the citizen in Nebraska must pay all of his medical expenses, [he is] taxed to pay the medical expenses of the citizen in New York with an earning capacity of much more. How would you justify that?[15]

New York liberals basically acknowledged that the purpose of their proposed liberalization was to distinguish Medicaid from cash welfare. Indeed, about 70% of New York's Medicaid budget went to medically needy claimants who did not receive cash assistance. Although it provided far more generous benefits than most other states, New York was hardly alone in wishing to distinguish Medicaid from welfare. The majority of Medicaid expenditures in eighteen other states also went to persons not on welfare. In Wisconsin, for example, 74% of total Medicaid payments were for medically needy recipients in 1967.[16]

In stopping New York's attempted liberalization in 1967, federal policy makers consciously decided to define Medicaid as a restricted welfare program, one that would be off limits to the employed. "The House is moving toward a program where you provide medical care to those who can't pay, and expect people to pay it if they are working and can earn income," stated one conservative senator in floor debate.[17]

Yet the 1967 legislation contained contradictions of its own. While it severely restricted the definition of "medically indigent," it nonetheless continued to allow states to make distinctions in their administration of the program between welfare recipients and those who needed health care but not cash assistance. More dramatically, the 1967 statute expanded a series of well-child care benefits for poor children, creating the Early and Periodic Screening, Diagnostic Treatment program. The practical effect was to make the Medicaid benefit package even more comprehensive than it was already.[18] Finally, the 1967 law established the so-called "freedom-of-choice" requirement, which specified that states could no longer create special clinics for welfare clients or require Medicaid recipients to use county hospitals. Now Medicaid administrators had to allow low-income citizens "to use providers of their choice, to enter the mainstream of American health care."[19] In sum, Congress in 1967 reinforced the tension between Medicaid's role as a residual program and its formulation as a more mainstream program. As many New York policy makers had warned, the practical effect of reducing income eligibility for the Medically Needy program was to force many families with large medical expenditures to "spend down" their resources. While federal law allowed states to distinguish Medicaid beneficiaries from welfare recipients, it ensured that many low-income persons who needed medical care would end up on cash assistance. Such political tensions would continue to surface throughout Medicaid's history.

Another crucial early development that led to significant downstream consequences was the creation in 1972 of the Supplementary Security Income (SSI) program. The establishment of SSI consolidated five separate state-run cash assistance programs for the aged, blind, and disabled into a single, federal, means-tested program.[20] Because SSI, unlike most means-tested benefits, is run as a *nationally uniform* program, a clear bifurcation among Medicaid beneficiaries was established. The elderly, blind, and disabled—who tended to be viewed as highly sympathetic groups—gained Medicaid eligibility based on a *federal* eligibility standard. In contrast, poor mothers and their children gained eligibility according to a (typically much lower) *state* eligibility standard.[21]

The establishment of SSI as a major entry point into Medicaid, together with Congress's decision to scale back state Medically Needy programs in 1967, set the contours for Medicaid's political trajectory over the following decade. These decisions reinforced the view of Medicaid as a residual program for a variety of low-income groups, each of whom obtained eligibility for benefits according to a different set of arcane rules and who were seen to have distinctive social characteristics. In sum, Medicaid emerged from its first decade of operation *marginalized politically, complex administratively, and fragmented socially.* Any discussion of Medicaid as the bridge to national health care reform was all but lost.

## Expansions within Welfare Medicine

In this section, we describe two main expansionary initiatives within Medicaid enacted in the 1980s: eligibility expansions for children and pregnant women and their infants, and Medicaid expansions for the elderly. We use these case examples to illustrate the dynamics of Medicaid politics for different clientele groups under a still-constrained welfare vision of the program's mission.

### Medicaid for Poor Women and Children

The federal government enacted incremental Medicaid expansions for children and/or pregnant women and infants in every year between 1984 and 1990. By the end of this 6-year period, up to 5 million children and 500,000 pregnant women had gained Medicaid eligibility.[22] What is most remarkable is that these Medicaid coverage expansions—which helped drive combined state and federal spending on health care for the poor (measured in 1996 dollars) from $75 billion in 1986 to almost $180 billion in 1996[23]—occurred during an era of general fiscal austerity. The federal government in particular was running large budget deficits. These program liberalizations followed significant cutbacks in Medicaid spending made under Ronald Reagan in 1981.[24] In sum, major targeted Medicaid expansions took place in the wake of an era of policy retrenchment.

Medicaid certainly did not fare well at the beginning of the 1980s. The Omnibus Budget Reconciliation Act of 1981 (OBRA-81), which carried out much of Reagan's budget-cutting agenda, reduced Medicaid spending largely through major reductions in spending for AFDC. More than 400,000 poor working families lost Medicaid coverage following their removal from the cash welfare rolls.[25] In addition, OBRA-81 restricted "categorical eligibility" for Medicaid benefits by (1) eliminating the state option to cover 19- to 21-year-old dependent children, (2) denying coverage of two-parent families in which only the secondary wage earner was unemployed, and (3) restricting the duration of Medicaid eligibility for first-time pregnant women. States were also given new discretion to restrict coverage under Medically Needy programs. For example, states could define the elderly, blind, and disabled with large medical expenses as medically indigent and therefore eligible for Medicaid, while denying coverage to equally poor families without these demographic or health characteristics.[26] In sum, states were invited to create yet more bifurcations among poor families, dividing the elderly, blind, and disabled from other financially strapped groups. The federal government also lowered the level of its financial contribution to state Medicaid programs, reducing the federal matching rate by 3%, 4%, and 4.5% over a 3-year period.[27]

Given the deep unpopularity of the cash welfare system among both the public and policy elites, it is not surprising that Medicaid has been damaged historically by its prior linkage to the AFDC program.[28] The Medicaid eligibility restrictions that were enacted in 1981 were actually mild relative to Reagan's original proposal, which would have terminated Medicaid's status as a budgetary entitlement by transforming it into a block grant program. Still, OBRA-81 manifested the basic tensions that seem to be endemic in Medicaid policy-making. While it sought to narrow Medicaid eligibility via its AFDC benefit cutbacks, OBRA-81 also promulgated a new federal mandate that required states to provide Medicaid coverage to adults who were removed from the welfare rolls for a 9-month transitional period. The federal government even offered to share the costs with any state that wished to extend this transition period for an additional 6 months. The main purpose of this new program was to help former AFDC recipients move from welfare to work by giving them a health care safety. Many states eventually opted for the extra 6-month option.

In addition to highlighting Medicaid's inevitable role in welfare reform efforts, the transitional coverage provisions of OBRA-81 illustrate—in this instance simultaneously within the same bill—the multiple and at times conflicting ways that Medicaid can be portrayed: (1) as assistance for the "totally indigent" (i.e., welfare dependents), (2) as a program to transition welfare dependents into work, and (3) as a policy carrot to discourage welfare dependency in the first place.

The targeted Medicaid expansions adopted from 1984 to 1990 increased the number of people receiving Medicaid benefits to 36 million in 1996, up from an average of 20–23 million between 1973 and 1989.[29] Obviously this constituted remarkable growth in the size of Medicaid's constituency. Three key political characteristics of the targeted expansions discouraged many Americans from noticing the cumulative impact of these expansions. In particular, the Medicaid expansions adopted in the 1980s and early 1990s were incremental, hidden, and portrayed as cost-effective.

*Incremental.* Many of the Medicaid expansions began as state "options" before being converted into federal mandates. National policy makers initially *allowed* states to receive federal matching funds for the cost of extending eligibility to a specific population, subject to certain federal standards. For example, coverage of pregnant women and infants up to 100% of poverty was a state option in 1986, but became a federal mandate in 1988. Similarly, the Medicare "buy in" (described in the next section) was optional in 1986 and required in 1988 (see Table 9.1). States that agreed to such options were generally not required to make any changes in their basic Medicaid eligibility definitions.

*Hidden.* Budget reconciliation bills were the main vehicles used to enact Medicaid expansions in the 1980s. Reconciliation bills are often massive omnibus measures that require changes in scores of federal spending programs and tax provisions. Creating new programs within the reconciliation process is politically attractive for two main reasons. First, reconciliation bills enjoy procedural advantages in the Senate that make them easier to pass. Second, their massive scope inhibits public scrutiny, at times allowing politicians to strike deals without having to go through the normal committee review process. Representative Henry Waxman

Table 9.1
Major Federal Expansions for Medicaid Eligibility,
Pregnant Women and Children: 1984–1990

| Legislation | Population Affected | Expansion |
| --- | --- | --- |
| DEFRA 1984 (Deficit Reduction Act of 1984, P.L. 98-369) | Infants and children | *Mandate*. Requires coverage of all children up to age 5 born after 9/30/83 who meet AFDC financial standards |
| | Pregnant women | *Mandate*. Requires coverage of first-time pregnant women and pregant women in two-parent families whose principal wage earner is unemployed (AFDC-UP) |
| COBRA 1985 (Consolidated Omnibus Budget Reconciliation Act of 1985, P.L. 99-272) | Pregnant women | *Mandate*. Requires coverage of all remaining pregnant women meeting AFDC financial standards (that is, those in two-parent families with an employed principal earner) |
| OBRA 1986 (Omnibus Budget Reconciliation Act of 1986, P.L. 99-509) | Children | *Option*. Allows coverage of all children up to age 7 born after 9/30/83 with family incomes up to 100 percent of poverty |
| | Pregnant women and infants | *Option*. Allows coverage of pregnant women and infants under age 1 if income is below a state-established income standard up to 100 percent of poverty (also allows states to pay for prenatal care while Medicaid applications are pending) |
| OBRA 1987 (Omnibus Budget Reconciliation Act of 1987, P.L. 100-203) | Children | *Mandate*. Requires coverage of all children up to age 7 born after 9/30/83 who meet AFDC income standards (extension of DEFRA 1984 mandate) *Option*. Allows coverage of all children up to age 8 born after 9/30/83 with family incomes up to 100 percent of poverty |

(*Continued*)

Table 9.1
(*Continued*)

| Legislation | Population Affected | Expansion |
|---|---|---|
| OBRA 1987 (*continued*) | Pregnant women and infants | *Option.* Allows coverage of pregnant women and infants with family incomes up to 185 percent of poverty |
| MCCA 1988 (Medicare Catastrophic Coverage Act of 1987, P.L. 100-360) | Pregnant women and infants | *Mandate.* Requires coverage of pregnant women and infants under age 1 with incomes under 100 percent of poverty |
| OBRA 1989 (Omnibus Budget Reconciliation Act of 1989, P.L. 101-239) | Children, pregnant women, and infants | *Mandate.* Requires coverage of pregnant women and all children (including infants) up to age 6 born after 9/30/83 if family income is below 133 percent of poverty |
| OBRA 1990 (Omnibus Budget Reconciliation Act of 1990, P.L. 101-508) | Children | *Mandate.* Requires coverage of all children up to age 18 born after 9/30/83 with family income under 100 percent of poverty (extends coverage to children age 7 to 18 under 100 percent of poverty; intent is to phase in coverage of all children in poverty by 2002) |

*Source:* CRS (1993, p. 36); Coughlin, Ku, and Holahan (1994, pp. 48–51).

(D-CA), the chair of the Health Subcommittee of the Energy and Labor Committee during this period, was a master at inserting incremental Medicaid expansions into reconciliation legislation. Waxman and his staff knew how to exploit budget-forecasting conventions. During the 1980s, budget estimators typically projected the cost of reconciliation spending for only 3 years. The Medicaid expansions, however, were usually phased in over a decade, thereby pushing most of their costs outside the official projection window.[30]

*Cost-Effective.* The fact that the populations targeted in these Medicaid expansions included pregnant women and their children was obviously crucial in rendering the expansions politically feasible. Yet proponents of the expansions actually did not appeal to moral arguments about the deservedness of these clientele groups. Rather, they argued that extending Medicaid coverage to these beneficiaries was *cost-effective*. While infant mortality had decreased, low birth weight had remained stubbornly high in the 1980s, especially for poor minority women. Health care costs associated with low birth-weight babies were rising dramatically. In part, this reflected technological improvements that allowed babies of lower and lower birth weight to be saved (at higher and higher costs). The increased spending also resulted from an exogenous increase in the rate of low birth-weight babies. Low birth-weight babies are at high risk for acquiring a permanent disability. They are not only expensive to cover while in the neonatal intensive care unit, but they are at greater risk for medical problems throughout their lives. Proponents argued that inexpensive prenatal care made good economic sense because it would reduce the need for expensive health care later on. A similar pragmatic argument was made for children: inexpensive immunizations and well-child care were portrayed as good investments for a healthy population and strong future workforce.[31]

## Expansions for the Elderly

The Medicaid expansions of the 1980s not only provided new benefits to women and children. They also provided valuable new protections to the low-income elderly. Congress mandated that states use their Medicaid revenues to pay for the Medicare premiums of eligible seniors. And Congress, in the ill-fated Medicare Catastrophic Coverage Act, raised the amount of money seniors in the community can keep when their spouses receive Medicaid benefits as residents of nursing homes. The adoption of the latter protection against "spousal impoverishment" reflects the emergence of Medicaid as America's de facto long-term care program. Medicaid's transformation into a key social support for the mainstream elderly requires careful scrutiny because it has fundamentally shaped both the program's internal operations and the character of its political dynamics.

While Medicaid's architects assumed that Medicaid would offer benefits to the indigent elderly, they did not expect the program to become the nation's main long-term care program. But the concepts of medical indigence and comprehensive benefits embedded in Medicaid's enabling legislation were sufficiently elastic that the program had a built-in potential to help fill the gaping long-term care hole in our patchwork national health care system. Medicare does not cover most of the costs of long-term custodial nursing home care. And relatively few Americans have been able or willing to purchase private long-term care insurance during their working years. As a result, citizens often arrive in old age unprepared to cover the expense of custodial nursing home care. When they need such care, they often fall back on Medicaid.

As early as 1975, Medicaid was paying the bills of more than half of all nursing home residents. Many seniors in nursing homes are not eligible for Medicaid at the time of their admission. At an average cost of $30,000 per year, however, nursing home care quickly depletes the resources of all but the most affluent seniors. Between 27%–45% of elderly nursing home residents become eligible for Medicaid after spending down their resources. A significant proportion of elderly nursing home residents on Medicaid are not poor by typical "welfare" standards.[32] Indeed, some spent their adult lives firmly in the middle class. States cover these "non-poor" persons under either their Medically Needy programs or under a special income rule called the "300% rule."[33] Together, these two sets of programs account for 88% of Medicaid's nursing home spending and 75% of total Medicaid spending on the elderly.

By the late 1980s, Medicaid was serving as the public support of last resort for many older Americans in nursing homes. Policy makers recognized, however, that many senior citizens remained anxious about their rapidly rising out-of-pocket medical costs and about the continuing lack of guaranteed protections in numerous areas (from acute hospital stays to long-term care). For those with serious conditions, out-of-pocket costs could reach catastrophic proportions. Low-income elderly persons not receiving Medicaid, for example, spent on average 25% of their income on medical bills.[34]

In 1988, policy makers from both parties saw a potential political gain in addressing seniors' anxieties about out-of-pocket medical costs. Given Medicaid's track record in long-term care, health reform advocates might have been expected to focus on it as the vehicle for adopting catastrophic coverage. Instead, reform proponents sought to expand benefits under Medicare. Advocates viewed Medicaid's demeaning asset tests, its welfare stigma, as well as the greater political uncertainty over its future trajectory, as reasons for focusing on benefit enlargements within Medicare. The Medicare Catastrophic Coverage Act (MCCA) was signed into law in July 1988. MCCA represented the largest expansion to the Medicare program since its inception in 1965. The new Medicare benefits included an outpatient prescription drug benefit, extended coverage of long-term hospital care, mammography screening, and hospice care. In a sharp break from prior social insurance legislation, Medicare beneficiaries themselves were asked to shoulder the financial burden by paying special premiums

pegged to family income. The main reason for this user fee approach—
and for the measure's failure to include the long-term custodial nursing
home benefits the elderly most wanted—was fiscal constraints. With an
increase in the payroll tax apparently unacceptable, and the federal government running large budget deficits, covering institutionalized nursing
home care within Medicare was simply not feasible. Health care reform
advocates nonetheless saw the passage of the catastrophic coverage measure as the foundation for future long-term care legislation.

It soon became clear that the adoption of the legislation had been a
"catastrophic" political mistake. While millions of Americans would benefit greatly from the new Medicare benefits offered under the legislation,
some upper-income seniors saw themselves as losers because they would
be paying for health benefits they apparently didn't want or need. In a
demonstration of the power of narrow constituencies, and the difficulty
of crafting explicitly redistributive reforms even within universal policy
structures, Congress repealed nearly the entire measure barely a year after
it was signed into law.

The new protection against spousal impoverishment (along with
the requirement that states pay the Medicare premiums, deductibles, and
copayments of seniors with incomes below the poverty level) was one
of the few major provisions to survive Congress's embarrassing policy
reversal.[35] One effect of the catastrophic coverage debacle was thus to
solidify Medicaid's de facto role as America's major long-term care program. The catastrophic coverage repeal demonstrated how difficult it
would be to create a significant long-term care benefit within Medicare
absent a willingness among policy makers either to raise payroll taxes or
tap federal general revenues. Yet allowing Medicaid to remain the main
source of governmental aid for nursing home residents created its own
set of political tensions. It signaled that Medicaid would permanently
serve a mainstream constituency—the institutionalized elderly—within a
means-tested policy design.

This situation created some tricky dilemmas for policy makers. On
the one hand, the deep reliance of the elderly created political pressures
to offer mainstream families greater security. Fearful of the potential electoral repercussions, Congress refused to repeal the spousal impoverishment protections in the catastrophic care repeal. On the other hand, some
wondered about the appropriateness of using a means-tested program to
support previously middle-class recipients. In sum, the fundamental tension between conceptualizing Medicaid as residual welfare program or
as broad public social support—which has shaped the politics of Medicaid for younger families—also reveals itself when policy makers consider

how to cover people at the end of the life cycle. While policy makers in 1988 tried to protect families from having to deplete their resources when a spouse requires long-term nursing home care, they have also sought to prevent middle-class children from "unfairly" taking advantage of the Medicaid program by transferring their parents' assets out of their name in order to maximize their inheritances and push their parents' future nursing home bills onto the government.

Medicaid's prominent role in supporting nursing home care has also led to new concerns about the program's implications for generational equity. While the elderly comprise less than 15% of Medicaid recipients, they account for more than 30% of the program's costs, in large part because of their nursing home care.[36] While concerns about generational equity in the American welfare state has focused mainly on Social Security and Medicare, some advocates for poor children began in the 1980s to argue that it was inappropriate for a disproportionate share of Medicaid dollars to support the elderly while younger people were struggling to pay for their health care.

It is with this backdrop—expansions for the "expensive" elderly and "cost-effective" expansions for pregnant women and children—that we move into the symbolically charged politics of Medicaid in the 1990s.

## The Contest over Medicaid's Image

During the presidential race in 1992, the U.S. economy was in recession. Despite a significant increase in Medicaid coverage over the 1980s, the number of uninsured Americans had climbed to a record high of 37 million as a result of a reduction in employer-sponsored coverage. With the economy weakening, many middle-class Americans who had health insurance were worried about keeping it. For a brief moment, it appeared that after 80 years, national health insurance was an idea whose time had finally come. Of course, as Mark Peterson discusses in chapter 7, Bill Clinton's health care reform plan failed. The politics of health policy-making did not remain static after comprehensive reform was defeated, however. In this section, we consider three main policy areas where there was substantial Medicaid activity in the 1990s: the growth of Medicaid managed care in the states, Clinton's successful effort to defeat the Republican Medicaid block grant proposal in 1996, and the creation of the State Children's Health Insurance Program (S-CHIP) in 1997. The big development in the 1990s has been a fundamental change in Medicaid's political framing and the very terms of the policy debate.

## Mainstreaming through Managed Care?

In the early 1990s, policy makers in many states readily characterized their Medicaid programs as administrative failures. To be sure, most policy makers acknowledged that Medicaid played a crucial role in providing health coverage for millions of Americans. Yet there was broad agreement—among Republican and Democratic officials alike—that Medicaid suffered from serious operational flaws. Medicaid still failed to cover many needy persons, and the health care it offered was too often of low quality and inefficiently provided. Numerous studies documented that Medicaid recipients were much *less* likely than Americans with private health insurance to have a relationship with a primary care doctor or to receive needed preventive care, and much *more* likely to receive their care in hospital emergency room settings or public clinics with long waiting lines.[37] Despite the targeted efforts to increase prenatal care and well-child care coverage in the 1980s, a large proportion of Medicaid women received no, or only minimal, prenatal care services. Many children enrolled in Medicaid were failing to receive needed immunizations. Layered atop these concerns about health care access and quality were concerns about Medicaid costs. While the annual growth rate of Medicaid spending declined immediately following the retrenchment period in the early 1980s, Medicaid costs rose steadily thereafter. As the program expansions for children and pregnant women and other legislative changes adopted in the 1980s and early 1990s were phased in, Medicaid expenditures shot up.[38] By the mid-1990s, Medicaid was the largest item in most states' budgets.

Yet if Medicaid spending was growing rapidly in the 1990s, so too were the ranks of the uninsured. Many state policy makers argued that it was simply inequitable to provide Medicaid coverage to the nonworking poor at a time when two thirds of uninsured Americans came from families with at least one working parent. When Medicaid was originally created, the assumption was that aid should be concerned with those who could not afford health insurance because of their lack of employment. By the 1990s, however, it was widely acknowledged that being employed does not guarantee affordable health insurance coverage. In sum, the inability of the working poor to obtain affordable health insurance is another reason for the emerging reconceptualization of Medicaid as a program distinct from welfare.

In light of these pressures to improve Medicaid services, rein in program costs, and expand access to the uninsured, states were ripe for considering a new administrative approach for Medicaid in the 1990s.

Medicaid managed care seemingly offered a "magic bullet" solution. It promised simultaneously to reduce costs, improve access, raise the quality of delivered services, and in some cases expand coverage to the uninsured. The basic idea behind Medicaid managed care is that states contract with managed care organizations at 95% of the current cost to run their Medicaid programs. Each state pays managed care organizations a preset monthly amount for each member in the plan, whether or not the member actually utilizes any medical care services during the month. The theory is that managed care organizations make money by emphasizing preventive care and reducing unnecessary utilization of expensive medical services, such as preventable emergency room use. Efficient managed care organizations may be able to provide services at only 85% of the cost baseline, allowing them to retain the 10% difference.

State policy makers have also been concerned about the continuing unwillingness of many physicians to provide services to Medicaid recipients. Despite the "freedom of choice" provision passed in 1967, few Medicaid recipients have ever really had access to "mainstream" medical care. As early as 1972, Medicaid was viewed as perpetuating a two-tiered system of health care in the United States: a lower Medicaid tier providing access to public clinics for the poor; and an upper, private-pay tier providing access to private office-based physician services for the middle and upper classes. This division continued to exist in the early 1990s, although a growing number of persons with nominally middle class incomes who had lost their health insurance were forced to obtain care from "lower tier" sources. Many state policy makers believed that Medicaid managed care would promote mainstreaming because it would offer physicians incentives to participate in the Medicaid program.[39]

Advocates for the poor also saw Medicaid managed care reform as a tool for ensuring more equal access to health care, believing it would remove the stigma associated with the traditional Medicaid program. For example, the director of a Phoenix-based philanthropy touted Arizona's Medicaid managed care program because "many Medicaid patients have access to mainstream private physicians whom they did not previously have access to. They don't feel like charity patients anymore."[40] "Medicaid managed care may offer the last, best opportunity to provide integrated health care for the nation's poor," wrote consumer advocate Geraldine Dalleck, author of *Health Care for America's Poor: Separate and Unequal.*[41]

In sum, Medicaid managed care promised to lower costs, improve quality, and widen access for the poor to mainstream health services. The only obvious alternative to this policy innovation, it appeared, was for states to stick with their antiquated, inefficient, state-run Medicaid programs. No approaches other than Medicaid managed care and the discredited status quo were even on the table for consideration. It is little wonder that the Medicaid managed care approach was subject to little political debate, or that it diffused rapidly across the nation once a few states adopted it.

With several years of administrative experience now behind them, policy makers' assessment of Medicaid managed care has become more ambivalent. Many commercial managed care organizations have stopped contracting with state Medicaid programs after experiencing problems. There is less talk now about the possibility of rapid mainstreaming. Access to some preventive services has improved in some states, but it is unclear whether there have been improvements in either the quality of care or in actual health outcomes. Finally, after temporarily stabilizing, Medicaid costs are again increasing at rates similar to those in the early 1990s. Clearly, there are no panaceas in the real world. In this light, Medicaid managed care simply promised too much too fast.[42]

More important, however, Medicaid may actually lose political clout if Medicaid managed care reinforces or increases the isolation of Medicaid beneficiaries from the health care systems experienced by the middle class. If state policy makers are willing to offer assistance to managed care organizations, Medicaid beneficiaries conceivably could be fully (or at least substantially) integrated into the mainstream managed care system. The divide between Medicaid and the private-sector health care would greatly narrow. Alternatively, if state policy makers fail to offer adequate assistance to managed care organizations, Medicaid could end up being treated not just as a welfare program, but as a second-class, *segregated*, service item distinct from the rest of the private sector. Only time will tell which of these courses policy makers will choose.

### The Clinton Spin: Your Parents' Medicaid

A second important development in the 1990s—one carried out at the level of high politics rather than at the level of program operations—was the attempt by President Clinton to recast Medicaid as a middle-class entitlement during his budget showdown with the Gingrich-Dole Republicans in 1995–1996. It would be difficult to exaggerate the political stakes for Clinton and the Democratic Party in this budget battle. Not only did the GOP budget package seek to undermine Clinton's ability to control the current policy agenda, but it sought to cripple the future possibilities for activist government.[43] Unsurprisingly, President Clinton sought to rally public opinion against the GOP package by arguing that it would entail huge cuts in spending for Medicare, education, and environmental protection—three federal programs with obvious appeal for middle-class voters. More startling was that Clinton also explicitly tied his political fate to support for *Medicaid*. Indeed, Clinton invoked this programmatic quartet—Medicare, Medicaid, education, and the environment—so often in the budget clash that observers dubbed it his "M2E2" strategy. Medicaid had evidently ascended to the status of most beloved federal programs. No other president had claimed that Medicaid, or any other means-tested program for that matter, carried the same importance as Medicare, whose political standing among both the public and policy elites was rivaled only by Social Security.

In explaining why protecting Medicaid was so vital, Clinton emphasized not that the program was an essential safety net for the economically disadvantaged, but rather that Medicaid was a key support for senior citizens residing in nursing homes. Clinton was at pains to emphasize that many of these seniors were middle-class before they depleted their resources and that they had middle-class children and grandchildren. In one address Clinton put it this way:

> Now, think about this—what about the Medicaid program? You hardly hear anything about Medicaid. People say, oh, that's that welfare program. One-third of Medicaid does go to help poor women and their poor children on Medicaid. Over two-thirds of it goes to the elderly and the disabled. All of you know that as well. [*Commenting on Republican proposals*] You think about how many middle-class working people are not going to be able to save to send their kids to college because now they'll have to be taking care of their parents who would have been eligible for public assistance.[44]

Clinton's statement revealed the huge political importance of the incremental expansions in the 1980s. By 1995, Medicaid's long-term care role was sufficiently recognized and well accepted that it was appropriate in a major public address for the president to talk about Medicare and Medicaid as comprising a health care *package* for the mainstream elderly. At the same time, Clinton evidently felt he could exploit the heterogeneity of the beneficiary groups within Medicaid for political advantage, using the recent increase in coverage for low-income pregnant women and poor children to direct attention away from any residual negative "welfare" connotations. In sum, Clinton sought to cast Medicaid as broad social entitlement that incorporated the middle class.

Clinton's strategy to reframe how Americans view Medicaid was not lost on his political opponents. "The White House insists on a Medicaid entitlement precisely because it wants to recast Medicaid as a middle-class property right perhaps as a prelude to another universal health care plan, or at least as a popular vote getter," observed the fiscally conservative Concord Coalition.[45] This strategic recasting also found expression in 1996 Democratic party platform language. The platform stated that securing both Medicare and Medicaid was a "duty for our parents, so they can live their lives in dignity," and it prominently pledged to protect Medicaid in particular from devastating cuts that "would jeopardize the health care of children and seniors."

Inspection of Democratic party platforms from 1984, 1988, and 1992 reveals that the platforms either did not mention Medicaid (1984 and 1988) or discussed the program only in the context of welfare reform and encouraging work. If the willingness to protect a program when the stakes are high is the test, then Medicaid had become a fundamental Democratic Party commitment. To be sure, Medicaid has long enjoyed more public support than certain other means-tested programs like food stamps and AFDC.[46] Policy makers' willingness to adopt significant Medicaid expansions in the 1980s suggests this political support can help motor significant program-building efforts. Until the 1995 budget battle, however, Democratic officeholders had been hesitant to defend Medicaid as a cornerstone of the American welfare state. What accounts for this shift in Medicaid's political standing? Was Clinton's vigorous support for Medicaid as a key program for the middle class indicative of a broader transformation of Medicaid's public image?

While Democrats have historically been more favorable toward protecting and expanding Medicaid than Republicans,[47] the Democratic Party had not presented a clear position on the program. During the battle over Medicaid spending in the 1981 budget battle, for example, House Democrats were initially confused about how to respond to Reagan's Medicaid retrenchment initiatives.[48] Ultimately, a consensus emerged among House Democrats on the need to protect public social spending for the poor. Medicaid was thus one of several low-income programs that merited a vigorous political defense. But there was no effort made in 1981 to reframe Medicaid as a middle-class entitlement or to distinguish Medicaid from efforts to protect other means-tested programs. In their public statements and media interviews, Democrats talked about Republican mean-spiritedness toward the poor more generally.[49] When Democratic lawmakers did mention Medicaid, they tended to focus on the burden

Reagan's block-grant proposal would place on state governments, not on the direct implications for Medicaid beneficiaries.

Clinton's decision to make a defense of Medicaid as an integral part of his political strategy in the 1995 budget showdown was anything but automatic. As in 1981, Democrats in 1995 did not immediately reject the GOP proposal to reduce Medicaid spending and abolish its legal status as a budgetary entitlement. Part of the confusion stemmed from uncertainty over how to respond to Republican proposals for welfare reform.[50] When Avis LaVelle, Assistant Secretary of Health and Human Services, was asked in early 1995 if she would defend the entitlement status of welfare and Medicaid, she said: "No, I can't. There is a re-evaluation going on throughout the department as to the whole concept of entitlement programs. It's just not smart for us to take an advocacy position one way or another. The ground is shifting under our feet."[51]

Debate over Republican health care proposals focused almost entirely on Medicare until September of 1995, when House Republicans formally unveiled their Medigrant proposal.[52] It was at this point that Clinton began to frame the proposed Medicaid changes not as an effort to reduce the traditional welfare caseload but rather as a serious threat to mainstream seniors who had previously worked and been taxpayers. In a speech before retirees in Miami Beach, Clinton said, "Do not take money from elderly people that barely have enough to live on, that have made their contributions all their lives, and give it to people who aren't even asking for a tax cut and don't need it."[53]

Clinton's high-profile defense of Medicaid's entitlement standing was all the more remarkable because many state officials, along with the National Governors' Association, favored the GOP block grant proposal. In sharp contrast, states were unanimously against Reagan's Medicaid block grant proposal in 1981. State forces aligned with the Republicans in 1995 for two reasons. First, unlike in 1981, when governors were coping with fiscal stress, many states were in excellent economic shape. The budgets of a number of states were in surplus. Less strapped for resources, state governors were attracted to the increased policy flexibility block grants promised. Second, states had gained experience with Medicaid managed care waivers over the 1980s and early 1990s, giving them confidence that they could manage block grants efficiently.

Republicans predicted that Clinton would quickly cave in to their budget-cutting demands in order to avoid being twice defeated in major social policy debates in a single presidential term. Instead, the President held his ground, steadfastly defending Medicaid's entitlement status. If

Clinton couldn't win the adoption of national health care reform, he refused to tolerate an erosion of existing federal health policy commitments. On one level, Clinton's effort to cast Medicaid as a middle-class entitlement can be seen as merely a pragmatic effort to draw attention to the most sympathetic groups within the program. On a deeper level, however, it signaled that Medicaid had been radically transformed since 1965 as a result of both incremental coverage expansions and a willingness of policy makers to tolerate efforts by seniors to render themselves eligible for nursing home benefits. By 1995, Medicaid could be credibly portrayed as something very different from "welfare medicine."

## Ambiguous Expansion: The State Children's Health Insurance Program

While Medicaid enrollment continued to rise through 1996, employer-sponsored health insurance declined to a greater degree. By 1997, 43 million Americans lacked health insurance. A window of opportunity opened in 1997 for a targeted coverage expansion due to the growing economy and an unexpected governmental revenue windfall as a result of tobacco litigation. As they had in the 1980s, elected officials decided to focus on reducing the number of uninsured children. The key administrative question was whether coverage expansion should take place exclusively within Medicaid. While eight major proposals were introduced, the debate quickly narrowed to two major alternatives: a major coverage expansion for children within Medicaid, and a state block grant proposal.[54]

Not surprisingly, the National Governors' Association favored the new block grant approach in large part because it offered state policy makers more control over eligibility levels and the benefit package. Many (although not all) social advocacy groups favored the Medicaid expansion approach for two main reasons. First, it guaranteed benefits for individual children; in contrast, the block grant approach would have provided an entitlement to the states, but not to individual beneficiaries. Second, expanding coverage for poor children through Medicaid would have further entrenched the existing Medicaid benefit package. Some activists were concerned that if states were given block grants, they might well expand coverage for children under a more restrictive benefit package. This restricted package would in turn become a negative policy precedent that might delimit and constrain future expansion attempts. Some even feared the block grant approach might allow conservatives to establish a beachhead in a future battle to dismantle Medicaid.[55]

Given Congress's tendency to deal with conflicts between multiple reform proposals not by splitting the difference but rather by accepting them all—which more or less captures how Medicaid came to be layered into the Social Security amendments of 1965—it is not surprising that Congress gave its blessing to both the block grant and Medicaid approaches in 1997. Under the State Children's Health Insurance Program (again, S-CHIP), states have the option to extend coverage to uninsured children (1) through Medicaid; (2) through the creation of an entirely new, separate program (with a restricted benefit package); or (3) through a combination of both. While 19 states opted for Medicaid expansions through 1999, more than half either implemented new (non-Medicaid) S-CHIP programs (13 states) or had combination (16 states) programs.[56]

While Clinton's defeat of the Republican's block grant proposal in 1996 clearly put Medicaid in a positively middle-class light, the political impact of S-CHIP on Medicaid—like Medicaid managed care reform—is more ambiguous. To the extent that many children in S-CHIP programs come from working families and are covered under Medicaid expansions, S-CHIP can be viewed as another form of middle-class incorporation under Medicaid. After all, the non-Medicaid children's health insurance programs are relatively small: as of January 2000, they served 2 million children, compared to approximately 20 million children enrolled in Medicaid nationally.[57] These enrollment numbers indicate that Medicaid is certain to remain much the larger program. Still, Congress did forgo an opportunity in 1997 to retain Medicaid as the *sole* administrative vehicle for children's coverage expansions—an approach that would have ensured that newly enrolled children would have been covered under a more comprehensive benefit package while further solidifying Medicaid's recent caseload growth.

## Conclusion

Medicaid stands at a crossroads. It could be the stepping stone to a universal system that incorporates large numbers of working- and middle-class Americans or it could revert to "welfare medicine," torn apart by divisions among different groups of lower-income beneficiaries. Groups as diverse as health insurance trade associations and liberal advocacy groups are proposing major expansions in Medicaid eligibility. Meanwhile, some policy makers are calling for the creation of new categorical health care programs like S-CHIP to serve only the most sympathetic constituencies, leaving Medicaid to provide coverage to the rest. The latter approach would only guarantee Medicaid's political marginalization.

Policy makers often argue that Medicaid's comprehensive benefit package makes further eligibility expansions too expensive. Yet Medicaid's inherited benefit package can be strategically revised to render future program expansions more affordable. The National Governors' Association, for example, has recently proposed an innovative Medicaid reform plan that would allow states to extend Medicaid coverage to millions of additional people under a restricted benefit package.[58] Under the National Governors' Association plan, Medicaid could provide health care security to many more American families (in all their multiple and varied forms) while continuing to serve the elderly and the disabled, thus broadening the overall size of Medicaid's political constituency. As the 1996 budget battle revealed, it is the incorporation of the middle-class elderly, the disabled, and families with children that endows Medicaid with political strength. In the rough and tumble of American politics, there are good, pragmatic reasons for preserving a degree of middle-class incorporation in Medicaid—and for not directing beneficiary groups into many different programs without a common political base. Viewed in this light, the shift to Medicaid managed care deserves praise not for its technical merits or potential cost savings, but rather for helping break down the welfare stigma by mirroring organizational changes in the private sector and thereby keeping Medicaid within mainstream patterns of health care delivery.

As a substantial number of Americans remain locked outside the private health insurance market and Medicare continues to fall short of providing needed services for the elderly, there is a welcome opportunity to reframe Medicaid's public image and transform the program into a core public social support. Creative policy reforms designed with an eye to politics could put Medicaid on the road toward a more universal program that is ultimately acceptable to "mainstream" America. As we strive to treat people more equally within our public programs, we can help reduce health inequalities.

# Notes

1. R. Stevens and R. Stevens, *Welfare Medicine in America: A Case Study of Medicaid* (New York: Free Press, 1974).

2. Charles N. Kahn and Ronald F. Pollack, "Building a Consensus for Expanding Health Coverage," *Health Affairs* 20.1 (2001): 40–48.

3. Robert Pear, "Governors Offer 'Radical' Revision of Medicaid Plan," *New York Times* (25 February 2001): A-1.

4. Karl Kronebusch, "Medicaid for Children: Federal Mandates, Welfare Reform, and Policy Backsliding," *Health Affairs* 20.1 (2001): 97–111.

5. Stevens and Stevens, *Welfare Medicine*; Theodore Marmor, *The Politics of Medicare* (London: Routledge & Kegan Paul, 1970).

6. Marmor, *Politics of Medicare*.

7. Sidney Fein, "The Kerr-Mills Act: Medical Care for the Indigent in Michigan, 1960–1965," *Journal of the History of Medicine* 53 (July 1998): 285–316.

8. Marmor, *Politics of Medicare*; Sandra J. Tanenbaum, "Medicaid Eligibility Policy in the 1980s: Medical Utilitarianism and the 'Deserving' Poor," *Journal of Health Politics, Policy and Law* 20.4 (1995): 933–954; Eric M. Patashnik and Julian E. Zelizer, "Paying for Medicare: Benefits, Budgets, and Wilbur Mills's Policy Legacy," *Journal of Health Politics Policy, and Law* 26.1 (2001): 7–36.

9. Stevens and Stevens, *Welfare Medicine*.

10. Congressional Research Service (CRS), *Medicaid Source Book: Background Data and Analysis (A 1993 Update)* (Washington, DC: U.S. Government Printing Office, 1993), 30.

11. Stevens and Stevens, *Welfare Medicine*.

12. This bizaare fractional percentage to determine eligibility is a testament to Medicaid's complexity.

13. U.S. Senate, 90th Congress, Congressional Hearing, "Social Security Amendments of 1967," Part 3, Committee on Finance, September 20–22 and 26, 1967. Based on testimony from George K. Wyman, Commissioner, New York State Department of Social Services, 1546.

14. U.S. Department of Health, Education and Welfare, Social and Rehabilitation Service, "Medical Assistance Financed under the Public Assistance Titles of the Social Security Act," November 1967, Table 15.

15. U.S. Senate, 90th Congress, Congressional Hearing, 1551.

16. Ibid.

17. U.S. Senate, 90th Congress, Congressional Hearing, 1547.

18. Sara Rosenbaum and Colleen A. Sonosky, "Child Health in a Changing Policy Environment: The Roles of Child Advocacy Organizations in Addressing Policy Issues," *Who Speaks for America's Children? The Role of Child Advocates in Public Policy*, ed. Carol De Vita and Rachel Mosher-Williams (Washington, DC: Urban Institute Press, 2001).

19. CRS, *Medicaid Source Book*, 1993, Appendix H, 1041.

20. Jill Quadagno, "From Old-Age Assistance to Supplemental Security Income: The Political Economy of Relief in the South, 1935–1972," *The Politics of Social Policy in the United States*, ed. Margaret Weir, Ann Shola Orloff, and Theda Skocpol (Princeton, NJ: Princeton University Press, 1988), 235–264.

21. There were some exceptions to the SSI federal standards. Some states were allowed to set lower state-defined SSI eligibility levels.

22. Sara Rosenbaum, "Medicaid Expansions and Access to Health Care," *Medicaid Financing Crisis: Balancing Responsibilities, Priorities, and Dollars*, ed. Diane Rowland, Judith Feder, and Alina Salganicoff (AAAS Publication, 1993), 45–82.

23. R. Shep Melnick, "The Unexpected Resilience of Means-Tested Programs," presented at the annual meeting of the American Political Science Association, August–September 1998.

24. Sandra J. Tanenbaum, "Medicaid Eligibility Policy in the 1980s."

25. J. Cohen and J. Holahan, "Medicaid Eligibility after the Omnibus Budget Reconciliation Act of 1981," Medicaid Program Evaluation Working Paper (Urban Institute, October 1985); C. N. Oberg and C. L. Polich, "Medicaid: Entering the Third Decade," *Health Affairs* Fall (1988): 83.

26. M. Ruther and T. Reilly, *The Medicare and Medicaid Data Book, 1988*, HCFA Pub. No. 03270, Office of Research and Demonstrations, Health Care Financing Administration (Washington, DC: U.S. Government Printing Office, 1988); B. O. Burwell and M. P. Rymer, "Trends in Medicaid Eligibility," *Health Affairs* (Winter 1987): 30–45.

27. Oberg and Polich, "Medicaid: Entering the Third Decade."

28. For a provocative argument that the political unpopularity of AFDC reflects racial coding, see Martin Gilens, *Why Americans Hate Welfare* (Chicago: University of Chicago Press, 1999). AFDC nothwithstanding, the political durablity of means-tested programs more generally is a matter of debate among welfare state scholars and practitioners. For contrasting views, see Theda Skocpol, "Targeting within Universalism: Politically Viable Policies to Combat Poverty in the United States," *Social Policy in the United States: Future Possibilities in Historical Perspective* (Princeton, NJ: Princeton University Press, 1995); and Robert Greenstein, "Universal and Targeted Approaches to Relieving Poverty: An Alternative View," *The Urban Underclass*, ed. Christopher Jencks and Paul E. Peterson (Washington, DC: Brookings Institution, 1991).

29. Melnick, *Unexpected Resilience*, 31.

30. Carol S. Weissert and William G. Weissert, *Governing Health: The Politics of Health Policy* (Baltimore: Johns Hopkins University Press, 1996).

31. Alice Sardell, "Child Health Policy in the U.S.: The Paradox of Consensus," *Health Policy and the Disadvantaged*, ed. Lawrence D. Brown (Durham, NC: Duke University Press, 1991), 17–53; Tanenbaum, "Medicaid Eligibility Policy in the 1980s."

32. CRS, *The Medicaid Sourcebook*, 1993.

33. The Medically Needy programs allow states to cover persons who have large medical expenses relative to their incomes. The 300% rule allows states (that so choose) to cover persons needing nursing home care whose income does not exceed 300% of the federally defined SSI level.

34. Rosenbaum, "Medicaid Expansions and Access to Health Care."

35. State governors balked at this new federal mandate, arguing that Medicare's shortcomings should be a federal responsibility; ibid.

36. Ibid.

37. Stephen M. Davidson and Stephen A. Somers, eds., *Remaking Medicaid: Managed Care for the Public Good* (San Francisco: Jossey-Bass Publishers, 1998). See also *Medicaid Source Book*, 1993.

38. T. Coughlin, L. Ku, and J. Holahan, *Medicaid since 1980* (Washington, DC: Urban Institute, 1994), 48–51; Rowland et al., eds., *Medicaid Financing Crisis*.

39. J. Holahan, S. Zuckerman, A. Evans, and S. Rangarajan, "Medicaid Managed Care in Thirteen States," *Health Affairs* 17.3 (1998): 43–63.

40. John K. Iglehart, "Health Policy Report: Medicaid and Managed Care," *New England Journal of Medicine*, 332.25 (1995): 1727–1731.

41. Geraldine Dalleck, "A Consumer Advocate on Medicaid Managed Care," *Health Affairs* 15.3 (1996): 174–177.

42. Davidson and Somers, *Remaking Medicaid*.

43. Paul Pierson, "The Deficit and the Politics of Domestic Reform," *The Social Divide*, ed. Margaret Weir (Washington, DC: Brookings Institution, 1998).

44. *U.S. Newswire* (15 September 1995).

45. *Facing Facts Alert* (19 February 1996).

46. Fay Lomax Cook and Edith J. Barrett, *Support for the American Welfare State: The Views of Congress and the Public* (New York: Columbia University Press, 1992).

47. Colleen M. Grogan, "The Political-Economic Factors Influencing State Medicaid Policy," *Political Research Quarterly* 47.3 (1994): 589–622.

48. Steven V. Roberts, "House Democrats Mounting Drive to Reduce Impact of Budget Cuts," *New York Times* (21 March 1981): 1-1.

49. Colleen M. Grogan and Eric M. Patashnik, "Universalism within Targeting: Nursing Home Care, the Middle Class, and the Politics of the Medicaid Program" (unpublished working paper, 2000).

50. Robert Pear, "Welfare Debate Will Re-Examine Old Assumptions," *New York Times* (2 January 1995): 1-1.

51. Ibid.

52. Peter Gosselin, "House GOP Proposes Medicaid as Payment to States under Plan, Mass. Would Get Less Aid than Weld Sought," *Boston Globe* (20 September 1995): 7; Elizabeth Shogren, "GOP Nursing Home Plan Holds Perils, Democrats Say," *Los Angeles Times* (13 October 1995): A-1.

53. Gosselin, "House GOP Proposes Medicaid as Payment," 7.

54. Alice Sardell and Kay Johnson, "The Politics of EPSDT Policy in the 1990s: Policy Entrepreneurs, Political Streams, and Children's Health Benefits," *Milbank Quarterly* 76.2 (1998): 175–205.

55. Rosenbaum and Sonosky, "Child Health in a Changing Policy Environment."

56. U.S. Department of Health and Human Services, Health Care Financing Administration, *A Profile of Medicaid: Chartbook 2000* (Washington, DC: Government Printing Office, 2000).

57. Ibid.; see also Cindy Mann, David Rousseau, Richard Garfield, and Molly O'Malley, "Reaching Uninsured Children through Medicaid: If You Build It Right, They Will Come" (Washington, DC: Kaiser Commission on Medicaid and the Uninsured, 2002).

58. Robert Pear, "Governors Offer 'Radical' Revision of Medicaid Plan," *New York Times* (25 February 2001): A-1.

# Kids and Bureaucrats at the Grass Roots

ELIZABETH H. KILBRETH AND JAMES A. MORONE

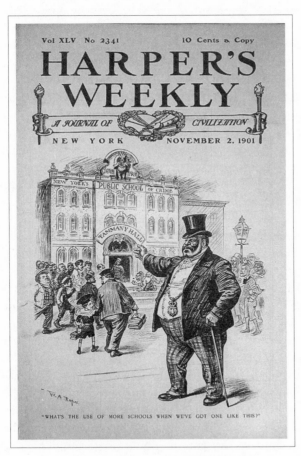

*What's the Use of More Schools When We've Got One*
*Like This? Harper's Weekly,* November 2, 1901.

Childhood inequity causes some discomfort in America—but not enough. Kids get preferential eligibility under Medicaid and are the target of the State Children's Health Insurance Program (S-CHIP)—the single largest health access initiative since the passage of Medicaid and Medicare. The Maternal and Child Health block grant program is a fixture of federal/state policy. Despite these large measures, children are swept along in the currents that separate Americans between wealth and economic insecurity. More children live in poverty, proportionately, than adults.[1] Millions lack health insurance and have no source of routine health care.[2] Chronic illnesses are on the rise, and injuries and deaths far surpass those among children in other nations.[3]

Inequities among children are readily apparent in the environment where children spend a good part of their waking hours—schools. Not only is resource allocation among schools hugely uneven, but also the demands made on schools can vary dramatically. Teachers in poor schools often face students who don't speak English or suffer from untreated illnesses such as asthma or depression. Poor children often come to school hungry, sleep deprived, or suffering from stress.

A small health program that addresses these problems suggests a new model, not just for getting health services to needy kids but also for forging political bonds between the middle-class and needy families. The program, flying below the national radar screen, seems an unlikely candidate for success, much less a model for other efforts. It has no federal funding. It regularly comes under withering attack from enraged political opponents; in fact, it has become a lightening rod for local culture wars. Yet it has survived and grown. How? Through political pressure exerted by an improbable coalition: state bureaucrats and parents.

The program sounds simple and uncontroversial. It places comprehensive primary care health care centers in schools, especially schools in poor neighborhoods. The school-based health center (SBHC) concept arose in the 1970s and caught on slowly. By 1990, there were just 150 centers nationwide. Then the centers took off. In the past decade, the number has increased tenfold to more than 1,400 operating in 48 states. The SBHCs are a small step in the overall effort to assure adequate health care to needy children. Their contribution seems modest, particularly when stacked up against the major federal programs like Medicaid and the S-CHIP. But the movement that created the SBHCs, nurtured them in the face of stiff opposition, and encouraged their spread across the country serves as a reminder that grassroots organizing can still be an important tool in the arsenal of political strategies for winning resources and services. And this grassroots story has an interesting twist—the organizing spark came from state bureaucrats. Perhaps, most important, the SBHC story shows how middle-class demands for services can be joined to the struggle to reduce inequality.

## Needs Trump Ideology

After a long series of high-profile battles, social conservatives on school boards and in state legislatures reflexively oppose SBHCs. Opposition frequently starts with many parents. Health care for high school students inevitably raises the difficult issues: sex, drinking, drugs, depression, and violence. The SBHCs conjure up visions of teen access to condoms and birth control pills. Parents worry about getting shut out of the most intimate aspect of their children's lives. Some centers promise even very young patients confidentiality, raising serious parental concerns when sex and drugs are not yet an issue.

The Religious Right and other social conservatives have powerful feelings about SBHCs. After all, children and schools are ground zero for culture wars. The centers touch all the explosive issues: what values to teach our children, how to respond to deviance among children, how to *define* deviance, and who bears responsibility for shepherding children safely to adulthood. Public programs that propose a public health and medical model for treating high-risk behaviors are anathema to the politically organized Right. In addition, bringing these services into schools runs directly counter to the "back to basics" movement for schools.

As so often happens, the conservative opposition mobilized in response to SBHCs' proponents. Some public health advocates suggested SBHCs as a response to teen pregnancy. Imagine the furor, for example, that erupted around future Surgeon General Joycelyn Elders when she held her first press conference as director of the Arkansas Department of Health. As she describes the event, reporters were sleepily going through the motions until she pledged to reduce teen pregnancy in the state. "How?" they asked, stirring to life. Elders responded: "We're going to have . . . school-based clinics. Now they were all wide awake. Somebody said, 'school-based health clinics? Does that mean you're going to distribute condoms in the schools?' I said, 'Yes it does. We aren't going to put them on the lunch trays. But yes, we intend to distribute condoms.'" Her boss, Governor Bill Clinton, looked like he was "trying hard to swallow something." But he stood by Elders and her views.[4] The combustible image of condoms on the cafeteria trays would haunt the program—

rousing conservative opponents, inspiring liberal advocates, and insuring bare-knuckle cultural politics across the country.

SBHCs won these battles in almost every community, liberal or conservative. Why? For the most basic political reason: The centers were responsive to parents' concerns. And, more important, they provided needed services. All SBHCs require parental authorization for children to access the health care services. This simple opt-out provision quells the fears of most parents. Then, parents find that they have a new and convenient source for the physical exams required for sports, that their child's asthma is successfully stabilized, and that a strep throat infection is promptly cultured and antibiotics prescribed. Teachers and school administrators discover that when a number of the most difficult children are diagnosed with posttraumatic stress disorder or depression and are referred , for appropriate treatment, life in the classroom gets much easier. It is the personal stories, the kids who are diagnosed and treated one at a time, the ground-level community scrutiny, that is at the core of the political success of SBHCs. The larger storyline is simple: On the local level, health care needs trumped ideology.

## Louisiana: A Snapshot of the Culture War

Louisiana politics illustrate the appeal of SBHCs. Here, the program has carved out a niche in an environment otherwise characterized by a punitive or neglectful approach toward poor or troubled children. Louisiana was recently sued by the U.S. Department of Justice over the treatment of children in its juvenile prisons.[5]

The public school system in Louisiana still suffers from the legacy of segregation. A 1981 court-ordered consent decree requiring student busing in Baton Rouge resulted in white flight and almost complete fiscal neglect of the school system by local officials. Until the mid-1990s, the most modern school in the parish had been built in 1977. During this 20-year hiatus, school buildings deteriorated, and the largely black school population burgeoned and spilled over into "temporary" classrooms with no plumbing or running water. The mobile classrooms were the only construction authorized under the city budget.[6]

SBHCs in Louisiana started as local projects in big city schools—collaborations between local officials and the State Department of Health. Funded in part through Maternal and Child Health block grant dollars, the projects were too small initially to catch the attention of the state legislature. But the Department of Health's interest in the model grew as state health officials watched the positive impact of the centers in the schools. Eventually, they took the program before the state legislature to recommend expansion and request general fund support. The history of neglected schools might have predicted a hostile reaction in the legislature. Moreover, the Christian Coalition is a powerful political force in Louisiana. It had ignored the move into black schools, but mobilized an energetic campaign when proponents sought to expand the model.

However, constituents vociferously supported SBHCs and legislators gravitated to the center of political strength. The noise and thunder of the Christian Coalition was drowned out by testimony from satisfied parents, grateful teachers and administrators, and even the children themselves. Some of the most riveting testimony came from a high school senior—a graduate of the SBHC anger management class. This student, the product of an abusive home, described to the legislators how he had obtained a gun and planned to shoot his stepfather for hitting his mother. It was the anger management class, he told them, that had offered him alternative mechanisms for coping with his situation. "Now," he testified softly to a packed legislative hearing, "I'm graduating from high school instead of doing time."

Evidence of effectiveness is persuasive across ideological lines. Even David Duke, a legislator with ties to the Klu Klux Klan, responded to testimony on the impact of SBHCs in New Orleans with the question, "Can we have some of those centers for our white children in Northern Louisiana?" One of the staunchest allies of SBHCs in Louisiana is the powerful Republican Speaker of the House.

The Christian Coalition, of course, did not give up without a long hard fight that lasted through the 1990s. The coalition threw its support behind Mike Foster and was, by many accounts, crucial to getting him elected as governor in 1996. He promised his backers that he would eliminate state support for SBHCs. The governor organized an investigative task force, confident that they would find evidence that the centers were providing birth control services—illegal in Louisiana. Just one case of illegal activity would shut the program down. To its surprise, task force members failed to unearth the criminal activity—birth control services in the schools. Instead, they ran into vocal support for the centers everywhere. A second task force creatively erected bureaucratic barriers. For example, it designed a seven-page parental consent form, written in dense legalese, requiring separate parental signatures for every conceivable health service.

The governor and his allies ran into unexpected opposition: first, the parents whose children were getting services, and second, the state's health officials. Even while the task forces were working to cut down the SBCHs, Governor Foster's own Children's Cabinet proposed to double the size of the program in the state. With time, a majority of the public began viewing the school centers as a valued service rather than a threat to families. In 1999, a voter initiative wrested control of the tobacco settlement dollars from the legislature. Through a popular referendum, citizens locked in tobacco settlement dollars for health and education services, including an explicit budget line for SBHCs.

## The Role of State Bureaucrats

Louisiana demonstrates that SBHCs can be successful in states where the climate is generally unfriendly to government programs and social service spending. But that success depends on transforming wary parents into satisfied constituents and satisfied constituents into political activists—a metamorphosis that does not happen spontaneously. Health professionals can win parents over by doing what they do: serving needy kids. But turning parents into forceful proponents is a more complicated matter. School parents are a socially disparate and ideologically heterogeneous group. A parent's interest in the services in any given school is relatively short-lived—the duration of a child's tenure in that school—making the boundaries of an "organizable" group fluid. Because school funding and policy is set locally, no organizational framework exists to rally parents around state policy debates. Furthermore, the primary target constituency for SBHCs, low-income and medically underserved families, is always difficult to mobilize.

Compare, for example, the differing response to two federal education initiatives. The Individuals with Disabilities Education Act sets the mandatory parameters for educational mainstreaming for children with disabilities. In response to this program, with a clearly defined (and frequently middle-class) constituency, state and nationally federated organizations representing affected parents have sprung up to assure state and local compliance. But Title One, which targets federal support to schools where 50% or more of the students are from low-income families, has not generated a similar organized response from communities. The program itself is diffuse—with monies put to a variety of programs from literacy enhancement to additional training for teachers—and the constituency, politically disorganized.

SBHCs start with this same politically disorganized base. The organizational energy and skill behind the centers' political success comes from bureaucrats within state departments of health. State agency advocates have astutely managed the political process using two strategies. The first is mobilizing statewide coalitions of organizations with a stake in the welfare of children. The second (building on the first) is orchestrating a grassroots campaign explicitly targeted at the state legislature.

Coalitions can be broad-based. In North Carolina, for example, a strategic coalition included representatives from the Pediatrics Association, Nurses Association, Teachers Organization, women's groups, and about 40 different advocacy groups representing the poor and uninsured. In 1998, when the legislature was debating implementation of S-CHIP, lobbyists for the Christian Conservatives succeeded in getting a sympathetic committee member to slip an eleventh-hour provision into the authorizing legislation—banning reimbursement for SBHCs. Catching the maneuver too late to stop it, coalition members vowed to get the SBHC reimbursement ban lifted in the next legislative session and threw the political weight of its many member organizations behind the effort. Despite the disparate political agendas of these groups, they stayed united around SBHC funding, dedicated lobbying efforts to the issue, and won. The conservative legislature buckled in the face of the concerted effort.

The most important asset to the political success of the SBHCs is ordinary voting constituents. Health department bureaucrats have proved surprisingly effective in mobilizing these folks. Parents, school principals and superintendents, local sheriffs, and the kids themselves have been recruited to come to the state capitol and testify before legislative committees and task forces. In one state, the Department of Health actually hired a trained consultant to coach community representatives in effective public speaking techniques before their presentations. Several states have developed professional and highly effective educational videos explaining the nature of SBHCs and presenting, on film, moving testimony from grateful students and happy parents. These videos are used as an organizing tool both in new communities, where SBHC development is under consideration, and with legislatures. Some program directors have organized legislative breakfasts to introduce and "sell" the SBHC concept and "field trips" where they have taken legislators to see, first hand, the SBHCs within their district and to talk to staff and school officials.

The political strategies of the bureaucratic "organizers" usually start with efforts to establish SBHCs, community by community. Many have extended their campaigns in efforts to establish and lock in state programs and funding. In one state, for example, where localized constituency demand had taken hold and legislators from districts across the state were supporting bills for funding SBHCs in their home district, a state public health employee had a more ambitious agenda. No one in the legislature was taking leadership to promote a program embedded at the state level with authority and funding to promote, license, and regulate SBHCs throughout the state. So she organized an inter-state meeting, putting her legislators in touch with legislators pursuing a more aggressive SBHC agenda. The strategy worked. Now the SBHC funding debate has moved from an individual school here and there to funding an expansive state program.

## Bureaucrats as "Rats"?

In the last presidential campaign, "The BureaucRATS decide" was a slogan Republicans expected would strike terror in American hearts. Bureaucratic agencies have suffered a lot of bad press over time, some of it deserved. Some public agencies hold the public captive—motor vehicle divisions, for example, or the Internal Revenue Service—and are famously indifferent to issues of consumer satisfaction. Agencies that serve a clearly defined clientele and have benefits to distribute can develop a very different relationship with "their" public. In distributive programs serving middle-class or corporate clients, a quiet (even stealthy) impulse to expand programs serves both the agency and its clients. The clients get subsidized goods or services; the bureaucrats get job security and a growing power base. These dynamics—typical of departments like agriculture or commerce—are not characteristic of agencies administering income-tested programs like Medicaid, where the clientele is stigmatized and politically disorganized. Nor does it characterize public health programs, even when they are broadly targeted to whole populations.

Health agency bureaucrats fit another paradigm—the powerful technocrats. The regulatory cost containment strategies of the 1980s and the adoption of managed care strategies in the 1990s triggered debates couched in highly technical and arcane terms that severely limit participation by anyone but regulators or the lobbyists of the powerful interest groups. Consumers and the traditionally dominant group in health policy—doctors—increasingly have been excluded from policy debates that look like technical "tinkering," but whose results can have devastating impact on provider income or consumer access.[7] The policy playing field has constricted even further with the practice over the past decade of rolling all policy changes related to the Medicaid and Medicare programs into the annual budget debate—the Omnibus Budget Reconciliation Acts and, most prominently, the Balanced Budget Act of 1997. This is a model that avoids broad-based political negotiation of health care rights and benefits through vesting the bureaucracy with unprecedented technical control, watchdogged by a few congressional staff and professional lobbyists with similarly rarified knowledge.

Despite the closed-door venue and exclusion of direct constituent demands, the bureaucratic health policy environment is densely populated with idealists. In the early 1990s, a substantial number of states turned bright policy entrepreneurs loose, convinced that through reformed insurance regulation and innovative reimbursement schemes they could squeeze enough "fat" from the seemingly bloated health care system to cover all the uninsured. Failing to divert any of the cash flow to providers and suppliers, and neglecting to build political support for increased public funding, most of these state-level efforts to expand access disappeared. President Bill Clinton's approach to the development of a national health reform proposal was the quintessential representation of advocacy through bureaucracy. Five hundred health policy experts, drawn from academia, think tanks, and government service, all eager to design the perfect system, gathered together in task groups—and met secretly. Providers were explicitly barred from the process. Consumers were treated to regional "town meetings," ostensibly to voice their opinions and "inform" the process, but with little meaningful influence on the actual work of system design.

The buildup of the health policy technocracy over the past two decades has given bureaucrats unprecedented control over health policy. However, as the outcome of the state efforts and the Clinton reform plan makes clear, the new bureaucratic power came at a terrible price. Cut adrift from public opinion, bureaucratic policy entrepreneurs lose their political bearings and spend their energy brokering insider bargains. However, the negotiated agreements only nibble at the margins of the health system enterprise because all the powerful stakeholders participating in the process are insulated from external, constituency-driven demands for significant reform.[8] When the public is excluded from the political process—and often finds it difficult to understand its outcomes—opponents find it easy to vilify the reform proposals. In 1991, according to one poll (2 years before Clinton undertook his reform effort), 91% of the public believed "there is a crisis in the health care system."[9] When Clinton set his task force to work, 71% approved of the undertaking.[10] When the final plan was unveiled, public support evaporated under the weight—the incomprehensibility—of the proposal itself.

## Politically Sensitive Bureaucrats?

What we saw in state health departments dealing with school clinics stands decidedly outside the technocracy model. The SBHC program managers in state public health departments emphasized strong constituency connections—they saw grassroots support as the key to their own success. Of course, one can argue about the direction of causation. Perhaps these bureaucrats put down roots in the community because they were forced to—if they wanted to get their programs into schools. Perhaps the SBHC program succeeded because these bureaucrats had constituency-building skills. Either way, the partnership between state bureaucrats, health care providers, community advocacy groups, public school personnel, and parents represents a most distinctive model of bureaucratic behavior.

There clearly is an element of good old-fashioned distributive politics in the dynamics at play with SBHCs. The health department puts in place a publicly funded service. Communities come to rely on the service and voice demands to the legislature when the service is threatened—or when communities that have been left out catch wind of what's going on in the neighboring school and demand their share. And, of course, that's the kind of language legislators get. After all, legislators are always keen to deliver concrete benefits to responsible services. And SBHCs are simple. They will not break the budget. They are easy to understand (a welcome relief from the usual health care brain busters). They are local. They offer fine photo opportunities. They can be doled out slowly, one school at a time.

But there is a whiff of insurgency in the work of these state health officials. SBHCs start as initiatives without legislative mandate, often with few local advocates, and sometimes without executive authorization. In some cases, as in Louisiana, the programs grow under the noses of expressly hostile governors. The program does not "create the lobby" under the protective aegis of executive or legislative mandate; rather, the lobby demands the legislative mandate—after the fact, after the first centers are up and running.[11]

More significantly, the health department officials—who look rather like the self-styled "guerillas" of the war on poverty—have successfully blurred the boundaries between distributive and redistributive politics. They have created an alliance between the middle-class "clientele" of legislative largesse (fighting for their kids) and the resented "have-nots" who soak up our tax dollars.[12]

## The Public Health Alternative to Zero Tolerance:
## A Platform for Unifying Communities

The take-home lesson from the story of the SBHCs may very well be the success this public health–based initiative has had in building community solidarity in a generally toxic political environment. Viewed initially as a targeted strategy applicable to medically indigent families, SBHCs turn out to be popular with kids and their parents across class and color lines. The constituency that puts them on legislators' agendas includes not just low-income parents, but organized physicians, nurses, teachers, school principals, women's groups, parents of children with special needs, and various low-income advocacy groups and—most importantly—middle-class parents. The fact that middle-class parents, the ones who vote in elections, join the ranks captures the attention of state legislators.

Some of the success in creating a broadly democratic movement comes from the democratic nature of children's needs. Children are equal opportunity hell-raisers, and the most prevalent and serious health problems—particularly among adolescents—are associated with high-risk behaviors. The primary causes of death in the United States for young people between the ages of 15 and 24 are traumatic injury (largely motor vehicle accidents), homicide, and suicide.[13] No community or school is immune to reckless drinking, other substance abuse, sexually transmitted diseases, or depression among its kids. Among younger children, the highly prevalent health problems are also universal: asthma, communicable disease, attention deficit disorder, and obesity.

Furthermore, school-aged children are underutilizers of health care services, regardless of insurance status or family income. Many older children resist seeing their pediatrician or family doctor because of newly felt needs for privacy and confidentiality. As mothers move (or are pushed) into the workforce, the problems get worse. Older children, left to their own devices, are unlikely to make or keep appointments with health care providers. Welfare reform has propelled many single mothers into low-wage, entry-level jobs, where taking time off for a child's health care visit might come at the cost of the job. The upshot is that centers located in schools are not only available to a heterogeneous population of children, but are *used* by a heterogeneous population and appreciated by a diverse parent body. Centers have proliferated in middle-class communities as well as poor ones. When the governor of Delaware offered to fund an SBHC for any interested high school in the state, every high school except one took him up on the offer. When the state of New Hampshire offered to fund a limited number, they were overwhelmed with applicants scrambling to "win" a school center. Both within schools and across communities, SBHCs have found a ready constituency. On average, across the country, over 60% of the students in schools with SBHCs are authorized by their parents to use them.[14]

The democracy of the community that comes together to demand school-based health services stands in contrast to the norm. Time and again, Americans transform social malaise into a morality play. The world is divided between those who stand on the side of the angels and those who consort with the Devil. This worldview reinforces and feeds on existing racial, class, and cultural schisms in society and views newcomers with suspicion and hostility. Fear-based policies infect the schools and other domains of child policy. We are currently experiencing the largest immigration since 1913 (and, in absolute numbers, the largest in American history). The new arrivals are nowhere so visible as in the public schools. Even in small cities across the country, schools are coping with student bodies that speak 40 (or more) different languages. In this climate, the culture wars that regularly characterize school politics become particularly intense. The advocates of division and repression seem to have the upper hand and zero tolerance is the policy of choice.

Incidents of violence, in particular, provoke panicked over-reaction. The Columbine tragedy was followed by a wave of state laws imposing curfews on youth, sanctioning corporal punishment by parents (spanking, paddling, and switching, in the case of Oklahoma) and—most significantly—increasingly shifting adjudication of juvenile offenses to the adult criminal justice system. All 50 states now try some juvenile crimes in adult courts.[15] At the national level, the gun control bill championed by President Clinton and congressional Democrats also included measures that empowered federal prosecutors to try 14-year-olds as adults, created harsh mandatory minimum sentencing provisions and loosened strictures on placing juveniles in adult prison facilities.[16] State legislatures and school systems across the country have adopted policies that sanction— and sometimes demand—inflexible and draconian penalties for childish behavior once handled through routine school disciplinary procedures. In some states and school districts, what started as a fairly confined approach to discouraging school violence has spun out of control. Drug possession and lesser infractions such as "disobeying rules," "insubordination," and "disruption" have been added to the list of mandatory punishable offenses. Some schools have suspended children for possession of aspirin, Midol, or Certs. Actionable weapons charges include possession of paper clips, nail files, and scissors.[17]

These policies exacerbate inequities among children. Both within the judicial system and at the school level, the penalties meted out to non-white children are harsher than to their white classmates—sometimes to an extraordinary degree. African-American children, while constituting 17% of public school enrollment, make up 32% of school suspensions.[18] Within the criminal justice system, disparities are even more pronounced. Among young people with no prior prison record, black teenagers who come before the juvenile court system are more than six times as likely as their white counterparts to be sentenced to prison. For those charged with equivalent drug offenses, black youths are 48 times more likely than whites to be sentenced to juvenile prison.[19]

Public health and health care providers offer an alternative way to think about and to treat illness, behavioral problems, and other manifestations of external stress that children bring into school with them. The SBHCs are proving to be an effective vehicle for winning families and communities away from the zero tolerance approach toward a health-based strategy. The universality of many children's health needs creates the acceptance of the public health model. The effectiveness of the health centers with children creates its own argument in favor of treatment of punishment. The shift in paradigm away from zero tolerance policies opens the door for community alliances between poor families and the mainstream middle class.

## A Model for Health Reform?

Nowhere is inequity in America more clearly delineated than in the divide between the insured and the uninsured in the health care system. The likelihood of decisive action from Washington in response to the current health care crisis seems bleak. The same old tired (and tiresome) rhetoric emanates from Washington. The Republicans accuse the Democrats of attempting "to impose government-run health care . . . by steadily taking health care choices away from the American people."[20] Liberals, in turn, accuse the Republicans of proposing health reform legislation that will "be of little benefit except to those in the highest tax brackets . . . While pretending otherwise, they would mainly help people who don't need it at the expense of those who do."[21]

In a policy environment where one frustrated safety net provider dubbed the government's motto as "Don't just do something, stand there!" the implementation and proliferation of SBHCs stands as a small triumph.

The program confounded expectations in several regards:

- Clinics targeted to poor and medically indigent children developed an enthusiastic support base among middle-class parents,
- Mid-level bureaucrats demonstrated political activism and skills that built community and broad-based coalition support for an initially controversial concept, and
- Controversial and publicly funded health services located in schools gained the support of socially conservative legislators.

The small victories of this program should re-energize those who have despaired of incremental reform. These school centers better children's lives, child by child and neighborhood by neighborhood. But their legacy may be a bit larger. They model a compassionate approach to responding to troubled children that—because it is effective—offers a real challenge to the zero tolerance ideology. And as a program that appeals across class and race boundaries, the SBHCs have "mainstreamed" a service originally targeted to the medically indigent and lent to the service needs of disenfranchised families the political respectability of middle-class constituent entitlement.

What is the secret? The guerrillas, who lurk in the public health bureaucracies, push concrete health services and build coalitions to support "their" programs: health care providers who trump culture war ideology with much-needed professional service, middle-class parents who will organize to protect their children's programs, and poor parents who—despite many more barriers to politics—are every bit as eager to speak out for their own kids and their services.

National discussions of inequality and poverty can have a depressing —not till the entire political universe changes—quality about them. Real reform seems unlikely in the fury of our new Gilded Age. And yet, a closer look at our communities offers a bit more optimism: Yes, the needs are great. But far below the media radar, broad local coalitions—bureaucrats, public health advocates, parents, doctors, health care clinics—organize and push. If nothing else, they testify that there is still plenty of political action at the American grass roots.

## Notes

1. Center for the Future of Children, "Children and Poverty—Executive Summary," *Children and Poverty* 7.2 (Summer/Fall 1997): 1–8.

2. In 2002, 7.8 million children were uninsured. Thirty-one percent of children received no well-child care and fifteen percent had no office visits. Data from the National Survey of America's Families as reported by G. Kenney, J. Haley, and A. Tebay, "Children's Insurance Coverage and Service Use Improvement," *Snapshots of America's Families No. 1.* (Washington, DC: Urban Institute, 2003).

3. *World Health Statistics Annual: 1996* (Geneva: World Health Organization, 1998). See also *1999 Annual Report on School Safety*, joint report prepared by the U.S. Departments of Education and Justice (Washington, DC: U.S. Government Printing Office, 2000).

4. Joycelyn Elders, MD, *From Sharecropper's Daughter to Surgeon General of the United States of America* (New York: Avon Books, 1996); for discussion, see James A. Morone, Elizabeth H. Kilbreth, and Katherine M. Langwell, "Back to School: A Health Care Strategy for Youth," *Health Affairs* 20 (January/February 2001): 1.

5. Fox Butterfield, "Louisiana Boy's Prison Is Epitome of Abuse and Neglect," *New York Times* (15 July 1998): 12.

6. Although the consent decree has not yet been lifted, there are encouraging signs of progress in Baton Rouge. A reform school board was elected in 1995, and a tax bond for a $287 million, 5-year system improvement program publicly authorized 2 years later. The local NAACP is encouraged by the efforts at education reform, but is taking a "wait and see" attitude toward the impact of these reforms on segregation.

7. James Morone, "The Bureaucracy Empowered," *The Politics of Health Care Reform: Lessons from the Past, Prospects for the Future,* ed. James Morone and G. S. Belkin (Durham, NC: Duke University Press, 1994).

8. Theda Skocpol, "Is the Time Finally Ripe? Health Insurance Reforms in the 1990s," *The Politics of Health Care Reform: Lessons from the Past, Prospects for the Future,* ed. James Morone and G. S. Belkin (Durham, NC: Duke University Press, 1994); See also J. B. Judis, "Abandoned Surgery: Business and the Failure of Health Care Reform," *The American Prospect* 21 (Spring 1995): 65–73 for a detailed description of how and why organized business groups walked away from the Clinton reform negotiations.

9. D. Yankelovich, "The Debate That Wasn't: The Public and the Clinton Plan," *Health Affairs* 4.1 (Spring 1995): 8–22.

10. R. J. Blendon, M. Brodie, and J. Benson, "What Happened to Americans' Support for the Clinton Health Plan?" *Health Affairs* 14.2 (1995): 7–23.

11. Samuel Beer, "Adoption of General Revenue Sharing," *Public Policy* 24 (Spring 1976).

12. This discussion draws on T. J. Lowi, "Decision Making vs. Policy Making," *Public Administration Review* 30 (1970): 314–325. On the war on poverty, see James Morone, *The Democratic Wish: Popular Participation and the Limits of American Government* (New Haven: Yale University Press, 1998), chapter 7.

13. *World Health Statistics Annual: 1996* (Geneva: World Health Organization, 1998).

14. National SBHC Census, 1998–99. The National Assembly on School-Based Health Care (NASBHC). Last accessed August 1, 2001, at http://www .nasbhc.org/census1.htm.

15. Jon Healy, *Los Angeles Times* (4 July 1999): A-6

16. Wendy Kaminer, *The American Prospect* (24 April 2000): 43.

17. The Civil Rights Project, *Opportunities Suspended: The Devastating Consequences of Zero Tolerance and School Discipline Policies.* Harvard University. Published in *Education Week* (June 21, 2000). Last accessed August 14, 2000, at http://www .law.harvard.edu/civilrights/conferences/zero/zt_report2.html.

18. Civil Rights Project, 7.

19. Fox Butterfield, "Racial Disparities Are Pervasive in Justice System, Report Says," New *York Times* (26 April 2000): A-1.

20. Dennis Hastert, letter to the *Washington Post* (20 October 2000): A-33.

21. *Washington Post* (18 October 2000): A-32.

# Part VI

## THINKING BIG

# 11

# Incrementalism Adds Up?

## LAWRENCE D. BROWN

The USA was a big operation, very
big. The more IT, the less WE.
—SAUL BELLOW, *Humboldt's Gift*

*Out of Work.* J. Macdonald, *Harper's Weekly*,
date uncertain.

Equality is one of the bigger ideas in Western political thought, and so it might seem natural (as in "natural right") that equality should be a bright guiding light in health (and other public) policy. And indeed, critics of U.S. health policy regularly lament that a nation so dedicated to egalitarian values in principle should compromise those values so glaringly in its health affairs.

The most parsimonious interpretation of this disconnect is of course to dismiss America's allegiance to equality as rhetorical wool that elites regularly pull over the eyes of the woolly headed masses. This chapter proposes a less cut-and-dried interpretation founded on the proposition that diminishing the scope of inequality in U.S. health care has little to do with comprehensive, enfolding Policy that routs Inequality. Rather, it has much to do with incremental measures won by myriad coalitions (typically separate and unequal in political inspiration and might) that work their way slowly down lists of inequities that are, literally, infinite. In health, inequality is not one thing but many, and this diffusion of egalitarian ends both sustains and justifies a ragged parade of incremental means. Incrementalism dominates U.S. health policy not because (or not *solely* because) Americans lack the policy wit and political guts to "maximize," but rather because it fits the complex character of the political challenges presented by the egalitarian "project."[1]

## Not Again?!

Twenty-first century paeans to the wisdom of incrementalism in health policy might seem to signify a failure of imagination, an inability to grow, an unwillingness to move on.[2] A doctrine that once sunk sharp teeth into hubristic over-reachings of discarded New Dealers is surely yesterday's news now that right-of-center regimes with little taste for any type of social innovation, still less "planning," have held national power for most of the past 35 years. As a policy theory, incrementalism has transparent limits: One observer's "increment" is another's bold step forward; adjudicating interpretations depends entirely on how one elects to characterize the "distance" between Point A(fter) and Point B(efore). It is also a suspect model of how policy gets made. Since the Great Society, public policies without solid incremental antecedents have popped up all over the place.[3] As a normative guide, incrementalism never recovered from its late 1960s conflation with "interest group liberalism"—a recipe for purposeless pluralism, path dependency on cruise control, and small-ish victories by selfish players unable to envision a broad public interest.[4]

It would seem to be equally outmoded as a blueprint for health policy: Everyone knows that the system's problems are deeply "systemic"; incremental Band-Aids merely protract the cost shifting and balloon squeezing that make comprehensive reform imperative.

And yet . . . perhaps the United States clings to incrementalism in health policy less because it has exhausted the alternatives than because it finds those alternatives exhausting and cannot make them work. If incrementalism turns out to be the best this society can do, one can lament the ensuing shortfalls and go around crooning "is that all there is?" Or one can celebrate the good it does, inquire respectfully into its dynamics, and work to make it as productive of social benefit as possible.

## Equalizing What?

Few would deny that inequality is a serious issue in health policy, but there is vigorous disagreement about what inequality means in this context and whom it is a serious issue *for*. Some disparities are unfair; some not (clearly) so. Some can be redressed; others cannot (clearly). Combining these dimensions yields a matrix that locates the scope of egalitarian policies. The distribution of some important influences on "life chances"—for instance, genetic endowment (including intelligence to some, perhaps very considerable, degree, and athletic ability)—is neither clearly unfair (except insofar as "life" is unfair) nor clearly redressable. Some conditions that may be partly redressable—for instance, differences in musical ability—are also not (clearly) unfair and so have little claim on public policy. Other circumstances plausibly classed as unfair—for example, inferior educational achievement, victimization by violent crime— may not be redressable (certainly not in full and probably not much). The remaining cell, which contains disparities that are both offensive and fixable—lack of adequate health coverage, malnutrition, exposure of workers to toxic chemicals, child abuse, and so forth—is the proper terrain and target of equity-promoting public policies.

This cell contains a great many highly disparate disparities, some of them intricately interconnected, which of course complicates decisions about what policies to design and how. Another disturbing monkey wrench is the continuously evolving debate about what social conditions make it across the border into the "favored" cell. The distribution of income and job opportunities is redressable, but the degree to which existing disparities reflect unfairness rather than merit and desert is hotly debated. Many people would agree that educational attainment is in some sense deeply unfair, depending heavily as it does on the quality of parenting and of schools, but how far it is redressable by public policy divides experts. Obesity, which has worrisome consequences for self-esteem, quality of life, health, and longevity, may or may not be unfair and may or may not be redressable. Defining and then shrinking the sphere of inequitable disparities is a political project the foundations of which are in constant normative and empirical flux.

Health policy fits this general picture. No one expects health outcomes (e.g., life spans), access (waiting times to see a doctor), or inputs (research dollars per disease) to be equal. Such differences are "disparities," some of which may lie beyond the range of social intervention (genetic contributions to longevity) or derive from individual choice (e.g., living a long way from a hospital). Some disparities, however, appear to be both unfair and amenable to amelioration. These are the "inequities" that public policy aims (or should aim) to reduce.

A short, simple list of inequities could include the following:

- "Society" spends research dollars out of proportion to the incidence of disease (for instance, more on cancer than on heart disease, more on breast cancer than on prostate cancer, and surprisingly little on pancreatic cancer).
- Income thresholds that define eligibility for Medicaid and State Children's Health Insurance Program (S-CHIP) vary considerably among the 50 states.
- Approximately 85% of Americans have health insurance, while the remaining 15% do not.
- A majority of the 43.6 million Americans who lack health coverage work and pay taxes that contribute to coverage for fellow citizens not much worse off financially than themselves.
- Some people (the uninsured, the underinsured, immigrants, and some Medicaid beneficiaries) have trouble securing specialty care, inpatient admissions, mental health and dental services, effective treatment for substance abuse, and access to the latest and best medical technology.
- Much more money is spent on curing disease than on preventing it or on promoting healthy behavior.
- Residents of rural, inner city, and other "underserved" areas may find it difficult to access care.
- Individuals who are neither part of an employer group nor eligible for public programs may have to pay a fortune to get health care coverage.

- Race seems to influence treatment patterns independently of income and clinical condition.
- Health status has "social determinants," which include the influence of other policy arenas (housing, education, job training), income distribution, and stress deriving from disparities in social rank (including but not limited to racial discrimination).
- The better off are much more able to secure adequate long-term (nursing home and home health) care than the less well off.
- Many providers contend that public programs, private plans, or both pay them less than fair rates.

This list could easily be expanded, as could the inegalitarian nuances within each item. The United States already spends more than 14% of its gross domestic product (and about $5,400 per capita) on health care—figures far above those of comparable Western nations that are generally said to have more equitable health systems. Addressing any subset of items on the dishonor roll would add appreciably to the U.S. health budget; tackling them all would increase it enormously. Different participants in the national policy debate—providers, consumer groups, researchers, insurers, people with chronic ailments, public office holders—argue for their own preferred priorities.

Meanwhile, the increasingly influential social determinants school contends that if the goal of health policy is indeed better health, then progress depends not on higher health care budgets but rather on better social services, more income redistribution, smoothing the sharper edges of social hierarchies, or some combination of these interventions. Egalitarian slopes are slippery indeed. Once social and psychological determinants and disparities get their due, why not grant that "spiritual (or immaterial) inequity is now as great a problem as material inequity, perhaps even more," and that "the most intractable misdistributions in rich countries such as the United States are in the realm of spiritual or immaterial assets."[5] Nor is national health insurance an all-purpose answer to these conundrums: Many issues on the list (extent of coverage for drugs, mental health services, and long-term care; how much to pay providers; how to ease access for those in underserved areas) would persist. The putative egalitarian agenda is, in short, little more than an (unprioritized) wish list. Philosophical principles that might guide priority setting—the greatest good of the greatest number, Rawlsian original positions and veils of ignorance, benchmarks of fairness, and so on—abound, but it is safe to say that none of these commands broad recognition (and still less broad agreement) among policy makers. The problem is not the absence of a constituency for equity but rather the presence of many such equity-promoting constituencies, which generally do not overlap, fail to cohere, cooperate intermittently and opportunistically, and compete vigorously for prominence and power.

## Equity by Increments

Absent some widely accepted unifying image of equitable health care, policies evolve from incessant pulling and hauling among values and interests of players and pundits—in a word, incrementally. Equity-promoting measures ride along on coalitions (sometimes ad hoc, sometimes more durable across programs and issues) that promote and protect them politically. The base from which these coalitions depart—the employer-based system of private health care coverage—is itself a (arguably evil) masterpiece of incrementalism: Foreswearing a compulsory, national system, the United States leaves health insurance for its working population and their dependents to the mercy of local employers, who decide whether to buy coverage at all and, if so, how much, on what terms, and from what carriers. Much of the history of U.S. health policy since World War II can be read as a quest to graft equity-enhancing public increments onto a private base inherently (and avowedly) indifferent to equity. Repeatedly, inequitable disparities catch political notice, generate demands for public redress, find programmatic solutions in Washington, sustain protective (and expansionary) coalitions, trigger anxieties about iron triangles and "pluralistic stagnation," and inspire debate on how policies may be "rationalized."[6]

Confronting chronic stalemate in the debate over national health insurance, coalitions of philanthropic entrepreneurs, disease-specific organizations, and academic medical researchers in the 1940s joined officials in the National Institutes of Health and advocates in Congress to attack inequalities between diseases by creating and expanding one national institute of health after another.[7] Meanwhile, congressional health leaders, supported by providers and state and local officials, worked to diminish regional inequalities by enacting the Hill-Burton program, which funded construction of new hospitals, mainly in underserved areas.[8] Community health centers (CHCs) and the National Health Service Corps (NHS) later joined this area-centered portfolio.[9] In the 1960s, Medicare and Medicaid tackled the most glaring disparities of employer-based coverage, namely, the plight of retired and unemployed people seeking affordable access to care, making a prominent dent in inequalities by class.[10] Medicare, created by a coalition led by the AFL-CIO (American Federation of Labor/Congress of Industrial Organizations) and groups representing the elderly, ensured that all seniors would have coverage for hospital and physician services.[11] Medicaid, born as a by-product of the political energies that created Medicare, transcended its troubled beginnings as a "poor people's program," (one expected mainly to benefit poor mothers and children), developing powerful political support from children's advocacy groups, health and human services coalitions, providers (hospitals, physicians, nursing homes, home health agencies), and a constituency of beneficiaries that encompasses not only the poor but also (people formerly known as) the middle class, who seek long-term care.[12]

In the late 1980s, providers (especially pediatricians) and advocates for children encouraged an odd couple of congressmen (Henry Waxman, a solid liberal, and Henry Hyde, an antiabortion leader who understood the case for easing access to prenatal and maternity care for pregnant women who chose not to terminate their pregnancies) to expand Medicaid coverage for lower-income women and children. A decade later, a comparable coalition supported another strange pair of political bedfellows (Edward Kennedy, liberal paragon, and Orrin Hatch, a conservative who recognized that better health care for kids has something important to do with promoting family values) in the enactment of S-CHIP, a program intended to bring new coverage to half the nation's 10 million or so uninsured children.[13] In their various fashions, all these programs are redistributive: They move money from the haves (or have mores) to the have-nots (or have lesses).

Public programs designed to "rationalize" these expensive expansionary commitments have often tried to hold protective coalitions at arm's length, but—partly because these coalitions give the programs clout and vice versa—these measures too have worked to win support by grafting egalitarian aims onto cost-containment plans. The federal and state governments have embraced managed care in Medicaid, for example, mainly to save money but also (so they say) to improve access and quality, which had suffered and slipped in the traditional fee-for-service program. State rate-setting programs worked both to slow the growth of hospital costs and to fashion cross subsidies that would keep troubled safety-net hospitals afloat financially.[14]

Incrementalism, in short, adds up. Several prominent chapters in the history of U.S. health policy tell of staggered but fairly steady additions of equity-promoting program increments that leave the United States far from "egalitarian" by cross-national standards, but far less inegalitarian than it would be in their absence. In health policy—as in the rest of the U.S. welfare state—public programs, beneficiaries, and benefits are smaller; taxes are lower; and cross-subsidies and redistribution are narrower than in "comparable" Western democracies. The glass is, classically, half empty, half full.

## Can Incrementalism Keep Pace?

The formidable gap-filling accomplishments of incrementalism co-exist alongside inequities that persist and widen. Pharmaceutical innovation aggravates the economic stress the elderly suffer in the absence of Medicare coverage for prescription drugs. Medicaid expands coverage, private employers contract it, and the number of American uninsured rises to 43.6 million. The federal government expands its support for CHCs, but local downturns in the economy increase demand and swamp many centers all the same. Increasing longevity raises the financial bar for adequate (not to say equitably available) long-term care (including home health care) benefits. As noted earlier, "true" equity (benefits that cover the true needs of all in need) would push U.S. health spending well above 14% of the gross domestic product and would doubtless drive the public portion of that spending far beyond its current nearly 50% plus.[15]

Incrementalism may also fail to add up because the need to enfold "targeted" benefits within broader political coalitions carries it off course. The founders of American social insurance understood from the start that means testing (income-based targeting) in Social Security and Medicare would weaken their political constituency and sap their power to serve the truly needy. The "choice between" universalism and targeting looked spurious: Only the former could adequately protect the latter.[16]

Whereas Medicare's coalition was born broad, Medicaid had breadth thrust upon it, as this "welfare program" came to commit nearly half its funds to long-term care for erstwhile middle-class seniors.[17] Winning right-of-center support for new coverage for lower-income groups may mean accepting labyrinthine eligibility determinations (for instance, long application forms to be filed in person at local welfare offices) that deter eligible applicants from enrolling.

The endless quest for incremental innovations in the employer-based system of coverage—for example, attractive but affordable coverage options, perhaps partly subsidized by government, that owners of small firms and their uninsured workers will buy—rarely yields results beyond ideological resuscitation of inherently inequitable arrangements. The case for incrementalism in U.S. health policy is not that it is the best, or even a very good, approach but rather that it is, politically, as good as it gets.

This case comes under attack from two sets of critics. First, analytical antagonists argue that enshrining incrementalism as a standard operating procedure of policy makes no intellectual sense because this method cannot begin to meet the central policy challenge of the day—namely, how to balance a limitless demand for benefits with a constrained stock of social resources. Second, political critics contend that incrementalism crimps the nation's policy style, narrows its horizons, and depletes its collective will to forge a health care system worthy of a genuine welfare state.

## Hard Choices, Explicit Priorities

A growing corpus of critics contends that the United States, like other Western nations, can "no longer afford" the system that it has; that hard, downright "tragic" choices must be made; that ubiquitous implicit rationing should be replaced by explicit rationing; that, in short, "society" should stiffen its upper lip, import some philosophically defensible system to "prioritize" the objects of health spending, and start allocating resources accordingly. The Oregon Health Plan (OHP) is often cited as a case in point. Cited, but not emulated. Ten years after its commencement, OHP remains a unique case, apparently because "societies" (including 49 American states) find its ambitious priority setting too philosopherkingly to swallow. A recent French report on the strategic road toward "benefit baskets" (le paniers de biens) shows why. Writing in 2001, Chabaud and Collombet unfurl the standard rhetoric of quiet desperation: spending cannot go on like this; tough choices are essential; and the rest.[18] They invoke OHP, even helpfully reproducing its lengthy priority list in an appendix. But, say they, that model is flawed. Truly explicit rationing must be democratic, participatory, equitable, and (everyone's term of art) transparent. Groups with greater needs (the elderly, the disadvantaged) should be weighted more heavily. Like most prioritizers, however, they miss the central point: Transparency cannot be detached from power, and such impeccably enhanced participation invites precisely the "pluralistic stagnation" that gave rise in the first place to demands for rigorous priorities.

This "problem" is ironically aggravated by a major coincident democratic victory, namely, steady growth in the organization and political mobilization of a range of groups—the disabled, people afflicted with particular clinical conditions (AIDS, mental illness, multiple sclerosis, breast cancer, etc.), and consumers—determined to join traditional business, labor, provider, and other interests in asserting their needs and ensuring that they stand high on everybody's priority list.[19] In Europe no less than in the United States, the practice (indeed the pondering) of prioritization ends by restoring, even revitalizing, incrementalism: Each increment of progress toward the priority list is matched and counterbalanced by an equal (or greater) increment of political organization among the "priorities" themselves. In Oregon, tough-minded souls put the disabled in their place; organizations of the disabled promptly persuaded the federal government (which had to approve the state's request for a Medicaid waiver) to change that place. Britain's National Institute for Clinical Excellence declines to endorse a new drug for multiple sclerosis; organizations of citizens afflicted with that condition join the drug's manufacturer in pressuring the NHS to overturn the decision.[20] Like voluntary organizations in general, these groups cohere and grow because they give voice to intensity of preferences—precisely the Achilles' heel, both philosophical and political, of doctrines that pursue the great good of the greatest number.

This political assimilation of prioritization to incrementalism could change, of course. If "societies" decide that health spending is really (not merely rhetorically) insupportable, they might turn a deaf ear to the advocacy groups, shut the doors at the Ministry of Health, cut to the chase, and impose a priority list from on high. Such radical departures from incrementalism do not look imminent anywhere, however, and in the meantime policy makers must begin to wonder how many more town meetings and forums one needs to prove that *of course* the public sets a higher priority on spending to prevent illness than on funding high-tech interventions near the end of life—unless and until (of course) the high-tech interventions prolong the life of parents, siblings, or others close to home.

## Universal Coverage at Last

Political critics of incrementalism urge a different Grand Strategy; namely, "comprehensive" reform that installs national health insurance or—better put, because everyone now acknowledges that cost is surely an object—affordable universal coverage. Equality may not be a simple concept or policy goal, but the absence of universal coverage is so plainly the heart of America's egalitarian shortfalls that achieving it is beyond question job one. The spectacular failure of the Clinton reform plan can be read as evidence that American politics are incapable of swallowing anything truly comprehensive—or as evidence merely that the planners went about it wrong.[21] Perhaps such staples of U.S. exceptionalism as culture, institutions, interests, and "path dependence" on the voluntary sector for health coverage put cross-national achievements beyond American reach.[22] Or perhaps the history of national health insurance in Europe and Canada is more pertinent to U.S. particulars than tends to be assumed. Other nations began with voluntary systems of coverage, instituted public coverage incrementally (generally starting with lower-income wage earners and moving "up" from there), fought pitched battles with providers, reconciled national systems with federalism (e.g., Canada, Germany, Australia, and Switzerland), and made hard choices among financing options (e.g., taxes, payroll, etc.).

The key exceptionalist variable is arguably that other nations entertain attitudes toward government's social role that encourage them to get on with these various tough jobs whereas deep-seated antistatism makes the United States throw up its hands at all but incremental reforms. It is far from certain, however, that the United States eternally lacks the political will to tackle big policy engagements. The New Deal and the Great Society are political facts and their policy legacies persist, conservative dominance since 1968 notwithstanding. Herbert Hoover was gone, and laissez-faire capitalism on the defensive a mere 3 years after the Great Depression changed the nation's political agenda. Charles Lindblom's classic exposition of incrementalism as the "is and the ought" of the U.S. policy process appeared in 1959—5 short years before Lyndon Johnson and a liberal Democratic Congress began enacting a cascade of measures previously dismissed as politically infeasible. In good economic times, a spasmodic commitment to social justice somehow swept the nation and, before the shaking and stirring stopped in 1968, changed the proverbial policy landscape. Election year 2004 will mark 36 years since 1968 (which conveniently arrived 36 years after 1932 and the New Deal)—precisely the "cyclical" interval sometimes said to trigger new generational tastes that give Left and Right their recurrent "turns" in politics and policy.[23] Might not lightning strike again—maybe soon—and retire incrementalism for at least a few politically productive years?

The question admits only guesswork: Health politics rolls with deep and mysterious currents imperfectly visible even to experienced (and perhaps especially to academically trained) eyes. (Accurate prediction of the Republican push for prescription drug benefits in Medicare in 2003, for example, would have had to foresee such more or less accidental "data" as the determination of the incumbent Republican president, who "won" election with fewer popular votes than his opponent, to pry away key

Democratic constituencies; Republican control of both houses of Congress; and the ascension of a physician to the position of majority leader of the Senate after his predecessor was forced to step down for making injudicious public comments on matters having nothing to do with health policy.) Meanwhile, this one good question leads to another: how big a political bang does how much expansion of coverage require? If the goal is a new system in which all citizens are covered by public right for all medically necessary and appropriate services, funded by national (or nationally prescribed) tax extractions and accompanied by national rules on payment to providers, the bang must need to be big indeed. If the goal, however, is reasonable coverage for the 43-plus million Americans who now lack it, a more modest bang—or a series of moderate-sized political explosions—might do the job.

In principle, income eligibility ceilings in Medicaid and S-CHIP could rise to embrace many of the currently uninsured and "buy ins" to these programs (or Medicare), which might incorporate tax credits, employer subsidies, or other favorite inducements and could reach most of the working uninsured and dependents who still would not qualify for Medicaid or S-CHIP. Incrementalism, in short, could carry the nation beyond the status quo—universal *care*—that is, a system in which most people have coverage, that coverage is uneven among the population, and those lacking coverage can (eventually) find care somehow at emergency rooms and other components of the safety net—to universal *coverage* (everyone has public or private health benefits, although disparities in coverage by employer, area, and age may persist), though probably not all the rest of the way to a universal *system* (everybody covered on uniform terms). Incremental extensions of coverage are vulnerable to economic ups and downs at the national, state, and local levels, as is evident today from the supplanting of contemplated expansions by tightened eligibility determinations and curtailed outreach initiatives. But that is beside the point. Those same economic doldrums, not to mention a $450 billion federal budget deficit, also surely deter bangs big enough to install a universal system.

## Rightsizing the Reform Vision:
## Is Bigger Thinking Better?

These incrementalist musings pose challenges for those convinced that thinking right about reform means Thinking Big. First, how does one hold the thought? What Big Thing(s) does one tackle? Universal coverage encapsulated in a universal system is pretty big, but not big enough for the social determinants school, for whom further spending on health care services, programs, and budgets means little unless accompanied by broad society-wide changes in the distribution of income (and perhaps social status). Nor will a universal system be big enough for the legions of special groups that will seek special standing (and funding) for their special needs within any such system. Absent (as argued earlier) any compelling analytical foundation for setting priorities among such claims, one is left with politics, which tends to digest big agendas by breaking them down into small, digestible policy pieces (i.e., increments).

Second, speeding aid to the digestive process is all the more important because Big Thinking invites Big Conflicts, as the unhappy history of internecine warfare among advocates for NHI reveals. Sighting of an open window of opportunity for reform not only invites the usual suspects on the opposing team (providers, business, insurers) to throw stones through it, but also inflames ideological purists, determined that History shall never say they did less than their best with this once-in-a-lifetime (generation, century) chance. If the stars finally have enough sense to align around a single-payer system, for instance, why settle for an employer mandate coupled to a jerry-built version of managed competition? If the question, however, is whether or not to support the insertion of (say) an expansion of Medicaid, S-CHIP, or school-based health clinics into the cavernous recesses of an annual budget bill, who needs or cares to squabble about single payer, managed competition, or other big polarizing possibilities?

Third, even if their ranks did not fragment, reformers would have trouble making Big Thoughts father to Big Deeds. Successful social movements with broad redistributive agendas are conspicuous mainly for their absence from American history. Social movements did not bring on the New Deal. The Great Depression did. The social movements that preceded and in some measure produced the Great Society pushed a focused, constitutionally grounded campaign for basic civil rights for African-Americans. Fallout from the civil rights movement (plus Kennedy's assassination, plus the Republican nomination of Barry Goldwater in 1964) contributed to political conditions that in turn generated Medicare and other progressive programs, but it takes a tortured reading to construe these programs as "products" of movement politics. The high-minded mid-1960s grafting of antipoverty and urban policy objectives onto civil rights goals in the war on poverty and Great Society arguably ferried the whole caboodle into perilous political precincts that soon conflated, confused, and confounded race, class, and area in ways that fractured both the new supportive coalition of the day and the New Deal Democratic coalition itself. Moreover, the main legacy of movement politics in the 1960s and 1970s was a proliferation of organizations seeking to win and advance the rights of myriad distinct groups—gays, women, prisoners, the disabled, divorced mothers seeking child support, and so on—that, by adding many new fragments to the reformist forces, further complicated the construction of bigger, broader reform agendas and coalitions and reinforced incrementalist norms that honor each fragment with programs and regulations roughly proportionate to its power.

No law says that these fragments must remain forever disconnected. But, fourth, progressive Big Thinking does not come out of nowhere, yet has been nowhere in the cards for 35 years (that is, since Nixon won the presidency in 1968). The Left could benefit from a "critical realignment" just around the corner, but one can hardly fail to notice that the one and only Big Idea to capture the public imagination since at least 1980 has been thoroughly anti-redistributive; namely, tax cuts that mainly favor the more affluent yet are broadly accepted as good for the economy, hence the public, at large. The prospect that reform groups, hitherto content to cultivate their particularistic gardens, will soon both assert and win public support for a broad progressive agenda does not look eminently imminent.

Fifth, the vast political windfalls repeatedly reaped by aggressive tax cutting offer a disquieting reminder: Big Thinking is alive and well today under the effective proprietorship of an anti-redistributive Right that both sincerely views economic growth as the cure for every social ailment and single-mindedly seeks to shrink government down to a size at which (in antitax crusader Grover Norquist's creepy image) it can be drowned in the bathtub. That government floats merrily along, and is likely to continue doing so, results not from the concerted countervailing power of progressive forces but rather from the subtle genius of incrementalism at translating redistributive issues that divide haves from have-nots into distributive and regulatory measures that blunt, disguise, and protect redistributive deeds executed within more malleable and manageable political confines. Dividing public programs (hence resources) among interested groups proves time and again to be an effective way of conquering conservative inhibitions on the growth of government, not least because every Henry Hyde and Orrin Hatch has his (or her) preferred constituencies and causes and stands ready to make "exceptions" that send public largesse their way.

Sixth, Big Thinking is hard to sustain because obscure but effective institutional mechanisms of equilibrium prevent the "crises" that supposedly must eventually impress one and all with the iron case for comprehensive change from developing truly compelling gravity. The ubiquitous depiction of the U.S. (non) system as a public-private mix fails to capture the complexity of what is in fact a three-legged configuration, the third leg of which is itself an intricate public-private mix called the safety net. The safety net—a mélange of public, private, and nonprofit hospitals, health centers, public and free clinics, and physicians funded by a pastiche of public, private, and nonprofit dollars—supplies care for 43.6 million uninsured Americans, a slice of the privately underinsured, and not a few Medicaid beneficiaries who cannot get timely access to "mainstream" care. By doing so, the safety net earns its name and fame not only as the port of first and last call for the disadvantaged, but also as a crucial source of political stability and insulation for the system as a whole.

In recurrent reformist dreams, comprehensive change awaits explosions that occur either endogenously (the system finally passes some breaking or tipping point—say, X% of uninsured, Y% of GDP spent on health care, or Z% public support for major change) or exogenously (electoral realignment sweeps health reform along on a tidal wave of pent-up political discontent that triggers policy innovation). In practice, however, these big bangs get snuffed out (at least to date) by steady incrementalist handoffs among the system's three sectors. Private coverage wanes marginally over time, public programs pick up some of the pieces (at least in relatively flush times), the number of uninsured rises a little higher, and the safety net performs triage.

To be sure, it does not do so painlessly: a steady stream of reports to the effect that the safety net is "afloat but endangered," "imperiled but intact," depict institutions that are chronically beleaguered but persistently bailed out. The peril is perpetual because payers must annually cough up new resources to cover rising safety-net costs. That they do so and keep bailing reflects a broad, albeit largely latent, social consensus on its value: the Left understands that the safety net is a matter of life and death for its clients, while the Right knows that its survival is itself a matter of life and death for the status quo. The safety net vindicates the comforting conviction that uninsured Americans "can still get care," the crucial normative antidote to the urgency of universal coverage in the minds of the (largely covered) polity. If the safety net crumbles so too does, to coin a phrase, the moral basis of a backward society.[24]

This pattern—marginal erosion of private insurance, incremental expansion of public coverage, and devolution of "the rest" to local safety-net providers—is no one's paradigm of rational policy, but, pace the inevitabilities of aficionados of endogenous and exogenous explosions, there is no reason why it cannot go on for the foreseeable future. The extreme opacity of the process is itself a force for persistence. Because safety nets are intrinsically local and highly variable across communities, no one really understands how "it" works. Because its funds derive, variously across sites, from myriad sources—state appropriations, federal 330 monies, Medicaid payments, foundation grants, income-related fees, time donated by providers, local taxes and more, the proportions among which shift from year to year—no one really understands whose money pays for what. The occasional impending collapse of an important safety-net institution somewhere or other may make front page news but by and large the safety net soldiers on outside the public spotlight, rearranging flows of patients and revenues and servicing the cast-offs of the larger system in an eternally recurring incrementalism that both steadies the system as a whole and stymies the calling of fundamental reformist questions.

Finally, Big Thinking in U.S. social policy is chronically, and perhaps fatally, hobbled by the nation's cultural and structural devotion to Governing Small. The egalitarian fellow feeling that Tocqueville celebrated in small town America does not presage so much as preclude the solidarity that cements a strong sense of national community. "Health is a community affair"—meaning, one in which local employers voluntarily decide whether their workers will have health coverage and, if so, how much and on what terms, and then contract for its supply with local insurance plans competing for profits or revenues in weakly regulated community markets. Housing is a community affair: having paid one's money one is disinclined to take chances that the arrival of discordant social types might depreciate the value of local real estate—hence zoning and other protections that limit socioeconomic heterogeneity. Education is a community affair that fits hand in glove with local housing markets. School quality varies pretty much with community wealth, and local control of schools is zealously defended. Administration of "welfare" benefits (Medicaid, food stamps, Temporary Assistance to Needy Families, and more) is an important part of community affairs in which the federal government yields substantial discretion to county and municipal officials to judge the eligibility of claimants.[25]

All these communitarian bulwarks are profoundly conservatizing: "The people" get (self) defined as covered lives seeking good rates in an insurance marketplace—homeowners and property tax payers, consumers chasing the competitive advantage conferred by educational excellence, arbiters of desert among the less advantaged—while "big" (federal and state) government gets defined as an enemy of the people. This self-satisfied localism relentlessly deconstructs the notion of national citizenship, confining it to formal-legal fundamentals, severing its connections to social policy, demolishing every blueprint for building atop it the diverse redistributive programs egalitarian social policies demand. And this chopping of civic identifications into communitarian bits and pieces duly reinforces the small-scale social thinking that reciprocally legitimizes the chopping itself. Incrementalism has the distinct strategic virtue of dealing directly with these bits and pieces as it finds them—easing the way of the working uninsured into Medicaid this much in one state, that much in another; accumulating programs of public housing, rental assistance, and support for homeownership by lower-income families in full foreknowledge that their implementation will vary markedly across venues; struggling to overlay statewide curriculum standards and "equalization" grants onto community-controlled school systems—instead of predicating policy on shifts of power among governments and redirection of resources among income groups that are too large to be (currently) plausible.

## Conclusion: Policy Models, Political Battles

The egalitarian "project" comes in two basic strategic styles that correspond closely to Lindblom's classic counterposition of root/ branch versus incremental methods of policy making.[26] The former, a comprehensive approach, gazes out holistically upon society, identifies inequitable disparities (always very numerous), summons moral philosophy to guide the ordering of priorities for amelioration, invokes social science to assign "root causes" of and connections among the items on the list, and seeks remedies that are (ideally) both fundamental and far-reaching. This method has it appeals, chief among them that it supplies stars to steer by, assurances that the big picture stays ever in view, and that, within it, first things come first. It also has its costs, notably, a strong risk of paralysis born of disappointed waiting for the feasible to align with the desirable.

The alterative method, incrementalism, canvasses the range of inequalities, examines the sources and scope of support for coalitions to address them, and seeks to forge exchange relations—quid pro quo—between those coalitions and policy makers. Although not obliged to lose sight of the whole, incrementalists seize their main chances where they find them and hope that their programmatic handiwork leaves objectionable disparities fewer, smaller, and less damaging. This strategy too carries both costs and benefits. Making so many little plans may give policy makers and the public a deceptive sense of progress that cannot be fairly tested without steady attention to big pictures, root causes, and systemic connections. It does, however, permit American society, in which economic individualism generally trumps social solidarity by a fairly wide margin, to limit the domain of inequality.

Whereas the abstract choice between comprehensive and incremental strategies has to do with the "true" requisites of a just society, the practical choice turns on the political battles one elects to fight. The battle—pretty much any battle—for comprehensive reform pits its proponents against providers, insurers, and business—and possibly also labor, the aged, and other potent interests heavily invested in the status quo. (Disunity within these blocs exists, but not enough to alter the basic political point.) The fate of the Clinton plan is but the latest demonstration that these battles are not winnable—at least not without dramatic change in configurations of political power. That public opinion polls show clear majorities for "reform," including universal coverage, means much less than meets the eye because public opinion is not static, but dynamic, perpetually a work in progress. Promisingly progressive poll numbers are an invitation to opposing groups to manipulate Americans' chronic ambivalence about government, reincarnate Harry and Louise and frighten the masses over trade-offs ("rationing" and such) they had not much pondered before.[27] Alas, this strategy works like a charm.

Incrementalist battles, which mainly aim not to rationalize "the system" but rather to expand the scope of public programs for the disadvantaged (more coverage, more CHCs, more medical research, and so forth) primarily confront small government, antitax forces, the political might of which no one who muddled through the last three and a half decades would deny. The conservative's lack of success in downsizing government's roles and duties, still less in drowning it, suggests, however, that progressive combatants in these struggles stand a decent fighting chance. With skill and luck, the terrors of the "T" word can be defused. Economic growth brings new public revenues that sustain broader programs without resort to tax increases. Fiscal federalism induces conservative leaders to expand public programs (Medicaid, for example) because, say, three federal dollars for each state dollar is an offer too good to refuse. New spending within one section of a budget bill can be justified by attribution of speculative (and perhaps specious) savings in another section. Electorates sometimes concur that one type of tax is less evil than another (for instance, the half-cent increase in the sales tax that officials in Hillsborough County, Florida, won in exchange for slowing increases in the property taxes that funded the local safety net). The mythology of social insurance—one simply gets back what one paid in—legitimates redistributions across generations from a range of revenue sources. Sinners (smokers, drinkers) are taxed as an incentive to "just say no," and serpents that led the sinners down the garden path (big tobacco companies) get hit for huge financial settlements that enter public coffers.

Political wills find fiscal ways. This mixed bag of revenues is, of course, precisely how the existing system of universal *care* is sustained—by employer contributions, employee premiums, consumer cost sharing, tax expenditures, payroll taxes (in Medicare Part A), general revenues (Medicare Part B, Medicaid, grants to community health centers, and so on). And it is precisely the prospect of continuing incremental innovation—infusion of new funds from some or all elements in this funding pastiche into the creation of new programs and expansion of older ones—that animates the vision of universal *coverage* (health insurance for all, albeit with possible disparities by state, age, or income). These battles are joined daily in Washington, state houses, county seats, and town halls. Progressives lose some and win some, and when they do win, the coalitions of beneficiaries, providers, philosophical allies, and constituency-minded public officials that quarterback these incremental victories become part of a policy "base" against which opponents find it increasingly futile or imprudent to launch fundamental objections and lethal political attacks. Fruitful government programs multiply, the risk that the State will succumb to an unfortunate household accident in some right-wing Bates Motel declines, and incrementalism grinds along its weary way.

## Notes

1. Herbert A. Simon, *Administrative Behavior: A Study of Decision-Making in Administrative Organizations* (New York: Macmillan, 1947).

2. "Incrementalism" is taken from Charles Lindblom, "The Science of 'Muddling Through,'" *Public Administration Review* 19 (Spring 1959): 79–88.

3. One case in point is clean air legislation, which moved Charles O. Jones to propose "speculative augmentation" as an alternative to incrementalism. See "Speculative Augmentation in Federal Air Pollution Policy-Making," *Journal of Politics* 36 (May 1974): 438–464.

4. Theodore J. Lowi, *The End of Liberalism* (New York: W. W. Norton, 1969).

5. Robert William Fogel, *The Fourth Great Awakening and the Future of Egalitarianism* (Chicago: University of Chicago Press, 2000), 1, 2.

6. This pattern is sketched in Lawrence D. Brown, *Politics and Health Care Organization: HMOs as Federal Policy* (Washington, DC: Brookings Institution, 1983), Introduction.

7. A. C. Cochrane, *Effectiveness and Efficiency* (London: Nuffield Provincial Hospitals Trust, 1972); Stephen P. Strickland, *Politics, Science and Dread Disease: A*

*Short History of United States Medical Research Policy* (Cambridge, MA: Harvard University Press, 1972).

8. Cochrane, *Effectiveness and Efficiency*; James E. Rohrer, "The Political Development of the Hill Burton Program: A Case Study in Distributive Policy," *Journal of Health Politics, Policy and Law* 12 (Spring 1987): 137–152.

9. Alice Sardell, *The US Experiment in Social Medicine: The Community Health Center Program, 1965–1986* (Pittsburgh: University of Pittsburgh Press, 1988); Eric Redman, *The Dance of Legislation* (New York: Touchstone, 1973).

10. Cochrane, *Effectiveness and Efficiency*.

11. Theodore R. Marmor, *The Politics of Medicare*, 2nd ed. (New York: Aldine de Gruyter, 2000); Jonathan Oberlander, *The Political Life of Medicare* (Chicago: University of Chicago Press, 2003).

12. Lawrence D. Brown and Michael S. Sparer, "Poor Program's Progress: The Unanticipated Politics of Medicaid Policy," *Health Affairs* 22 (January/February 2003): 31–44.

13. Alice Sardell and Kay Johnson, "The Politics of EPSDT Policy in the 1990s: Policy Entrepreneurs, Political Streams, and Children's Health Benefits," *Milbank Quarterly* 76.2: 175–205.

14. Robert Hackey, *Rethinking Health Care Policy: The New Politics of State Regulation* (Washington, DC: Georgetown University Press, 1998).

15. If tax expenditures are counted as spending, the public share runs closer to 60%. Daniel M. Fox and Paul Fronstin, "Public Spending for Health Care Approaches 60 Percent," *Health Affairs* 19 (March/April 2000): 271–273.

16. Nor is such diffusion merely an artifact of American exceptionalism, as Peter Baldwin's account of the importance of middle-class support in the expansion of European welfare states makes plain. See *The Politics of Social Solidarity: Class Bases of the European Welfare State 1875–1975* (Cambridge: Cambridge University Press, 1990).

17. Medicare too gains strength not only from its voting constituency but also from suppliers and myriad other non-beneficiary interests. See Bruce C. Vladeck, "The Political Economy of Medicare," *Health Affairs* 18 (January–February 1999): 22–36.

18. Sophie Chabaud and Catherine Collombet, "Le panier de biens et services medicaux rembourses par l'assurance maladie obligatoire et complementaire: d'une realite implicite a une redefinition explicite" (Paris: CNESSS, 2001).

19. Michael Moran, *Governing the Health Care State: A Comparative Study of the United Kingdom, United States and Germany* (Manchester, UK: Manchester University Press, 1999).

20. Keith Syrett, "A Technocratic Fix to the 'Legitimacy Problem'? The Blair Government and Health Care Rationing in the United Kingdom," *Journal of Health Politics, Policy and Law* 28 (August 2003): 715–746.

21. Theda Skocpol, *Boomerang: Clinton's Health Security Effort and the Turn Against Government in US Politics* (New York: W. W. Norton, 1997); Walter Zelman and Lawrence D. Brown, "Looking Back on Health Care Reform: 'No Easy

Choices,'" *Health Affairs* 17 (November/December 1998): 61–68; Jacob Hacker, *The Road to Nowhere* (Princeton, NJ: Princeton University Press, 1997); Mark Peterson, chapter 7 in this volume.

22. Seymour Martin Lipset, *American Exceptionalism: A Double-Edged Sword* (New York: W. W. Norton, 1996); Sven Steinmo and John Watts, "It's the Institutions, Stupid: Why Comprehensive National Health Insurance Always Fails in America," *Journal of Health Politics, Policy and Law* 20 (Summer 1995): 329–372; Colin Gordon, *Dead on Arrival: The Politics of Health Care in Twentieth-Century America* (Princeton, NJ: Princeton University Press, 2003); Paul Starr, *The Social Transformation of American Medicine* (New York: Basic Books, 1982).

23. Walter D. Burnham, *Critical Elections and the Mainsprings of American Politics* (New York: Oxford University Press, 1970); Byron E. Shafer, ed., *The End of Realignment?: Interpreting American Electoral Eras* (Madison: University of Wisconsin Press, 1991).

24. Edward Banfield, *The Moral Basis of a Backward Society* (New York: Simon and Schuster, 1958).

25. Thomas J. Sugrue, "All Politics Is Local: The Persistence of Localism in Twentieth-Century America," *The Democratic Experiment*, ed. Meg Jacobs, William Novak, and Julian Zelizar (Princeton, NJ: Princeton University Press, 2003), 301–326.

26. Lindblom, "The Science of 'Muddling Through.'"

27. Lawrence R. Jacobs, "Health Reform Impasse: The Politics of American Ambivalence toward Government," *Journal of Health Politics, Policy and Law* 18 (Fall 1993): 629–655.

335

# What Government Can Do

## BENJAMIN I. PAGE

THE MEPHISTOPHELES OF TO-DAY — HONEST LABOR'S TEMPTATION.

*The Mephistopheles of Today* tempts the worker
with labor unions and riches. Joseph Keppler,
*Puck*, date uncertain.

The health of Americans—and health inequalities among Americans—are affected not only by people's access or non-access to medical care (notably the lack of medical insurance coverage for some 43 million mostly lower-income people), but also by a wide range of social conditions, many of which can be influenced by government policies. Such policies include public health–related programs to control epidemics, improve workplace health and safety, and reduce dangers from automobiles, guns, or drugs like tobacco and alcohol. They also include programs that help provide good nutrition and shelter and that improve the physical, mental, and social development of children.

More broadly still, as Ichiro Kawachi pointed out in chapter 1, health is significantly affected by overall inequalities in the distribution of income and wealth. One obvious reason is that poor people often cannot afford good nutrition, safe environments, medical care, and other things they need to stay healthy (a form of *absolute* deprivation.) A second reason is that (at least in the United States) poverty tends to deprive people of the political power needed to get government to help. Third, however, even non-poor people who fall economically below their fellow citizens tend to suffer from a variety of social and psychological tensions and stresses that apparently impair their health. That is, *relative* deprivation appears to matter as well. Through all of these pathways, severe inequalities of income and wealth produce severe inequalities in health.

Thus health inequalities are affected not only by government policies that directly and straightforwardly deal with the prevention or treatment of injury and disease, or that provide basic nutrition and shelter to the poor, but also by the even broader set of policies that affect overall inequalities in the distribution of income and wealth. Such policies include social insurance and "safety net" programs; progressive (or regressive) taxes; public schools, day care, and educational assistance; macroeconomic policy, public service employment, the minimum wage, income subsidies like the Earned Income Tax Credit (EITC); and even policies related to immigration, international trade, birth control, and prisons.

James Simmons and I have discussed many actual and proposed government policies that can affect or (in many cases) *do* now affect the extent of poverty and inequality in the United States.[1] We argue that inequalities of income and wealth have reached extremely high levels that damage our sense of national community, contribute to crime and disorder, undermine the ideal of equal opportunity (when families have highly unequal resources, it is hard for their children to get an equal start), and reduce the aggregate welfare of Americans. We maintain that government can and should do a great deal to reduce these inequalities. We believe it can do so effectively and efficiently, without infringing on personal liberties or interfering with economic growth and prosperity.

If more egalitarian government programs are desirable, why haven't they been enacted? What stands in the way? The answer to this question should help us understand not only the medical care policies discussed in much of this volume (including the absence of universal health insurance in the United States), but also the much broader range of public policies that directly or indirectly affect health inequality.

## Obstacles to Egalitarian Policies

One myth is that the weakness of egalitarian programs is simply a result of democratic decision-making: A majority of U.S. citizens opposes such policies. According to this myth, most Americans are strongly and persistently antigovernment; they reject the sorts of pro-equality government policies that characterize much of the rest of the advanced industrial world.

Various pundits and observers assert this to be true, but the evidence for it is surprisingly scanty. When one looks closely at nationally representative polls and surveys—the best available source of evidence—it turns out that, yes, majorities do endorse various sorts of antigovernment rhetoric, and pluralities or majorities identify themselves as "conservative." Yet when it comes to concrete policies, large majorities of Americans favor government help with jobs, education, medical care, and other matters, and large majorities say they want to spend more on such egalitarian programs.[2]

Take the case of Social Security, our most important antipoverty program. (According to budget analysts, if Social Security payments were subtracted from the incomes of unmarried elderly beneficiaries, some 61% of them would fall below the meager official poverty line.[3]) Despite years of negative rhetoric about Social Security and proposals to privatize it, survey after survey shows more than 90% of Americans say they want to keep spending on the program steady or increase it. There is substantial support for such progressive changes as limiting the benefits of the wealthiest recipients, or removing the regressive "cap" on payroll taxes that currently completely exempts all earnings above $85,000 or so from taxation.[4]

As to medical care, eventual public disillusionment with the Clinton managed-care, employer-mandate plan that fizzled in 1993–1994 should by no means be taken as signaling public opposition to a government role in providing universal health insurance. In fact, large majorities of Americans—often reaching 60%–70% of the public—have expressed support for universal coverage, comprehensive benefits, tax-based financing, regulation of medical fees and drug prices, and a Canadian-style single-payer system.[5]

Most Americans are willing to pay taxes for popular progressive programs, want taxes to be moderately progressive, and favor closing loopholes. True, most people say their own taxes are "too high," and most say they favor tax cuts of almost any sort as opposed to the status quo; this includes the Bush administration cuts in 2001 and 2003. When questioned more closely before enactment of those cuts, however, substantial majorities thought the Bush plan was "very" or "somewhat" likely to cause a federal budget deficit (56% thought so, with 39% saying "not too likely" or "not at all likely"), likely to "take money away that is needed to protect Social Security" (56% vs. 40%), and likely to "mostly benefit the rich" (75% vs. 22%). Large majorities said they wanted the Senate to change the House bill so as to "significantly" lower the total amount of cuts (59% to 36%), "stop the cuts" if it looked like they would create a budget deficit in the future (63% to 33%), and adjust the plan so that "more of the tax cuts go to lower-income taxpayers."[6] By a large margin (55% to 30%), most people said they would prefer a Democratic alternative "about half as big, with more money devoted to spending on domestic programs such as Medicare and education and reducing the debt."[7]

To be sure, there are definite limits to the egalitarianism of the American public. Most Americans see some degree of income inequality as necessary or desirable in order to provide material incentives for the work, savings, and investment that are essential to economic prosperity and growth. And Americans, on average, do express less egalitarian views than most Europeans and others abroad.[8] But there exists so much actual or potential public support for new and expanded egalitarian programs that it would be perverse to attribute the absence of such programs to public opposition. Public opinion is *not* a major obstacle to moving U.S. public policy in a more egalitarian direction.

A second myth is that nothing can be done for reasons of cost, economic efficiency, or the constraints of global economic competition.

The argument that "we cannot afford it" makes no sense. This was particularly obvious at the beginning of 2001, when official government forecasts projected some $5.6 *trillion* (that is, $5,600 *billion*) in federal budget surpluses over the following decade.[9] To be sure, much of the projected surplus was hastily dissipated by the large tax cut—heavily tilted toward the highest-income taxpayers—that was expected (if fully implemented) to take up some $1.6 trillion. But the point is that abundant public resources can be available if we are willing to pay the taxes. Our current tax rates are much lower than those of other advanced industrial countries, and there is considerable evidence of public willingness to pay more for popular programs. It would clearly be possible to fund many redistributive programs that were rejected or starved for appropriations during the Clinton era of deficit cutting.

The much-feared "race to the bottom," in which all countries of the world were supposed to compete to offer the lowest taxes, feeblest regulation, and lowest public spending in order to lure capital and manufacture low-cost exports, has not occurred. True, the social democracies of Northern Europe, including Sweden, underwent some retrenchment, but the core of the modern welfare states has barely been touched. Nearly all the nations of Europe—indeed, nearly all advanced countries of the world except for a few (predominantly Anglo-American) holdouts—maintain extensive egalitarian government policies that reduce their levels of poverty and inequality considerably below those of the United States. And most of those countries are doing quite well economically, with per capita gross domestic products and long-term growth rates comparable to (and in some cases higher than) those of the United States.[10]

Nor is it the case that egalitarian government programs are inherently wasteful, inefficient, or entangled in red tape, or that they are bound to undermine work and savings incentives and cause great economic losses. Some of the antigovernment rhetoric of the 1980s lingers in the public mind, but recent research has indicated that negative effects were grossly overstated. Progressive taxes, for example, have much less tendency to discourage work or savings than was once believed.[11] Moderate minimum wages do *not* (contrary to conventional economic wisdom) increase unemployment.[12] Social Security does not greatly discourage private savings.[13]

Of course, different kinds of egalitarian policies vary markedly with respect to economic efficiency and vulnerability to global competitive pressures. The old Aid to Families with Dependent Children (AFDC) "welfare" program, for example, did indeed provide perverse incentives not to work. (The reason: policy makers refused help to those above the most desperate levels of poverty, so that those who worked could lose more in benefits than they gained in wages.) The remarkable thing, however, is how little this actually reduced work efforts.[14] Similarly, as Germany has learned to its regret, overly generous unemployment benefits are far less efficient than programs that provide abundant jobs and subsidize wages. Corporate income taxes are particularly vulnerable to global competition: capital can flee to low-tax countries, and companies can use accounting tricks to shift apparent profits to those countries.

On the positive side, however, many egalitarian programs can actually *lower* net production costs, increase productivity, and increase economic efficiency.

This is most obviously true of "human capital" programs that upgrade the skills and productivity of the disadvantaged, especially those that focus on young children and bring life-long benefits. But it may also be true of wage subsidies (like the EITC) that encourage low-income people to work longer and harder by ensuring that they get decent net wages as a result. And the cross-national evidence indicates that a single-payer system of universal health insurance, in which the single (government) payer has the bargaining clout to hold down medical costs, could actually cost a much *lower* fraction of our gross domestic product than our current public/private hodgepodge system does, while providing better medical care for the average American and much less health inequality.[15]

Thus, it is a myth that either public opposition or economic considerations can explain the lack of strong egalitarian policies in the United States. So what does explain it?

I see the main obstacles to egalitarian policies as lying chiefly in two interrelated realms. One is the decentralized nature of American politics, characterized by separation of powers and federalism, which provides multiple veto points for stopping new programs. The second, and even more fundamental, factor is a high degree of *political inequality* that enables small but active and affluent groups of individuals and corporations to dominate those veto points and prevent major egalitarian policy changes.

Europeans and U.S. students of comparative politics often fasten on the unusually decentralized nature of American politics as the major reason for different policy outcomes in the United States.[16] There is clearly some truth to this. The independence of our legislative branch from the executive; the existence of two distinct chambers of Congress that must both approve legislation (as well as the relatively strong system of committees within them); the weakness of the political parties; the substantial independence of the bureaucracy and the Supreme Court; and the dispersion of much policy responsibility to 50 separate states—all these factors do obviously make it easy to prevent the enactment or implementation of major new policies. One president, one chamber of Congress, sometimes just one determined congressional committee chairman, can effectively veto change. Such vetoes may be particularly likely when the parties divide control of government.

Yet a simple thought experiment demonstrates that decentralization of government and multiple veto points do *not*, in themselves, necessarily lead to the obstruction of egalitarian policy changes. Suppose that the officials occupying each veto point were chosen at exactly the same time, in exactly the same way—through genuinely democratic elections in which each citizen had exactly equal ("one person, one vote") influence on the outcome—and that the officials then paid attention to nothing but the wishes of the general public when they made policy. Clearly, differences among officials' policy stands would be minimal; multiple veto points would lose their significance; and the public would regularly get its way on whatever egalitarian (and other) policies it wanted.

This thought experiment makes clear that multiple veto points will obstruct popular policies only when one or more of those points is dominated by non-majoritarian political influences. To some limited extent, that could occur simply as a result of institutional inertia due to indirect appointments and staggered elections. The will of the majority, for example, might be embodied in today's House of Representatives but might be thwarted by yesterday's president or senators (elected years earlier), or by the day-before-yesterday's Supreme Court, appointed and confirmed during a previous decade. Again, however, if all elected public officials were chosen through fully democratic elections and responded only to public majorities, appointments and staggered elections might delay responsiveness to changing public majorities, but they would only cause delays, not long-term obstruction.

Thus I see *political inequality*—in which the selection and/or the influencing of public officials occurs under something other than one citizen/one vote circumstances—as constituting the most fundamental obstacle to the enactment of egalitarian policies.

Given the existence of multiple veto points, political inequality could create serious obstacles even if it impinged on only one or two major institutions (e.g., the Supreme Court). But in fact, it impinges on all of them. As Lawrence Jacobs points out in chapter 2, political inequality is pervasive throughout the American political system. Of particular importance are severe class-based inequalities in voting turnout and political participation. The abysmally low turnout of voters in the United States involves especially low turnout rates among low-income citizens: only 52% reported turning out, compared with 86% of their high-income fellows.[17] In the United States, unlike nearly all the rest of the advanced world, there is a marked class bias in turnout and therefore a marked class bias in whom politicians must pay attention to. In the United States, those of higher income—who tend to be much less enthusiastic about egalitarian government policies—have a much louder electoral voice.

It is sometimes argued that low turnout makes little difference because the expressed candidate choices and policy preferences of those who do not vote closely resemble those of the people who do vote.[18] True, surveys often show the expressed preferences of the two groups to be similar. (Not always, though: A marked counterexample came in 1994, when the voters who elected the Newt Gingrich–led Republican House of Representatives were much more conservative than the American citizenry as a whole.) But this does not dispose of the matter, because there is every reason to think that *if* lower-income Americans voted in large numbers—especially if they were mobilized to do so by a workers' party of the European Social Democratic type—they would become more aware of the class-based aspects of their political interests and would express different, more progressive preferences. American politics would look quite different.[19]

Political inequality is even more stark in types of participation that go beyond voting. Americans with higher incomes, more prestigious occupations, and more formal education are much more likely than their lower-income fellow citizens to go to political meetings, take an active part in campaigns, write letters to public officials, and the like. The class bias in each of these activities further magnifies the disproportionate voice of higher-income Americans—those least likely to favor egalitarian programs—in elections and policy-making.

Political inequality is by far greatest when it comes to contributing money to political candidates. Sidney Verba, Kay Schlozman, and Henry Brady's data indicate that those with family incomes over $75,000 were about *nine times* as likely as those with incomes under $15,000 to give campaign contributions, and their donations on the average were more than four times as big, so that the average high-income person gave at least *thirty-five times* as much money as the average low-income person did.[20] It would be surprising if big money givers did not have more influence on the selection of officials and their behavior in office. Again, such unequal political influence by the well-to-do is likely to lead to public officials showing less sympathy to egalitarian programs.

The increasingly blatant role of money in American elections, where many hundreds of millions of dollars are required for media advertising, not only tends to fill the U.S. Senate with multimillionaires (many of whom have reservations about progressive taxes or egalitarian spending programs); it also forces all politicians, including Democrats, to pay attention to big money givers who tend not to embrace egalitarian policies.[21]

Many studies have indicated that the organized interest groups active in American politics predominately represent corporations, businesses, and professional people, not ordinary workers and their families—let alone poor people. (Schlozman and John Tierney, for example, found that 64% of all the organizations with Washington representation were corporations [46%] or trade associations [18%].[22]) As E. E. Schattschneider put it, the heavenly chorus of interest groups that pluralist scholars used to celebrate "sings with a strong upper-class accent."[23] Organized interest groups not only wine and dine policy makers, bombard them with press releases and self-serving "studies," testify at hearings, and even draft legislation; increasingly groups also pursue "outside" strategies of stirring up public opposition, sometimes arousing public fears of new programs through misinformation. Thus, small businesses and a segment of the insurance industry were able to wreak havoc with the Clinton health care proposals in 1993–1994.[24]

To be sure, political scientists have spilled a great deal of ink debating how much influence interest groups actually exert, and some have doubted whether they have any impact at all.[25] It turns out to be very difficult to ascertain; this is not an area where quantitative social science has been very illuminating. But virtually all well-informed observers of the policy-making process judge that—while politicians sometimes extort money from groups rather than submitting to bribery, and while the wealthiest interest groups by no means always prevail—more often than not, abundant money and armies of lobbyists confer advantages in policy influence. Given the pro-producer biases of the interest-group universe, these advantages tend to push against the enactment of egalitarian policies. The existence of multiple veto points makes it particularly easy for a few moneyed, well-organized groups to obstruct the enactment of anything new.

## What Can Be Done?

Should we take these formidable obstacles as ruling out any possibility of enacting major egalitarian reforms of the sort that would reduce U.S. poverty and inequality? No. Leadership and energetic action can accomplish a great deal.

Political scientists are particularly susceptible to the "inevitability" fallacy. We want to believe that the political world is governed by simple, uniform, enduring laws. We hope to win fame (and, less likely, fortune) by discovering such laws. Since we are in the business of finding laws and regularities, we tend to explain past events as the result of the inexorable working of fixed processes. We tend to think that whatever happened in the past was inevitable, and that the same inevitability governs the future. If it never happened before—or has not happened recently—we doubt that it will happen in the future. Thus we might conclude that pervasive political inequalities in the United States, and the absence of strong (or, as Marie Gottschalk points out in chapter 5, clear-sighted) labor unions or a Social Democratic Party,[26] may make it impossible ever to enact substantial egalitarian programs.

This, I think, would be quite mistaken. In fact, obsession with what seems politically feasible at the moment can be quite harmful, if it discourages efforts at change. Human agency matters. I believe that progress is possible through four mutually complementary political strategies: (1) organize, particularly at the grass roots; (2) build incrementally toward long-term goals; (3) think big and seize opportunities when they arise; and (4) reform the political process itself.

## Organize

The very importance of organized interest groups in our political system suggests an obvious strategy: form, nurture, and deploy progressive groups and organizations. I am impressed by the presence now in Washington of a plethora of progressive groups and think tanks, many of them small (like the Indian Law Resource Center), some middle-sized (the Economic Policy Institute, the Center for Budget and Policy Priorities), and some quite large (Common Cause). These groups are usually out-spent, out-lawyered, and out-lobbied by big corporations (pharmaceuticals, health insurers, and tobacco companies come to mind), but they can have surprisingly significant impacts. One punchy, fact-filled press release faxed to the media can often change public discourse and affect policy.

Progressive groups can magnify their influence further by mobilizing at the grassroots level, pestering (and sometimes unseating) politicians in their home constituencies, and forming networks and alliances with like-minded organizations. True, as Elizabeth Kilbreth and James Morone points out in chapter 10, the Right Wing organizes too, and sometimes only idealistic bureaucrats can counter their pressures. True also, as Constance Nathanson discusses in chapter 6, it is generally harder to mobilize movements on behalf of lower-income citizens. But it can be done. The "living wage" campaigns in many cities provide one recent example. There are many opportunities to organize progressives.

## Build Incrementally

Lawrence Brown in chapter 11 argues—correctly, I believe—that small new programs and small changes in existing programs can add up to something big. A wonderful example is the EITC, which was enacted and expanded under presidents of both parties. The EITC won bipartisan backing because it encourages work while raising the incomes of low-income families, and it has recently grown to become one of our most important egalitarian programs. In fiscal year 2002, the EITC paid about $5 billion in tax credits and $27 billion in cash to roughly 19 million workers and their families. EITC's total expenditure of $32 billion easily outweighed, for example, the $21 billion spent on Food Stamps.[27]

Clearly it is well worthwhile to work away at the margins, improving the programs we have, coming up with clever but small new ideas that may grow bigger, and making things better in as many little ways as possible.

At the same time, there are dangers in a purely incrementalist strategy. For one thing, incremental change is not invariably positive. It is possible to "muddle backward" rather than forward—or to backslide badly in some areas while moving forward modestly in others. In 2001, for example, while many progressives seemed to be looking the other way—perhaps focused on hopes for incremental gains on education, prescription drugs, and the like—the Bush administration's bold, enormous tax cut tossed away more than a trillion dollars of revenue that could have been used for egalitarian programs and at the same time sharply reduced the progressivity of the tax system. (According to the best available estimate, the Bush plan, if fully in place, would give 44% of its dollars in cuts to the top 1% of households: those earning $373,000 or more per year. The top 1% of households would average $28,000 each annually in cuts, while 60% of U.S. households would get less than $316 each.[28]) This can only be viewed as a catastrophe for progressive policies in the United States.

In addition, an exclusive focus on incremental improvements can lead us to ignore the need for major transformation and fundamental change when dispassionate analysis would indicate that such transformation is called for. To a non-expert like myself, for example, the U.S. system of delivering medical care appears clearly in need of fundamental transformation. It seems bizarre, truly outlandish, that we spend such enormous amounts of resources while so poorly serving so many of our citizens. This mess probably results from our commitment to public subsidy of private profits and our decentralization of insurers. Reliance on multiple private insurers has led to wasteful private bureaucracies and red tape, severe difficulty in controlling costs (realistically, only a single payer may be able to do it), and scandalously incomplete coverage. Given the problems of adverse selection and "creaming," complete coverage can probably be achieved only through universal, government-provided insurance.[29]

If I am right about the deficiencies of the present U.S. medical care system, small changes by themselves are unlikely to make much difference. To focus exclusively on small changes could be to forgo any chance of reshaping the whole system. The best strategy may be, as Colleen Grogan and Eric Patashnik recommend in chapter 9, to think big while initially acting small. We could consider incrementally lowering the eligibility age for Medicare, for example, with the aim of eventually providing a framework for universal health insurance for all Americans. Or, as Grogan and Patashnik suggest, Medicaid's provision of long-term care for the middle class could be expanded as another vehicle for universality.

It may be that some non-medical program areas are also ripe for incremental egalitarian changes that aim for big long-term effects. We might, for example, make the personal income tax more progressive a small step at a time (as was done in 1993), gradually undoing regressive Bush cuts before they phase in. The regressivity of payroll taxes might also be lessened a step at a time, rather than trying to remove entirely, all at once, the "cap" that exempts high incomes from taxation. We might gradually expand EITC benefits to childless workers, fund Head Start fully and include more 3-year-olds in the program, restore the universality of Food Stamps, improve public elementary schools, ready a modest program of public service employment for recessions, and the like. Such incremental measures could be very helpful indeed in reducing poverty and inequality generally and health inequality in particular.[30] If properly designed, each of them could lead toward major long-term improvements in U.S. public policy.

Success on such matters could well cumulate into a major policy shift in an egalitarian direction. It is also necessary to think big, however, if we want to avoid backsliding, increase the probability of success for each small move, ensure that the small moves actually cumulate into something, and be ready to make bigger changes if the opportunity arises. We need to analyze fundamental policy changes that may be needed; to formulate, promote, and publicize bold progressive ideas; to mobilize and build constituencies for them; and to seize (or create) opportunities to make comprehensive changes in policy.

## Think Big

Even a passing acquaintance with American history indicates that big changes *do* sometimes occur in U.S. social policy. The most notable examples in recent times are the New Deal of the 1930s, when the Social Security Act, the National Labor Relations Act, and other fundamental new programs were enacted; and the Great Society of the middle and late 1960s, which included the enactment of the Civil Rights Act of 1964, Medicare, Medicaid, and a number of smaller antipoverty and equal-opportunity programs—followed by a major expansion of Social Security in the early 1970s.

The New Deal, of course, came only amidst the extraordinary circumstances of the Great Depression, when social disorder and radical movements gave upper-income citizens and politicians reason to fear for the stability of their system. American business was under the gun, and key business elements cooperated to an unprecedented extent with a progressive agenda.[31] (One lesson of American social policy may be that support from at least some key segments of business is necessary for any major policy initiative.) It would certainly not be prudent to do nothing while waiting for another such calamity—though it would be equally foolish to ignore the possibility of crises altogether. The new, highly interdependent global economy may be newly vulnerable to multinational depression. Progressives would be wise to be prepared with sweeping programs in the event of an economic crash.

Of more immediate relevance, however, is the experience of the 1960s. For those who consider political patterns to be fixed and immutable, it might be instructive to look back at the remarkable contrast between the politics of 1963—when Congress was deadlocked by the "conservative coalition" and when white southerners, seething with resentment over the civil rights movement, were vowing to impeach President Kennedy—and the politics of 1965, just 2 years later, when Lyndon Johnson, enjoying overwhelming Democratic majorities in both houses of Congress, rammed through his Great Society legislation. What a difference 2 years can make.

To be sure, those were very eventful years. The assassination of Kennedy in 1963 and the Republicans' blunder in nominating Barry Goldwater for president in 1964, together with Johnson's immense energy and his regionally based advantages in working with conservative Democrats, altogether transformed the political landscape. We should not expect exactly such a configuration of events to occur again. But the point is that accidents *do* happen in politics, and that political accidents can have big policy consequences. It makes sense to be prepared for all sorts of events that may suddenly alter the political equation.

Indeed, even rather small, unexpected events can have important consequences. A shift in party control, even by a very narrow margin, can change committee chairmen and legislative leaders; alter the agenda of policies under consideration; change the thrust of investigations, hearings, and the like; significantly change the voices heard in the media; and shift the terms of public discourse.

If only to *be ready* for such changes in the political environment, it is important—even in the worst of times—to keep thinking big, to work out ambitious progressive ideas, so that they can be deployed when circumstances become propitious.

But the argument for thinking big goes well beyond that. To think big is also crucial for the success of our first strategy, "organize." As Schattschneider long ago suggested, the best hope for overcoming the class bias in the interest group system may be to "expand the scope of the conflict": to get ordinary citizens involved and mobilized.[32] But citizens have many things to do, and it is hard to mobilize them around small ideas. (Millions are unlikely to storm the barricades under a banner reading, "Raise the income cap a bit on FICA.") Big ideas can capture the imaginations of millions of people and give them hope for a better life. Big ideas can energize social movements.

For this reason, I believe that those of us who are progressively inclined should think through not only what is politically feasible right now, but also what is *really desirable*—exactly what sorts of public policies we would want enacted under ideal conditions. We should work out and refine such ideas and publicize them as widely as we can, challenging the narrowness of within-the-Beltway discourse. We should use these ideas as organizing tools and use them also to design incremental measures that will actually lead to something, while being prepared to move fast at propitious moments when comprehensive policy changes might be enacted.

## Reform the Political System

I have saved for last a strategy that may actually deserve first priority, because it affects everything else: namely, to weaken or remove the political obstacles against egalitarian programs by reducing political inequality. Clearly, egalitarian programs of all types would be easier to enact, and regressive backsliding would be less likely, if the political power of money were curtailed and if the lower-income segment of our population were mobilized into political activity.

Remedies for political inequality are not hard to formulate. If, for example, we were to join most of the rest of the world in holding elections on holidays and automatically registering everyone—instead of imposing on individuals the burden of traveling to the right place at the right moment in order to register and stealing time from their jobs or families in order to vote—we could probably raise election turnout rates from our anemic 50% or less to the European levels of 70% to 80%. This would also greatly reduce our unique class bias in turnout and would empower our lower-income citizens, particularly if we also ensure that they have attractive choices to vote for. Furthermore, if we provide free airtime and public funding for election campaigns while severely restricting private expenditures, we can substantially reduce the power of money in politics. To increase the political power of low-income citizens and to reduce the power of money would undoubtedly make progressive policies far easier to enact.

Of course, many politicians who have been elected under the current system of money-driven politics and a demobilized citizenry will bitterly resist changes that might drive them out of office. (Some of that resistance is cleverly disguised, particularly among Democratic senators and representatives who are afraid to defend a corrupt status quo openly.) Moreover, U.S. political inequalities have deep historical roots in such factors as our weak labor movement, racial and ethnic divisions among American workers, and the dominance of huge, minimally regulated business corporations. But it does not follow that nothing can be done about political inequality.

Some progress may be made incrementally through skillful policy design and advocacy and through hard political work, as was true of the "Motor Voter" Act providing for voter registration in motor vehicles departments and other government offices, and state laws permitting expanded absentee ballots or general voting by mail.[33] Continued outrage over widespread disenfranchisement in the 2000 election provides a good opportunity for improving citizens' access to the polls and ensuring that their preferences are accurately tallied. The very prevarications and "proreform" disguises used by many politicians can be used against them, if legislative votes are structured so as to be too embarrassing to duck.

But fundamental changes will probably require extensive mobilization of the citizenry—along the lines of our first and third strategies—through social movements that target political reform along with substantive policy measures. Assertive political leadership can be important, as exemplified by the attention that Senator John McCain won for campaign finance reform. The Beltway wisdom that the public "doesn't care" that money is corrupting American politics could very well be disconfirmed by an energetic campaign. Moreover, each successful step in reducing political inequality would alter the effective electorate and thereby ease further steps, ultimately perhaps including the institution of a more representative, worker-friendly political party, or at least a reduction in the Democratic Party's distracting dependence on Goldman Sachs, communications conglomerates, and other big investors.

In politics, as in other realms, a division of labor often makes sense. Some progressives, including those employed in the trenches of day-to-day policy making, quite properly focus on particular policy areas and spend most of their time working for small-scale changes. But it is important that others work on organizing and mobilizing the citizenry on behalf of large causes, and that everyone—including those who work on small things—keeps the big picture in mind.

## Notes

1. Benjamin I. Page and James R. Simmons, *What Government Can Do: Dealing with Poverty and Inequality* (Chicago: University of Chicago Press, 2000).

2. Fay Lomax Cook and Edith J. Barrett, *Support for the American Welfare State: The Views of Congress and the Public* (New York: Columbia University Press, 1992); Benjamin I. Page and Robert Y. Shapiro, *The Rational Public: Fifty Years of Trends in Americans' Policy Preferences* (Chicago: University of Chicago Press, 1992), chapter 4.

3. U.S. Office of Management and Budget, *Budget of the United States Government, Fiscal Year 1999* (Washington, DC: Government Printing Office, 1998), 229. Of course, this 61% figure probably overestimates how many would actually stay poor after workers had time to adjust to the absence of Social Security, but sharp drops in poverty rates among the elderly after expansions of Social Security indicate that its antipoverty effects are real. See Rebecca Blank, *It Takes a Nation: A New Agenda for Fighting Poverty* (Princeton, NJ: Princeton University Press, 1997), 19–20.

4. Fay Lomax Cook and Lawrence R. Jacobs, "Assessing Assumptions about Americans' Attitudes toward Social Security: Popular Claims Meet Hard Data," paper presented at the annual conference of the National Academy of Social Insurance, Washington, DC, January 24, 2001; Page and Simmons, *What Government Can Do*.

5. Lawrence Jacobs and Robert Shapiro, *Politicians Don't Pander* (Chicago: University of Chicago Press, 2000), chapters 3, 7, esp. 94–102, 228–229. See also Page and Shapiro, 129–132.

6. CNN/*USA Today*/Gallup Poll, March 9–11, 2001. N = 1,015 adults nation-wide; expectation questions asked of a subsample of 530.

7. *Los Angeles Times* Poll, March 3–5, 2001. N = 1,449 adults nationwide. A narrower majority (53% to 43%) preferred, instead of a "large tax-cut plan that provides an across-the-board tax cut for everyone," "a smaller tax cut plan that provides targeted tax cuts mainly for lower- and middle-income people." ABC News/*Washington Post* Poll, February 21–25, 2001. N = 1,050 adults nationwide.

8. Sidney Verba, Steven Kelman, Gary Orren, Ichiro Miyake, Joji Watanuki, Ikuo Kabashima, and G. Donald Ferree, *Elites and the Idea of Equality: A Comparison of Japan, Sweden, and the United States* (Cambridge, MA: Harvard University Press, 1987), chapters 4 and 6; Jennifer L. Hochschild, *What's Fair?: American Beliefs about Distributive Justice* (Cambridge, MA: Harvard University Press, 1981).

9. U.S. Office of Management and Budget, *A Blueprint for New Beginnings: A Responsible Budget for America's Priorities* (Washington, DC: Government Printing Office, 2001), 11.

10. Page and Simmons, *What Government Can Do.*

11. Joel Slemrod, ed., *Tax Progressivity and Income Inequality* (New York: Cambridge University Press, 1996).

12. David Card and Alan B. Krueger, *Myth and Measurement: The New Economics of the Minimum Wage* (Princeton, NJ: Princeton University Press, 1995).

13. Page and Simmons, *What Government Can Do*, 80.

14. Blank, *It Takes a Nation*, 100–102, 146–148.

15. Michael J. Graetz and Jerry L. Mashaw, *True Security: Rethinking American Social Insurance* (New Haven, CT: Yale University Press, 1999), chapter 7; Page and Simmons, *What Government Can Do*, 89–100.

16. Sven Steinmo and Jon Watts, "It's the Institutions, Stupid! Why Comprehensive National Health Insurance Always Fails in America," *Journal of Health Politics, Policy and Law* 20.2 (1995): 329–389; see also Mark Peterson, chapter 7 in this volume.

17. Sidney Verba, Kay Lehman Schlozman, and Henry E. Brady, *Voice and Equality: Civic Volunteerism in American Politics* (Cambridge, MA: Harvard University Press, 1995), 190; Frances Fox Piven and Richard A. Cloward, *Why Americans Don't Vote* (New York: Pantheon, 2000); Alexander Keyssar, *The Right to Vote: The Contested History of Democracy in the United States* (New York: Basic, 2000).

18. For example, Raymond E. Wolfinger and Steven J. Rosenstone, *Who Votes?* (New Haven: Yale University Press, 1980), 109–114.

19. Higher turnout among lower-income Americans and the existence of a workers' party would likely influence each other; to start with either one would encourage the other.

20. Verba, Schlozman, and Brady, *Voice and Equality*, 190, 192; in my calculations from Verba, Schlozman, and Brady's figures, I have conservatively treated the contributions of the few respondents with incomes over $125,000 (which actually averaged $1,183) as if they were the same as the next lowest income

group ($322), so that the ratio between high- and low-income contributions is somewhat understated.

21. Thomas Ferguson and Joel Rogers, *Right Turn: The Decline of the Democrats and the Future of American Politics* (New York: Hill and Wang, 1986); Thomas Ferguson, *Golden Rule: The Investment Theory of Party Competition and the Logic of Money-Driven Political Systems* (Chicago: University of Chicago Press, 1995).

22. Kay Lehman Schlozman and John T. Tierney, *Organized Interests and American Democracy* (New York: Harper & Row, 1986), 67.

23. E. E. Schattschneider, *The Semi-Sovereign People: A Realist's View of Democracy in America* (New York: Holt, Rinehart and Winston, 1960), 35.

24. Darrell M. West and Burdett A. Loomis, *The Sound of Money: How Political Interests Get What They Want* (New York: W. W. Norton, 1998), chapter 4; but see Lawrence R. Jacobs, "Manipulators and Manipulation: Public Opinion in a Representative Democracy," draft paper (Minneapolis: University of Minnesota, 2001).

25. For example, Fred S. McChesney, *Money for Nothing: Politicians, Rent Extraction, and Political Extortion* (Cambridge, MA: Harvard University Press, 1997).

26. See Dietrich Rueschemeyer, Evelyne Huber Stephens, and John D. Stephens, *Capitalist Development and Democracy* (Chicago: University of Chicago Press, 1992).

27. U.S. Office of Management and Budget, *Budget of the United States Government, Fiscal Year 2002* (Washington, DC: Government Printing Office, 2001), 112, 199, 200, 219.

28. Citizens for Tax Justice, "House Committee Approves Bush Income Tax Rate Cuts; Republicans and Democrats Disagree on Tax Breaks for the Rich," press release (Washington, DC: Citizens for Tax Justice, 2 March 2001).

29. Page and Simmons, *What Government Can Do*, 56–59, 98–100, 117–119, 269–273; Michael J. Graetz and Jerry L. Mashaw, *True Security*, chapter 9, offers an interesting alternative.

30. A number of such proposals are spelled out and given an appealing rationale in Theda Skocpol, *The Missing Middle: Working Families and the Future of American Social Policy* (New York: W. W. Norton, 2000).

31. Ferguson, *Golden Rule*; Peter Swenson, *Capitalists against Markets: The Making of Labor Markets and Welfare States in the United States and Sweden* (New York: Oxford University Press, 2001).

32. Schattschneider, *The Semi-Sovereign People*, especially chapter 1.

33. See Piven and Cloward, *Why Americans Don't Vote*.

# Conclusion: Prospering in the Age of Global Markets

## LAWRENCE R. JACOBS AND JAMES A. MORONE

*Stop Thief! The Ram's Horn,* April 18, 1896.

W e live in new economic times. The remarkable sway of markets in the United States is not an accident, nor is it inevitable. It is the product of conscious decisions made by American government officials confronting a rapidly changing global economy. All advanced industrial countries face the same challenges. The American difference lies in the choices that our leaders have made—and the alternatives they have rejected. These decisions—about whether to buffer people from the economic storm—have profound consequences for both the wealth and the health of nations.

## The New Global Economy

T wo of the most important changes in the structure of the world economy are expanded trade (and investment) and the growing demand for technologically skilled workers. The changes offer every nation great economic opportunities—and the threat of expanding inequality.

A look at imports and exports provides a snapshot of the fast opening of the international economy. As a proportion of gross domestic product, foreign trade in the United States rose from 3% in 1970 to 10%–12% by the mid-1990s; in higher-income countries more generally, it rose from 12% in 1965 to 20% in 1990.[1] Although there is some debate over the degree to which international investment and, especially, trade contributes to rising economic inequality, most observers agree that they are important factors.

At the same time, the growing role of technology (from computers to bioengineering) has reduced the demand for less skilled workers and increased the demand for technologically savvy labor—a demand that outstrips the growing supply. Another snapshot will convey the rapid shift to a more skilled workforce in the United States: the proportion of the adult population over 24 years old that completed college doubled from 11% in 1970 to 22% by 1993. The shift toward more skill-based jobs puts premiums on better educated workers and fuels a disparity in earnings: the ratio of average weekly wages of college grads to those of high school grads almost doubled in the past two decades, rising from 38% in 1979 to 71% in 1998.[2]

The American experience is not unique. Nearly all industrialized countries witnessed massive economic changes that widened inequality in income and wealth during the 1980s and 1990s. Tim Smeeding has mapped changes in income inequality across industrialized countries from the 1970s to the 1990s and found that in Germany and Sweden—with comparatively well-developed welfare states—income inequality dipped by 1% to 6% during the 1970s but modestly increased by the same proportion in the 1980s and 1990s; France and Canada had similar records. Income inequality also grew in the United States. What is striking, however, is that it grew at a much faster rate and without interruption across the entire period—expanding by a consistent pace of 7% to 15%.[3]

Changes in the global economy created a common set of influences that help to explain the acceleration in economic inequality across countries. These countries were also affected by demographic and social changes like aging, the growth of single-parent households, and changing patterns of labor force participation (such as the increased presence of women in the workforce).[4]

## The American Difference

The dawn of the new economy in the 1970s and 1980s generated predictions of a worldwide "race to the bottom" as international trade, finance, and demand for ever more valuable skilled workers forced draconian cuts in government taxes as countries elbowed each other to stand out as the most friendly to increasingly mobile business and skilled workers. Those were the predictions. The reality of the past two decades has been quite different. Although changes in the global markets did produce a common pattern of widening inequality (as we just observed), there were important differences in how individual countries and groups of countries responded to the common economic changes.

One big difference jumps out: how quickly and radically inequality widened in the United States compared to its allies. By the 1990s, economic inequalities in household income were far sharper in the United States than in any other advanced industrialized country.[5]

The critical question is why. Why did inequality increase so much more rapidly in the United States than in Europe and Canada? Answering this question will provide a roadmap to how to respond to the structural changes in the economy.

### The Secret to Success in Europe and Canada

Government policy is not the only remedy for the rise in economic inequality, but it is an important influence and one of the few that we can control through our collective decisions. Markets, along with demographic and social changes, generate inequality; the question is whether and how the government will step in to offset and filter out disparities in earnings that markets produce. Advanced industrialized countries face a choice: Do citizens and their government accept market outcomes or step in and modify them?

Three types of government programs are particularly important for offsetting inequality in Europe and Canada. The first set of efforts is the most obvious—social welfare programs: cash transfers in the form of public assistance to the poor as well as family and housing allowances that are widely distributed; health care; and generous pensions.

The effect of these programs is large and impressive. The impact of markets on widening inequality is most apparent in earnings—how much workers get in their paycheck. Some European countries interfere directly in the labor market to prevent disparities in earnings. But other European countries and Canada do not; their strategy has been to use taxes, government services, and cash to counteract the outcomes of labor markets. For instance, Canada experienced large increases in earnings inequality but used transfers and taxes to balance out the effects of growing inequality. As a result, Canadians have experienced only very modest increases in inequality in family or household income.[6] The most active welfare states in northern Europe (namely, Sweden, the Netherlands, Norway, Finland, and Denmark), as well as France and Germany, intervene by providing services, cash, and tax credits to keep the households with the lowest 10th percentile of income at about 55% to 60% of the income of the households in the middle of the income distribution; they hold the wealthiest households (in the highest 10th percentile of income) to about 150% to 180% of the middle household.[7]

A second type of policy pursued by European and Canadian governments is aimed at structuring labor markets to the advantage of labor—and, indirectly, business. In response to the growing importance of skilled labor in a technological age, these governments invest in human capital by expanding the supply of skilled labor to better satisfy business needs. For instance, government funding to substantially increase the supply of workers with a college education in the Netherlands contributed to reducing the premium for skilled labor found in other countries. In addition, European governments regularly adjust the minimum wage and encourage centralized wage bargaining between business and labor to hold off increases in inequality (as in Germany) or to mitigate them (as in Sweden and the Netherlands).[8]

Faced with a worldwide fall in demand for less skilled workers, European governments decided that their first priority was to fend off the downward pressure on wages and the accompanying rise in inequality.

They (and their voters) accepted higher unemployment rates as a price of protecting the compensation of lower skilled workers. Although the unemployment rates in Europe had been lower than those in the United States for most of the post–World War II period, its rates became higher in the 1980s.[9]

The third policy was to maintain (rather than reduce) taxes in order to provide a steady stream of revenues. The new global economy was expected to spark dramatic tax cuts as governments competed with each other to create an attractive business climate and lure investment and skilled labor. In Europe and Canada, international pressures did not bring about the doomsday scenario; economic changes did not eviscerate the government's capacity to raise revenues. Government officials were apparently constrained from entering into a tax-cut bidding war by domestic pressure and budgetary commitments to maintain revenues that addressed rising needs while avoiding government debt.[10]

Overall, then, America's allies in Europe and Canada faced up to the gales of the new global economy that, if ignored, would have dramatically widened economic disparities. Instead, these countries designed government policies that offset or moderated the income disparities generated by private markets.

A common complaint about extensive government social and labor policy is that it prevents economic growth by draining the country of money through taxes and burdening business with responsibilities. Few complaints are as often repeated and as lacking in evidence. Critical measures of economic activity (per capita gross domestic product) and long-term rates of economic growth in Europe are similar or better than those in the United States. As one compilation of data on economic inequality concluded, other advanced industrialized countries "spend more on both poverty reduction and family-friendly policies… while maintaining competitive rates of productivity and income growth."[11]

## America's Choice: Too Little, Too Late

The United States has not protected its own citizens from the new global economic maelstrom. Changes in the labor and financial markets since the 1980s have had an immediate, powerful, and unbuffered impact on income and wealth distribution. Other industrial nations protected their citizens from the consequences. The United States did not.

American policy makers did make some efforts to offset the widening economic divide by providing help to low-income workers. Tax rebates to this group of workers under the earned income tax credit

(EITC) were substantially expanded beginning in the 1980s and continuing through the 1990s. Tax expenditures (the total cost of the tax breaks) hovered just over $2 billion from 1975 to 1986. With the Tax Reform Act of 1986, President Reagan and Congress started reforming tax policy toward low-income families; by the late 1990s, the cost of the earned income tax credit had risen to $21 billion. The expansion of EITC lifted millions out of poverty. Policy makers took other steps. State legislatures and Congress helped reduce the hurdle of child care a bit by expanding subsidies for low-income workers.[12] Chapters 9 and 10 discuss steps to widen access to health insurance among poor or near poor families with children.

The problem was not inaction but inadequate action. The response of American policy makers to economic pressures was not enough to prevent the sharp expansion of the disparity in household income to a level not found in any other industrialized country.[13]

The three types of government interventions pursued by the European and Canadian governments to mitigate the sharp rise in economic inequality and the associated erosion of health—policies on social welfare, labor markets, and taxation—have been used in different or less extensive ways in the United States.

First, the United States lacks the kind of social welfare safety net that would have protected American workers from market-generated inequalities. Compared to Canada and Europe, the United States has (by far) the most unequal household income *after* the government intervenes through taxes and the distribution of services. Recall that northern European countries and France and Germany lifted the income of the poorest households to about 55% to 60% of those in the middle of the income distribution and held the wealthiest households to about 150% to 180% of middle income households. By contrast, the lowest tenth percentile of household income in the United States is only 38% of the households in the middle of the income distribution and the wealthiest households (the top 10%) balloons to 214% of the middle household.[14] In other words, the household income of those at the bottom is about a third poorer than in Europe, while those at the top are 20% to 40% richer.[15]

Not surprisingly, poverty rates are substantially higher in the United States. No industrialized country matches the proportion of the American population (16.9%) or American children (22.3%) who live in poverty. The rates in Germany, France, and northern Europe are a half or a third of our rates.[16] Americans stand a far better chance of being billionaires (almost impossible in some European countries)—or of being homeless—than the citizens of other wealthy nations.

In the United States, government assistance has long been criticized as wasteful, even harmful, by undermining self-sufficiency and independence. Even so, the government provides enormous assistance to some groups. Seniors have benefited spectacularly from Social Security and Medicare. In 2001, before the government intervened with social assistance and tax benefits, 49% of Americans age 65 and over were poor and slightly fewer (41%) citizens living in families with children headed by a woman were poor. Government intervention, however, slashed poverty among poor seniors to 8% (an 84% reduction), while poverty in female-headed families remained quite high at 25% (a smaller—but still significant— 38% decline).[17]

Government has also stepped in to assist children. We recognize that feeding, educating, and keeping them healthy are all essential to insuring children an opportunity to get as far as they can with their own skill and effort. Public assistance for children and their mothers is one of the oldest forms of government provision in the United States.

Even with these efforts to give children an equal opportunity, the United States does far less for its children than its allies. Other countries allow parents to stay home with newborns in the critical weeks after birth, support quality child care for working parents, and prevent families from sliding into poverty due to the costs of caring for children. For instance, the United States government pays about 25% to 30% of child care costs compared to rates of 70% to over 85% in France, Norway, Sweden, and other European countries.[18] The United States is alone among its allies in Western Europe and Canada in not mandating paid maternity or paternity leave. The result should be more widely acknowledged: the birth of a child pushes nearly 9% of American families into poverty, at least double the rate in nearly all Western European countries.[19] As one authoritative study concludes: "The United States stands out as the country with the lowest [government] expenditures and highest child poverty rate."[20]

Second, the United States has not pursued a coherent and coordinated policy to address the structural changes in labor markets. Abandoned to face the global economic gale, less skilled workers in the United States have experienced startling declines in their real wages.[21] Between 1979 and 1993, the real hourly wages of males with 12 years of education fell by a fifth; those with entry-level jobs declined by a third.[22] These are staggering changes and they happened in a flash.

Europeans rejected the idea of leaving large numbers of workers behind, unprotected in the global economic storm. Governments—left, right, and center—moved firmly to shield their people from sharp economic deprivation. In contrast, the United States has allowed itself to be

split in two. On the one side are the winners of the new global economy—the better-educated and more skilled workers. On the other side
are the losers—the less educated and less skilled.

Third, progressive tax policy was scaled back during the 1980s and in
the early 2000s, curtailing the government's capacity to generate revenue.
A cottage industry set up shop after the Reagan administration tax cuts to
study their effects on income distribution. The verdict is in: Tax cuts failed
to counteract the inequalities generated in the private markets.[23]

One study of 14 advanced industrialized countries during the 1980s
and 1990s found that the United States stood out for having the lowest
taxation at all levels of government (as a percentage of gross domestic
product).[24] Even if the government officials decided to adopt the policies
of its allies, they lacked the revenues to offset the growing inequalities
generated by the private sector. American government went into the new
global economy cutting back its own capacity to protect its citizens.

Europe and Canada made a series of decisions in the 1980s and 1990s
to respond to structural changes in the global economy; the United States
failed to act, took half steps, or acted in ways that tied its own hands—
such as reducing its progressive income tax. The previous chapters have all
grappled with the stark consequences: The United States sports far higher
rates of economic inequality, poverty, and ill health compared to those
experienced by its allies.

The lesson here is simple: Global markets push us toward increased
inequalities as employers compete for highly skilled labor, but most governments can and do step in to protect their people. Other countries
offset rising inequality.[25]

The Austrian economist Joseph Schumpeter described modern
capitalism as a great "storm of creative destruction." That storm grows
increasingly fierce as the world economy becomes more open and interconnected. Citizens in Europe and Canada have erected barriers to protect their entire community—especially the most vulnerable and the less
skilled—from the winds of global economic activity. The United States
has chosen an alternate route. America's comparatively modest protections against the consequences of the global economy have allowed a few
individuals to profit fantastically even as a great many have languished or
seen their economic position decline.

In short, other nations band together. Americans seem to turn on
one another. They reduce health insurance coverage (even for workers), starve local governments (thanks to tax cuts), and promote tough-
minded policies that land more than 2 million people in jail. Our crime

rates are roughly the same as the crime rates in other industrial countries (murder aside); but with one out of thirty-three Americans in prison or jail, under probation, or on parole, no other country is as tough on its citizens.[26]

## Toward the Good Community

During the second half of the nineteenth century, industrialization brought new factories making new products—from railroads and automobiles to efficient oil processing and steel production. A handful of people made staggering new fortunes. By the late nineteenth century, John D. Rockefeller, J. P. Morgan, and Andrew Carnegie had amassed wealth without parallel in American history. That period became known as the Gilded Age.

We are now living through the Second Gilded Age of wealth accumulation.[27] In 1868, Cornelius Vanderbilt boasted America's largest fortune: $40 million—about 80,000 times greater than the wealth held by the middle family or household. In 1999, Bill Gates held the distinction of being the wealthiest American with a fortune of $85 billion—1,416,000 times more than the wealth of the median family or household.

The rapidly changing global economy has reshuffled the distribution of money in American society and unsettled the life circumstances that nurture and protect the health of a population. A few individuals have grown fantastically wealthy, but America as a whole has struggled as it separated into two groups—the wealthy and everyone else. The consequences for health are significant, as Ichiro Kawachi shows in chapter 1.

Maintaining the health of Americans amidst structural economic change requires bold policy change. Incremental changes can add up. They improve the lives and the health of millions of Americans. But narrowing the large and growing inequality in income, wealth, and health that exists in the United States—and in no other industrial nation—will require something more: a set of policies addressing the structural changes in the global economy.

The arsenal for fending off inequality is the tried and proven trio found in Europe and Canada, though they will need to be tailored to American institutions and practices. Restructuring government to reflect the new economic order and build on the experiences of America's allies requires carefully balancing protections for American workers without reducing the incentives to work.[28] Economists speculate that generous benefits for the unemployed would decrease disparities in income; but they might also lessen the incentives to earnestly search for a new job and accept it (especially if it is unattractive).[29] But in many areas, this is a false choice. The sensible path forward is to focus policies on protecting and expanding opportunity for motivated individuals—insuring health care, improving education, training (or retraining) workers, and ensuring that wages allow full-time workers to escape the shadow of poverty.

The following suggestions—drawn from American experience as much as foreign successes—point the way to a society that is healthier, wealthier and fairer.

## Insure Health Care

The place to begin is by making a just health care system. In Europe and Canada, the government has dominated the financing of health (even while doctors and hospitals largely remained in private hands); in the United States, employers doled out health insurance for the great majority of Americans who were not elderly or poor. Far from operating as a "free" market, the private welfare state that provided health insurance in the United States over the past half-century was supported by massive tax breaks for businesses (amounting to the third largest federal health care expenditure—after Medicare and Medicaid) and by the contributions of employers in lieu of wages.

Global economic pressures are contributing to the steady unraveling of the employer-based health insurance system. Businesses scramble to cut the wages and benefits of workers—at a minimum, employers are passing more health costs to their workers. Stagnating real wages makes it increasingly difficult for many workers to pay the premiums and coinsurance of their employers' health plans. America's employer-based health insurance system is cracking.

How can we respond? A century of failure has left reformers timidly seeking "plausible," incremental solutions. But the American health system is thick with interested parties—primed to fend off threats to their own turf. Addressing a social problem this large—one out of eight Americans does not have health insurance—will take bold action. Only a powerful reform will rally the kind of support that might push serious change on a reluctant health care system.

Of course, there are many approaches to insuring health care—Democratic and Republican ideas, private-sector plans and large government programs. The key is a clear commitment to the goal: insuring all Americans. And the most important lesson from the great reforms in American history—from Social Security to civil rights—is unambiguous: think big, define the core principles, negotiate the details, and never stop pushing.

Our own policy preference draws on one of America's most successful and popular social programs: Medicare. Medicare has transformed the health care—and the health—of older Americans. It is a major reason why the United States has caught up to the rest of the world in the senior brackets of the health Olympics—our life expectancy rises to the very top of the international charts for very old people.

We would expand Medicare to the entire population.[30] Certainly Medicare would have to be reformed: Its procedures would have to be simplified, its finances overhauled, the benefits package reconfigured, and the administrative practices streamlined (a good idea even if the program is not expanded).[31] Every American would be permitted to pay premiums and enter the revised Medicare program.

The program would be expensive. It would require significant new taxes. However, Medicare For All has no real prospects if its proponents duck the responsibility of paying for it. Perhaps a value-added tax could be earmarked for health care. An expanded tax credit could offset the costs for low- and even middle-income consumers (a health care tax credit for anyone making less than $35,000 would keep the tax progressive and, incidentally, help push back the tide of inequality).

In any case, expanding Medicare is one of many possibilities. The key point is not selecting the perfect plan but agreeing on a national goal: affordable health care coverage for all Americans.

## Help Americans Help Themselves: Education

Expanded government action in the labor market can enable motivated Americans to train themselves and earn a good living. Seriously facing up to America's rising inequality in wealth and health will take a lot more than health care policies; it will also require significant efforts to respond to the structural pressure for skilled labor that has fueled growing economic inequality.[32] Education is the drawbridge to the American dream. The passage of the G.I. Bill after World War II inaugurated federal and state government policies to open access to postsecondary education based on a student's motivation and talents and not his or her ability to pay. Continuing and expanding these policies would offer a tested and popular approach to expanding the supply of skilled labor.

Over the past two decades, higher education has become increasingly tied to income: gaining access to community colleges, technical schools, and 2- and 4-year colleges is more difficult for lower-income Americans at precisely the moment that it has become more important for economic security. Between 1980–1982 and 1992, the entrance of low-income students to college did not significantly increase despite its growing importance in the global economy; by contrast, attendance rose dramatically among students with the most income and modestly among those in middle-income groups.[33] Access to education is increasingly influenced by income rather than intelligence and hard work.

The National Center for Public Policy and Higher Education has monitored the affordability of higher education by comparing its costs (i.e., tuition plus other expenses) to the income of the student's family.[34] It reports that from 1980 to 2000, the costs of higher education have grown faster than family income, placing a particularly heavy burden on lower income groups. During this two-decade period, the share of family income necessary to pay for tuition at public 4-year institutions doubled for students in the lowest quintile of income (from 13% in 1980 to 25% in 2000) while holding steady at about 3% for students in the highest income quintile.

Federal and state governments did significantly increase their spending on higher education and on student financial aid, but these increases largely bypassed the students in greater financial need. From 1986 to 1999, the proportion of tuition costs per student paid by the federal government's Pell grants (which is based on financial need) fell from 98% to 57%; the proportion of state financial aid that took need into account declined from 91% to 78%.[35] In addition, the new resources that the federal government has put into higher education since the mid-1990s has been targeted at families with income too high to qualify for financial aid through federal tax credits, education savings plans, and federal income tax deductions; these are not available to financially needy students whose families do not pay taxes. As higher education and labor skills have become more important to employers, education after high school has become less affordable, especially to low-income students.

Since the mid-1980s, federal and state policies have established an impressive and expensive set of programs to reduce the financial squeeze on middle-income families. Attention now needs to turn to making the opportunity of higher education equally available for low-income Americans, like the G.I. Bill did for an earlier generation. According to the National Center, state policies vary significantly in their generosity toward need-based financial aid. Five states (two of which are at or below the national average regarding per-capita income) stand out for their efforts to make higher education affordable and offer models for other states. California and North Carolina provide low-cost community colleges to serve a majority of their state's postsecondary students; Utah maintains low tuition; and Minnesota and Illinois have boosted financial aid as they increased tuition.[36] Increasing the federal Pell grants and state funding for need-based state financial aid, combined with support for less expensive community colleges, are concrete options for expanding the supply of skilled labor.

Both Democrats and Republicans have embraced the idea of national service. A broad new national service—open to every young adult—might form the basis for a modern G.I. Bill—with full tuition benefits for every American who served his country by devoting a year to national service.

### Protecting the Wages of Less Skilled Workers

The United States should also learn from its allies and protect the wages of less skilled workers. Two proposals deserve attention. One focuses on the minimum wage. The law to establish a national minimum wage was first enacted in 1938 but the wage has not been increased by Congress to keep up with inflation. The result is that it has lost more than 24% of its value since 1979—which helps explain why workers earning the minimum wage (that is, those who tend to have less skill) have seen their earnings fall behind that of more skilled workers. Except for a brief period in the mid-1980s, the real value of the federal minimum wage has not been as low as it is today since the 1950s. The minimum wage could be indexed to inflation—like Social Security benefits—and removed from the vicissitudes of congressional politics. Proposals to increase the minimum wage are often met with charges that employers will cut jobs and move their operations overseas rather than pay the additional wages. Although some job loss may happen, the worst scenarios have not transpired and are unlikely. Businesses that are most inclined to offer low wages (such as fast food restaurants) rely on local customers. McDonald's is not likely to abandon Boston for New Delhi.

In fact, an analysis of the most recent increase in the minimum wage during 1996–1997 found no evidence that jobs were lost among workers normally covered by the law—teenagers and adult workers with less than a high school education. And some studies comparing adjacent states when one raised its minimum wage suggest few lost jobs.[37]

Another strategy is the living wage ordinance adopted by cities and localities. Businesses that have received government contracts and economic development subsidies are required to pay a wage that would keep a full-time worker above the poverty line. Over 70 localities have enacted living wages, ranging from 100% to 130% of the poverty line. The wages range from a low of $6.25 in Milwaukee to a high of $12 in Santa Cruz. Although employers (eager to save money) have criticized the strategy for destroying jobs, one study of the living wage ordinance in Baltimore found that it did not cause loss of employment. Indeed, employers in Baltimore reported that the wage increase was offset by lower rates of turnover and less expense in training.[38]

Proposals to expand government involvement in wages are criticized as inappropriate interference in the private sector. What this argument ignores is that the global economy has introduced a new age; government is continuously involved in the private sector—doling out subsidies, offering tax breaks, negotiating with other nations to open markets, and providing many other forms of assistance.

Americans in mid-century may well look back on our time as a moment of economic transformation. Incremental adjustments in government policy and the action of voluntary associations and employers can do a great deal to protect people amidst the disruptive changes. But government also needs to create a new structure of social and economic protections for its citizens. Making these changes is essential to securing the economic well-being and health of the country.

For now, Americans continue watching their communities split— some thrive, while others fall behind. Our terrible health data is just one symptom of national trouble. The global economic transformation exacerbates our divisions. But we are not helpless before this "storm of creative destruction." Other nations have successfully protected their people. So can we.

# Notes

1. J. David Richardson, "Income Inequality and Trade: How to Think, What to Conclude," *Journal of Economic Perspectives* 9 (Summer 1995): 33–55.

2. Robert Lawrence, "Inequality in America: The Recent Evidence," *The Communitarian Network* 10.2 (Spring 2000); Richard Freeman and Lawrence Katz, "Rising Wage Inequality: The United States vs. Other Advanced Countries," *Working under Different Rules,* ed. Richard Freeman (New York: Russell Sage Foundation, 1994), 29–62.

3. Timothy Smeeding, "Globalization, Inequality, and the Rich Countries of the G-20: Evidence from the Luxembourg Income Study," Luxembourg Income Study, Working Paper No. 320, July 2002, Table 5.

4. For a concise summary of some of the multiple reasons that income inequality has increased, see Gary Burtless, "Growing American Inequality:

Sources and Remedies," *Setting the National Priorities: The 2000 Election and Beyond*, ed. Henry Aaron and Robert Reischauer (Washington, DC: Brookings Institution, 1999), 137–165; Peter Gottschalk and Timothy Smeeding, "Cross-National Comparisons of Earnings and Income Inequality," *Journal of Economic Literature* 35 (June 1997): 633–687; Sheldon Danziger and Daniel Weinberg, "The Historical Record: Trends in Family Income, Inequality, and Poverty," *Confronting Poverty: Prescriptions for Change*, ed. Sheldon Danziger, Gary Sandefur, and Daniel Weinberg (Cambridge, MA: Harvard University Press, 1994), 18–50; Roberto Korzeniewicz and Timothy Moran, "World-Economic Trends in the Distribution of Income, 1965–1992," *American Journal of Sociology* 102 (January 1997): 1000–1039.

5. Larry Mishel, Jared Bernstein, and Heather Boushey, *State of Working America, 2002–2003* (Ithaca, NY: Cornell University Press, 2002), 411–412; Edward N. Wolff, "Recent Trends in the Size Distribution of Household Wealth," *Journal of Economic Perspectives* 12 (Summer 1998): 131–150; Gottschalk and Smeeding, "Cross-National Comparisons."

6. Peter Gottschalk, "Inequality, Income Growth, and Mobility: The Basic Facts," *Journal of Economic Perspectives* 11 (Spring 1997): 21–40, 35.

7. Mishel, Bernstein, and Boushey, *State of Working America*, 411–412.

8. Gottschalk, "Inequality, Income Growth, and Mobility"; Freeman, and Katz, "Rising Wage Inequality."

9. Richard Freeman, "Are Your Wages Set in Beijing?" *Journal of Economic Perspectives* 9 (Summer 1995): 15–32.

10. Duane Swank and Sven Steinmo, "The New Political Economy of Taxation in Advanced Capitalist Democracies," *American Journal of Political Science* (July 2002): 642–655.

11. Mishel, Bernstein, and Boushey, *State of Working America*, 422.

12. Burtless, "Growing American Inequality."

13. Mishel, Bernstein, and Boushey, *State of Working America*, 411–412.

14. Ibid.

15. Ibid.

16. Ibid., 416. Poverty rates in comparative research are often measured in terms of the proportion of the population living below 50% of the median income in each country.

17. Ibid., 340.

18. Ibid., 419–422.

19. Ibid., 419.

20. Ibid., 411–412.

21. Freeman and Katz, "Rising Wage Inequality."

22. Freeman, "Are Your Wages Set in Beijing?"

23. Edward Gramlich, Richard Kasten, and Frank Sammartino, "Growing Inequality in the 1980s: The Role of Federal Taxes and Cash Transfers," *Uneven Tides*, ed. Sheldon Danziger and Peter Gottschalk (New York: Russell Sage Foundation, 1993) 225–249.

24. Swank and Steinmo, "The New Political Economy."

25. Gottschalk, "Inequality, Income Growth, and Mobility," 35.

26. For an analysis of the crime war, see James Morone, *Hellfire Nation: The Politics of Sin in American History* (New Haven: Yale University Press, 2003), chapter 15.

27. The phrase comes from Kevin Phillips, *Wealth and Democracy: A Political History of the American Rich* (New York: Broadway Books, 2002).

28. Arthur Oken, *Equality and Efficiency: The Big Tradeoff* (Washington, DC: Brookings Institution, 1975).

29. Gary Burtless and Christopher Jencks, "American Inequality and Its Consequences" (Luxembourg Income Study, Working Paper No. 339, March 2003).

30. For a detailed version of this proposal, see James A. Morone, "Medicare for All," *Covering America: Real Remedies for the Uninsured*, vol. II, ed. Jack Meyer and Elliot Wicks (Washington, DC: ERSDI, 2002).

31. For a description of what was essentially an effort to fast-track the Clinton administration proposal, see Lawrence Jacobs and Robert Shapiro, *Politicians Don't Pander* (Chicago: University of Chicago Press, 2000).

32. Freeman and Katz, "Rising Wage Inequality."

33. David Ellwood and Thomas Kane, "Who Is Getting a College Education? Family Background and the Growing Gaps in Enrollment," *Securing the Future: Investing in Children from Birth to College*, ed. Sheldon Danzinger and Jane Waldfogel (New York: Russell Sage, 2000).

34. The National Center for Public Policy and Higher Education, *Losing Ground: A National Status Report on the Affordability of American Higher Education* (San Jose, California, 2002). Last accessed June 1, 2003, at http://www.higheredu-cation.org.

35. Ibid., 6.

36. Ibid., 10, appendix.

37. Jared Bernstein and John Schmidt, *Making Work Pay: The Impact of the 1996–97 Minimum Wage Increase* (Washington, DC: Economic Policy Institute, 1998); David Card and Alan B. Krueger, *Myth and Measurement: The New Economics of the Minimum Wage* (Princeton, NJ: Princeton University Press, 1995); Card and Krueger, "Minimum Wages and Employment: A Case Study of the Fast Food Industry in New Jersey and Pennsylvania," *American Economic Review* 84.4 (1994); Card and Krueger, "Minimum Wages and Employment: A Case Study of the Fast Food Industry in New Jersey and Pennsylvania: Reply," *American Economic Review* 90.5 (December 2000): 1397–1420.

38. Christopher Niedt, Greg Ruiters, Dana Wise, and Erica Schoenberger, *The Effects of the Living Wage in Baltimore*, Working Paper No. 119 (Washington, DC: Economic Policy Institute, 1999).

# Essential Reading

American Political Science Association, Task Force on Inequality and American Democracy. "Democracy in an Age of Rising Inequality." http://www.apsanet.org/inequality.

Auerbach, James A., and Richard S. Belous, eds. *Inequality Paradox: Growth of Income Disparity.* Washington, DC: National Policy Association, 1998.

Blank, Rebecca. *It Takes a Nation: A New Agenda for Fighting Poverty.* Princeton, NJ: Princeton University Press, 1997.

Brown, Lawrence D. *Politics and Health Care Organization: HMOs as Federal Policy.* Washington, DC: Brookings Institution, 1983.

Burtless, Gary. "Growing American Inequality: Sources and Remedies." In *Setting the National Priorities: The 2000 Election and Beyond*, edited by Henry Aaron and Robert Reischauer, 137–165. Washington, DC: Brookings Institution, 1999.

Campbell, Andrea L. *How Policies Make Citizens: Senior Political Activism and the American Welfare State.* Princeton, NJ: Princeton University Press, 2003.

Cohen, Cathy J. *The Boundaries of Blackness: AIDS and the Breakdown of Black Politics.* Chicago: University of Chicago Press, 1997.

Cook, Fay Lomax, and Edith J. Barrett. *Support for the American Welfare State: The Views of Congress and the Public.* New York: Columbia University Press, 1992.

Daniels, Norman, Bruce Kennedy, and Ichiro Kawachi. *Is Inequality Bad for Our Health?* Boston: Beacon Press, 2000.

David, Richard J., and James W. Collins. "Differing Birth Weight among Infants of U.S.-Born Blacks, African-Born Blacks, and U.S.-Born White Women." *New England Journal of Medicine* 337 (1997): 1209–1214.

Ehrenreich, Barbara. *Nickel and Dimed: On (Not) Getting By in America.* New York: Metropolitan Books, 2001.

Ellwood, David, and Thomas Kane. "Who Is Getting a College Education? Family Background and the Growing Gaps in Enrollment." In *Securing the Future: Investing in Children from Birth to College*, edited by Sheldon Danziger and Jane Waldfogel. New York: Russell Sage, 2000.

Epstein, Steven. *Impure Science: AIDS, Activism, and the Politics of Knowledge.* Berkeley and Los Angeles: University of California Press, 1996.

Ferguson, Thomas. *Golden Rule: The Investment Theory of Party Competition and the Logic of Money-Driven Political Systems.* Chicago: University of Chicago Press, 1995.

Fogel, Robert William. *The Fourth Great Awakening and the Future of Egalitarianism.* Chicago: University of Chicago Press, 2000.

Freeman, Richard, ed. *Working under Different Rules.* New York: Russell Sage Foundation, 1994.

Geronimus, Arline, John Bound, Timothy Waidmann, Marianne Hillemeier, and Patricia Burns. "Excess Mortality among Blacks and Whites in the United States." *New England Journal of Medicine* 335 (1996): 1552–1558.

Gilens, Martin. *Why Americans Hate Welfare.* Chicago: University of Chicago Press, 1999.

Gordon, Colin. *Dead on Arrival: The Politics of Health Care in Twentieth-Century America.* Princeton, NJ: Princeton University Press, 2003.

Gottschalk, Marie. *The Shadow Welfare State: Labor, Business, and the Politics of Health Care in the United States*. Ithaca, NY: Cornell University Press, 2000.

Graetz, Michael J., and Jerry L. Mashaw. *True Security: Rethinking American Social Insurance*. New Haven, CT: Yale University Press, 1999.

Hacker, Jacob S. *The Road to Nowhere: The Genesis of President Clinton's Plan for Health Security*. Princeton, NJ: Princeton University Press, 1997.

Hochschild, Arlie. *The Time Bind: When Work Becomes Home and Home Becomes Work*. New York: Metropolitan Books, 1997.

Hochschild, Jennifer L. *Facing Up to the American Dream: Race, Class and the Soul of the Nation*. Princeton, NJ: Princeton University Press, 1995.

Hochschild, Jennifer L. *What's Fair?: American Beliefs about Distributive Justice*. Cambridge, MA: Harvard University Press, 1981.

House, James. "Relating Social Inequalities in Health and Income." *Journal of Health Politics, Policy and Law* 26(3).

Institute of Medicine. *Unequal Treatment: Confronting Racial and Ethnic Disparities in Health Care*. Edited by Brian D. Smedley, Adrienne Y. Stith, and Alan R. Nelson, Report of the Institute of Medicine Committee on Understanding and Eliminating Racial Differences in Health Care. Washington, DC: National Academy Press, 2003.

Jacobs, Lawrence R. *The Health of Nations: Public Opinion and the Making of American and British Health Policy*. Ithaca, NY: Cornell University Press, 1993.

Jacobs, Lawrence R. "The Politics of America's Supply State: Health Reform and Technology." *Health Affairs* 14 (Summer 1995): 143–157.

Jacobs, Lawrence R., and Robert Shapiro. *Politicians Don't Pander: Political Manipulation and the Decline of Democratic Responsiveness*. Chicago: University of Chicago Press, 2000.

Jacobson, P. D. *Strangers in the Night: Law and Medicine in the Managed Care Era*. New York: Oxford University Press, 2002.

Jencks, Christopher. "Does Inequality Matter?" *Daedalus* 131 (Winter 2002): 1.

Kahn, K. L., M. L. Pearson, E. R. Harrison, K. A. Desmond, W. H. Rogers, L. V. Rubenstein, R. H. Brook, and E. B. Keeler. "Health Care for Black and Poor Hospitalized Medicare Patients." *Journal of the American Medical Association* 271.15 (1994): 1169–1174.

Kawachi, Ichiro, Bruce P. Kennedy, and Richard G. Wilkinson. *Income Inequality and Health: A Reader*. New York: The New Press, 1999.

Keyssar, Alexander. *The Right to Vote: The Contested History of Democracy in the United States*. New York: Basic, 2000.

Kuttner, Robert. *Everything for Sale: The Virtues and Limits of Markets*. Chicago: University of Chicago Press, 1996.

Lipset, Seymour Martin. *American Exceptionalism: A Double-Edged Sword*. New York: W. W. Norton, 1996.

Lowi, Theodore. *The End of Liberalism*. New York: Norton, 1979.

Marmor, Theodore. *The Politics of Medicare*. 2nd ed. New York: Aldine de Gruyter, 2000.

Marmot, Michael, and Richard G. Wilkinson, eds. *Social Determinants of Health*. Oxford, UK: Oxford University Press, 1999.

Masters, Marick F. *Unions at the Crossroads: Strategic Membership, Financial, and Political Perspectives*. Westport, CT: Quorum Books, 1997.

Mellor, Jennifer, and Jeffrey Milyo. "Re-examining the Evidence of an Ecological Association between Income Inequality and Health." *Journal of Health Politics, Policy and Law* 26 (2001): 487–522.

Mishel, Larry, Jared Bernstein, and Heather Boushey. *State of Working America, 2002–2003.* Ithaca, NY: Cornell University Press, 2002.

Morone, James A. "The Bureaucracy Empowered." In *The Politics of Health Care Reform: Lessons from the Past, Prospects for the Future*, edited by James A. Morone and Gary S. Belkin. Durham, NC: Duke University Press, 1994.

Morone, James A. *The Democratic Wish: Popular Participation and the Limits of American Government.* New Haven, CT: Yale University Press, 1998.

Morone, James A. "Enemies of the People: The Moral Dimension to Public Health." *Journal of Health Politics, Policy and Law* 22 (1997): 993–1020.

Morone, James A. *Hellfire Nation: The Politics of Sin in American History.* New Haven: Yale University Press, 2003.

Morone, James A. "The Ironic Flaw in Health Care Competition: The Politics of Markets." In *Competitive Approaches to Health Care Reform*, edited by Richard Arnould, Robert Rich, and William White, 207–222. Washington, DC: Urban Institute Press, 1993.

Nathanson, Constance A. "Social Movements as Catalysts for Policy Change: The Case of Smoking and Guns." *Journal of Health Politics, Policy and Law* 24 (June 1999): 421–488.

The National Center for Public Policy and Higher Education. *Losing Ground: A National Status Report on the Affordability of American Higher Education.* 2002. http://www.highereducation.org.

Oberlander, Jonathan. *The Political Life of Medicare.* Chicago: University of Chicago Press, 2003.

Ott, Katherine. *Fevered Lives: Tuberculosis in American Culture since 1870.* Cambridge, MA: Harvard University Press, 1996.

Page, Benjamin I., and Robert Shapiro. *The Rational Public: Fifty Years of Trends in American's Policy Preferences.* Chicago: University of Chicago Press, 1992.

Page, Benjamin I., and James R. Simmons. *What Government Can Do: Dealing with Poverty and Inequality.* Chicago: University of Chicago Press, 2000.

Phillips, Kevin. *Wealth and Democracy: A Political History of the American Rich.* New York: Broadway Books, 2002.

Peterson, Mark A. "From Trust to Political Power: Interest Groups, Public Choice, and Health Care Markets." *Journal of Health Politics, Policy and Law* 26 (October 2001): 1145–1163.

Piven, Frances Fox, and Richard A. Cloward. *Why Americans Don't Vote.* New York: Pantheon, 2000.

Powe, L. A. *The Warren Court in American Politics.* Cambridge, MA: Harvard University Press, 2000.

Putnam, Robert. *Bowling Alone.* New York: Simon and Schuster, 2000.

Quadagno, Jill. "From Old-Age Assistance to Supplemental Security Income: The Political Economy of Relief in the South, 1935–1972." In *The Politics of Social Policy in the United States*, edited by Margaret Weir, Ann Shola Orloff, and Theda Skocpol, 235–264. Princeton, NJ: Princeton University Press, 1988.

Reeher, Grant. *Narratives of Justice: Beliefs about Distributive Justice.* Ann Arbor: University of Michigan Press, 1996.

Roosevelt, Franklin Delano. "Inaugural Address. March 4, 1933." In *The Public Papers and Addresses of Franklin D Roosevelt*, vol. II, 11–16. New York: Random House, 1938.

Rosenbaum, Sara, Anne Markus, and Julie Darnell. "U.S. Civil Rights Policy and Access to Health Care by Minority Americans: Implications for a Changing Health Care System." *Medical Care Research and Review* 57.1 (2000): 236–259.

Rosenbaum, Sara, and Colleen A. Sonosky. "Child Health in a Changing Policy Environment: The Roles of Child Advocacy Organizations in Addressing Policy Issues." In *Who Speaks for America's Children? The Role of Child Advocates in Public Policy*, edited by Carol De Vita and Rachel Mosher-Williams. Washington, DC: Urban Institute Press, 2001.

Rosenberg, G. N. *The Hollow Hope: Can Courts Bring About Social Change?* Chicago: University of Chicago Press, 1991.

Rosenblatt, Rand E., Sylvia A. Law, and Sara Rosenbaum. *Law and the American Health Care System.* Westbury, NY: Foundation Press, 1997.

Schattschneider, E. E. *The Semi-Sovereign People*. Hinsdale, IL: Dryden Press, 1970.

Schlesinger, Mark, and Richard R. Lau. "The Meaning and Measure of Policy Metaphors." *American Political Science Review* 94 (2000): 611–626.

Schlozman, Kay Lehman, and John T. Tierney. *Organized Interests and American Democracy.* New York: Harper & Row, 1986.

Schneider, Anne, and Helen Ingram. "Social Construction of Target Populations: Implications for Politics and Policy." *American Political Science Review* 87 (June 1993): 334–347.

Skocpol, Theda. *Boomerang: Clinton's Health Security Effort and the Turn against Government in U.S. Politics.* New York: W. W. Norton, 1996.

Skocpol, Theda. *Diminished Democracy: From Membership to Managed in American Civic Life.* Norman: University of Oklahoma Press, 2003.

Slemrod, Joel, ed. 1996. *Tax Progressivity and Income Inequality*. New York: Cambridge University Press.

Smeeding, Timothy M. "U.S. Income Inequality in a Cross-National Perspective: Why Are We So Different?" In *Inequality Paradox: Growth of Income Disparity*, edited by James A. Auerbach and Richard S. Belous, 194–217. Washington, DC: National Policy Association, 1998.

Smith, David Barton. *Health Care Divided.* Ann Arbor: University of Michigan Press, 1999.

Smith, Susan L. *Sick and Tired of Being Sick and Tired: Black Women's Health Activism in America, 1890–1950.* Philadelphia: University of Pennsylvania Press, 1995.

Starfield, Barbara. "Is U.S. Health Really the Best in the World?" *Journal of the American Medical Association* 284 (2000): 483–484.

Starr, Paul. *The Social Transformation of American Medicine.* New York: Basic Books, 1982. (See especially 58.)

Steinmo, Sven, and Jon Watts. "It's the Institutions, Stupid! Why Comprehensive National Health Insurance Always Fails in America." *Journal of Health Politics, Policy and Law* 20 (Summer 1995): 329–372.

Stevens, Robert, and Rosemary Stevens. *Welfare Medicine in America: A Case Study of Medicaid.* New York: The Free Press, 1974.

Stone, Deborah. "The Doctor as Businessman: The Changing Politics of Cultural Icon." *Journal of Health Politics, Policy and Law* 22.2 (1997): 533–556.

Stone, Deborah. *Policy Paradox: The Art of Political Decision Making.* New York: Norton, 1997.

Stone, Deborah. "The Struggle for the Soul of Health Insurance." *Journal of Health Politics, Policy and Law* 18.2 (1993): 267–317.

de Tocqueville, Alexis. 1835. *Democracy in America*. Garden City, NY: Doubleday, 1969.

Verba, Sidney, Kay Lehman Schlozman, and Henry E. Brady. *Voice and Equality: Civic Volunteerism in American Politics*. Cambridge, MA: Harvard University Press, 1995.

374

Vladeck, Bruce. "The Political Economy of Medicare: Medicare Reform Requires Political Reform." *Health Affairs* 18:1 (January–February 1999): 22–36.

Watson, Sidney. "Reinvigorating Title VI: Defending Health Care Discrimination—It Shouldn't Be So Easy." *Fordham Law Review* 58 (1990): 939–978.

Weir, Margaret, ed. *The Social Divide: Political Parties and the Future of Activist Government.* Washington, DC, and New York: Brookings Institution and Russell Sage Foundation, 1998.

Weisman, Carol S. *Women's Health Care: Activist Traditions and Institutional Change.* Baltimore: Johns Hopkins Press, 1998.

West, Darrell M., and Burdett A. Loomis. *The Sound of Money: How Political Interests Get What They Want.* New York: W. W. Norton, 1998.

White, Joseph. *Competing Solutions: American Health Care Proposals and International Experience.* Washington, DC: Brookings Institution, 1995.

Williams, David. "Race and Health: Trends and Policy Implications." In *Income, Socioeconomic Status and Health*, edited by James Auerbach and Barbara Kivimae Krimgold, 67–85. Washington, DC: National Policy Association, 2001.

# Index